Automating Microsoft® Access®
with Macros

Susann Novalis

SYBEX®

San Francisco • Paris • Düsseldorf • Soest

Acquisitions Manager: Kristine Plachy
Developmental Editor: Melanie Spiller
Editor: Julia Kelly
Project Editor: Bonnie Bills
Technical Editor: Helen Feddema
Book Designer: Suzanne Albertson
Book Design Director: Catalin Dulfu
Technical Artist: Alan Smith
Desktop Publisher: Deborah A. Bevilacqua
Production Coordinators: Renee Avalos, Kimberley Askew-Qasem
Indexer: Nancy Guenther
Cover Designer: Archer Design
Cover Illustrator: Richard Miller

Screen reproductions produced with Collage Complete.
Collage Complete is a trademark of Inner Media Inc.

Nizhoni University graphic produced with VISIO.
VISIO is a trademark of Shapeware Corporation.

SYBEX is a registered trademark of SYBEX Inc.

TRADEMARKS: SYBEX has attempted throughout this book to distinguish proprietary trade-marks from descriptive terms by following the capitalization style used by the manufacturer.

Every effort has been made to supply complete and accurate information. However, SYBEX assumes no responsibility for its use, nor for any infringement of the intellectual property rights of third parties which would result from such use.

Library of Congress Card Number: 95-72705
ISBN: 0-7821-1856-9

Manufactured in the United States of America
10 9 8 7 6 5 4 3 2 1

Warranty

SYBEX warrants the enclosed disk to be free of physical defects for a period of ninety (90) days after purchase. If you discover a defect in the disk during this warranty period, you can obtain a replacement disk at no charge by sending the defective disk, postage prepaid, with proof of purchase to:

SYBEX Inc.
Customer Service Department
2021 Challenger Drive
Alameda, CA 94501
(800) 227-2346
Fax: (510) 523-2373

After the 90-day period, you can obtain a replacement disk by sending us the defective disk, proof of purchase, and a check or money order for $10, payable to SYBEX.

Disclaimer

SYBEX makes no warranty or representation, either express or implied, with respect to this medium or its contents, its quality, performance, merchantability, or fitness for a particular purpose. In no event will SYBEX, its distributors, or dealers be liable for direct, indirect, special, incidental, or consequential damages arising out of the use of or inability to use the medium or its contents even if advised of the possibility of such damage.

The exclusion of implied warranties is not permitted by some states. Therefore, the above exclusion may not apply to you. This warranty provides you with specific legal rights; there may be other rights that you may have that vary from state to state.

Copy Protection

None of the files on the disk is copy-protected. However, in all cases, reselling or making copies of these files without authorization is expressly forbidden.

This book is dedicated to my mother and father who helped me to believe that there are no limits.

Nizhoni means beautiful land in the Navajo language.

Acknowledgments

Heartfelt thanks to everyone who has helped me, in one way or another, to write this book.

Thanks to James Kelley, Marci Manderscheid, and San Francisco State University for supporting my work with Microsoft Access.

Thanks to the guiding lights of Microsoft Access—some of you don't even know me, but you have taught me in your books and articles—especially Rob Krumm, Miriam Liskin, John Viescas, Ken Getz, Stan Leszynski, Mike Gunderloy, and Paul Litwin. Special thanks to Helen Feddema whose technical editing made this a better book.

Thanks to the people at Microsoft Corporation who gave me encouragement, included me in the Access for Windows 95 Beta testing program, and answered all of my questions.

Thanks to Rick Fisher for creating Find and Replace: a wonderful gift to all of us.

A special thanks to Roger Jennings who taught me how a book goes together and is my role model.

Thanks to those who are teaching me how to write, especially Melanie Spiller, my developmental editor at SYBEX, and others whose writings are my teachers, including Susan Schwartz, Ken Atchity, and William Brohaugh.

Thanks to everyone at SYBEX for their careful production of this book, especially Julia Kelly and Bonnie Bills.

Special thanks to Cameron and Greer, and particularly to Rich who gave me full support and understanding when my book took precedence over ... everything. I love you, guys. And, thanks to my bicycle buddies, especially Leo and Lisa, for the weekly sanity sessions in the hills.

CONTENTS AT A GLANCE

TABLE OF CONTENTS

11 Finding Records to Print 417

12 Handling External Data 443

15   Controlling the User Interface   543

16   The Finishing Touches   577

Introduction

About This Book

Microsoft Access is an extremely powerful desktop database management program with features designed to satisfy the needs of all users—novice end users, power users and professional database developers.

No matter what kind of user you are, you started out by using Microsoft Access *interactively*—that is, you ran a built-in Access command by choosing the command from a menu, clicking a button on a toolbar, or pressing a shortcut key combination. You can do quite a lot by running one command at a time, but there are good reasons for moving on to the next level and learning to *automate* Microsoft Access. When you automate your Access database, a single user action runs a whole set of commands instead of just a single command. Here are some reasons for automating a database:

Eliminate the manual labor of routine operations.   After you have worked interactively with Microsoft Access for a while, you realize there are many routine repetitive procedures you don't want to do interactively anymore. For example:

- Finding and opening forms
- Finding specific records
- Updating forms to display the most current data
- Printing routine reports
- Importing and modifying data
- Archiving data

You would like to automate routine tasks so that the computer does more of the work by looking up information, synchronizing and updating forms automatically, or running a whole set of commands for a particular task.

Improve data protection. You are creating a database for yourself or someone else to use, and you want to build in more protection for your data, along with more techniques to make data entry faster and more accurate.

Create an application for novice users. You want to create a custom database application that a novice can use without having to learn Microsoft Access first.

Because it's there. You've read about the power of Microsoft Access and want to use it to make your database more attractive and easier to use.

Two Automation Tools

Microsoft Access provides two related sets of tools you can use to automate your databases: macro programming and a programming language, Visual Basic for Applications (VBA).

A *macro action* is an instruction built into Microsoft Access that you can use to automate tasks. For example:

This macro action	instructs the computer to
OpenForm	open a form
Close	close an object
GoToControl	move to a control
SetValue	set the value of a control or property

Microsoft Access provides a set of 49 macro actions. Many of these actions duplicate the familiar menu commands and mouse actions. Other macro actions provide new capabilities, such as the **Beep** macro action that instructs the computer to "beep" and the **MsgBox** macro action that instructs the computer to display a custom message.

A *macro* is a set of instructions that runs one or more macro actions. In addition to running macro actions, you can create macros that make decisions—a macro can test a condition and carry out different actions depending on the outcome of the test. While macro programming is a powerful automation tool, its powers are limited. In contrast, the power of Visual Basic programming is nearly limitless.

Visual Basic for Applications is a complete programming language which allows you to carry out calculations and operations that are awkward or impossible to carry out with macros alone. Along with the increased power comes a longer learning period and longer sessions writing the programs. In VBA you create *procedures* (analogous to macros) to perform operations or calculate values.

In Microsoft Word, Microsoft Excel, and many other applications that have a programming language, there is a recorder you can use to record menu selections, keystrokes, and mouse actions for an operation. You view the recorded steps in a separate programming window, where the recorded program is saved as text in the application's programming language. In Microsoft Word you record the steps in Word Basic, while in Excel your record program is in Visual Basic for Applications. When you edit in the programming window, the full capability of the programming language is available so you can remove unnecessary steps and add steps that can't be recorded. A recorder is an excellent tool for learning a programming language because the recorder automatically creates simple programming code with correct commands, spelling, and grammar. Access does not have a recorder for either of its languages, but it has several other features to help you automate a database:

- Macro programming is easy to learn because the design of the macro window provides point-and-click programming.

- Macro programming is a separate automating tool. You can create sophisticated applications using macros without having to write any code.

- You can convert macros to VBA code if you want the additional power of VBA.

- You can use several commands to create VBA code automatically for many simple operations. In a limited sense, these wizards play the role of a recorder by creating simple code that you can edit.

Visual Basic and macro programming are not completely independent. Certain tasks require macros whether you are using macro programming or Visual Basic. Macro programming may require Visual Basic to deal with errors that occur when you use the database, and VBA procedures must occasionally run macro actions. Even if you are an emerging power user or an accomplished developer, you still need to know about macro programming.

This book shows you how to create a complete custom application, using macro programming and one simple VBA procedure to handle errors. Whether you need to progress beyond macro programming depends on what you want to do—if you are creating applications for your own use or for coworkers, macro programming alone may satisfy all of your needs, while developers creating complex professional applications need the additional power of Visual Basic. Nevertheless, macro programming can provide the developer with the tools to complete a prototype in the shortest time.

This book concentrates on using macros to automate your interactive database. You learn how to create a custom application with custom menus, toolbars, and keyboard shortcuts. Additionally, you learn intermediate and advanced database techniques that don't require either macros or Visual Basic, but that help to make your data more useful.

Who Should Read This Book?

This is an intermediate-level book about Microsoft Access. You should be familiar with the basic concepts and techniques of interactive Access, including creating a simple Access database complete with related tables, queries, forms, and reports. This book shows you how to put these pieces together into an application. You do not need any prior experience with another macro language or a programming language. Although it is an intermediate-level Access book, it is also a beginning-level macro programming book. For help with interactive Access, study the manuals or an introductory text such as *Mastering Access for Windows 95* by Alan Simpson and Elizabeth Olson (SYBEX, 1996).

How to Use This Book

This is both a hands-on tutorial and macro programming reference. As a tutorial, this book leads you through each step needed to turn an interactive database into a sophisticated automated application. As a macro programming reference, this book provides detailed explanations of concepts, reference tables of macro actions and events, and macro programming techniques for typical database operations.

This book uses a sample database for managing information in a college, so we'll be working with students registering for classes and paying fees, instructors teaching classes and assigning grades, and academic departments approving course outlines.

People use computer databases to manage all sorts of information. The list of database templates that the Database Wizard can create provides only a glimpse of the possibilities, including resource scheduling, asset tracking, time and billing, contact management, order entry, inventory control, and membership. You can use the book's database example as a model for the databases you work with in your professional or personal life. Database operations are essentially the same for all databases—only the names change. Customers order products, students register in classes, consultants work on several projects, a part is used in many products—these activities are all quite similar in terms of database functions.

Each of the sixteen chapters builds on material covered in the previous chapters. Chapters 1 through 4 teach the basics of macro programming and user interface design. Chapters 5 through 7 focus on the mechanics of looking up information and moving around through controls and records. Chapters 8 and 9 teach skills for data entry. Chapters 10 through 14 focus on techniques for working with groups of records, including importing and archiving data. Chapters 15 and 16 focus on topics in application design, including controlling the interface and protecting the application. To get the most out of this book, you should work through each chapter—performing the steps *at the computer*—before continuing to the next chapter. You learn macro programming only by writing macros; there just isn't any other way.

Most chapters have optional exercises provided for additional practice. There are two kinds of exercise problems:

- Adding to the Application
- Extending the Concepts

"Adding to the Application" exercises duplicate the techniques covered in the lesson but put you more on your own. By applying the techniques of the current and previous chapters to other database objects in the sample database, these exercises allow you to practice the techniques in the current chapter and integrate current chapter techniques with those in previous chapters.

"Extending the Concepts" problems go beyond the concepts covered in the chapter, either by introducing related techniques and concepts not covered explicitly in the chapter or by introducing concepts from Visual Basic.

Conventions Used in the Book

This book uses the following conventions:

Key Combinations   Key combinations that you press are indicated by joining the keys with a plus sign. For example, SHIFT+F2 indicates that you hold down the SHIFT key while you press the F2 function key.

Menu Choices   Sequences of menu commands are indicated by the symbol ➤. For example, File ➤ Close indicates the Close command on the File menu. To select a menu item with the keyboard, you hold down the ALT key and press the first underlined letter to display the drop-down menu, and then press the next underlined letter to activate the command.

Bold Type   Words, phrases and names that you must type or enter are shown in **bold** type. For example, name the form **frmStudents**

Programming Fonts   `Bold program font` is used for the special words in macro programming: the names of macro actions and their arguments.

For example:

Macro Name	Action	Action Arguments
cmdSave_Click	`DoMenuItem`	`Menu Bar`: Form
		`Menu Name`: Records
		`Command`: SaveRecord

Most of the macros in the book are listed in tables like this one and indexed in Appendix E.

Monospace type is used for examples of Visual Basic programming code, as in the following:

```
Private Sub Form_Error (DataErr As Integer, Response As Integer)
    If DataErr = 3058 Then
        MsgBox "You must enter a StudentID, please enter it now. The
        ➥ StudentID must have the same format as a Social Security
        ➥ number."
        Response = acDataErrContinue
    Else
        Response = acDataErrDisplay
    End If
End Sub
```

In Visual Basic code examples, the symbol ➥ indicates a line of program code that is too long to fit on a single line of the printed page but is to be typed as a single line in the Module window. Alternatively, you can break a line in the Module window by typing a space followed by an underscore (_) as a continuation character and then continuing the line of code on the next line in the window.

Keywords of SQL statements are shown in uppercase (for example, DISTINCTROW).

Definitions The first time a new word or phrase is introduced and defined, it is displayed in *italic* type.

Flow Diagrams The book makes extensive use of macro flow diagrams to depict macros and uses diagram symbols that are based on the diagramming techniques in *Principles of Object Oriented Analysis and Design* by James Martin (PTR Prentice Hall). The diagram symbols include:

The shadowed operation box with the event triangle indicates the direct user operation that causes the event shown above the event triangle.

The operation box with the event triangle indicates the indirect operation that causes the event shown above the event triangle.

The operation box indicates a single macro action and includes an English phrase to describe the action (the macro action is in italics).

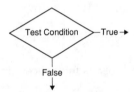

The rounded termination symbol indicates the end of the macro.

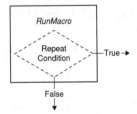

The decision diamond indicates a branching to one of two alternative sets of actions, depending on the outcome of the test shown in the diamond.

The loop symbol indicates an action that runs another macro repeatedly as long as the test shown in the dashed decision diamond is true.

Naming Standard This book uses the Leszynski/Reddick naming standard for naming tables, queries, forms, reports, and macros and for many of the form controls (see Chapter 1, "Making Your First Decisions"). If you haven't been using a naming standard, you'll need to deal with the problem of changing names in your partially created databases. Unfortunately, Microsoft Access doesn't provide a way to propagate name changes (except in Visual Basic modules). Whenever you want to change a table name, field name, query name, form name, report name, macro name, control name, etc., you have to go through all of your tables, queries, forms and reports and make all of the changes manually. Without a utility that propagates name changes, the basic Access rule of thumb is "Don't make any name changes!" A solution is to use one of the third-party utilities currently available. Particularly recommended is Find and Replace, the shareware Access utility developed by Rick Fisher. The Find and Replace utility installs as an add-in to Access and lets you make changes easily, almost too easily. Be very careful when you use any name-changing utility, and back up your database first. More information is available in Rick Fisher's article "Using the Global Find and Replace Utility" (*Access Advisor*, Feb./Mar. 1994). The latest version of his software can be found on CompuServe and can be downloaded from the MSAccess forum, library 15, filename REPL7.ZIP. The software is also available on the Internet at ftp.winsite.com (IP 199.26.178.13) in the Access directory (/PUB/PC/WIN3/ACCESS) or on the World Wide Web at http://www.winsite.com. The REPL7.ZIP file contains the utility Replace7.mda, the online help file Replace7.hlp, and a text file called Replace7.wri that explains how to install the files and also explains the shareware requirements.

Getting Ready

This section prepares you for using the disk provided with this book, and includes a list of the files on the disk and instructions for installing the files.

Software Requirements

Using the disk and working through the steps of the book require that you have Windows 95 and Microsoft Access for Windows 95 installed on your computer.

What's on the Disk?

Included with this book is a disk with two folders, Automate and Gallery.

The Automate Folder   The Automate folder contains the three files you work with in the book:

College.mdb contains all the tables, queries, forms, and reports for the College database example. You must install this file in order to be able to work through the chapters.

Offsite.xls is the spreadsheet file you import in Chapter 12. You don't need to have Microsoft Excel installed on your computer.

Students.txt is the text file you import in Chapter 12.

The Gallery Folder   The Gallery folder contains the gallery.mdb database that includes the form masters, and the galleries of reusable controls and macros that you create in the book. You'll be creating everything in the gallery.mdb database while you work through the book; the file is included on the disk for reference.

Installing the Files

1. Start Windows 95.

2. Insert the disk from the back of the book into your floppy disk drive.

3. In My Computer, click the floppy disk drive, and then click the Automate folder.

4. Choose Edit ➤ Copy.

5. In My Computer, click the disk where you want to put the copy. In this book the Automate folder is placed in the C drive, but you could place the folder inside the Access folder.

6. Click Edit ➤ Paste.

7. Click the Automate folder. The college.mdb database file, the offsite.xls spreadsheet file, and the students.txt text file appear.

8. Close the folder window.

Endnotes

Thank you for selecting this book to help you learn about macro programming and application development in Microsoft Access. I really enjoyed writing the book and hope you enjoy learning with it. Please send your comments, suggestions, and corrections to me at novalis@sfsu.edu, Compuserve 73312,3437, or on the World Wide Web at http://userwww.sfsu.edu/~novalis.

CHAPTER

ONE

Making Your First Decisions

- Why automate a database?

- Macro programming as an automation tool

- Choosing names to make objects self-documenting

- Ways to customize the Microsoft Access environment

- Form masters to speed development

A *database* is a collection of records and files. When you create a database, you need a system that will help you to store, retrieve, and sort your data, as well as analyze and convert it into useful information. If the database is large or complex, you'll probably use a commercial computer database application, such as Microsoft Access, to help with these tasks. Since you are reading this book, you are using, or plan to use, Access—congratulations on an excellent choice! Access has a terrific set of tools and wizards to help you create a database, including:

- tables to store data

- queries to retrieve data

- forms to enter and view data

- reports to print information

What Is a Database Application?

An Access database is an *interactive database*, which means you initiate each action the computer carries out by running one of the built-in commands, so you have to know the Access commands and capabilities. Further, if a task has many steps, you have to know the correct sequence of steps so that you can issue the correct sequence of commands. In an interactive database, you have complete control. You have the power to use the interactive database in meaningful, productive ways; but you also have the power to corrupt your data and damage the database by selecting the wrong command at the wrong time.

In order to protect the database, and at the same time make your database easier to use, you can take the next step beyond an interactive database and customize your database using the tools that Access provides. With these tools you can turn your interactive database into a custom database application.

A *custom database application* is a database that you've automated so that it can be used by any computer user (even by someone who doesn't know Access). Users don't have to know the sequence of steps required for a task, nor do they have to know the Access commands. They need only click a single button to execute a complicated task. But unless you've designed the custom database application properly, users can still corrupt the data and damage the database.

This book is about creating custom database applications according to the following principle:

> *The fundamental purpose of a custom database application is to protect the data by controlling how the user can work with the data.*

The database application you create using this book gives power to the user, but puts the application itself in control by

- ensuring the accuracy of the data

- organizing and controlling the work flow to prevent tasks from being done out of order

- guiding the user through the application while providing help and feedback

The guidelines this book follows for developing an Access application are spelled out in "Application Development Guidelines," which follows.

Application Development Guidelines

Following are the guidelines used in this book for developing an Access application. They are based on an article by Stan Leszynski called "Building Bulletproof Access Applications" (*Access Advisor*, February/March 1994).

1. Give your application a separate identity by creating a shortcut icon on the Windows 95 desktop that launches both Access and your application (so users don't have to search through folders).

2. Give your application a custom opening act by setting startup conditions such that users can begin productive work immediately.

3. Hide the Database window so that your tables, queries, and macros are not directly available.

(continued)

4. Hide the Access built-in menus and toolbars; display custom menus and toolbars that contain exactly the commands users need to do productive work.

5. Let users see the basic organization of the application at a glance. Display a main menu form, or switchboard, with a list of the tasks they can carry out with the application.

6. Control how users work with the forms in order to avoid data integrity problems. Allow users to work with only one form at a time—usually this means displaying only one form at a time. If two forms are displayed, this means preventing users from changing data using both forms.

7. Test sample data to ensure that changes and new data are validated before saving.

8. Design forms for maximum data protection by removing or disabling features that could lead to data corruption.

9. Provide help and feedback by using ToolTips, status bar messages, message boxes, visual cues and instructions on forms.

10. Provide a log-in form to track the use of the application.

You'll learn how to implement the guidelines as you transform an interactive database into a custom database application. The path from one to the other requires dealing with two major issues:

- automating database tasks so as to pass the maximum amount of manual labor to the computer

- controlling how users work with the application

These issues require a seemingly endless series of design decisions; the charm of Access is that so many alternatives are available.

Selecting an Automation Tool—Macros or Access Visual Basic?

Access provides two sets of tools to automate database tasks: macro programming and Visual Basic for Applications (VBA). Both tools write instructions that shift the labor burden from you to the computer. Visual Basic for Applications is a full-featured programming language and is the more powerful tool, but it is also a lot harder to learn. This book refers to Visual Basic for Applications as either VBA or Visual Basic. When you write a Visual Basic program, you begin with a blank Module window (see Figure 1.1). Before you can create Visual Basic programs, you must master the spelling, grammar, and syntax of the Visual Basic language.

FIGURE 1.1:
The Module window used to write Access Visual Basic programs.

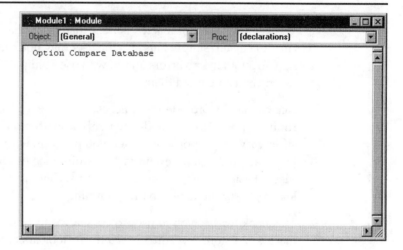

In contrast, you create Access macros in a Macro window (see Figure 1.2) by pointing and clicking to provide the additional information Access needs to carry out the action. Figure 1.2 shows the Macro window.

The structure of the Macro window minimizes your need to learn the syntax of macro programming. With nearly 50 macro actions to choose from, Access macro programming is powerful enough to create sophisticated custom applications.

FIGURE 1.2:

The Macro window used to write
Access macros.

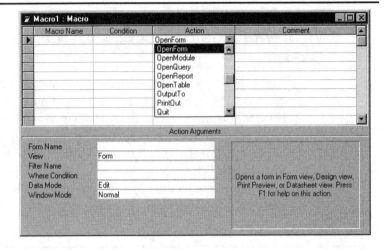

The key limitation of macros is their inability to handle errors; when an error occurs, the macro simply fails and the user may not know why. This book shows you how to avoid macro errors and how to use a simple VBA program to handle errors when you can't avoid them.

Access macros provide the quickest way to get an application prototype up and running. Power users and developers use mixtures of Access macros and Visual Basic in varying proportions. When you program with Visual Basic, you still need to know about macros; certain tasks require macros and others are programmed in Visual Basic by using macro actions. Everyone who automates an Access database learns at least some macro programming.

This book teaches you to use Access macros to automate your database. You create macros to customize menu commands and toolbars, automate database tasks, navigate among the tasks in your application, test conditions and make decisions, and carry out repetitive tasks. Along the way I'll note the limitations of Access macros so that you'll know when your application needs the additional power of Access Visual Basic.

Deciding on a Naming Standard

Even the simplest Access database has hundreds of objects: tables, fields, indexes, queries, forms, controls, reports, and properties. The main purpose of a naming standard is to make clear, at first glance, the type and purpose of the object. A naming standard can also suggest the relationship between different objects. Using a consistent naming standard helps to bring order to your database and makes your application easier for both you and others to understand.

The Leszynski/Reddick Guidelines

This book uses a naming standard that follows, with a few exceptions, the conventions first introduced by Stan Leszynski and Greg Reddick in "Naming Objects in Access: Version 2 of a Proposed Standard" (*Smart Access Journal*, Aug. 1993), and updated in "Revisions to the Leszynski-Reddick Naming Standard for Access 2.0" (*Smart Access Journal*, May 1994). We'll refer to these guidelines as the L/R naming standard. New versions of the standard for Microsoft Access for Windows 95 should be available shortly.

According to the standard, you give each of your objects a name with at least two parts, a *tag* and a *base name*. The tag refers to the type of the object and is usually three or four lowercase letters. The tag is followed by the base name. The base name is the name you would use if you weren't following a naming convention. Here are some examples:

Object Name	Tag	Base Name
tblInstructors	tbl	Instructors
qryEnrollmentSummary	qry	EnrollmentSummary
frmAppointments	frm	Appointments
rptClassList	rpt	ClassList
cboScheduleNo	cbo	ScheduleNo
qfltEnrollmentBySize	qflt	EnrollmentBySize

Capitalize the first letter of the base name, and don't use spaces. If the base name contains more than one word, capitalize each word. It is preferable to spell out words entirely, but abbreviations are okay if they are long enough to be memorable (or better still, recognizable by someone else trying to understand your work). After working with the naming convention for a while, you'll find that your eye quickly glides over the tag to the base name. This book uses the tags listed in Tables 1.1 and 1.2.

TABLE 1.1: Tags for objects in the Database window.

Object	Tag	Example
Table	tbl	tblStudents
Table(linking) [1]	tlnk[table1][table2]	tlnkClassStudent
Query	qry	qryEnrollment
Query(autolookup) [2]	qalk[oneside][manyside]	qalkStudentClass
Query(append)	qapp	qappClasses
Query(delete)	qdel	qdelClasses
Query(filter) [3]	qflt	qfltEnrollmentBySize
Query(parameter) [4]	qpar	qparCourseClass
Query(lookup) [5]	qlkp	qlkpInstructorName
Query(update)	qupd	qupdClassSchedule
Query(totals)	qtot	qtotMissingGrades
Form	frm	frmRegistration
Form(dialog)	fdlg	fdlgEnrollment
Form(sub) [6]	[formname]Sub	frmRegistrationSub
Report	rpt	rptClassSchedule
Report(sub) [6]	[reportname]Sub	rptClassListSubStudent
Macro [7]	mcr	mcrToolbars
Macro(for form)	m[formname]	mfrmRegistration
Macro(for report)	m[reportname]	mrptEnrollment
Macro(menu)	mmnu[name]	mmnuMenuBar
Module	bas	basFunctionLibrary

[1] The *linking table* of a many-to-many relationship

[2] The *autolookup query* for two tables in a one-to-many side relationship. An autolookup query requires that the join field for the table on the one side of the relationship has a unique index and that the query includes the join field from the many side.

TABLE 1.1: Tags for objects in the Database window *(continued)*.

[3] A query used to filter a form's (or a report's) underlying table or query.

[4] A query with criteria specified interactively or specified by a form.

[5] A query used to provide lists for combo boxes and list boxes.

[6] Sub is called a *qualifier* (not a tag). Qualifiers are placed after a base name and have the first letter capitalized. Here the qualifier Sub is used so that the form and its subform will appear together in the Database window. When a form has more than one subform, an identifying word follows Sub, as in rptClassListSubStudent and rptClassListSubInstructor. The L/R naming standards provide an alternate way to name subforms and subreports by using tags fsub and rsub; for example, fsubRegistration.

[7] There are two special macros without tags called *AutoExec* and *AutoKeys,* which must have exactly these names in order to be recognized by Access.

TABLE 1.2: Tags for controls on forms and reports.

Object	Tag	Example
Label	lbl	lblTotalFee
Combo box	cbo	cboScheduleNo
List box	lst	lstSession
Command button	cmd	cmdCancel
Option group	grp	grpLocation
Check box	chk	chkCancelled

NOTE

If you want to change the name of an object in your database, use the Find and Replace add-in (described in the Introduction) so that you find all instances of the object name and all changes are spelled correctly.

What the User Sees

When you create a custom database application using the guidelines and techniques in this book, the users see only forms and reports. They see the form and report captions, but not the coded object names you use when you create the application. The captions the user sees should be informative and free of jargon.

Here are some examples:

Object Name	Caption
frmClassList	Class List
frmRegistration	Class Registration
rptStudentProgram	Program Verification Report
rptMailLabelsStud	Mailing Labels: Students

Since we'll be working behind the scenes most of the time, I'll usually refer to a form or report by its object name. When we look at an object from the user's perspective, I'll often use the caption instead.

Getting to Know the College Database

This book assumes that you already know how to create an interactive database complete with tables, queries, forms, and reports. To illustrate the automation of an interactive database, we'll work with the example database contained on the disk. The best approach to learning a new technique is to work through it using the example database first and then try it out with your own database.

The example database, College.mdb, is a model for tracking information at a college. Here are the basic characteristics that are modeled:

- The college offers classes at three locations: a main campus, a downtown campus, and a set of off-campus sites.

- A *program* (also called a department) consists of the full-time faculty members who teach in a specific subject area. Examples of programs are Biology, Business, Microsoft Training, Multimedia Studies, and Cinema. Programs are also the administrative units that hire part-time instructors, appoint teachers to classes, develop courses and offer the courses as classes.

- A *course* is a plan of instruction for a narrowly defined topic in the subject area. Faculty in the program define a course by describing its concepts and objectives and writing a detailed outline of the topics and a plan for the lectures, recitations, and laboratory. Each course is assigned a unique course number. Courses are described in a college *bulletin* or *catalogue* printed annually. Examples of courses in the College database are:

> Biology 300, Nature Study
>
> Cinema 310, Workshop in Film Production
>
> Business 682, The Environment of Business

- A *class* is an individual offering of a course at a specific time and place, and taught by a specific instructor.

- The college divides the year into four *sessions* as follows:

> Winter session—January
>
> Spring session—February through May
>
> Summer session—June through August
>
> Fall session—September through December

- During each session a program may schedule and offer a class at a specific time and place. For example, during Spring 1996, the Biology program offers two classes of Biology 300 as follows:

> Biology 300, section 1; 10:00 Monday, Wednesday, Friday; 100 Low Hall
>
> Biology 300, section 2; 11:00 Tuesday, Thursday; 100 Low Hall

- The college publicizes the classes in a *class schedule* printed for each session. Each class has a unique schedule number assigned by the college. Classes may be team-taught by two or more instructors. Classes may be offered for academic credit (which counts toward degree requirements), for continuing education credit (which does not count toward degree requirements), or for no credit at all.

- An *instructor* is a full-time faculty member or a part-time person appointed to teach a class. Instructors are identified by social security number. Instructors are assigned, or *appointed*, to teach one or more classes during a session. Their duties are to teach the course material as described in the course outline and evaluate the performance of the students.

- A *student* is a person who enrolls or *registers* in a class and participates in the lectures and laboratory. Students are identified by social security number. Typically, students register for several classes during a session. At the end of a session, the instructor evaluates the performance of the students registered in the class and assigns grades.

I chose this particular example database because it contains familiar examples of both one-to-many and many-to-many relationships. Many-to-many relationships are more complicated to work with and you may not have mastered them yet, so you'll have another opportunity here. In fact, the College database has two of each kind of relationship; the tutorial deals with one pair and the optional exercises cover the other pair. Here are the relationships in the College database:

- A program lists many courses in the college bulletin and each course is owned by only one program, so there is a one-to-many relationship between programs and courses.

- A course is offered during a session as one or more individual classes, so there is a one-to-many relationship between courses and classes.

- A student may enroll in many classes and a class has many students (classes with only one student are cancelled), so there is a many-to-many relationship between students and classes.

- Classes may be team-taught. Because a class may have more than one instructor and an instructor may teach several classes, there is a many-to-many relationship between classes and instructors.

As you work with different databases, you quickly realize that database models for most real-life business and personal situations have similar kinds of data and similar kinds of relationships and database tasks. The techniques you learn while working with a specific database are transferable to others by simply changing the names of the objects. This book uses specific terminology and operations for an educational model (such as registering students in classes and testing that all grades have been assigned before archiving records at the end of a session) to teach you how to automate database operations; however, you can use the same methods to automate analogous operations in other scenarios, such as taking customers' orders and testing that all invoices have been approved before payment checks are printed.

Fundamental to all relational database management systems is the way they store data. A *relational database management system* stores facts for different subjects in separate tables. The College database stores facts for programs, courses, classes, instructors, and students in five main tables. A relational database can produce information based on two or more tables if you relate the tables correctly. The data tables, together with the relationships that you define between them, form the *structure* of your database. It is fair to say that your database is only as good as its database structure. Deciding what facts to store and how to organize them into separate tables requires careful thought and planning. You simply can't analyze the data in all of the ways needed and produce the kinds of reports you want if the database structure is faulty.

Characteristics of a Relational Database

These are the three basic characteristics of a well-designed relational database:

- Each table contains information about a single subject.

- The information in two tables can be related so that they appear as if they were one table. You can relate two tables if each has a matching field with values in common. The process used to relate the tables, called a *join*, uses the duplicated information in the matching fields to relate the records in the two tables.

- The only fields that must have duplicated information are the matching fields. Thus, a relational database can be designed to minimize the duplication of information.

To organize the facts into separate tables and achieve the minimum amount of duplication you use a process called *normalization*. Normalization is part of the complex mathematical theory of relational database design. For most databases, you can achieve a reasonable degree of normalization by following a simple set of rules when you design.

1. Each field in a table contains a single kind of information. As an example, you should have separate fields for a person's first name and last name.

2. Each table has a field or combination of fields (called the *primary key*) with values that uniquely identify a record. There can be no duplicate records. As an example, there can be only one record in the instructors table for each instructor; each record is uniquely identified by an instructor ID number.

3. The information in each (non-primary key) field must be relevant to the subject of the table. As an example, you should not store information about the classes that a student takes in the student table; the student table should store only information about the student.

4. The information in each (non-primary key) field must depend on all parts of the primary key. As an example, the table that stores registration information has a two-field primary key composed of a student number and a class number; this table must not have a field for student name data because student name data depends only on the student number and not the class number.

5. Each field in a record contains only one value. As an example, if you intend to store both work and home telephone numbers for instructors, a single telephone field isn't sufficient and you'll need separate work and home telephone fields in the instructor table.

6. Each record in a table has the same number of fields. In the telephone number example, each record in the instructors table must have the same number of fields for storing telephone numbers, so if you know that some instructors have several phone numbers while others have only one or two, it would be more efficient to move the telephone fields into a separate telephone table instead of creating additional fields in the instructors table.

7. The information in each (non-primary key) field must be independent of all other fields. As an example, you should not include any calculated fields such as the total fees due from a student (the sum of the class fees for all classes a student is registered in).

NOTE

In Microsoft Access for Windows 95, there are two new wizards that can help you create a normalized database: the Database Wizard and the Table Analyzer Wizard. You can use the Database Wizard to create a simple database application (for more than 20 sample scenarios) complete with normalized tables and relationships, queries, forms, and reports. If you are starting from scratch, you can use the Table Analyzer Wizard to help you normalize a table that you have already set up.

Observing the Structure of the College Database

1. Start Access, and choose File ➤ Open Database.
2. In the Database window, locate and double-click the Automate folder to open it.
3. Double-click College.
4. Choose Tools ➤ Relationships. Figure 1.3 shows the Relationships window.

The Tables

Tables store the facts for each of the five subjects: tblPrograms, tblCourses, tblClasses, tblInstructors, and tblStudents. Each of the five basic data tables has a DateModified field for keeping track of when you edit a record. The primary key for each of these tables, indicated in bold in the field list, is a *single field*. The techniques you learn in this book work without modification only if the primary key is a single field for each of the basic data tables. (Although you can modify most of the techniques for multiple-field primary keys, there is usually little reason to deviate from this database design guideline.)

When you create two tables that have a many-to-many relationship you must also create a *linking table* between them. You use the linking table as a go-between to convert the many-to-many relationship into a pair of one-to-many relationships between the two tables and their linking table. Put the primary key fields of each of the two data tables into the linking table, then designate these fields as the *composite primary key* for the linking table. Add to the linking table any additional fields that

FIGURE 1.3:

The Relationships window displays the five basic data tables of the College database, two linking tables, and the relationships between them.

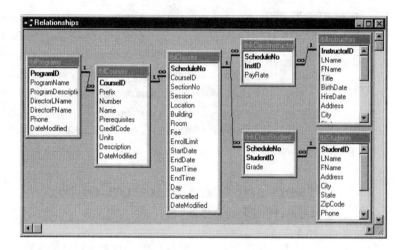

describe the relationship itself. Name a linking table with the tag "tlnk" and a base name that includes at least a part of each of the base names of the two tables. Figure 1.4 depicts the many-to-many relationship between classes and students, and Figure 1.5 demonstrates the resolution of the many-to-many relationship into a pair of one-to-many relationships.

The tlnkClassStudent table is the linking table for the many-to-many relationship between the tblClasses and tblStudents tables. The tlnkClassStudent table contains three fields: the primary keys from tblClasses and tblStudents, as a two-field primary key, and a field to store the grade the student receives in the class. Each record in the linking table corresponds to a student enrolled in a class. In the same way, the tlnkClassInstructor table is the linking table for the many-to-many relationship between the tables tblClasses and tblInstructors. This table contains the primary keys from tblClasses and tblInstructors, as a two-field primary key, and a field to store the instructor's pay rate for teaching the class.

The Relationships window displays the relationships among the five basic tables and the two linking tables (see Figure 1.3). The relationship join lines with their 1 and ∞ symbols reflect the decision to have Access enforce the *referential integrity rules* for each relationship.

The referential integrity rules prevent you from creating records in the table on the many (child) side of a relationship unless there is a corresponding record in the table

FIGURE 1.4:

The many-to-many relationship between Classes and Students.

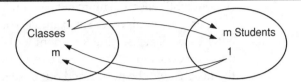

FIGURE 1.5:

The linking table tlnkClassStudent links the tblClasses table to the tblStudents table.

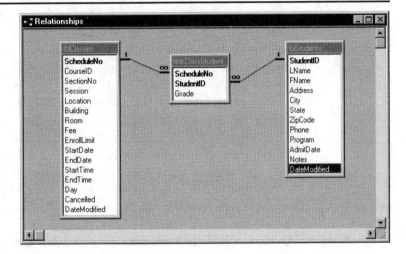

on the one (parent) side. For example, you can't add a class unless there is an approved course and you can't register a student until the class is scheduled. When you enforce referential integrity, you are not allowed to create "orphan" records in the child table. This means

- You can't add a record to the child table unless there is a corresponding parent record in the parent table.

- You can't delete a record from the parent table if the record has corresponding child records in the child table.

- You can't change the primary key value for a record in the parent table if the record has corresponding child records in the child table.

Enforcing the referential integrity rules protects the data by preventing inconsistencies such as a student registered in a non-existent class.

A more subtle effect of enforcing referential integrity is that a specific order for data entry operations is imposed. For example, you must enter data for a new class before you enter data for registering a student in it. In designing the navigation between the data entry operations, you need to build in the required data entry sequence so that the tasks cannot be performed out of sequence.

The Relationships window doesn't indicate whether the Cascade options have been chosen. The Cascade options let you modify the restrictions while still preventing "orphan" records. When you check Cascade Update Related Records, you can change a primary key value of a parent record and Access automatically updates the matching value in the related child records. When you check Cascade Delete Related Records, you can delete a parent record with corresponding child records and Access automatically deletes the child records. You can view the Cascade options by right-clicking a relationship line, then choosing the Edit Relationship command. Figure 1.6 shows the Relationships dialog, with Cascade settings, for the relationship between tblCourses and tblClasses. The Cascade Update Related Fields checkbox is checked, which indicates that you can change the CourseID for a course and Access will update its scheduled classes automatically (the data change will be "cascaded" to other tables). The Cascade Delete Related Records options is not checked, which means that you can delete a course only if there are no classes scheduled for it, but you can't delete a course if you've already scheduled classes for it (the data change will not be "cascaded" to other tables).

FIGURE 1.6:

The Cascade options for the relationship between tblCourses and tblClasses. With these options you can change the Course ID, but you can't delete a course if you've already scheduled classes for it.

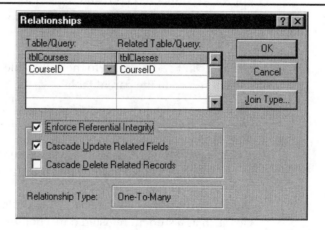

There are several other tables in the database in addition to the five basic data tables and two linking tables:

- Two lookup tables, tblCreditType and tblLocation, provide text equivalents for the numerical values that result from using option groups on the data entry form for courses (frmCourses) and classes (frmClasses).

- The tblDays table stores the various combinations of the days of the week that classes are offered; this table provides the list for the combo box used on the data entry form for classes (frmClasses).

- The tblSession table stores the values of the sessions, e.g., Spr 96 and Sum 96.

The Historical Tables

There are three historical tables, which store archived data from the three data tables that change each session: tblClassesHist, tlnkClassStudentHist and tlnkClassInstructorHist. At the end of each session, you complete your work by closing out the session. *Closing out* is a series of database operations: testing that all classes have been assigned instructors and all grades have been given, calculating session summary totals, posting the records for the session to the corresponding historical tables (*archiving the records*), and deleting the records from the current session tables. By removing the records for a completed session from the tables that hold the current sessions, you protect the historical data from inadvertent changes.

In addition to the historical tables for the data tables, there is a historical table that stores enrollment summary information for each session, tblEnrollmentSummaryHist.

The Queries

Queries serve a wide variety of purposes in any database. The College database uses queries for the following:

- To combine data from two or more tables into a recordset with temporary records. For example, qryCourses combines fields from tblCourses and tblCreditType to create records with course and credit information.

- To select records that satisfy specified criteria. For example, qryClasswoInstructors selects classes for which no instructors have been appointed.

- To sort records in a single table. For example, qlkpStudentName selects fields from tblStudents and sorts the records by last name.

- To perform calculations on each temporary record in the dynaset. For example, qryInstructorName includes the last name and first name fields from tblInstructors and concatenates these fields into a new name column.

- To perform calculations on groups of records. For example, qryEnrollment-Summary counts the number of students registered in a class.

- To look up information automatically. For example, qalkCourseClass is an autolookup query that combines fields from tblCourses, tblClasses, tblPrograms, tblCreditType and tblLocation and looks up course information when the CourseID is specified.

- To append and delete groups of records. For example, qdelClasses deletes records from tblClasses for a specified session. This query also deletes the related records in tlnkClassStudent and tlnkClassInstructor, since the Cascade Deleted Records option has been selected for the relationships between tblClasses and the two linking tables.

Query Performance Considerations

It's a good idea to index the fields on both sides of a query join, in order to speed the execution of a query that joins two or more tables. When you index the fields on both sides of a join, Access uses the index in the second table to find the records in the second table that match the index in the first table.

Access has several ways to perform a join. In order to optimize query performance, Access rearranges the query internally and then selects one of several join strategies to run the query in the shortest time. Indexing the fields on both sides of the join allows Access to select a faster join strategy. Access automatically creates an index for primary key fields. When you create a relationship in the Relationship window, Access automatically creates an index for the matching fields.

Additionally, you can index the fields that you use for setting multiple selection criteria in order to take advantage of another optimization capability, called *Rushmore query optimization*. Rushmore query optimization involves an internal reordering of the steps used to execute a query to take optimal advantage of indexes.

The Forms

An Access database uses forms to enter, edit, and review the data stored in fields in the tables. Forms have *data controls* that act like windows into the fields to let you see the values stored there.

The College database allows you to work on multiple sessions, but only one session at a time. You use the frmSwitchboard form to select the session you want to work with.

The College database uses forms in three distinct ways: for *entering data* into the five basic data tables, for entering data into some of the data controls while reviewing data in the rest, and for *reviewing data*. Controls used for review are locked and disabled. You use forms with different editing capabilities to protect data from inadvertent changes, and also to control the sequence of data entry into related tables that have the Enforce Referential Integrity option checked.

FIGURE 1.7:
The form used to select records for a session.

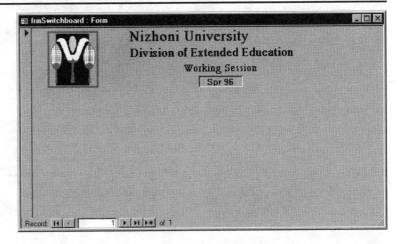

The Data Entry Forms

You should design data entry forms so that data can be entered or edited in data controls only if the data meets the validation rules you set. Access automatically checks for uniqueness of the primary key values and enforces your referential integrity options. In addition to data entry controls, the form may have a few locked controls that you use to keep track of when and by whom the record was last edited.

The College database has data entry forms for four of the five basic data tables: frmInstructors, frmStudents, frmCourses, and frmPrograms, respectively. Figure 1.8 shows the frmCourses data entry form.

The Review-Data Entry Forms

In review-data entry forms, you can add or edit data in some, but not all, controls. The controls that display information for review only are disabled and locked to protect the data. To give the user a visual clue, they may have a different back color from editable controls.

Use review-data entry forms for data entry into linking tables. The key to understanding a linking table is this: a linking table is always on the many side of a one-to-many relationship, and referential integrity requires that the record for the table on one side must be entered and saved before you can enter a record into the table on the many side. One way to control the sequence of data entry into related tables is to use a review-data entry

FIGURE 1.8:

The frmCourses data entry form.

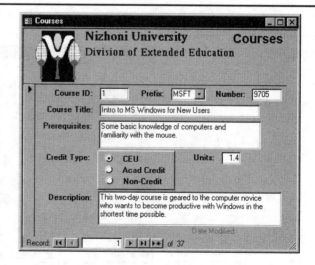

form with the controls from the one side locked and the controls from the many side available for editing.

The College database uses review-data entry forms for both of the linking tables. You use the frmAppointments form to appoint instructors to classes (see Figure 1.9). This is the data entry form for the tlnkClassInstructor linking table. The referential integrity rules require that you enter and save the record for an instructor (in the tblInstructor table) before you appoint the instructor to a class (by creating a record in the tlnkClassInstructor table). One way to preserve the required order of operations is to require that you enter and save new instructor information (with the frmInstructors data entry form) before letting you appoint the instructor to a class (with the frmAppointments form). The frmAppointments form displays review information for an instructor and for each class as soon as you make the assignment. You can change only the two controls associated with the appointment.

The frmRegistration form, used to register students in classes, is another review-data entry form with disabled and locked controls; it displays information about the student and classes and has a single enabled control to do the registration. This is the data entry form for the tlnkClassStudent linking table.

Other review-data entry forms are frmClasses (the data entry form for the tblClasses table, which also displays information from the tblCourses table), and frmClassList (which has a single enabled control to assign grades, and also displays review information for the class, the instructor(s) and the students registered in the class).

FIGURE 1.9:

The frmAppointments form is the data entry form for the tlnkClassInstructor linking table.

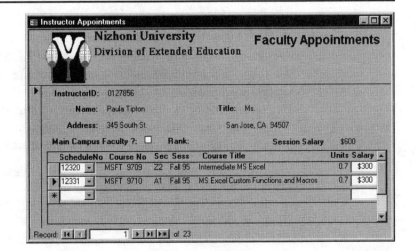

The Review Forms

In a review form, all of the data controls are locked and disabled. To provide a visual cue the background color may match the form color.

In the College database, review forms include frmListofClasses (a list of classes), frmClassSchedule (which provides class schedule information in a tabular form), frmCourseList (a list of approved courses), and frmEnrollmentSummary (which provides the current enrollment figures for each class). Figure 1.10 shows the frmClassSchedule form.

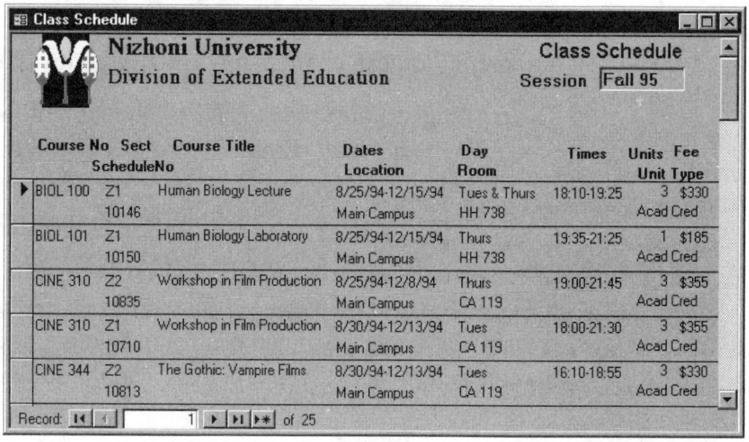

FIGURE 1.10:

The frmClassSchedule form is used to review, but not edit, data.

The Reports

The College database has a variety of reports to publicize the offerings of the college. As examples, the rptCourseList report is a list of courses along with course descriptions and prerequisites; the rptClassSchedule report is a list of class schedule information including times, dates, location, and instructors; the rptMailLabelInstructor and rptMailLabelStudent reports generate mailing labels; and the rptStudentProgram report generates written verification of the student's program.

The College database contains most of the tables, queries, forms, and reports needed for the instructional database tasks. Spend a little time becoming familiar with the tables, queries, forms and reports in the College database. Appendix D provides more information about these objects.

Customizing Your Working Environment

You can be more efficient and shorten development time by changing how you work with Access. This section shows you ways to customize your Access working environment.

Setting Options

Access allows you to make a number of changes in the way that it operates.

1. Choose Tools ➤ Options, then click the View tab. The tabs in the Options dialog box indicate the categories of options you can change. You can get online Help for any of the options by pressing F1. Figure 1.11 shows the View options and on-screen help for the Macro Design grouping.

FIGURE 1.11:
The Tools ➤ Options dialog box, showing the ways you can change the Access environment.

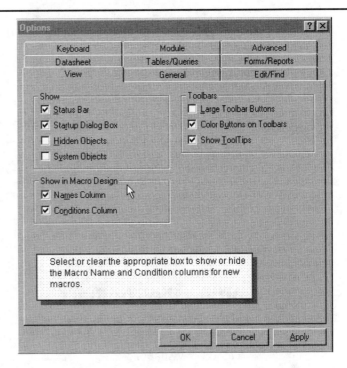

2. With the View tab displayed, make sure the Status Bar, Startup Dialog Box, Color Buttons on Toolbars and Show ToolTips checkboxes are checked, then check the Names Column and the Conditions Column checkboxes.

3. You can click Apply to apply the changes immediately or click OK to close the dialog and apply the changes.

The changes you make with the Tools ➤ Options command are not part of the current database (your .mdb file); instead, they are stored in a file called the *workgroup information file*. The workgroup information file stores information about the options you set and any security restrictions you make.

CAUTION   The options you set become part of your Access environment and will affect all of the databases created by anyone who is using the same workgroup information file. You can't change these settings without affecting other databases.

You can make other changes that affect only the database you are working on. For example, you can control how your database starts up by using the Startup dialog. Chapter 2, "Building a User Interface," shows you how to set startup options.

TIP   While you are developing an application, you can improve performance by opening the database in exclusive mode. This avoids the overhead necessary to manage a multi-user database. For example, in exclusive mode, Access doesn't have to take time to lock and unlock a data page each time you edit a record, and doesn't have to create the locking information (.ldb) file. You can set the Exclusive option in the Tools ➤ Options dialog box, Advanced tab.

Customizing the Toolbars

You can customize the built-in toolbars by adding, deleting, and rearranging the buttons; the buttons can be built-in, or custom buttons that you create with macros and/or Access Visual Basic.

NOTE   Information regarding changes to the built-in toolbars is also stored in the workgroup information file, so when you customize a built-in toolbar, the changed toolbar appears in all the databases created by anyone using the same workgroup information file. If you add a custom button, the button will appear in the other databases, but it won't be functional unless you copy the macro or Access Visual Basic program to the other databases.

1. Choose View ➤ Toolbars. A list box displays the built-in toolbars, with a checkmark next to any toolbar that is visible (see Figure 1.12).

2. Click the check box for the Print Preview toolbar to display the toolbar. Unless this toolbar has already been customized, it won't include a Design View button. When you are designing a report, it is convenient to be able to toggle between Print Preview and Design View. You can add a Design View button to the Print Preview toolbar.

3. On the Toolbars dialog, click the Customize button. The Customize Toolbars dialog displays a list box with categories of built-in buttons (see Figure 1.13). When you select a category, the box to the right displays the available buttons. The Design View button is in the View category.

FIGURE 1.12:
Use the Toolbars dialog to show or hide toolbars.

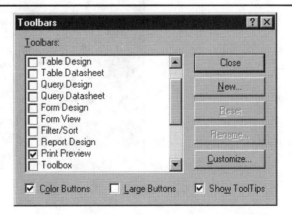

4. Select the View Category. Click the Design View button and drag it onto the Print Preview toolbar. Drop it just to the right of the Close button.

5. Click the Close button on the Customize Toolbars dialog box.

6. Choose <u>V</u>iew ➤ Tool<u>b</u>ars, and clear the Print Preview check box.

In the same way, you can add any button to any toolbar; however, if the button runs a command that is not available for a particular view, it will appear dimmed. For example, you can add a Build button to the Form View toolbar, but the button will remain dimmed.

Customize the built-in toolbars by adding the Run button to several of them. You use the Run button to update the records in any Datasheet view or in Form view.

1. In the Toolbars dialog, check the Form View, Table Datasheet, and Query Datasheet checkboxes, then click Close.

FIGURE 1.13:

Drag the Design View button from the Customize Toolbars dialog onto the Print Preview toolbar.

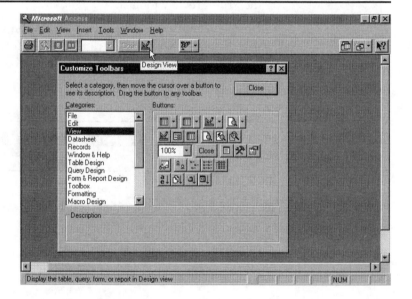

2. Using the steps described above, customize the toolbars as follows:

Toolbar	Category	Add	Reason
Form View	Records	Run	To update the data in the underlying records (equivalent to SHIFT+F9)
Table Datasheet	Records	Run	To update the datasheet
Query Datasheet	Records	Run	To update the datasheet by running the query

3. Choose View ➤ Toolbars and clear the check boxes for each of these toolbars (to hide them in Database view), then click Close.

NOTE When you manually select a toolbar in the Toolbars dialog for a view other than the view currently displayed, the toolbar you select is displayed in all views. To show or hide the toolbar for a particular view only when that view is current, make sure that view is current when you open the Toolbars dialog. For example, to show or hide the Form View toolbar in Form view only, open a form in Form view, then choose View ➤ Toolbars and check or clear the Form View check box. To show the Form View toolbar at all times, make sure Form view is not the current view when you show or hide the toolbar.

Designing for Consistency

When you design an application, one of the most important design considerations is consistency. Consistency makes your application much easier to learn and use.

- Your application should be consistent with other Windows applications. Windows users expect controls to look and behave in familiar ways. For example, Windows typically uses a sunken textbox control for data entry and a raised button for issuing commands.

- Your application should have internal consistency. Color schemes and placement of controls should be consistent throughout your forms, and data entry controls and review controls should provide different visual cues. Your reports should have standardized headers and fonts.

There are two techniques that can help you maintain a consistent approach in your application. First, you can customize the templates that Access uses when you create a new form or report without using a Form Wizard. The second method is to create a set of your own "masters" for each application and then use the masters to create new forms and reports. The masters contain your own default settings and the specific controls you want on forms and reports.

Creating Custom Form and Report Templates

When you create a form without using a wizard, Access uses a template called Normal to define the default characteristics of the form (including the property settings for the controls, the form sections, and the form itself). When you create a report from scratch, Access uses a report template, also called Normal. You can create your own custom form and report templates and replace the built-in templates.

Observing the Normal Form Template

You can observe the built-in Normal form template by creating a new blank form.

1. On the toolbar, click the arrow on the New Object button, then select New Form from the dropdown list. Make sure the combo box is empty and click OK.

2. Switch to Form view. When you create a new form, Access includes a set of *default form controls* arranged around the perimeter of the form, including control box, minimize, maximize, and close buttons, vertical and horizontal scroll bars, navigation buttons, a new records button, and a record selector. Figure 1.14 shows the default form controls.

3. Switch to Design view. The displayed form has neither Header nor Footer and only a Detail section which is 5" wide and 1" tall. The Back Color is light gray. Place a sample of each control type on the form in order to observe the default control properties in the Normal form template.

FIGURE 1.14:
The default form controls around the perimeter.

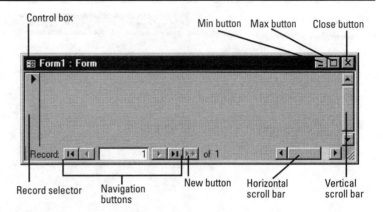

4. If necessary, deselect the Control Wizards tool in the toolbox by clicking the Control Wizards tool so that it is not pressed in.

5. For each of the following controls: text box, option group, toggle button, option button, check box, combo box, list box and command button, select the corresponding tool from the toolbox and draw the control on the form. Observe the default control properties in the Property sheet for each control. Figure 1.15 shows the Normal form template and the default properties for a text box.

6. Switch to Form view. Observe the default controls, then close the form without saving.

Creating a Custom Form Template

The database application design guidelines given earlier in the chapter include guidelines for designing forms to help to protect data and to control navigation among the database tasks. You can create custom form templates that follow these guidelines. For example, you can remove several of the default form controls from the new template in order to control how the user works with your forms. As one step in controlling how a form is closed, you can remove the Control Box and the Close Box. To control the form's display, you can remove the Min button and the Max buttons.

FIGURE 1.15:

The Normal form template.

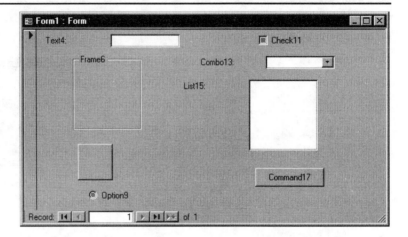

You often use forms to set validation rules for new or changed data (form-level validation) in addition to the rules you set in Table design view (table-level validation). You can restrict the user to Form view in order to enforce the form-level validation rules by disabling Datasheet view. Finally, you should size your forms to fit the screen and minimize scrolling around to view the data; this makes the horizontal scroll bar unnecessary. (The forms in the College database are designed for a VGA screen.)

You can also change the default settings for several of the control tools in the toolbox, to realign labels, close the gap between controls and their labels, and to remove label colons. When you are finished making changes, save the form as a new form template.

1. Switch to Design view, then choose View ➤ Form Header/Footer. Access displays Header and Footer sections 0.25" tall.

2. Select the form and change the default form properties as shown below. (With the Control Box and the Close button removed you have to use File ➤ Close or CTRL+F4 to close the form.)

ViewsAllowed	Form
ScrollBars	Vertical Only
ControlBox	No
MinMaxButtons	None
CloseButton	No

3. In the toolbox, click the Text Box tool and change its default properties as follows (then do the same for the Combo Box tool and the List Box tool):

AddColon	No
LabelX	-0.05
LabelAlign	Right

4. In the toolbox, click the Option Group tool and change its default properties as follows:

LabelX	-0.05
LabelY	0.0
LabelAlign	Right

5. Change the default properties of the Option Button and Check Box tools as follows:

LabelX	0.15

6. Save the form as **zsfrmTemplate** (see Figure 1.16).

The name for the template uses the *prefix* feature of the Leszynski/Reddick naming guidelines. A prefix can precede some tags and is used to provide additional information. The four prefixes are showr. in Table 1.3.

TABLE 1.3: Prefixes in the Leszynski/Reddick naming standard.

Prefix	Description
zs	For system objects that are part of the development and maintenance of your application but are not used by end users. The system objects sort to the bottom of the database container lists.
_	For objects that are under development. These objects sort to the top of the database container lists.
zz	For objects you are no longer using but want to keep for reference or reuse.
zt	For temporary objects such as test objects.

FIGURE 1.16:

The features of the new form template.

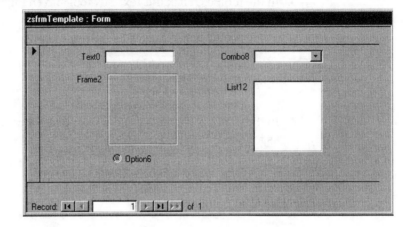

Creating a Custom Report Template

You can observe the built-in Normal report template by creating a new blank report.

1. On the toolbar, click the arrow on the New Object button and select New Report. Make sure the combo box is empty, then click OK. Access displays the Normal report template (see Figure 1.17). The default template has Page Header, Page Footer, and Detail sections, but no Report Header or Report Footer. You can place a sample of each type of report control on the template in order to observe the default control properties. Normally, only text box, label, line and rectangle controls are placed in reports.

2. In the toolbox, click the Text Box tool and draw a text box in the Detail section. Observe the default text box and label properties.

3. Change the default properties of the Text Box tool to close the gap between the control and its label as follows:

AddColon	No
LabelX	-0.05
LabelAlign	Right

4. Save the report as **zsrptTemplate**

FIGURE 1.17:

The Normal report template.

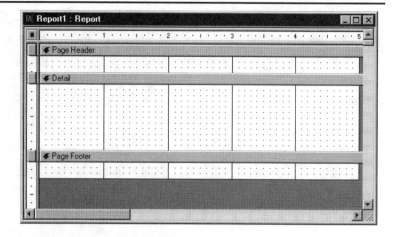

Replacing the Normal Templates

Now replace the Normal templates with the revised templates you just created.

1. Choose <u>T</u>ools ➤ <u>O</u>ptions, then click the Forms/Reports tab.

2. Click in the Form Template textbox and change Normal to **zsfrmTemplate**

3. Click in the Report Template textbox and change Normal to **zsrptTemplate** (see Figure 1.18).

4. Click OK.

Access saves the settings for the new templates in the workgroup information file, and uses the new templates for any other database you create as long as zsfrmTemplate and zsrptTemplate are copied into that database. If the custom templates are not copied into a database, then Access uses the default Normal templates (but continues to display the names of the custom templates in the <u>T</u>ools ➤ <u>O</u>ptions dialog box).

Creating Masters to Shorten Development Time

When you create a database, two important considerations are visual consistency of the forms and reports, and ease of development. The forms should have the same color scheme and font properties, and consistent visual cues for controls. You can accomplish this by using a custom form template. In addition, many of your forms

FIGURE 1.18:

The new template settings in the Options dialog box.

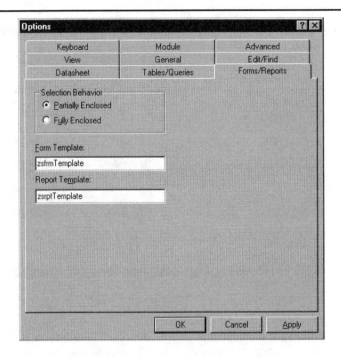

have similar functions and should have several identical controls (for example, you may include a logo and the corporation name, or a label displaying the purpose of the database, on all of your forms). Also, data entry forms should have the same command buttons to automate routine data entry operations, and the buttons should be in the same place on the forms for ease of use. A custom form template can't produce forms with custom controls, so you need to create a *form master* for each of the types of forms you plan to use. The form master will have specific logos, labels, command buttons, and other custom design features that you want for a particular type of form. To create a new form of a specific type, you need only copy the form master and add the specific data controls necessary for the new form.

By creating a set of form and report masters when you begin designing your application, you speed the process of creating the forms and reports and, at the same time, ensure visual consistency. In the College database many of the forms have been created, but we'll create a set of three masters for additional forms we create.

Since you'll be working with the forms in the College database, you first need to open the frmSwitchboard form to make sure the records for one session are selected. Leave the form open and minimized throughout the remainder of this chapter. In Chapter 2, "Building a User Interface," you'll learn how to start up the database with the frmSwitchboard form opened automatically.

> **CAUTION** If the frmSwithchboard form isn't open when you try to display the Form view of a form that depends on it, Access displays a dialog box prompting for the value of Forms ! frmSwitchboard ! WorkingSession. Click Cancel, open frmSwitchboard in Form view, and then open your form again.

1. In the Database window, click the Forms tab, then double-click frmSwitchboard.

2. Click the Minimize button on frmSwitchboard.

Creating a Form Master to Display a Single Record

The first form master is for displaying a single record.

1. In the Database window, click the Forms tab, then click the New button and click OK. A new blank form using the custom template properties is displayed.

2. In the Database window, double-click the frmStudents form. The frmStudents form is the data entry form for student information; the form header contains the logo and information labels that appear on all the College database forms (see Figure 1.19).

3. Switch to Design view, then press SHIFT while selecting the logo and the information labels and copy to the clipboard.

4. Click in the header of the new form and paste the controls (reposition as necessary).

5. Switch to Form view (see Figure 1.20).

6. Save the form as **zsfrmMaster**

FIGURE 1.19:

The frmStudents data entry form.

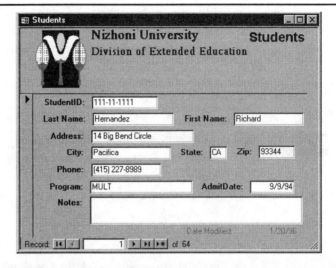

FIGURE 1.20:

The form master to display a single record. A form master can contain the specific controls such as a logo and labels that you want on all forms.

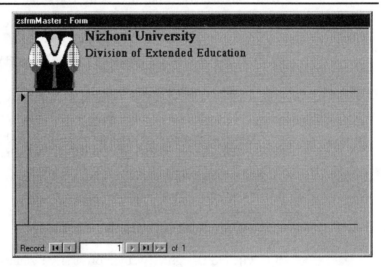

Creating a Form Master for a Tabular Form

The second form master is for displaying multiple records in a tabular format. A tabular format is good for reviewing information in as many records as will fit on the screen. Create a tabular form master by modifying the master you just created to shrink the logo and change the default view.

1. Switch to Design view, then select the logo and resize it so that the new dimensions are approximately two-thirds the original; decrease the Header section height to approximately 0.67", and decrease the Detail section height to 0.2".

2. Select the form and change the DefaultView property to Continuous Forms.

3. Save the form as **zsfrmMasterTabular** (see Figure 1.21).

FIGURE 1.21:

The form master for a tabular form.

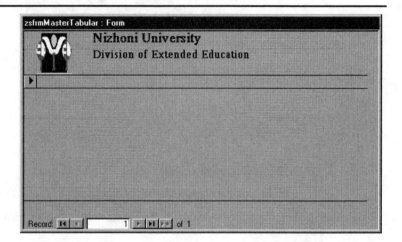

Creating a Form Master for a Subform

The third form master is for displaying subform records in a tabular format. When you use the Form Wizard to create a subform, the Wizard displays default navigation buttons in the lower right corner of the subform. For a more polished look, you can remove the subform navigation buttons (which can be especially confusing if the main form also displays navigation buttons). Create a subform master by modifying the tabular form master.

1. In the Database window, double-click frmRegistration. Observe that the subform displaying the instructor information has a tabular style and there are no navigation buttons or horizontal scroll bars (see Figure 1.22).

FIGURE 1.22:

The frmRegistration form with a subform in tabular form style, without navigation buttons.

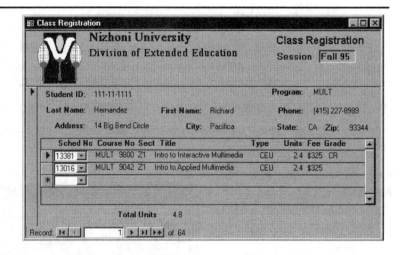

2. Close frmRegistration.

3. Select and delete the controls in the Header section of the open tabular form master, then set the height of the Header section to 0.2" and the height of the Footer section to 0.0".

4. Select the form and set the Navigation Button property to No.

5. Save the form as **zsfrmMasterSub** (see Figure 1.23), then close the form.

FIGURE 1.23:

The zsfrmMasterSub form master.

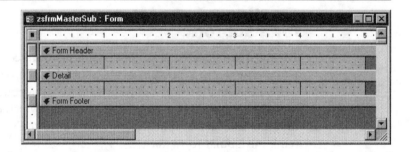

Create a New Form/Subform Using the Masters

To see how the masters work, create a new form with a subform to display the courses in each program.

Create the Main Form

The main form is created first, followed by the subform.

1. In the Database window, select zsfrmMaster, then copy and paste it with the name **frmCoursesByProgram**

2. Open frmCoursesByProgram in Design view; set the RecordSource property to tblPrograms, the Caption property to Courses By Program, and the Height property of the Footer section to 0.0".

3. From the field list, drag ProgramName to the upper left corner of the form's Detail section.

4. Select the ProgramName text box, then set the Enabled property to No and the Locked property to Yes.

5. On the toolbar, click the arrow on the Back Color button and select light gray (to match the form color).

Create the Subform

1. In the Database window, select zsfrmMasterSub, then copy and paste it as **frmCoursesByProgramSub**

2. Open frmCoursesByProgramSub in Design view, and set the RecordSource property to tblCourses and the AllowAdditions property to No. (The purpose of this form is to display records, and setting the AllowAdditions property to No avoids displaying a blank record at the bottom of the course list.)

3. One by one, drag the Prefix, Number and Name fields from the field list to the Detail section; select the three labels, then cut and paste them into the Header section.

4. Resize the text boxes for Prefix and Number to 0.5″ and the Name text box to 2″; move and align the text boxes below the corresponding labels.

6. Move the text box–label pairs to the left to minimize the width and set the width of the form to 3.25″ (see Figure 1.24).

7. On the toolbar, click the arrow on the Back Color button and select light gray (to match the form color).

8. Save and close the form.

FIGURE 1.24:

The frmCoursesByProgramSub form.

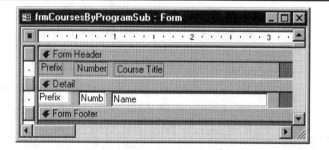

Creating the Form/Subform Combination

1. In the Database window, select frmCoursesByProgramSub, then drag the icon to the frmCoursesByProgram form and drop it just below the Program Name label (see Figure 1.25). (Access automatically sets the linking properties because the relationship between tblPrograms and tblCourses was defined in the Relationships window.)

2. Delete the label for the subform control, and set the subform control height to 2″ and width to 3.75″.

3. Switch to Form view and choose <u>W</u>indow ➤ Si<u>z</u>e to Fit Form (see Figure 1.26).

4. Save the result.

FIGURE 1.25:

Access uses the linking properties for the subform control to link the records of the subform to the records of the main form.

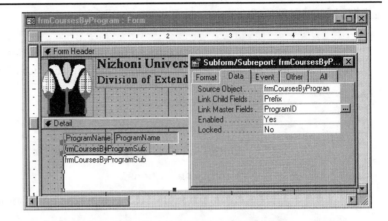

FIGURE 1.26:

The Courses By Program form.

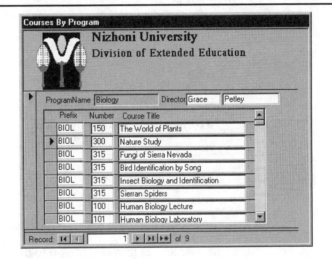

The form masters created in this chapter are just the beginning. As you learn new ways to use forms to control application flow in the chapters to come, you'll add new features to the masters. As examples, you add a command button to close a form in Chapter 2, "Building a User Interface"; and you add a combo box to navigate to a specific record in Chapter 7, "Using Macros to Navigate"; and you add command buttons to automate data entry operations in Chapter 8, "Data Entry Operations."

Endnotes

This chapter has introduced important guidelines to follow and decisions to make as you design and create a database application. The main ideas we looked at are:

- Tips and guidelines for

    controlling data entry

    controlling data integrity

    naming conventions

    customizing the Access working environment

- Modifying

    templates

    toolbars

- Creating

    masters for new forms

    a convenient work environment

- Concepts

    interactive databases

    custom database applications

    relational database management systems

Also, this chapter has introduced you to the College database, the interactive database you use throughout the book to learn the automating techniques. In the next chapter you begin the creation of a new face for your application.

On Your Own

In the exercises you use the form masters to create a new form/subform, and explore the difference between one-to-many and many-to-many relationships.

Adding to the Application

In this exercise you use the form masters to create a new form/subform to display the classes offered for each course. This form is intended for display purposes only.

1. Use the form masters to create a new form/subform.

   a. Create the main form by copying and pasting the form master zsfrmMaster as **frmClassesByCourse**. Set the RecordSource property to **tblCourses** and the Caption property to **Classes By Course**. This form should display the Course Prefix, Number, Name, Credit Code and Units. Set the properties of the data controls as appropriate for display only.

   b. Create the subform by copying and pasting the subform master zsMasterSub as **frmClassesByCourseSub**. Set the RecordSource property to **tblClasses**. This form should display the class Schedule No, Section No, Session, Start and End Dates, Day, and Start and End Times. Rearrange the controls so that the subform has minimal width. Set the properties of the data controls as appropriate for display only. Save the subform.

   c. Drag the subform onto the main form. Size and save the form (see Figure 1.27).

FIGURE 1.27:
The frmClassesByCourse form.

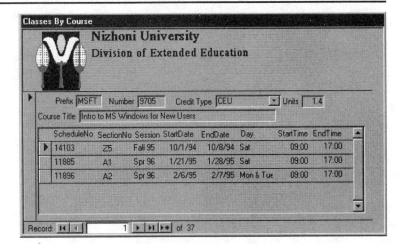

Extending the Concepts

The instructor of a class decides on a reading list composed of one or more books or journal articles. A book or article may be selected for use in several classes. A table, tblResources, can be created to store information about each book or article listed.

1. Exploring relationships

    a. What would be a good candidate for a single-field primary key?

    b. What are other fields you should include in the table?

    c. What table or tables should you relate tblResources to?

    d. For each relationship, determine whether the relationship is one-to-one, one-to-many, or many-to-many. One relationship you may have decided upon is the many-to-many relationship between tblResources and tblClasses.

    e. Create a linking table for the relationship. A common error is to place too many matching fields; make sure that tblResources does not contain a matching field for ScheduleNo.

2. Suppose instead that each class can have only one book on the reading list. A book or article may be selected for use in several classes. How does this change your answers?

CHAPTER

TWO

Building a User Interface

- Interface design guidelines

- Switchboard design

- Macros and events

- Macro flow diagrams

- Navigating between forms

- Reusable objects and macros

- Custom startup options

The *user interface* includes what you see on the screen and how you use the keyboard and mouse to communicate with the computer.

The User Interface

In your custom application's new user interface, you click command buttons to navigate between tasks, perform data entry operations, find records, and print reports. In Access, you can't place buttons on tables or queries and you can't enforce complex validation rules using tables or queries alone; therefore, you build the new user interface entirely out of forms and reports in Print Preview.

The new interface is where the user "lives" in your database application. From the user's perspective, the interface *is* your database application. When creating the new interface, you supply tools to open forms, perform data entry, locate specific records or groups of records, and print records. You also provide a choice of paths for navigating through your database, making sure that users always know where they are and how to backtrack along the path. At each stage of interface construction, your goals are to build in ease of use and intuitive understanding of the application.

User Interface Design Guidelines

Our goal is to design for the person who wants to use your application but doesn't want to spend a lot of time learning *how* to use it—a person who uses your application infrequently and doesn't want to have to relearn it each time. To make your user interface as satisfactory to this person as possible, build it according to the design guidelines shown in "User Interface Design Guidelines", which follows.

An excellent resource for additional information is *Mastering Microsoft Windows 95 User Interface Design* (Microsoft Press, 1995).

User Interface Design Guidelines

The following guidelines will help make your application easier to learn and use:

1. Consistency

   - Be consistent with the standard Windows look and feel so that users can leverage what they already know.

   - Use the standard Windows controls correctly. For example, use option groups when the user can select only one option, but use check boxes when the user can select several options; use command buttons to initiate actions; use a combo box when the user can enter data that is not already on the list; for data that users can enter or edit, use a sunken text box with a contrasting background, but when the data can't be edited, use a background the same color as the form.

   - Use the Microsoft standard menu items, maintain the standard menu order and use the assigned standard menu positions for commands.

2. Directness

   - Provide direct and intuitive ways to accomplish tasks. The interface itself should indicate the choices.

   - Use the tab order to reinforce the visual order of the controls.

   - Organize data controls logically and consistently.

   - Add keystroke shortcuts to command buttons, to menu command buttons and to labels on forms.

3. Feedback (clear, brief instructions)

   - Create status bar messages with short phrases, usually starting with a verb.

   - Create ToolTip messages with two or three words of help.

   - Use message boxes with a short sentence and an appropriate icon to display instructions (rather than error messages).

(continued)

- Use message boxes with short questions to ask for confirmation only when an action has irreversible consequences.

- Incorporate an hourglass with a status bar message when an operation will take more than a few seconds.

- Use color and sound where appropriate (these are useful, but shouldn't be relied on as the only means of conveying information).

4. Aesthetics

- Simple is better for promoting visual clarity.

- Avoid the use of too many colors (it's visually confusing).

- Avoid using more than two or three different fonts or different font properties on the same form.

- Align controls.

- Use rectangles to organize information.

Organizing the Tasks

Before designing the new interface, list the tasks you want to carry out with the database. Some questions that will shape your interface are:

- What tasks do you perform?

- How often are those tasks performed?

- Are any tasks related?

- Must related tasks always be performed together?

- Is there a sequence you must follow in performing certain tasks?

- Which of the tasks are represented by forms or reports in the application?

The answers to these questions need to be reflected in the interface.

A *main task* is any task that is represented by a form or report in the application. For the College database, the main tasks and the forms and reports to carry them out are:

Task	Form or Report
Maintain course information	frmCourses
Schedule classes	frmClasses
Maintain program management information	frmPrograms
Maintain personal information for students	frmStudents
Maintain personal information for instructors	frmInstructors
Register students in classes	frmRegistration
Prepare student program verification reports	rptStudentProgram
Appoint instructors to classes	frmAppointments
Produce an annual college bulletin	rptCourseList
Produce a quarterly class schedule	rptClassSchedule
Prepare class lists of enrolled students	frmClassList, rptClassList
Review class enrollment summaries	frmEnrollmentSummary
Record final grades	frmClassList
Prepare session grade reports for students	rptStudentProgram
Prepare summary enrollment reports	rptEnrollmentSummary
Import data	(form to be created)
Archive session information	(form to be created)

There are two ways you can organize the tasks: by task flow, and by user work flow.

Organizing by Task Flow

One way to organize tasks is according to the sequence in which the tasks must be performed. In Chapter 1 you saw that enforcing referential integrity rules imposes an order on data entry (for example, before you can register a student in a class you must first have entered information for the student in tblStudents and information for the class in tblClasses). You can lay out the major tasks in a *database task flow diagram* that displays the underlying sequence, or *flow*, of the tasks. Figure 2.1 is the database task flow diagram for the College database.

We'll use this diagram to analyze and automate individual tasks.

FIGURE 2.1:

The task flow diagram for the College database shows the sequence in which tasks must be performed.

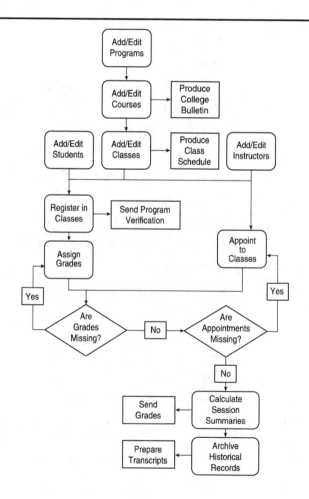

Organizing by User Work Flow

Another way to organize the tasks is according to how they are actually carried out on a daily basis. Each time you start the application, you may want to work on a few different tasks (for example, you may need to enter a new Biology course, register several students in existing classes, and review current enrollments for the Cinema classes). Organize the tasks by selecting those that should be available as choices when the database opens, then arrange them into groups by topic, and determine which main form or report you need to begin each task. For the College database, you can arrange the tasks into three groups: classes, students and instructors, and courses and programs (see Table 2.1).

TABLE 2.1: The College database tasks.

Task	Form Name
CLASSES	
Edit/Add Class	frmClasses
Review Class Lists/Assign Grades	frmClassList
Review Class Schedule	frmClassSchedule
Review Enrollments	frmEnrollmentSummary
Close Out a Session	form to be created
Reports	form to be created
STUDENTS AND INSTRUCTORS	
Edit/Add Student	frmStudents
Register in Classes	frmRegistration
Edit/Add Instructor	frmInstructors
Appoint Instructor	frmAppointments
Import Data	form to be created
Reports	form to be created
COURSES AND PROGRAMS	
Edit/Add Course	frmCourses
Review Course Information	frmCourseList
Edit/Add Program	frmPrograms
Reports	form to be created

Notice that each group in Table 2.1 includes a Reports task that represents the group's reports. In Chapter 11, "Finding Records to Print," you learn how to create a form to select reports.

The new interface must allow you to navigate easily from one task to another. There are many navigation styles—the sample applications that come with Microsoft Access for Windows 95 demonstrate three: a switchboard with command buttons, a switchboard with list boxes, and a task form with navigation toolbar buttons. Each of the sample applications opens with a *splash screen*. Typically, a splash screen provides information about the database, and perhaps the organization, and has no other navigation function. A splash screen gives the user something to look at while Access is running the queries that are needed by the forms that open when the database starts up. The splash screen for the Northwind Traders sample database is shown in Figure 2.2.

Switchboard with Command Buttons   The Northwind Traders application (Northwind.mdb) uses a single form, called a *main menu form* or a *switchboard*, to guide the flow between tasks. This switchboard form uses command buttons to navigate to the main tasks in the application (see Figure 2.3). To view the switchboard, double-click the Main Switchboard form in the Database window.

Switchboard with List Boxes   The Solutions application (Solutions.mdb) opens with a pair of *splash screens*; the first displays the name and a graphic, and the second displays instructions for using the database to learn database techniques. After you close the second splash screen, the Solutions application displays

---

FIGURE 2.2:

The splash screen for the Northwind Traders application.

a switchboard form with synchronized list boxes that provide navigation to any of the numerous examples in the application (see Figure 2.4).

Task Form with Navigation Toolbar Buttons   The Northwind Order Entry application (Orders.mdb) opens with a splash screen and then displays one of the main task forms. This application displays the order form and uses custom buttons in the toolbar for navigation to the other tasks (see Figure 2.5).

FIGURE 2.3:

The switchboard for the Northwind Traders application uses command buttons for navigation to the main tasks.

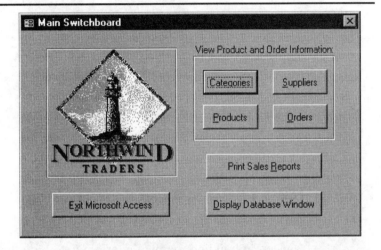

FIGURE 2.4:

The switchboard form for the Solutions application uses synchronized list boxes to navigate to the examples.

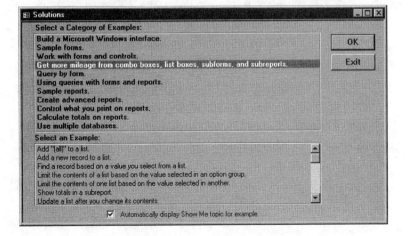

FIGURE 2.5:

The startup orders form and custom toolbar navigation buttons for the Northwind Order Entry application.

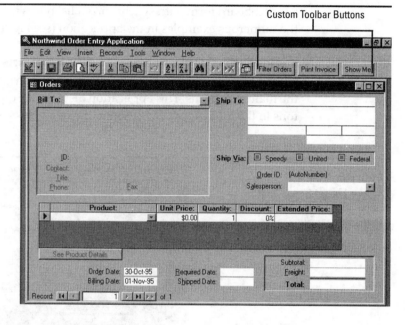

Designing the Switchboard

When you open an Access database file, the Database window appears. The first step in building the new interface is to hide the Database window and display instead the first form—either a splash screen or the first form in the application—and indicate the navigation method you've decided on. We'll use a switchboard form, similar to the switchboard in the Northwind Traders application, and a simple navigation design as follows:

- The switchboard is the first form that opens and remains open until you close the database.

- The switchboard displays the three task groups, with the main tasks listed for each group.

- To select a task to work on, you click its button to open the task's form and hide the switchboard.

- After completing a task, you click a button on the task's form to close the form and unhide the switchboard.

- When you are finished using the database, you click a button on the switchboard to close the application.

In Chapter 1 you learned about a special form that the College database uses to select records for a particular session. We'll modify this form and use it for navigation as well.

1. In the Database window, click the Forms tab.

2. Open frmSwitchboard (or click Restore if the form is already open and minimized).

This form, which I named frmSwitchboard in anticipation of its function as a main menu, already has some of the features desirable for a switchboard: labels to provide the name of the organization, and a logo. The form also displays the value of the selected session. The College database is designed so that you can work with data for more than one session, which allows you to register students for classes in the current session and also begin scheduling classes and appointing instructors for the next session. But you can work with only one session at a time; the chosen session is called the *working session* (refer to Figure 1.25).

NOTE   In most organizations there is an analogous division of time into intervals, usually quarters or fiscal years. If you need to work on records for one time interval, you can select and display only the records for that interval. Chapter 10, "Finding a Group of Records," shows how the selection technique works.

In this Chapter you place command buttons on the frmSwitchboard form for two of the tasks: registering students in classes, and reviewing the class schedule. In order to restrict the user to working with one form at a time, you hide the switchboard form when the main task form opens. A third command button will allow you to quit the application. (In Chapter 4, you replace the command buttons with a more efficient design that uses option groups.)

> **NOTE**
>
> You can also use the Switchboard Manager, a new feature in Microsoft Access for Windows 95, to create a switchboard form. This add-in creates a switchboard form with command buttons that are automated using VBA, and stores information about the buttons in a Switchboard Items table. While it is easy to create a switchboard form with the Manager, it is not very easy to customize the form that is created.

Place Command Buttons to Open the Task Forms

First, create a rectangle to group the command buttons that open the forms.

1. Switch to Design view.

2. In the toolbox, select the Rectangle tool and create a rectangle 5.75" wide and 2" tall. Place it just below the Working Session text box.

3. Make sure that the Control Wizards tool is deselected, and then click the Command Button tool. (If the Control Wizards tool is pressed in when you click the Command Button tool, the Command Button Wizard starts.)

> **TIP**
>
> You can use the Command Button Wizard to create buttons for a large selection of simple tasks. When you use the Wizard, Access creates the instructions using Visual Basic for Applications.

4. In the upper left corner of the rectangle, click and hold down the left mouse button, and drag to create a button 1.5" wide and 0.5" tall.

5. Select the button and choose Edit ➤ Duplicate. Access places a second button below and aligned with the first button.

6. Click the second button, and with the left mouse button pressed, drag the second button to the right of the first button; then select both buttons and choose Format ➤ Align ➤ Top to align the top edges.

7. Select the second button, then copy and paste to create a third button.

8. Click the third button, and with the left mouse button pressed, drag the third button above the rectangle and near its right edge.

9. Resize the third button to be 0.75" wide and 0.25" tall (see Figure 2.6).

FIGURE 2.6:

The Switchboard with Command Buttons.

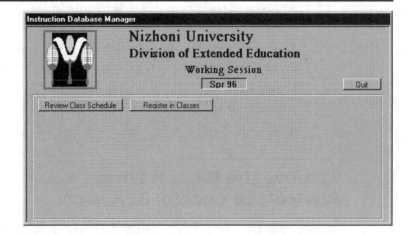

Naming the Command Buttons

Every control placed on a form or report has a name (either you assign it or Access assigns it by default).

1. If necessary, open the property sheet by clicking the Properties button on the tool bar or by selecting View ➤ Properties, then click the All tab.

2. Click several controls on the form and observe the default names such as Box7, Embedded0, and Text8.

3. Click in the text box—the control is named WorkingSession. I named this control when I created the database.

4. Click the first command button—the Name property is Button2 (your computer may indicate a different number) which is the default name.

> **NOTE**   If there is any chance that you will need to refer to the control, replace the default name with a name that reflects the control's type and purpose. Because you refer to a button when you assign a macro to it, you should always rename a command button.

5. Name the button **cmdClassSchedule** and set the Caption property to **Review Class Schedule**

6. Select the other button in the rectangle, then set the Name property to **cmdRegistration** and the Caption property to **Register in Classes**

7. Select the small button outside the rectangle, then set the Name property to **cmdQuit** and the Caption property to **Quit**

8. Save the form.

Remove the Default Form Controls to Control Behavior

When you create a form using a Form Wizard or the Normal template, Access places a set of default form controls along the perimeter that allow you to scroll around in the window, navigate through the records that underlie the form, select a record, and close, minimize, or maximize the form. In order to control the work flow and prevent tasks from being done out of order, you design your own navigation paths and restrict the user to them by eliminating all other navigation methods. In the case of a switchboard, you want the switchboard to remain open and to close only when you quit the application. There is no need for scrolling since you are designing the switchboard to fill the screen without the need for scrolling. Navigation buttons and record selectors are unnecessary. Additionally, you don't want the user to minimize or maximize the form. You change several layout properties to reflect the special nature of the switchboard form.

1. Select the form by clicking in the form selection box in the upper left corner, at the intersection of the rulers (the selection box is available only when you display the rulers), or by choosing Edit ➤ Select Form, or by clicking outside the form's boundary.

2. Set the form properties as listed below. (Without a Control Box or Close button on the form, you have to choose File ➤ Close or press CTRL+F4 to close the form.)

Property	Setting
Caption	Instruction Database Manager
DefaultView	Single Form
ShortCutMenu	No
ScrollBars	Neither
RecordSelectors	No
NavigationButtons	No
ControlBox	No
MinMaxButtons	None
CloseButton	No

3. Switch to Form view and choose Window ➤ Size to Fit Form. If necessary, switch back to Design view to realign buttons and rectangles and save your changes. Figure 2.6 shows the modified switchboard.

4. Click one of the command buttons. The dotted line surrounding the caption indicates the button is selected, but no action occurs because you haven't created any macros.

Macros and Events—An Overview

The next task is to tell Access what action to take when you click a command button on the switchboard. When you click a command button, you change the *state* of the button from unclicked to clicked. Whenever you use the keyboard or the mouse, you *change the state of some object*. The state of an object is the list of all of its characteristics that Access keeps track of. For instance, when you double-click a form in the Database window, you change the form's state from closed to open; when you click in another open form, the state of the first form changes from active to inactive.

Access sets aside several of the changes in the state of an object as opportunities for you to interrupt the normal processing that follows each change. These special changes in the state of an object are called events.

An *event* is a change in the state of an object for which you can define a response.

When an event occurs we say the object *recognizes the event*. For example, when you click a command button, the button recognizes the **Click** event.

What

You tell Access what to do by creating a macro. A *macro* is an action or a series of actions that you instruct Access to carry out. You create a macro by selecting *macro actions* from a list of 49 possible actions. Many of the macro actions are equivalent to choosing commands from menus; other actions provide capabilities not available as menu commands, such as the **Beep** action to "beep" and the **Requery** action to update data; and many of the actions mimic manual user interactions, such as the **SelectObject** action to select a specified database object and the **OpenForm** action to open a specified form. Table 2.2 shows the macro actions grouped by the kinds of tasks they perform.

TABLE 2.2: The macro actions grouped by task.

Category	Task	Macro Action
Manipulating objects	Copying or renaming a Database window object	**CopyObject**, **Rename**
	Deleting a database object	**DeleteObject**
	Opening a table, query, form, report, module	**OpenTable**, **OpenQuery**, **OpenForm**, **OpenReport**, **OpenModule**
	Closing a Database window object	**Close**
	Saving a Database window object	**Save**
	Printing a Database window object	**PrintOut**, **OpenForm**, **OpenQuery**, **OpenReport**
	Selecting a Database window object	**SelectObject**
	Updating data or updating the screen	**RepaintObject**, **Requery**, **ShowAllRecords**
	Setting the value of a field, control, or property	**SetValue**

TABLE 2.2: The macro actions grouped by task *(continued)*

Category	Task	Macro Action
Execution	Carrying out a menu command	`DoMenuItem`
	Running a query	`OpenQuery`, `RunSQL`
	Running a macro or a Basic procedure	`RunMacro`, `RunCode`
	Running another Windows or DOS application	`RunApp`
	Stopping execution of the macro or all currently running macros	`StopMacro`, `StopAllMacros`
	Stopping execution of Access	`Quit`
	Stopping execution of default behavior following an event	`CancelEvent`
Working with data in forms and reports	Selecting or sorting records	`ApplyFilter`
	Finding a record	`FindRecord`, `FindNext`
	Moving to a particular location	`GoToControl`, `GoToRecord`, `GoToPage`
Importing and export-ing data	Outputting data from a table, query, form, report or module in xls, rtf or txt formats	`OutPutTo`
	Including data from a table, query, form, report or module in xls, rtf or txt formats in an e-mail message	`SendObject`
	Transferring data between Access and other data formats	`TransferDatabase`, `TransferSpreadsheet`, `TransferText`
Miscellaneous	Creating a custom menu bar or modifying the display of a menu command	`AddMenu`, `SetMenuItem`
	Sounding a beep	`Beep`
	Displaying or hiding a toolbar	`ShowToolbar`
	Sending keystrokes to Access or a Windows application	`SendKeys`
	Displaying an hourglass	`Hourglass`
	Displaying or hiding screen updates or system information	`Echo`, `SetWarnings`
	Displaying custom messages	`MsgBox`

How, Which, Where...

Most macro actions require additional information before Access can carry them out. The additional information required, specified as *action arguments*, varies with the action and may include, for example, the name of the object you take the action on, or the criteria for selecting records to take action on.

Before you can decide on the appropriate macro action, you need to be familiar with the capabilities of the macro actions. Table B.1 in Appendix B provides an alphabetical listing of the macro actions together with their arguments and guidance on selecting the appropriate action. Online Help provides in-depth information about macro actions. To get help on a particular macro action, choose Help ➤ Microsoft Access Help Topics, then click the Index tab and enter the macro action (see Figure 2.7).

FIGURE 2.7:

Getting online Help for the MsgBox macro action.

When

You can tell Access when to carry out a macro by linking the macro to a specific event of an object. When you click a command button, the button recognizes the **Click** event. When a form receives the focus and becomes the active window, the form recognizes the **Activate** event. When you tab out of control into a second control on the same form without making any changes, the two controls recognize the following sequence of events:

1. The first control recognizes the **Exit** event.
2. The first control recognizes the **LostFocus** event.
3. The second control recognizes the **Enter** event.
4. The second control recognizes the **GotFocus** event.

If you changed the data in the first control before tabbing out, then two additional events are recognized by the first control before the four listed above are recognized:

- The **BeforeUpdate** event is recognized by a control when Access detects changed data in the control buffer and before updating the changed data to the record buffer.

- The **AfterUpdate** event is recognized by a control when Access detects changed data in the control buffer and after updating the changed data to the record buffer.

If you assign a macro to an event, then when the event occurs Access interrupts its default behavior, carries out the macro, and returns to normal processing. For some events, your macro can even terminate the default processing that would normally follow the event.

In all, 39 events are defined in Access. One way to organize events is according to what causes the event to occur. Table 2.3 shows the events grouped by cause.

Because an event is a change in the state of an object, another way to organize events is according to object. Table 2.4 shows the events for each object.

The Update Process

Access uses a two-buffer system to track changes in data: When a record is first displayed, Access places a copy of the data contained in its controls into a temporary storage location called a *record buffer*; when you type a character into a control, Access places a copy of the data you typed into another temporary storage location called a *control buffer*.

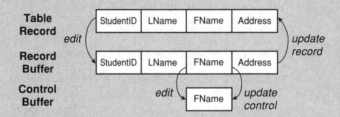

When you try to move out of the control, Access compares the data in the two buffers to determine if you have made any changes.

If you have made a change, the following sequence occurs: the control recognizes the `BeforeUpdate` event, then Access *updates the control* by copying the changed data from the control buffer to the record buffer, and finally the control recognizes the `AfterUpdate` event. If you haven't changed the data in the control, the control update process doesn't occur.

When you attempt to save the record, Access compares the data in the record buffer with the data stored in the table. If you have made changes to at least one control, the following sequence occurs: the form recognizes the `BeforeUpdate` event, then Access *updates the record* by copying the changed data from the record buffer to the table fields, and finally the form recognizes the `AfterUpdate` event. If you haven't changed the data, the record update process doesn't occur.

Cancelling the Default Behavior Following an Event

After an object recognizes an event, Access carries out default behavior. Sometimes the default behavior is to stop and wait for the next user action. For example, when a command button recognizes the `Click` event, Access looks to see if you have assigned a macro to the `OnClick` event; if you have, then Access runs the macro, but if you haven't, Access stops and waits for your next action. Other times, Access goes through a series of default operations either before or after running the macro assigned to the event. For example, when you change the data in a control and then tab to the next control, the changed control recognizes the `BeforeUpdate` event. In response, the following default behavior occurs:

1. Access updates the control to the record buffer.

2. The changed control recognizes the `AfterUpdate` event.

3. The changed control recognizes the `Exit` event.

4. The changed control recognizes the `LostFocus` event.

5. The next control recognizes the `Enter` event.

6. The next control recognizes the `GotFocus` event.

For some events, including the `BeforeUpdate` event, Access runs the macro *before* the default behavior takes place. For these events you can include the `CancelEvent` action in the macro to cancel the subsequent default behavior. The events with default behavior that can be cancelled are:

ApplyFilter	Filter	Error
BeforeDelConfirm	Format	Print
BeforeInsert	KeyPress	Exit
BeforeUpdate	MouseDown	Unload
DblClick	NoData	
Delete	Open	

For the remaining events, Access runs the macro *after* carrying out the default behavior so the default behavior can't be cancelled.

TABLE 2.3: The Access events grouped by cause.

Category	Occur in Response to	Events
Mouse events	the user creating mouse actions, such as moving the mouse pointer over a form, form section or form control, or clicking a mouse button when the mouse pointer is over a form object.	`Click`, `DblClick`, `MouseDown`, `MouseUp`, `MouseMove`
Keyboard events	the user typing on the keyboard or when keystrokes are sent with `SendKeys`, while a form or form control has the focus.	`KeyDown`, `KeyUp`, `KeyPress`
Window events	the opening, closing, or resizing of a form or report window.	`Open`, `Load`, `Unload`, `Close`, `Resize`
Focus events	a form or form control losing or gaining the focus or when a form or report becomes active or inactive.	`Enter`, `GotFocus`, `Exit`, `LostFocus`, `Activate`, `Deactivate`
Data events	changes in the data in a form control and a record displayed in a form, or when the focus moves from one record to another in a form.	`Current`, `BeforeInsert`, `AfterInsert`, `Delete`, `BeforeDelConfirm`, `AfterDelConfirm`, `BeforeUpdate`, `AfterUpdate`, `Change`, `Updated`, `NotInList`
Filter events	opening or closing a filter window, and when the user applies or removes a filter.	`Filter`, `ApplyFilter`
Print events	when selecting or arranging data for printing in a report section or a report.	`Format`, `Print`, `Retreat`, `NoData`, `Page`
Error events	an error being generated and the form or report has the focus.	`Error`
Timing events	a specified amount of time passing.	`Timer`

TABLE 2.4: The events recognized by each object.

Object	Mouse	Keyboard	Window Focus	Data and Filter	Print	Error and Timing
Label	Click DblClick MouseDown MouseUp MouseMove					
Text Box	Click DblClick MouseDown MouseUp MouseMove	KeyDown KeyUp KeyPress	Enter GotFocus Exit LostFocus	BeforeUpdate AfterUpdate Change		
Option Group	Click DblClick MouseDown MouseUp MouseMove		Enter Exit	BeforeUpdate AfterUpdate		
Toggle Button	Click DblClick MouseDown MouseUp MouseMove	KeyDown KeyUp KeyPress	Enter GotFocus Exit LostFocus	BeforeUpdate AfterUpdate		
Option Button	Click DblClick MouseDown MouseUp MouseMove	KeyDown KeyUp KeyPress	Enter GotFocus Exit LostFocus	BeforeUpdate AfterUpdate		
Check Box	Click DblClick MouseDown MouseUp MouseMove	KeyDown KeyUp KeyPress	Enter GotFocus Exit LostFocus	BeforeUpdate AfterUpdate		
Combo Box	Click DblClick MouseDown MouseUp MouseMove	KeyDown KeyUp KeyPress	Enter GotFocus Exit LostFocus	BeforeUpdate AfterUpdate Change NotInList		

TABLE 2.4: The events recognized by each object *(continued)*.

Object	Mouse	Keyboard	Window	Focus	Data and Filter	Print	Error and Timing
List Box	Click DblClick MouseDown MouseUp MouseMove	KeyDown KeyUp KeyPress		Enter GotFocus Exit LostFocus	BeforeUpdate AfterUpdate		
Graph	Click DblClick MouseDown MouseUp MouseMove			Enter GotFocus Exit LostFocus	Updated		
Subform/-Subreport				Enter Exit			
Object Frame	Click DblClick MouseDown MouseUp MouseMove			Enter GotFocus Exit LostFocus	Updated		
Bound Object Frame	Click DblClick MouseDown MouseUp MouseMove	KeyDown KeyUp KeyPress		Enter GotFocus Exit LostFocus	BeforeUpdate AfterUpdate Updated		
Line							
Rectangle	Click DblClick MouseDown MouseUp MouseMove						
Page Break							

TABLE 2.4: The events recognized by each object *(continued).*

Object	Mouse	Keyboard	Window	Focus	Data and Filter	Print	Error and Timing
Command Button	Click DblClick MouseDown MouseUp MouseMove	KeyDown KeyUp KeyPress		Enter GotFocus Exit LostFocus			
Form Sections	Click DblClick MouseDown MouseUp MouseMove						
Form	Click DblClick MouseDown MouseUp MouseMove	KeyDown KeyUp KeyPress	Open Load Unload Close Resize	Activate GotFocus LostFocus Deactivate	Current BeforeInsert AfterInsert Delete BeforeDelCon firm AfterDelConf irm BeforeUpdate AfterUpdate Filter ApplyFilter		Error Timer
Report Page Header/ Footer						Format Print	
Group Header/ Footer						Format Print Retreat	
Report Detail						Format Print Retreat	
Report			Open Close	Activate Deactivate		NoData Page	Error

Timing is Everything...

You must decide the correct event to link the macro to. When a series of events is recognized, such as editing data in a control and tabbing to another control, you need to know which of the events is the appropriate one for your macro. Sometimes you have a choice and selecting any of several events will cause the action to be carried out as you intended. More often, there is only one event that gives the result you want—your task as the macro programmer is to determine that single correct event. Online help is available by selecting Help ➤ Microsoft Access Help Topics, clicking the Contents tab, and then clicking in succession Microsoft Access Programming and Language Reference, Events and Event properties (see Figure 2.8).

FIGURE 2.8:

Getting online help for event properties.

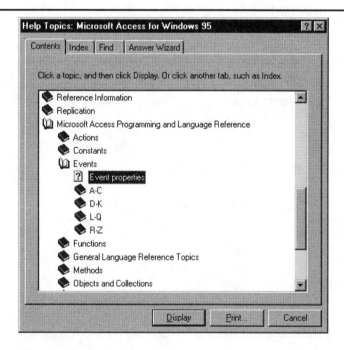

The following Appendix C tables provide descriptions of the timing of events recognized by controls, forms and reports, and guidance for selecting events:

Table C.1: The focus and data events for controls on forms

Table C.2: The mouse and keyboard events

Assigning a Macro to an Event

Access defines events for forms and reports, for sections on forms and reports, and for controls on forms, all of which are listed in Table 2.4. (There are no events defined for tables and queries.) For each event associated with an object there is a corresponding *event property*. Event properties are listed as a separate category in the object's property sheet. You assign a macro to an event by setting the event property to the name of the macro.

When the event occurs, it *triggers* the macro, which means that Access runs the assigned macro when the event occurs. When you assign a macro to an event by entering the macro's name in the event property for the object, you are *trapping* the event. When you set an *event trap* by assigning a macro to an event, you interrupt the default processing that Access would normally carry out following the occurrence of the event. For example, you can trap the `AfterUpdate` event of a combo box by assigning a macro for Access to find the record corresponding to the value in the combo box before stopping.

Observing Event Properties

The event properties are listed in the property sheet.

1. Switch to Design view, then click the Event tab at the top of the Property Sheet. The form's event properties are displayed. (For most events, the related event property is the name of the event preceded by the word "On;" for example, the `Delete` event corresponds to the OnDelete event property.)

2. Click in the text box with the Working Session label. The event properties for a text box are displayed.

3. Click in one of the command buttons. The event properties for a command button are displayed.

Ways to Run a Macro

There are many ways to run a macro other than by using an event to trigger it. Other ways include:

from the Macro design window

from any active window

from the Database window

from another macro

from a custom toolbar button

from a custom menu command

from a shortcut key

by trapping an event on a form or report

at startup

from the Debug window

from a VBA procedure

Creating a Macro

You create macros in a Macro window.

1. In the Database window, click on the Macro tab, and then the New button. Access opens a new Macro window and displays a *macrosheet* (see Figure 2.9).

The upper pane of the Macro window contains four columns. (By default, Access displays only two columns: Action and Comments. In Chapter 1 you set the View option to display all four columns.) Typically, you store several macros in a macro sheet and enter the name of an individual macro in the Macro Name column. The Condition column is where you enter test conditions to control whether a part of the macro runs. The Action column is where you select actions by choosing from a list. The Comments column is for recording the purpose or reason for the action and additional helpful comments (Access ignores the Comments column).

FIGURE 2.9:

The Macro window.

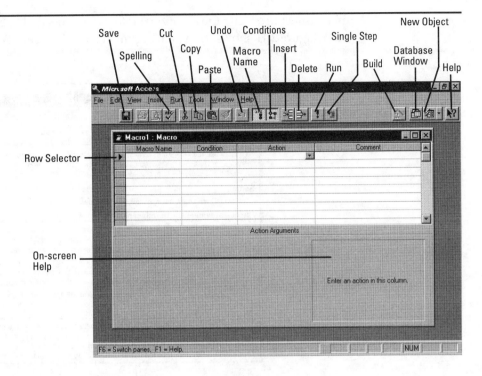

The Macro toolbar contains familiar editing tools to help you create and edit macros, including the Save, Cut, Copy, Paste, Undo, Insert Row, and Delete Row buttons. Additionally, the toolbar contains buttons to show or hide the Macro Names and Condition columns, a Run button which runs the first macro listed in the macrosheet, a Single Step button to help in troubleshooting macros, and a Build button which helps you create expressions in the Condition column and also in any action arguments that take expressions.

1. Click in the first Action cell, and press ALT+↓ or F4 to open the list. The list displays the available macro actions. To get help on an action, select the action, then click the Help button in the toolbar and click in the selected action cell (or press F1).

2. Select the **OpenForm** action, click on the Help button in the toolbar and then click in the first action cell. Online Help displays information about the action and its arguments (see Figure 2.10). You use the lower pane in the

macrosheet to specify the additional information needed to carry out the action. Figure 2.11 shows the action arguments for the **OpenForm** action.

FIGURE 2.10:

Online Help for the **OpenForm** action.

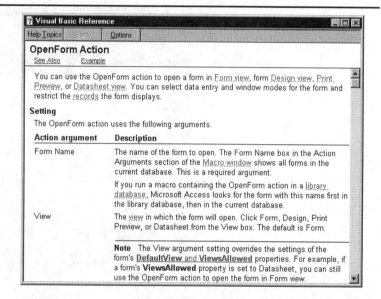

FIGURE 2.11:

Action arguments for the **OpenForm** action.

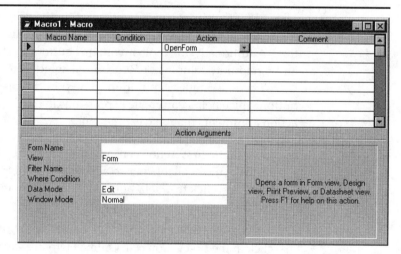

The action arguments for the **OpenForm** action are:

Form Name to specify the name of the form to be opened.

View to specify whether to open the form in Form, Design, Print Preview, or Datasheet view.

Filter Name or the **Where Condition** to specify whether you want to restrict the records that the form displays.

Data Mode to specify whether you want to allow adding new records without the ability to edit existing records, editing existing and new records, or viewing only.

Window Mode to specify whether the form is hidden, minimized, behaves like a dialog box, or has the mode set in its property sheet.

Editing in the Macrosheet

Editing in the macrosheet is similar to editing in a datasheet. You can navigate around the macrosheet using the mouse or the normal Windows editing keys.

The rules for editing individual cells follow the normal Windows and Access editing rules. Tab into a cell to select its entire contents; press F2 to switch to editing mode or for longer expressions; press SHIFT+F2 to open the Zoom Box and display the entire contents in a separate edit window. The ← and → keys allow you to move the insertion point; the DELETE key lets you delete the character to the right of the insertion point and the BACKSPACE key lets you delete the character to left of the insertion point.

You can copy individual characters or the entire contents of the cell to the clipboard by selecting what you want to copy, then pressing CTRL+C, choosing Edit ➤ Copy, or clicking the Copy button on the toolbar. To paste the selection into another cell, click in the paste cell (place the insertion point where you want the contents to be pasted), then press CTRL+V, choose Edit ➤ Paste, or click the Paste button on the toolbar. When you copy the contents of a macro action cell, only the action (not the action arguments) is copied to the clipboard.

You can change the height of rows and the widths of columns just as you do in a datasheet, but the rules for editing rows and columns in the macrosheet are somewhat different because you can select a row but not a column. You select a row by clicking into the row selector; you select several contiguous rows by clicking into the first row selector and dragging to the last row or by pressing the SHIFT key and clicking into the last row selector (you cannot select discontiguous rows). After selecting one or more rows, you can delete the selection by pressing the DELETE key, or insert the same number of rows above the selection by pressing the INSERT key, or copy the selection to the clipboard. When you copy a row the entire macro action is copied, including the action arguments you set.

Additionally, you can move rows by pressing the left mouse button as you click in the selection and dragging to the rows where you want to insert the selection; a bold horizontal line indicates the new boundary of the selection (the new upper boundary if you are moving the selection up and the new lower boundary if you are moving the selection down).

You can copy a macro to another macrosheet by copying the rows of the macro to the clipboard and then pasting the selection to a new location in the other macrosheet. You can use the clipboard to paste a macro into another Access database, but since you have to close the current database and open the other one in order to paste, it is usually more convenient to export the macrosheet to another database or import it from another database using the usual Access methods (File ➤ Save As/Export, or File ➤ Get External Data/Import).

Customizing the Macro Toolbar

The Run button on the toolbar runs the first macro listed in the macrosheet. You can run any macro listed by choosing Tools ➤ Macro to display the Run Macro dialog (see Figure 2.12) and entering the name of the macro you want to run.

You can customize the Macro toolbar (or the toolbar of any view) by adding a Run Macro button. Since it is convenient to test macros when a form is active, add the Run Macro button to the Form view toolbar, also.

1. Right-click on the toolbar and select the Customize command. Figure 2.13 shows the built-in buttons for the File category.

2. From the File category, drag the Run Macro button onto the Macro toolbar, and drop it to the right of the Single Step button. Close the Customize Toolbars dialog.

3. Right-click the toolbar and select the Toolbars command.

FIGURE 2.12:

The Run Macro dialog.

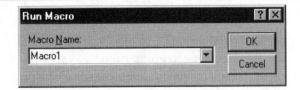

FIGURE 2.13:

The built-in toolbar buttons for the File category, including the Run Macro button.

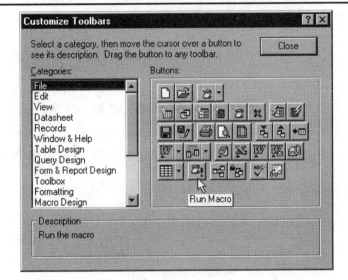

4. Select the Form view toolbar, click the Customize button, drag the Run Macro button to the Form view toolbar and drop it to the right of the Run button, then close the Customize Toolbars dialog.

5. Right-click the Form view toolbar, select the Toolbars command, clear the Form view check box, and close the Toolbars dialog.

Storing Macros in Macro Groups

There are two ways you can store macros: you can use a macrosheet to create a single macro with one or more macro actions and save the macro as a macro object that appears in the list of macros in the Database window, or you can use a macrosheet to define several individual macros, in which case the set of macros stored in the macrosheet is called a *macro group*. Only the name of the macro group is displayed as a macro object in the Database window (not the names of the individual macros in the group). Organize the various macros you create for a form or report into a single macro group called a *form macro group* or a *report macro group* and name the macro group to reflect the form or report as follows:

> *m[formname]* for a form macro group

> *m[reportname]* for a report macro group

As an example, you can store all of the macros for the switchboard in a form macro group named mfrmSwitchboard.

Naming Individual Macros

You use an individual macro to trap an event recognized by an object. Name the individual macro by combining the object name and the event name separated by an underscore, as follows:

> *objectname_eventname*

As an example, the individual macro named

> cmdRegistration_Click

contains the actions you want to carry out when you click the command button named cmdRegistration. The macro named

> Form_Activate

contains the actions you want to take when the form becomes the active window.

Referring to a Macro in a Macro Group

To refer to an individual macro in a macro group, use the name of the macro group followed by a dot (.) followed by the name of the macro:

> *macrogroupname.macroname*

As an example,

mfrmSwitchboard.cmdClassSchedule_Click

refers to the macro in the group mfrmSwitchboard assigned to the **Click** event of
the cmdClassSchedule button.

Create the Switchboard Macros

In this section you create three macros, store them in a form macro group called
mfrmSwitchboard, and assign each macro to a button on the frmSwitchboard form.

Using Macro Flow Diagrams

When you click the command button cmdClassSchedule you want to open the
frmClassSchedule form and hide the frmSwitchboard form. Figure 2.14 is a macro
flow diagram for this operation.

A *macro flow diagram* is a diagram that represents the macro actions you want to run
in response to an event. The first operation box indicates the operation that causes
the event and the small solid triangle attached to the operation box represents the
event (see Figure 2.15).

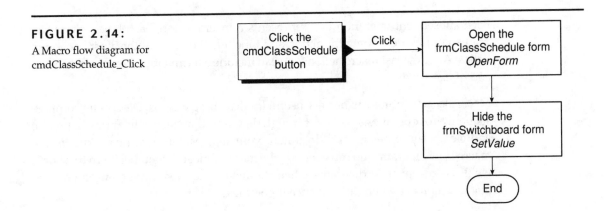

FIGURE 2.14:
A Macro flow diagram for
cmdClassSchedule_Click

FIGURE 2.15:

Diagramming an operation that causes an event.

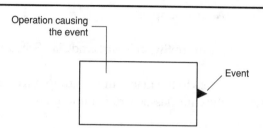

Your action can directly or indirectly cause an event. For example, when you click a command button, your action directly causes the button to recognize the **Click** event. When you open a form you cause a series of events: the form recognizes the **Open, Load, Resize,** and **Activate** events, the first record recognizes the **Current** event and the first control recognizes the **Enter** and **GotFocus** events. While your action directly causes the **Open** event, you cause the subsequent events only indirectly. When direct user action causes the event, we'll use an operation box with a shadow (see Figure 2.16).

FIGURE 2.16:

Diagramming a user operation that directly causes an event.

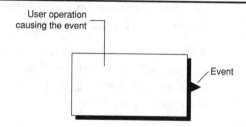

Each subsequent operation box represents a macro action; each box includes an English phrase describing the action and I include the name of the macro action in italics. After the last macro action, you can include a termination box to indicate the end of execution.

Macro flow diagrams can be very useful for designing macros. Describing complex sequences of operations is easier through diagrams than text; a diagram is a precise and clear way to design and document your macros. Once you have drawn the macro flow diagram, you can generate the macro almost automatically. In this book, we'll use macro flow diagrams when the macro requires more than one or two macro actions or when the sequence is complex.

Create a Macro to Open the frmClassSchedule Form

We'll use drag-and-drop to create a macro that opens a form from the Database window.

1. Save the macro group and name it **mfrmSwitchboard**

2. Resize and move the Macro window to display both the Database window and the Macro window.

3. Type **cmdClassSchedule_Click** in the first Macro Name cell, then click in the Comment cell in the same row and enter the comment **Open frmClassSchedule and hide the switchboard**. The first row of the new macro now contains the name of the macro and a brief comment explaining its purpose.

> **TIP**
>
> When you create a macro, place only the macro name and a general comment in the first row and enter the first macro action in the second row. This macro design makes it easier to modify a macro later if you want to insert a new first action or copy the actions of the macro to another macro.

4. In the Database window, click the Forms tab, then select frmClassSchedule, drag the icon to the Action cell in the second row, and enter the comment **Open frmClassSchedule**. Access automatically sets the action to OpenForm, and sets default arguments including setting the `Form Name` to frmClassSchedule.

> **NOTE**
>
> When you drag a table, query, form, or report to the Macro window, Access inserts a row with an action to open the object, and sets default arguments. When you drag a macro object, Access inserts a row with the `RunMacro` action.

Referring to a Form Property in a Macro

The next step in the macro is to hide the switchboard form by setting its Visible property to No. You use the **SetValue** action to set the form's Visible property. In the **Item** argument you need to refer to the form's Visible property. When you refer to a form in a macro you must follow the Access rules for referring to objects. (While you use a naming standard, such as the Leszynski/Reddick standard, to help to distinguish the objects you create, Access has its own rules for referring to objects. You must follow the Access rules when you create macros.)

When you first open a database, Access creates two collections: *Forms* is the collection of all open forms and *Reports* is the collection of all open reports. Access updates each collection as you open or close individual forms and reports. You can refer to a form or report only if it is open. Since Access allows you to use the same name for a form and a report, Access can't tell the type of the object by name alone. Therefore, when you want to refer to a form or a report, you must first tell Access whether the object is a form or report by specifying the collection name. The collection name is followed by the exclamation point operator and then the name of the form or report:

> *Forms![formname]* for a form
>
> *Reports![reportname]* for a report

Use the *exclamation point operator* to separate the collection name from the object name. Following these rules,

> Forms!frmSwitchboard

refers to the switchboard form. To refer to a property of an object, you follow the object name with the *dot operator* and then the property:

> *Forms![formname].propertyname*

Use the *dot operator* to separate the object name from the property name. Therefore,

> Forms!frmSwitchboard.Visible

is the required reference for the Visible property of the switchboard form.

Setting Values

You use the `SetValue` action to set the value of a field or control, or to set a property of a control, form or report. The `SetValue` action has two arguments: `Item` is the name of the field, control or property you want to set and `Expression` is the expression to which you want to set the object's value.

When you enter the `Expression` argument, note that Access assumes the value you enter is an expression (so you don't need an equal sign). If you do include an equal sign, Access evaluates the expression first and uses the result as the argument. Using an equal sign when it is not needed can cause the macro to fail—for example, if you want to set the value of a text box to "John Smith" and you enter ="John Smith", Access evaluates the expression and treats the result as the name of a control; when Access can't find the [John Smith] control, the `SetValue` action fails.

You can use the `SetValue` action for a form to set the value of a bound control or of an unbound control that is not a calculated control. When you set the value of a control, the control's form-level validation rule isn't tested; however, if the control is bound, the field's table-level validation rule is tested. You can also set the value of a field in the underlying table, even if there is no control bound to the field.

You can use the `SetValue` action for a report to set the value of an unbound control that is not a calculated control, but you can't set the value of abound control. You can set the value of a field in the underlying table only if there is a control that is bound to the field or refers to the field in a calculation.

1. Click in the next action cell and choose the `SetValue` action.

2. Press F6 and set the action arguments as follows:

Item	Forms!frmSwitchboard.Visible
Expression	No

3. Enter the comment **Hide the switchboard**, select the row with the `SetValue` action, and copy the row to the clipboard. You'll be pasting this macro action into another macro.

4. Save the macro.

Test the Macro

1. Click the Run button on the toolbar or choose <u>R</u>un ➤ <u>S</u>tart. When you "run" a macro object using the Start command, the first macro in the group runs. In this case, there is only a single macro, so Access opens the frmClassSchedule form and hides the frmSwitchboard form.

2. Choose the <u>F</u>ile ➤ <u>C</u>lose command, then choose <u>W</u>indow ➤ <u>U</u>nhide, and click OK. The frmClassSchedule form closes and the switchboard is visible.

Create a Macro to Open the frmRegistration Form

When you click cmdRegistration, you want to open the frmRegistration form and hide the frmSwitchboard form .

1. Click in the macrosheet, skip a row, click in the Macro Name cell of the new row, enter **cmdRegistration_Click** and enter **Open frmRegistration and hide the switchboard** in the Comment cell.

2. In the Database window, select frmRegistration, drag its icon to the Action cell in the next row, and enter the comment **Open frmRegistration**.

3. Click in the next row and paste the contents of the clipboard. The `SetValue` action that hides the switchboard is pasted.

Create a Macro to Quit the Application

1. Skip a row, click in the Macro Name cell of the new row and type **cmdQuit_Click**, then click in the comment cell and type **Close the database**

2. Click in the Action cell of the next row and click the arrow to display the list of macro actions. Access provides a list of the available macro actions. There is no Close Database action in the list; however, there is a `Quit` action which exits Access itself.

3. Select the **Quit** action. Figure 2.17 shows the macro group with the three macros.

4. Save and close the macro group.

FIGURE 2.17:

The mfrmSwitchboard macro group.

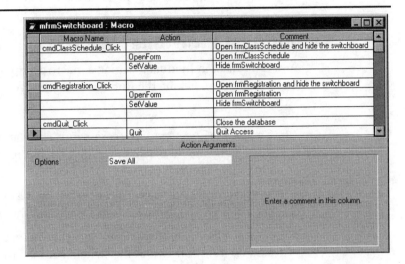

Running Macros

We've created a few simple macros. This section explains how Access executes a macro and how you tell Access when to run one.

The Flow of Macro Execution

Access starts the execution of a simple macro with the first row containing the macro name, executes the action in this row if there is one, and ignores any comments in the row. Then Access looks for the next row that is not blank and moves to it. If there is an entry in the Macro Name cell, Access interprets this row as the beginning of another macro and stops execution. If the Macro Name cell is blank, Access moves to the Action cell to the right. If there is an entry in the Action cell, Access executes the action, ignores the comment and moves to the next row that is not blank. If the Action cell is blank, Access moves to the next row that is not blank. Access continues to move down the rows of the macrosheet examining one row at a time, until it finds a row with an entry in the Macro Name cell, or until there are no more non-blank rows. In either case, the macro ends. You don't have to end a macro with a specific end action. Since Access ignores blank rows you can insert them between the macro actions of an individual macro and between the individual macros in a macro group to make them easier to read.

Running an Individual Macro

You can run an individual macro in a macro group by choosing the Tools ➤ Macro command or by clicking the Run Macro button you added to the toolbar earlier in this chapter.

1. Choose the Tools ➤ Macro command. The combo list displays the mfrmSwitchboard macro group and the full name of each macro in the group (see Figure 2.18).

2. Select mfrmSwitchboard.cmdRegistration_Click from the combo list and click OK. The Registration form opens and the switchboard is hidden.

3. Choose File ➤ Close, then choose Window ➤ Unhide and click OK. The Registration form closes and the switchboard is visible.

Once you have tested a macro to be sure the macro works the way you intended, assign the macro to an event. This process is outlined below in "Steps for Assigning a Macro to an Event".

FIGURE 2.18:

Selecting a macro to run.

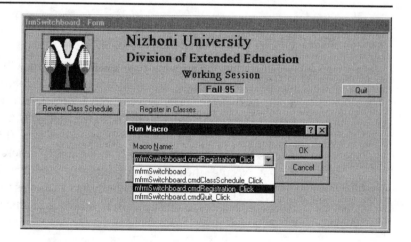

Assigning a Macro to a Command Button

You want one of the macros to run when you click the appropriate command button, so you set the OnClick property of the button to the name of the macro that the button should run.

1. Select the button with caption Review Class Schedule.

2. Click the Event tab in the property sheet. Access displays a list of the event properties for the command button.

3. Choose the OnClick property and click the arrow. A list of the macro group and the full names of the individual macros is displayed.

4. Select mfrmSwitchboard.cmdClassSchedule_Click. The macro is now assigned to the OnClick property of the command button (see Figure 2.19).

FIGURE 2.19:
Assigning a macro to the **OnClick** event property of the cmdClassSchedule button.

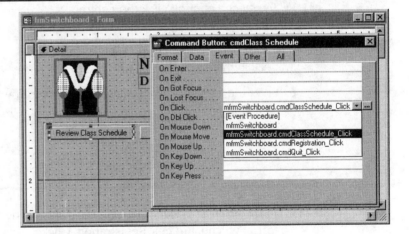

Assigning the Other Switchboard Macros

We'll use the same steps to assign the other switchboard macros.

1. Click in frmSwitchboard and select the button captioned Register in Classes.

Steps for Assigning a Macro to an Event

Once you have tested a macro and it is working correctly, assign the macro to an event following these steps:

1. Open the form or report in Design view.

2. Display the property sheet (by clicking the Properties button in the toolbar or choosing View ➤ Properties).

3. Select the object that recognizes the event.

- To select the form: choose Edit ➤ Select Form, or click the form selection button at the intersection of the rulers, or click outside the form.

- To select the report: choose Edit ➤ Select Report, or click the report selection button at the intersection of the rulers, or click outside the report.

- To select a control: click the control.

4. Click the Event tab in the property sheet.

5. Click in the event property for the event.

6. Enter the full name of the macro by typing or by clicking the arrow and selecting the macro from the list. Use the syntax *macrogroupname.macroname*.

7. Save the form or report.

2. In the property sheet, choose the OnClick property and select the macro mfrmSwitchboard.cmdRegistration_Click.

3. Click in frmSwitchboard and select the button captioned Quit.

4. In the property sheet, choose the OnClick property and select the macro mfrmSwitchboard.cmdQuit_Click.

5. Save the form.

Test the Macros

You should always test a macro to make sure Access carries out the steps you intended.

1. Switch to Form view.

2. Click the Class Registration button. The form frmRegistration opens and the switchboard is hidden.

3. Choose File ➤ Close, then choose Window ➤ Unhide and click OK.

4. Click the Class Schedule button. The form frmClassSchedule opens and the switchboard is hidden.

5. Choose File ➤ Close, then choose Window ➤ Unhide and click OK.

6. Click the Quit button. Access quits.

7. Start Access and open the College database.

Guidelines for Macro Programming

Throughout this book you create dozens of macros, many as simple as these, and others quite complex. "Steps in Creating Macros," below, provides you with a list of the basic guidelines for creating macros.

Documenting Macros

When you are working in a macrosheet you can see the arguments for only one action at a time, and you have to click in the row that contains the action. This limitation makes understanding how the macro works more difficult. You can compensate for this limitation at least partially by using comments for every action that has arguments and including the most important information from the action arguments in your comments. While the effort required to comment nearly every action is substantial, you will find the rewards equally substantial. In this regard, Visual Basic code has the advantage by displaying all of the details of your program as text so that you can see the entire program at a glance. Using flowcharts to document your macros is another way to see the flow of the macro at a glance. But if you want to see all the arguments for all the macros in a macrosheet, you can print the

Steps in Creating Macros

Here is a list of the basic guidelines for creating macros:

1. Determine which object and event you want to trigger the macro execution.

2. Design the macro (use a macro flow diagram if necessary). For simple macros you can design the macro mentally and may not need to sketch the macro flow diagram. For more complex macros you should draw the macro flow diagram, to document the macro as well as to help with the design.

3. Determine the macro actions. If you are using a macro flow diagram, each operation box in the diagram translates into a separate macro action.

4. Create and save the macro. You must save a macro before you can run it.

5. Assign the macro to the corresponding event property.

6. Test the macro. Use the Tools ➤ Macro command or click the Run Macro button to run the individual macro, and see if it accomplishes the intended task. Some macros require that specific forms and reports be open and that a specific object is active when you run the macro— make sure these conditions are satisfied before you run the macro. Also, you should test the macro in context by causing the event to occur (for example, by clicking the command button). Testing a macro in context allows you to observe how the macro interacts with other macros. Often the interaction of two or more macros gives unexpected results, requiring you to either redesign a macro or choose a different event to trigger an interacting macro.

macro's definition for reference (choose File ➤ Print, click OK on the macro Definition dialog box). This printout shows all the conditions and arguments for all the macros in a macrosheet.

Navigating between a Form and the Switchboard

After completing a task using one of the main task forms, you close the form, return to the switchboard, and select another task or close the application.

Creating Reusable Objects

Each of the main task forms needs a command button to close the form and unhide the switchboard. Since several forms need exactly the same command button, you can avoid having to recreate the button and its macro for each form by creating the button and its macro just once and reusing them on other forms. Create the command button and its macro, taking care to avoid using names of specific objects, and place the button in a *controls gallery*, named zsfrmGallery, and the macro in a *macro gallery*, named mcrGallery. Then, when you need the button, you can just copy it from the controls gallery.

Creating a Controls Gallery

1. Create a new blank form, delete the header and footer sections, and save the form as **zsfrmGallery**

2. In the toolbox, with the Control Wizards tool deselected, select the Command Button tool.

3. Click in the form and create a button 0.5" wide and 0.25" tall. Set the Name property to **cmdReturn**

4. Set the Caption property to **&Return**

5. Save the form.

NOTE You can provide an *access key* that can be used in place of clicking a command button. Assign a keyboard combination ALT+*letter* where *letter* can be any letter in the button's Caption property. Specify your choice by typing the ampersand (&) immediately before the letter in the Caption property. For example, set the Caption property to &Return to have the keyboard shortcut be ALT+r.

Creating a Gallery Macrosheet

1. Create a new macrosheet and save it as **mcrGallery**

You use this macrosheet to store the macros for the objects you place in zsfrmGallery. When you have completed the application, you can remove the zsfrmGallery from the database; however, the macrosheet must remain because it contains all of the macros triggered by the objects you copied from the controls gallery to the forms in the database.

Create the Macro

When you click the cmdReturn command button, the window closes and the frmSwitchboard form becomes visible. Figure 2.20 shows the macro flow diagram.

1. Click in the first cell of the Macro Name column, and name the new macro **cmdReturn_Click**

2. Click in the Action cell of the next row and select the **Close** action. You can use the **Close** action to close a particular window by entering the type and name of the database object in the arguments; however, you can also use the action to close the active window by leaving the arguments blank. When you create a gallery macro, it should not refer to a specific form or report by name.

3. Click in the next action cell and select the **SetValue** action.

FIGURE 2.20:

A macro flow diagram for cmdReturn_Click

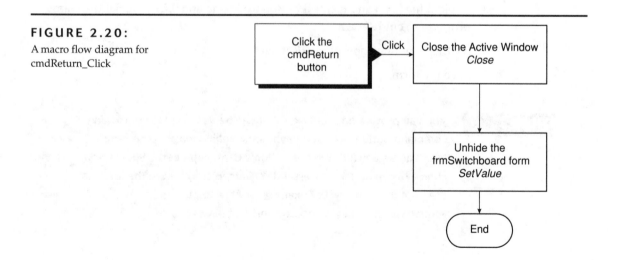

4. Press F6 and set the action arguments as shown below. Referring to the frmSwitchboard form in this action doesn't prevent the macro from being reused in this application, because you want to unhide the switchboard whenever you close a main task form.

Item	Forms!frmSwitchboard.Visible
Expression	Yes

5. Save the macrosheet. Table 2.5 shows the macro.

NOTE   In this book, the default action arguments are not included explicitly in the tables that show the macros.

TABLE 2.5: The cmdReturn_Click macro to close a form and unhide the switchboard.

Macro Name	Action	Action Arguments
cmdReturn_Click		
	Close	
	SetValue	Item: Forms!frmSwitchboard.Visible
		Expression: Yes

Attach and Test the Macro

1. Click in zsfrmGallery and select the Return button.

2. Click in the OnClick event property and select the macro mcrGallery.cmdReturn_Click (see Figure 2.21).

3. Save the form, switch to Form view and click the Return button. The gallery closes and the switchboard is displayed.

4. In the Database window, select zsfrmGallery and click the Design button. You can leave the gallery open in Design view so that you have ready access to the controls in the gallery.

FIGURE 2.21:

Creating reusable objects in the controls gallery and the gallery macro group. To reuse a control in the gallery, you copy and paste to its new location. The attachment to the macro is pasted with the control.

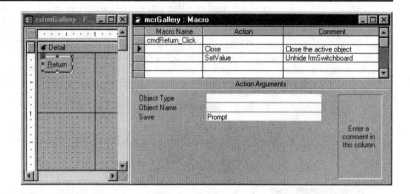

5. Resize the Window and move the gallery to the side of your screen (or minimize the form).

Using the Controls Gallery

You can copy and paste the cmdReturn button to other forms in your database. When you paste a control, you paste its properties, too; this means that macros attached to the control's event properties are also pasted.

1. Select the Return button and copy the button to the clipboard.

2. Open frmRegistration in Design view, click in the Form Header and paste the button. Verify in the property sheet that the pasted button has the pasted properties including the Name property cmdReturn, the Caption property &Return and the OnClick property mcrGlobal.cmdReturn_Click.

3. Move the button to the lower right of the header and save the form.

4. Open frmClassSchedule in Design view, click in the Form Header, and paste.

5. Move the button to the lower right of the header and save the form.

Pasting the Return Button to Other Task Forms

This is a good time to paste the Return button to the other main task forms.

1. One by one, open each of the following forms in Design view, paste the Return button into the form header, move the button to the lower right corner, and save and close the form.

frmAppointments	frmClasses
frmClassesByCourse (created in Chapter 1)	frmClassList
frmCourseList	frmClassSchedule
frmCourseList	frmCourses
frmCoursesByProgram (created in Chapter 1)	frmCoursesView
frmEnrollmentSummary	frmInstructors
frmListofClasses	frmPrograms
frmRegistration	frmStudents

Adding the Return Button to Form Masters

You can also paste the button to the form masters you created in Chapter 1.

1. Open zsfrmMaster in Design view, click in the form header, paste, and move the Return button to the lower right corner.
2. Save and close the form.
3. Open zsfrmMasterTabular, paste the button into the form header, move the button to the lower right corner.
4. Save and close the form.

New forms you create with these form masters will have a return button that closes the form and unhides the switchboard.

Setting Form Properties to Control Form Behavior

You can set the form properties of both task forms in order to control how the user can work with them.

1. Click in frmClassSchedule and set the following Form properties:

Form Property	Setting
ViewsAllowed	Form
ScrollBars	Neither
ControlBox	No
MinMaxButtons	None
CloseButton	No

2. Save and close the form.

3. Click in frmRegistration and set the same form properties as in the first step.

4. Save and close the form.

Starting Up Your Application

You can create a special macro to start up your application, or use the Startup dialog which is a new feature in Microsoft Access for Windows 95.

Using the Startup Dialog

Access provides tools that you can use to control how your application starts up. You can use the Startup dialog to hide the Database window, display a custom title and icon in the title bar, and display your own form to greet the user. The changes you make with the Startup dialog are stored with your application. Figure 2.22 shows the Startup dialog.

You enter the new title in the Application Title text box, and the full path to the bitmap (.bmp) or icon (.ico) file that you want to display as the new title bar icon in the Application Icon text box. The Display Form combo box lists the forms in the application and you can select the form you want to display. You can prevent the user from having access to the tables, queries, macros, and modules by clearing the Display Database Window check box. But don't clear the Display Status Bar check box if you use the Status Bar to provide custom on-screen help. The title bar changes take place as soon as you click the OK button; the other settings take effect the next

FIGURE 2.22:
Use the Startup dialog to control
how your application starts up.

time you open the database. Chapter 16 "Controlling the User Interface" shows you
how to use the additional Startup features.

1. Select Tools ➤ Startup.

2. In the Application Title text box, enter new title **Instructional Database Manager**.

3. Select frmSwitchboard in the Display Form combo list.

4. Clear the Display Database Window check box.

5. Click OK. The Startup dialog closes.

6. Select the Database window and click its Close button. The College database closes.

7. Choose File ➤ Open Database and select the College database in the Open Database dialog. The database opens with the switchboard displayed and the Database window hidden.

Creating a Startup Macro

You can set additional startup conditions by creating a special macro in a separate
macrosheet and saving the macrosheet as **AutoExec** (spelled exactly this way; case
doesn't matter). For example, you can use the AutoExec macro to open and hide additional forms or to import and modify data from an online source when the database first opens.

When you open a database, Access first uses the Startup dialog settings and then looks for a macro named AutoExec. If there is an AutoExec macro, Access runs it.

Bypassing the Startup Options

If you don't want the startup options you set with the Startup dialog or the AutoExec macro to take effect, just hold down the SHIFT key when you open the database.

Creating an Application Icon for the Desktop

You can give your application a separate identity by displaying a custom icon on the Windows 95 desktop to represent your database application.

1. Double-click the My Computer icon on the Windows 95 desktop, then locate and open the Automate folder containing the College database.

2. Right-click the College database file and select the Create Shortcut command. Windows 95 creates a shortcut icon named Shortcut to College (see Figure 2.23).

3. Right-click the Shortcut to College file, select the Properties command and click the Shortcut tab.

FIGURE 2.23:

Right-click the College database file and select the Create Shortcut command to create a custom icon for the file.

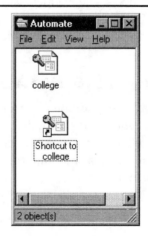

4. Click the Change Icon button. Figure 2.24 shows the Change Icon dialog with the default Windows system icon file displayed.

5. If another file is shown, click the Browse button, locate the Windows\System\Shell32.dll file, and click Open.

FIGURE 2.24:

Choosing an icon to represent the application.

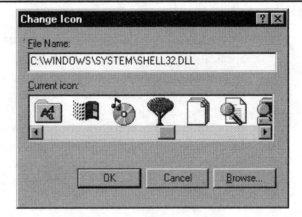

6. Select the tree icon, click OK, and then click OK again to close the Shortcut to College Properties sheet.

7. Right-click the shortcut icon and choose the Rename command.

8. Change the name of the shortcut file to **College** (see Figure 2.25) and drag the startup icon to the desktop.

FIGURE 2.25:

The custom application icon.

When you click the custom application icon, Access starts up, displays the Access splash screen, and opens the College database.

Endnotes

In this chapter you've given your application a separate identity of its own. You open the application from the Windows 95 desktop by clicking a special icon. The application opens with its own title in the title bar and displays a switchboard. The switchboard identifies the application with a logo and information labels, and displays the jobs you can perform with the application. You scan the application's capabilities, select a job, and click a button to open the form and begin the job. After completing the job, you click a button to return to the switchboard to select another job or quit the application. This chapter brought you to the beginning of a database job and returned you to the switchboard when you finished the job. The next several chapters show you how to use macros and other Access techniques to do the job itself.

In the next chapter you learn how to use Access to make decisions.

On Your Own

In these exercises you add a command button and macro to the switchboard and explore how the Command Button Wizard works.

Adding to the Application

1. Adding frmAppointments to the Switchboard

    a. Add a command button to the frmSwitchboard form with Name **cmdAppointment** and Caption **Appointment**s

    b. Create a macro named **cmdAppointment_Click** within the macro group mfrmSwitchboard to open frmAppointments and hide the switchboard. Assign the macro to the OnClick property of cmdAppointment.

    c. Set the form properties to control how the user interacts with the form just as you set them for frmRegistration.

Extending the Concepts

1. Exploring the Command Button Wizard

    a. Open a new blank form in Design view. Activate the Control Wizard, select the Command Button tool and place a command button on the form. The first dialog of the Wizard displays the categories of operations for which predefined buttons are defined.

    b. Select Form Operations to display the set of buttons available for operating with forms. Select Open Form.

    c. Select frmClasses in the next dialog and accept the next two defaults. Name the button **cmdClasses**. Access builds the instructions using VBA and stores them with the form in a unit called an *event procedure*. To view the instructions, click in the OnClick property of the button and click the Build button at the right. A window displaying the instructions appears. The procedure includes 12 lines of code including, near the bottom, instructions for what Access should do if an error occurs when Access tries to run the procedure. In the middle are two lines

```
stDocName = "frmClasses"
DoCmd.OpenForm stDocName, , , stLinkCriteria
```

These lines instruct Access to run the **OpenForm** macro action and open frmClasses.

Event procedures for all of the controls on the form and the form itself are stored together in a *form module* which is stored with the form.

    d. Close the form module, switch to Form view and click the button. The form frmClasses opens. After testing the button, close frmClasses, and discard the new form.

CHAPTER

THREE

Handling Conditions

- Make decisions to run different actions in a macro

- Improve the switchboard design by using option groups

- Use a built-in function to change null values to zero

- Use built-in functions with option groups to display text

Often you want to carry out different tasks depending on current conditions in the database. For example, when registering a student in a class you need to determine if the class is full. If the class isn't full, you can register the student in the class, but if the class is full, you don't register the student.

A *condition* is a logical expression that is either true or false.

Here are some examples of conditions:

Enrollment = EnrollLimit

Enrollment < 5

Date() ≤ 12/31/96

Prefix = "MULT"

Access has several ways to test a condition and then carry out different activities depending on its value. In this chapter you learn two ways to handle conditions: by using macros, and by using the built-in decision functions.

Conditions in Macros

The macros we created in Chapter 2 consisted of actions executed one after the other—the *flow of execution* in these macros is *sequential*—but sometimes you want to perform a macro action only if a certain condition is true. A *conditional macro* provides a way to test the value of a condition and take different actions depending on the value. A conditional macro contains a condition and two alternate sets of macro actions: one set of actions is carried out only when the condition is true, and another set only when the condition is false. In a macro flow diagram the condition is represented as a diamond-shaped decision box with two alternative paths, as shown in Figure 3.1.

If there isn't a separate set of actions that is carried out only when the condition is false, the conditional macro has one alternative (as shown in Figure 3.2).

FIGURE 3.1:

The flow diagram for a conditional
macro with two alternatives.

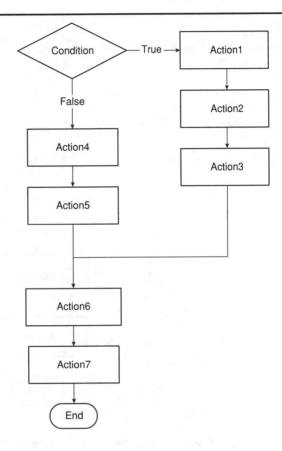

Controlling the Flow of a Macro with Conditions

You enter the condition you want to test into a Condition cell in the macrosheet. If the condition is true, Access executes the action that is in the same row and then moves to the next row; if the condition is false, Access skips the action that is in the same row and moves directly to the next row. If the next row has a condition, the testing procedure is repeated; if the next row doesn't have a condition, Access takes the action in that row.

FIGURE 3.2:

The flow diagram for a conditional macro with one alternative

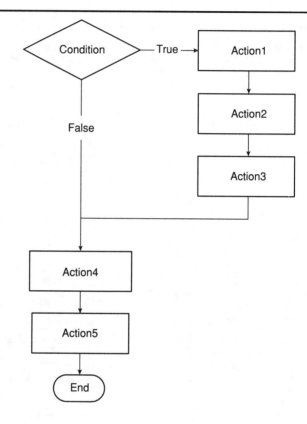

If you want to execute several consecutive actions when the condition is true, you can repeat the condition, or simply enter an ellipsis (…) in the Condition cell for each of the subsequent actions you want executed. The ellipsis acts like a ditto mark. When a consecutive subsequent row has an ellipsis in the Condition cell, Access executes the action if the condition is true, skips the action if the condition is false, and then moves to the next row.

The Conditional Macro with One Alternative

By design, the macrosheet handles a conditional macro that has one alternative with ease. You enter the condition you want to test into a Condition cell, and enter the action you want to take if the condition is true in the same row. If there is more than one action you want to take if the condition is true, enter the actions in consecutive rows, with an ellipsis in each Condition cell. Then enter the actions you want to take regardless of the value of the condition. Table 3.1 shows a conditional macro with one alternative (in a macrosheet layout). If the condition is true, Access runs all five actions one after another; if the condition is false, it runs only the last two.

TABLE 3.1: A conditional macro with one alternative in the macrosheet. If the condition is true, all actions are run; if the condition if false, only Action4 and Action5 are run.

Condition	Action
Condition	Action1
...	Action2
...	Action3
	Action4
	Action5

The Conditional Macro with Two Alternatives

When a conditional macro has two alternatives (as shown in Figure 3.1), you can convert the macro into an equivalent macro with a pair of one-alternative conditions, as shown in Figure 3.3, in which the second condition is the opposite of the first.

Here are some examples of conditions and their opposites:

Condition	Opposite Condition
[Amount] ≤ 9	[Amount] > 9
[Name] = "Jones"	[Name] <> "Jones"
[EmployeeID] Is Null	[EmployeeID] Is Not Null
[Counter] < 4	Not [Counter] < 4
[Price] Between $.30 And $.50	Not [Price] Between $.30 And $.50

FIGURE 3.3:

Flow diagram for a macro with a pair of one-alternative conditions that is equivalent to a macro with a single two-alternative condition.

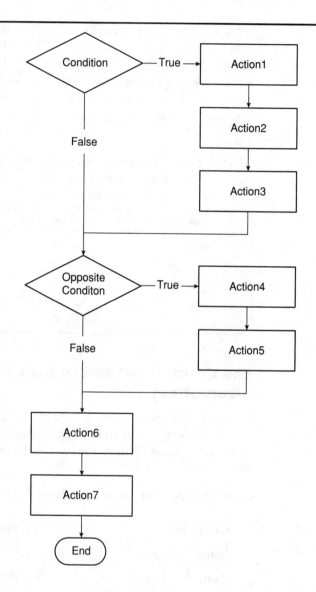

To create the *opposite condition* of a condition, you can either change the operator in the condition or just place the *Not* operator to the left of the condition as in the last two examples. You can use the Not operator to test the opposite of a condition as follows:

> If *condition* is true then *Not condition* is false, and
>
> if *condition* is false then *Not condition* is true.

When a condition is false, its opposite condition is true.

In the macrosheet, you enter the condition in a Condition cell and enter the set of actions you want to take if the condition is true in consecutive rows, with an ellipsis in the Condition cell of each subsequent row. In the next row, you enter the opposite condition and then enter the set of actions you want to take if the condition is false (that is, if the opposite condition is true) in consecutive rows, with an ellipsis in the Condition cell of each subsequent row. Finally, enter the actions you want to take regardless of the value of the condition. Table 3.2 shows a conditional macro with two alternatives (in a macrosheet layout). If the condition is true, Action1, Action2, Action3, Action6, and Action7 are run; if the condition is false, Action4, Action5, Action6, and Action7 are run.

TABLE 3.2: In the macrosheet, a pair of one-alternative conditions is equivalent to a single two-alternative condition.

Condition	Action
Condition	Action1
…	Action2
…	Action3
Opposite Condition	Action4
…	Action5
	Action6
	Action7

Handling Option Groups with Conditional Macros

You can use an option group and a conditional macro to provide the user with choices between different actions. In this section you improve the switchboard by replacing the two command buttons that open forms with option groups that allow you to choose any one of the tasks in the database. Using option groups instead of command buttons allows the switchboard to offer a larger number of choices within a compact organized design. Figure 3.4 shows the final design of the switchboard.

FIGURE 3.4:
Using option groups in the switchboard provides a larger number of choices within a compact design.

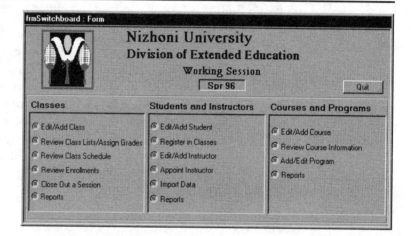

1. Select frmSwitchboard and switch to Design view.

2. Select and delete the two command buttons with captions Review Class Schedule and Register in Classes.

Create an Option Group for a Switchboard Task List

The database tasks for the Classes category are listed in Table 2.2. You create an option group for these tasks.

1. In the toolbox (with the Control Wizards tool selected), select the Option Group tool, then click in the rectangle just below the logo. The Option Group Wizard starts. The first dialog requests the label you want for each option.

2. Type the labels as follows, then click the Next button:

> Edit/Add Class
>
> Review Class Lists/Assign Grades
>
> Review Class Schedule
>
> Review Enrollments
>
> Close Out a Session
>
> Reports

3. The next dialog asks if you want to select one option as the default choice. Without selecting a default, click the Next button.

4. The next dialog displays the default numerical values the Wizard assigns. You can change the values, but the values you assign must be numbers. Accept the default values and click the Next button.

5. The next dialog asks whether you want to save the value for later use or to store the value in a field in the underlying table. You want to save the value for later use. With this choice, the option group acts simply as a location to hold the value selected temporarily. With the first option selected, click the Next button.

6. The next dialog presents choices for the appearance of the option group. Select the Sunken style and click the Next button.

7. Type **Classes** as the label for the option group and click the Finish button.

8. Minimize the width of the option group by adjusting both left and right sides. You can also select the option button labels and move them closer to the buttons. You will be duplicating this group twice and placing the three option groups side by side, so the width of this option group should be about 1.6" wide.

9. Move the option group to the left.

10. Drag the label up slightly so that it doesn't overlay the option group.

11. Set the Font Size to 10 and the Font Weight to Bold.

Create Option Groups for the Other Tasks

In the same way, you can create option groups for the tasks in the Students and Instructors and Courses and Programs categories.

1. Click on the option group border to select it, then choose the Edit ➤ Duplicate command.

2. Select the new option group and drag it just to the right of the first one, aligning the top edges, then choose the Duplicate command again. The switchboard now contains three option groups.

Name the Option Groups and Change the Labels

Modify the properties of the two duplicated option groups.

1. Select the first option group by clicking on the sunken border, then set its Name property to **grpClasses**.

2. Select the second option group and set its Name property to **grpStudentsInstructors**; then select its label and change the Caption to **Students and Instructors**

3. Select the third option group and set its Name property to **grpCoursesPrograms**; then select its label and change the Caption to **Courses and Programs**

4. Select a few option buttons in turn and observe the value of the OptionValue property.

5. Change the option button labels in the second and third option groups as follows (and delete the unused buttons):

Students and Instructors	Courses and Programs
Edit/Add Student	Edit/Add Course
Register in Classes	Review Course Information
Edit/Add Instructor	Edit/Add Program

Students and Instructors	Courses and Programs
Appoint Instructor	Reports
Import Data	
Reports	

6. Switch to Form view. The switchboard is now quite full, but the design is simple and the user can view the available tasks in a single glance (see Figure 3.4). Once the option buttons are empowered with macros to open the task forms, the switchboard will provide the user with a means of navigating to the desired task with a single click.

7. Click one of the option buttons for the Classes task list. When you click an option button, the button appears to be selected, but no actions occur because you haven't yet told Access what actions to take.

Create the Macro for the Option Group

When you select a button in an option group, the value of the option group changes to the button's value. For example, if you select the Review Class List/Assign Grades button (whose value is 2), the option group takes the value 2. You want this choice to open the frmClassList form and hide the switchboard. For each option button choice you want to open the corresponding form and hide the switchboard. You'll create a macro to test the value of the option group, open the correct form, and hide the switchboard; the macro runs whenever you change the value of the option group. The option group control recognizes the **AfterUpdate** event when you change its value, so the macro is named for the first option group, grpClasses_AfterUpdate.

Using the Value of an Option Group as a Condition

You use the value of the option group in a set of conditions to control which form is opened.

1. In the Database window, click the Macro tab, then select mfrmSwitchboard and click the Design button.

2. Delete the rows containing the macros named cmdClassSchedule_Click and cmdRegistration_Click.

3. Click in the first empty row and name the new macro **grpClasses_After-Update**

4. Click in the Condition cell of the next row and enter the condition **grpClasses = 1**. A value of 1 corresponds to selecting the Add/Edit Class option button. If this condition is true, you want to open frmClasses.

5. In the Action cell to the right, click the drop-down arrow, select **OpenForm** and enter the comment **Open frmClasses**; then select frmClasses from the drop-down list in the **Form Name** argument.

6. Type **grpClasses = 2** into the next empty Condition cell. A value of 2 corresponds to selecting the Review Class Lists/Assign Grades option button. If this condition is true, you open frmClassList.

7. Select **OpenForm** from the Action cell list, and enter the comment **Open frmClassList**; press F6, and select frmClassList from the list in the **Form Name** argument.

8. From the Database window, drag the frmClassSchedule icon to the next Action cell. Access automatically sets the action to **OpenForm** and sets default arguments, including setting the **Form Name** to frmClassSchedule.

9. Type **grpClasses = 3** into the Condition cell in the same row, and enter the comment **Open frmClassSchedule**

10. Type **grpClasses = 4** into the next empty Condition cell, and enter the comment **Open frmEnrollmentSummary**

11. From the Database window, drag the frmEnrollmentSummary icon to the Action cell on the right of the condition grpClasses = 4. When you drag an object to the Macro window and drop it into a row where the Condition cell or the Macro Name cell is not empty, Access inserts a row above the desired row and places the **OpenForm** action in the inserted row. To correct this, press CTRL+X to cut grpClasses = 4, then click in the Condition cell above and press CTRL+V to paste the expression.

Next, enter the action you want Access to run regardless of the value of the option group.

12. In the next row, select the **SetValue** action, enter the comment **Hide frmSwitchboard**, and set the arguments as follows:

Item	Forms!frmSwitchboard.Visible
Expression	No

13. Save the macro. Figure 3.5 shows the macro.

FIGURE 3.5:

The option group macro for the grpClasses option group.

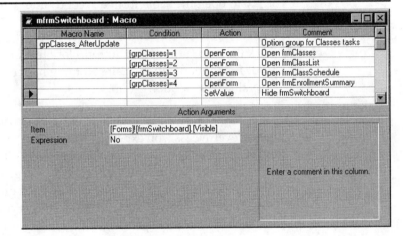

Attach and Test the Macro

1. Click in frmSwitchboard, select the option group grpClasses, and click the Event tab in the property sheet.

2. Choose the AfterUpdate property and select the macro mfrmSwitchboard.grpClasses_AfterUpdate.

3. Save the form.

4. Switch to Form view.

5. Click the Add/Edit option button. The form frmClasses with caption Classes opens.

6. Close the frmClasses form using the Return button you created in Chapter 2, then click the remaining option buttons and close each form in turn. For the first four buttons, the corresponding form opens. There is no response when you click either of the last two buttons because you haven't included them in the macro yet.

Resetting the Option Group

If you try to open the same form a second time without selecting another option button first, the form doesn't open.

1. Click the Add/Edit option button, close the form frmClasses, then click the Add/Edit option button again. Nothing happens because you didn't change the value of the option group.

The **AfterUpdate** event is triggered only when the value of the option group changes. Nevertheless, you expect a form to open in response to clicking an option button, even if it is only to reopen the same form. To make the option group react as you expect, modify the behavior of the option group by setting its value to null after the task form opens. If the value of the option group is null, the option buttons are grayed out. This is the visual cue that prompts you to select any button (including the button selected just previously). You add a row and use the **SetValue** action to reset the value of the control.

2. Click in the mfrmSwitchboard Macro window, then click in the row following the last row of the grpClasses_AfterUpdate macro; select the **SetValue** action and enter the arguments below, then enter the statement **Reset the option group to null** in the Comment cell.

Item	grpClasses
Expression	Null

3. Select the row and copy it.

4. Insert a row before each **StopMacro** action and paste the copied row into each inserted row.

5. Save and close the macro.

Test the Macro

1. Click in frmSwitchboard.

2. Click the Add/Edit option button, and then click the Return button to close the frmClasses form. The switchboard is displayed with the option group reset to null.

3. Click the Add/Edit option button again. This time frmClasses opens in response.

4. Click the Return button to close frmClasses.

Empowering the Remaining Option Groups

You create macros for the other two option groups in the same way.

1. Click in the macrosheet mfrmSwitchboard, then click in a new row and enter a new macro named **grpStudentsInstructors_AfterUpdate**

2. Enter the macro conditions and actions that are shown in Table 3.3.

3. Click in a new row and enter a new macro named **grpCoursesPrograms_AfterUpdate**.

4. Enter the macro conditions and actions that are shown in Table 3.4.

5. Save and close the macrosheet.

6. Click in the frmSwitchboard form , then switch to Design view; select the grpStudentsInstructors option group, then click in the AfterUpdate property and select the mfrmSwitchboard.grpStudentsInstructors_AfterUpdate macro.

7. Click in the frmSwitchboard form, then select the grpCoursesPrograms option group; click in the AfterUpdate property and select the mfrmSwitchboard.grpCoursesPrograms_AfterUpdate macro.

8. Save the form and switch to Form view.

9. Test the option groups by choosing an option button. The selected form opens and the switchboard is hidden.

10. Click the Return button. The form closes and the switchboard is unhidden (with the option group reset).

TABLE 3.3: A macro to empower the grpStudentsInstructors option group.

Macro Name	Condition	Action	Action Arguments
grpStudents-Instructors _ AfterUpdate			
	grpStudentsInstructors=1	OpenForm	Form Name: frmStudents
	grpStudentsInstructors=2	OpenForm	Form Name: frmRegistration
	grpStudentsInstructors=3	OpenForm	Form Name: frmInstructors
	grpStudentsInstructors=4	OpenForm	Form Name: frmAppointments
		SetValue	Item: Forms!frmSwitch-board!Visible
			Expression: No
		SetValue	Item: grpStudents-Instructors
			Expression: Null

Controlling the Flow with Macro Loops

Using conditions in macros gives you a way to define different results depending on the value of an expression—this is referred to as a *decision structure*. A decision structure allows you to control which actions Access executes. Access provides another way to control the flow by providing the ability to run a macro repeatedly; the macro actions that are repeated are called a *loop*. By using the **RunMacro** action, you can run a macro a specified number of times or until a given condition becomes true or false. You use the first action argument, **Macro Name**, to specify the name of the macro to be run, and use either of the remaining arguments to repeat the macro. You use the second argument, **Repeat Count**, to enter the specific number of times

TABLE 3.4: A macro to empower the grpCoursesPrograms option group.

Macro Name	Condition	Action	Action Arguments
grpCoursesPrograms_After-Update			
	grpCoursesPrograms=1	OpenForm	**Form Name**: frmCourses
	grpCoursesPrograms =2	OpenForm	**Form Name**: frmCourseList
	grpCoursesPrograms =3	OpenForm	**Form Name**: frmPrograms
		SetValue	**Item**: Forms!frmSwitch-board!Visible
			Expression: No
		SetValue	**Item**: grpCoursesPrograms
			Expression: Null

you want the macro to run, and the third argument, **Repeat Expression**, to enter an expression that evaluates to true or false as a repetition condition. If you leave both repeat arguments blank, the macro runs only once. Using either of the repeat arguments to run a macro repeatedly is an example of a *loop structure*.

In Chapter 9, "Techniques for Review and Data Entry," we'll explore a macro loop that "loops" through the controls on a form and changes their property settings.

The Built-in Decision Functions

Using conditions in macros is one way to generate different results depending on the value of an expression. Access also provides another way: using built-in functions.

Access provides three *decision functions* you can use to make decisions. A decision function returns different values depending on the value of an expression. The first argument is the expression and the remaining arguments are the possible values

Functions

A *function* is a procedure that returns a value (a very large set of functions is built into Access). For example, the Sum() function returns the total of the values in a field on a query, form, or report. Usually you have to specify one or more pieces of information, called the *function arguments*. The Sum() function requires only a single argument to specify the field that contains the data—for example, Sum([Fee]) will calculate the total fees. You can use functions in field, criteria, and update cells in queries and filters, and in calculated controls and property settings on forms and reports. You can also use functions in macros and Visual Basic modules. You can also create your own functions using Visual Basic if you don't find the function you need in the list of built-in functions.

that the function can return. The three functions IIf( ), Choose( ), and Switch( ) are closely related; nevertheless, they allow you to make different kinds of decisions. The IIf( ) function (the Immediate If Function) is extremely useful; if you aren't already familiar with using this function so you should study the next section. The Choose( ) and Switch( ) functions are less commonly used, but are particularly useful in working with option groups, so you should at least browse through the later sections dealing with them.

The Immediate If Function

The IIf( ) function lets you make decisions by testing a condition and returning one of two different values depending on whether the condition is true or false. The function has three arguments: the first is the condition, the second is the result you want if the condition is true, and the third is the result you want if the condition is false.

IIf(condition,true,false)

For example, in the function

IIf(Enrollment<5,"Underenrolled","OK")

the condition is Enrollment<5; if this condition is true, the function returns the text expression Underenrolled, while if the condition is false, the output is the text expression OK. You can visualize the Immediate If function by using a diamond-shaped decision box to represent the condition and rectangular result boxes to represent the two possible results (see Figure 3.6).

FIGURE 3.6:

A flow diagram for the IIf( ) function

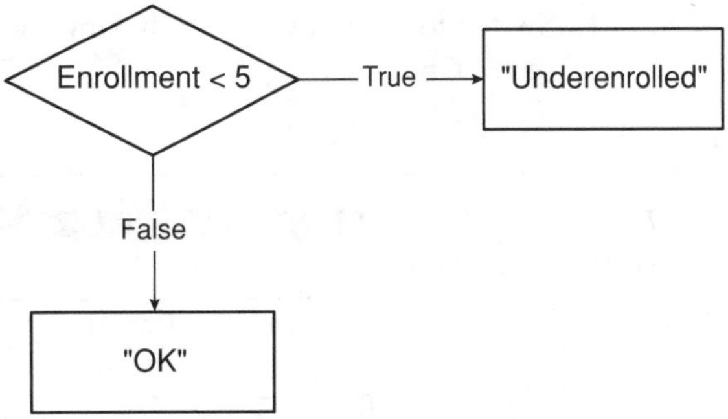

Using the IIf( ) Function to Embellish a Report

You can use the IIf( ) function in a calculated control on a report, to highlight information by printing a message that emphasizes exceptional values.

1. If the Database window is hidden, press F11 to display it.

2. Press the Report tab, then double-click rptEnrollmentReport .

> **TIP**
>
> The Startup options you set in Chapter 2 hide the Database window when the database opens. You can display the Database window by pressing the F11 Function Key, provided you haven't disabled this feature using the Advanced Startup options.

The Enrollment Report provides the current enrollment and enrollment limit for each class (see Figure 3.7). You can make this report more useful by drawing attention to the classes that are fully enrolled—use the IIf( ) function to compare current enrollment to the enrollment limit and display the word Full if they are equal (display nothing otherwise). You can display the result in a new calculated control.

Add a Calculated Control to the Report

The next step is to place a calculated control on the report.

1. Switch to Design view by clicking the Design button you added to the toolbar in Chapter 1.

FIGURE 3.7:
The rptEnrollmentReport.

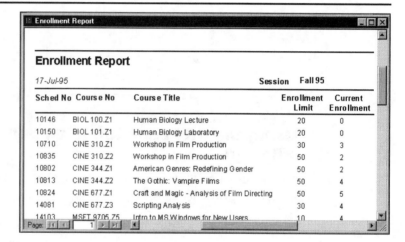

2. In the toolbar, select the Text Box tool, then draw a rectangle 0.5" wide and 0.25" tall to the far right of the Detail section.

3. Set the Name property of the new text box to **Status**, then click in the ControlSource and enter the expression below.

   =IIf(Enrollment=EnrollLimit,"Full","")

Access evaluates the condition in the first argument. If the expression if true, the IIf( ) function returns the text value "Full" and displays this value in the control. If the expression is false, the IIf( ) function returns the *zero-length* string, "" (without a space between the quotation marks), and displays this value (that is, nothing).

4. Set the format properties to match the other text box controls.

5. Switch to Print Preview. The full classes are highlighted with the word Full.

Using a Nested IIf() Function

You may want to highlight additional enrollment information, for example, to indicate classes with enrollments less than 5 as "low" enrolled. You can modify the IIf() function to handle this additional condition. When the condition Enrollment = EnrollLimit is false, test the condition Enrollment < 5 using another IIf() function as the third argument.

1. Switch to Design view and select the Status control.

2. Click in the ControlSource property and replace the third argument in the IIf() function as shown below.

   =IIf(Enrollment=EnrollLimit,"Full",IIf(Enrollment<5, "Low",""))

   This expression is called a *nested IIf() function* because one IIf() function is placed inside another. Make sure to include both parentheses for the inner IIf() function.

3. Save the report and switch to Print Preview. The full classes are highlighted with the word Full and the classes with low enrollments are highlighted with the word Low.

4. Save and close the report.

Changing a Null Value to Zero

When a field contains no value, it contains the *null value* (empty). A common use of the IIf() function is to test the value in a control or field and, if the value is null, replace the value with zero (if the field contains numbers) or the zero length string (if the field contains text).

1. In the switchboard, click the Register in Classes button.

2. Browse through the records using the navigation buttons. Note that the Total Units control displays numerical values when the student is registered in at least one class, but displays nothing when the student has not registered in any classes (see Figure 3.8).

FIGURE 3.8:

The Total Units control is null when the student isn't registered in any classes.

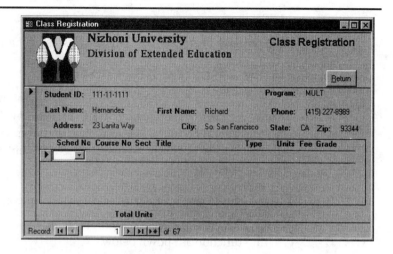

You should replace these null values with zeros for two reasons:

- The records lack visual consistency—you expect to see a zero if the student has not registered in any classes.

- Access cannot use a null value in numeric calculations. If you use an arithmetic operator in an expression and one of the values in the expression is null, the result of the calculation is null; this is called *propagation of nulls*. For example, if you calculate the average enrollment for all students using the division operator, Access will return a null value for the average if even one student has not registered in classes. If you use an aggregate function such as Sum( ), Count( ), or Avg( ) to determine a result for a specified field, records with null values in the field aren't included in the calculation.

1. Switch to Design view, click once outside the subform control to deselect it, then double-click the subform control. The form frmRegistrationSub opens in Design view. The form header contains a hidden calculated control that determines the total by summing the values in the Units field.

2. Click on the text box in the form header and note the properties below. The function Sum([Units]) determines the total of the units for all of the records displayed by the form. When the form is used as a subform, its records are linked to the record displayed in the main form. The subform displays only the classes that the student is registered in, so the Sum( ) function calculates

the total units for these classes. If the student is not registered in classes there are no records to sum, so the Sum function returns the null (empty) value.

Name	TotalUnits
ControlSource	=Sum([Units])

3. Select the TotalUnits control. Use the IIf( ) function to replace the value with zero when the total is null and to display the total otherwise.

4. In the property sheet, click in the ControlSource property and replace the expression as follows:

=IIf(IsNull(Sum([Units])), 0, Sum([Units]))

The modified expression uses another built-in function, IsNull( ). The IsNull( ) function returns True if the argument is null and returns False otherwise (see Figure 3.9).

5. Save and close the form.

6. Switch to Form view. Observe the replacement of the null values.

FIGURE 3.9:

Using the IIf( ) function to replace the null result for the Sum( ) function with 0.

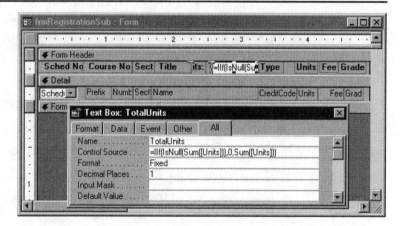

The Choose() Function

The Choose( ) function lets you pick a value from a list depending on the position of the value in the list. The Choose( ) function takes several arguments. The first argument, called *indexnumber*, takes an integer value of 1 or greater. The remaining arguments make up the list of values the function can return.

Choose(indexnumber, value1, value2,...)

If indexnumber = 1, value1 is returned, If indexnumber = 2, value2 is returned, and so on.

The returned value must be a number, date, or string, or a function that returns a number, date, or string. There can be at most 13 values in the list. You can visualize the Choose( ) function as a set of decision diamonds for testing the value of the index number, as shown in Figure 3.10.

Using the Choose( ) Function with an Option Group

The Choose( ) function is particularly useful when you use option groups in data entry, because option groups restrict the field to a limited number of values. One problem with using an option group in data entry, however, is that the value of an option group can only be a number. Unless you do something to convert the option group's numerical value into a text value, the number is stored in the table. For example, the form used for data entry of course information, frmCourses, uses an option group for the course credit type (refer to Figure 1.8). When you select one of the three text values, the option group stores the corresponding number in tblCourses. When the course information is displayed in another form, such as frmClasses, the number corresponding to the credit type is displayed (see Figure 3.11).

Using the Choose( ) Function to Display Text Instead of an Integer

You can use the Choose( ) function to display the corresponding text instead of the number.

1. In the Database window, double-click frmClasses; browse through the records. Observe that the Credit Type is 1, 2, or 3. You can use the Choose( ) function to display corresponding text values instead:

CreditCode	Credit Type
1	CEU
2	Acad Credit
3	Non-Credit

FIGURE 3.10:

A flow diagram for the Choose( )
function.

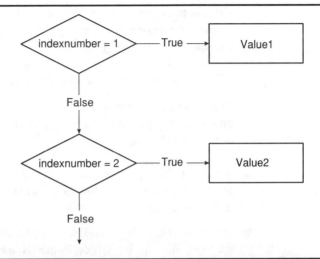

FIGURE 3.11:

The frmClasses form displays an
integer code for the Credit Type
because the value is entered using an
option group.

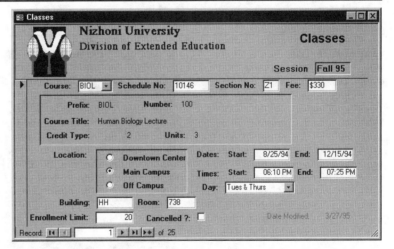

2. Switch to Design view, then select and delete the CreditCode text box and its
   label.

3. Place an unbound text box in place of the deleted text box, and set the Name
   property of the text box to **CreditType** and the Caption property of the label
   to **Credit Type**

4. Click in the ControlSource property of the text box and enter the expression below (you must include the quotation marks because the Choose() function requires text values to be strings).

=Choose(CreditCode, "CEU","Acad Credit","Non-Credit")

This function determines the value in the CreditCode field, and depending on whether the CreditCode is 1, 2, or 3, the function returns the first, second, or third text string.

5. Set the Enabled property to No and the Locked property to Yes, then set the layout properties of the text box and label controls to match the other controls on the form.

6. Switch to Form view. The Choose() function substitutes the appropriate text value for the number stored in the table (see Figure 3.12).

FIGURE 3.12:

Using the Choose() function to substitute text for a number.

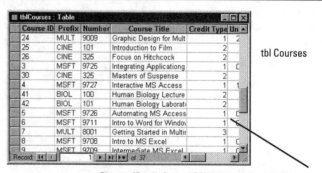

tbl Courses

Choose (Credit Code, "CEU", "Acad Credit", "Non-Credit")

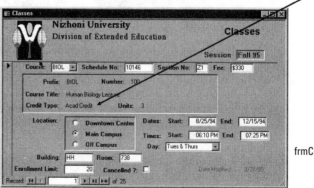

frmClasses

The Switch() Function

The Switch() function takes pairs of expressions as its arguments:

Switch(condition1, value1, condition2, value2,...)

The first member of each pair of arguments is a condition that evaluates to true or false, and the second member of the pair is the value that is returned if the first member is true. The Switch() function evaluates the conditions, and for the first condition that is true, the Switch() function returns the corresponding value. If none of the conditions is true, the Switch() function returns a null value. You can visualize the Switch() function as a set of decision diamonds, as shown in Figure 3.13.

You can use the Switch() function with option groups to switch back and forth between the numerical value of the option group and the corresponding text value. Switching back and forth requires two Switch() functions, one for each switch direction.

As an example, the data entry form for instructors, frmInstructors, has a text box for the instructor's title: Ms., Mr., or Dr. (see Figure 3.14). The text value entered in the text box is stored in the table in a field named Title.

You can replace the text box with an option group, named grpTitle, and use the Switch() function to convert the text value in the Title field into the corresponding integer value for the option group grpTitle. When you change the value of the option group, you need a second Switch() function to convert the changed option group value to its text equivalent in the Title field. In Figure 3.15, notice how the two Switch() functions switch back and forth between the numerical values in the form and text values stored in the table.

FIGURE 3.13:
A flow diagram for the Switch() function.

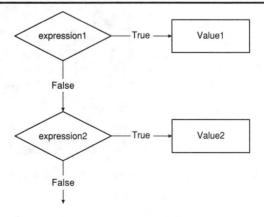

131

FIGURE 3.14:

The frmInstructors form.

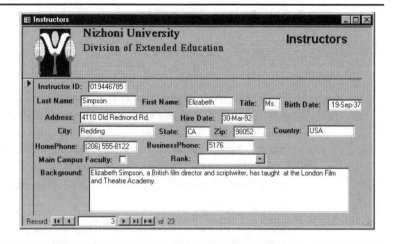

FIGURE 3.15:

Using a pair of Switch( ) functions with an option group.

Switch (Title="Ms.", 1, Title="Mr.", 2, Title="Dr.", 3,) **Macro:** Form_Current

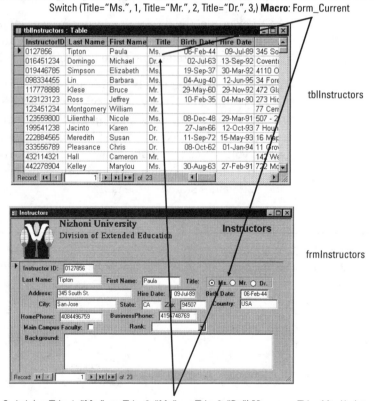

tblInstructors

frmInstructors

Switch (grpTitle=1, "Ms.", grpTitle=2, "Mr.", grpTitle=3, "Dr.") **Macro:** grpTitle_AfterUpdate

Using a Pair of Switch() Functions to Drive an Option Group

First, you replace the Title text box with an unbound option group.

1. In the Database window, select frmInstructors and click the Design button.

2. Select and delete the Title text box and its label.

3. In the toolbox (with the Control Wizards tool selected), click the Option Group tool, and then click in the form where the title text box had been.

4. Enter the label names: **Ms., Mr., Dr.**; do not choose a default value; accept the default values shown in Figure 3.16; do not store the value in the table; and set the label to **Title**. The option group must be an unbound control since you aren't storing the values of the option group in the Title field in tblIn-structors. Instead, you'll create macros to link the numerical option group values and the text field values. The option group in the form and the field in the table will be linked by the macros you create.

5. Set the Name property of the option group to **grpTitle**

FIGURE 3.16:

Setting option group values with the Option Group Wizard.

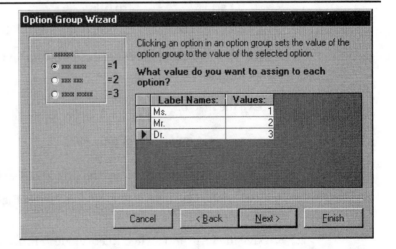

133

Create a Macro to Switch a Value from Text to Numeric

You can pass the value from the Title field in the table to the option group control on the form by using a macro. Use the `SetValue` action to set the value of the option group control to the number corresponding to the text value in the Title field by using the Switch( ) function to determine the correct number:

Switch(Title="Ms.",1,Title="Mr.",2,Title="Dr.",3)

You set the value of the option group whenever an instructor's record is displayed (that is, becomes the current record). When the focus moves to a record (making it the current record), the form recognizes the `Current` event. Name the macro Form_Current.

1. On the toolbar, select the New Object button, then select New Macro and save the macrosheet as **mfrmInstructors**

2. In the first MacroName cell, enter **Form_Current**

3. In the next row, select the `SetValue` action and set the arguments as follows:

Item	grpTitle
Expression	Switch(Title="Ms.",1,Title="Mr.",2,Title="Dr.",3)

   The Switch() function passes the text value in the table to the option group in the form as the corresponding integer.

4. Save the macro.

Attach and Test the Macro

1. Click in the form and choose the Edit ➤ Select Form command.

2. Click in the OnCurrent property and select the macro mfrmInstructors.Form_Current.

3. Save the form and switch to Form view. Browse through the records and observe that the option button corresponding to the text value for Title is filled in. But if you try to change a title by clicking a different option button, the value in the Title field does not automatically change; you have to create a macro to update the field value.

The macro Form_Current sets the value of the option group to the numerical equivalent of the text value in the Title field. The link goes in one direction only: from the table field to the form's option group. To have the link go in both directions, so that when you click a different option the table updates, you need a second macro to pass the value from the form to the table.

Create a Macro to Switch a Value from Numeric to Text

You can create a second Switch( ) function to set the value of the Title field to the text equivalent of the option group value:

Switch(grpTitle=1,"Ms.",grpTitle=2,"Mr.",grpTitle=3,"Dr.")

You run this macro whenever you change the value of the option group. The option group recognizes the **AfterUpdate** event whenever its value has been changed; name this macro grpTitle_AfterUpdate.

1. Click in the macrosheet, skip a row and create a new macro named **grpTitle_AfterUpdate**

2. In the next row, select the **SetValue** action, and set the arguments to:

   Item   Title

   Expression   Switch(grpTitle=1,"Ms.", grpTitle=2,"Mr.",grpTitle=3,"Dr.")

3. Save the macro and close the macrosheet.

Attach and Test the Macro

1. Click in the form and switch to Design view.

2. Select the option group, then click in the AfterUpdate property and select the macro mfrmInstructors.grpTitle_AfterUpdate.

3. Save the form and switch to Form view. Select a different title using the option group, and observe that the field changes to reflect your choice.

The two macros use the Switch( ) functions to switch back and forth between the table and form values, as shown in Figure 3.15, with each macro providing one direction of the link between the field and the option group.

Advantages and Limitations of the Built-in Decision Functions

As the diagrams suggest, the Choose( ) and Switch( ) functions are really just specialized versions of nested IIf( ) functions. For example, the two functions

IIf(CreditCode=1,"CEU",IIf(CreditCode=2,"Acad Credit","Non-Credit"))

Choose(CreditCode, "CEU","Acad Credit","Non-Credit")

give the same result, and the two functions

IIf(Title="Ms.",1,IIf(Title="Mr.",2,"Dr."))

Switch(Title="Ms.",1,Title="Mr.",2,Title="Dr.",3)

give the same result in this case.

Use a built-in decision function when you want to test a condition and return different values depending on the condition. You can use these functions in the property sheet of an object on a form or report. When you use one of these functions as the control source of an object on a form or report, you can view your "code" directly in the form's Design view; you can understand how the form works more easily than if you have to switch to a macrosheet to look at the macros that make the form work. On the other hand, when you use one of these functions as the control source, the resulting calculated control is read-only. If you want to use the control in data entry you have to be able to change its value, so instead of entering the function in the control's ControlSource property, you leave the ControlSource blank and link the control and the field using macros (as explained in the previous section).

You can use the decision functions in queries to create calculated fields, to define query criteria, and to create a query update expression; in macros to define action arguments and to handle conditions in macros; and in VBA modules.

NOTE

Access carries out the decision functions in different ways. When you use the IIf() function on a form or on a report, Access evaluates the condition and then evaluates either the true or the false expression, but not both. The Choose() and the Switch() functions work differently. The Choose() function evaluates every value in the list, even though it returns only one value. Likewise, the Switch() function evaluates every condition and every value, even though it returns only one value. Because Access is evaluating all of the expressions, these functions may be slow. Also, since all expressions are being evaluated, there can be undesirable results. For example, if one of the expressions that is not being returned results in a Division By Zero error, Access reports the error anyway.

Endnotes

In this chapter you've learned how to use macros and the built-in decision functions to give your application some intelligence. When you include decision capabilities, your application can test current values and respond accordingly. For example, in Chapter 8, "Data Entry Operations," you use a conditional macro in data entry to test the value of the primary key as soon as you enter the value, and if you've entered a non-unique value, to display the stored record with the same primary key.

Before continuing to explore how to use this new decision capability, we focus next on the problem of dealing with errors in macros. Macro errors are a fact of life in application development—rarely does a macro with more than a few actions work perfectly the first time. When you see a program written either with macros or VBA that carries out complicated operations, you can be sure that someone spent time finding errors in the program, troubleshooting the causes, and figuring out how to eliminate them. In the next chapter you'll learn that the best way to deal with macro errors is to learn how to avoid them in the first place.

On Your Own

In these exercises you'll use the IIf( ) function to highlight low-enrolled classes and the Choose( ) function to display the text equivalent of the numerical Credit Code. You'll use a conditional macro to alter navigation through the controls on a form.

Adding to the Application

1. Creating a Low Enrollment Class List using IIf( )
   You can use the IIf( ) function to highlight the enrollment summary report for low-enrolled classes.

   a. In the Database window, copy frmEnrollmentSummary and paste it as **frmLowEnrollment**

   b. Select and delete the text boxes and labels containing current enrollment and enrollment limit data.

   c. Create an unbound text box in the far right side of the Detail section for frmLowEnrollment.

   d. Enter an expression into this control, using the IIf( ) function, that will display the text "Under enrolled" if the value in the Enrollment control is less than 5, and displays nothing otherwise.

   e. Set the Name property to **Status**. Set the control's properties to match the other controls in the Detail section.

   f. In the Form Header, place a label with the text **Status** just above your calculated control.

2. Using the Choose( ) function
   Use the Choose( ) function in frmClassList to display the text equivalent to the Credit Code.

Extending the Concepts

1. Using a condition to navigate through the controls

   When you enter instructor information, you record a value for rank only if the instructor is also a Main Campus faculty member.

   a. Draw a macro flow diagram to test the value in the Main Campus Faculty check box on frmInstructors and jump to the Bio memo field if the value is No.

   b. Decide the event that will trigger the macro and create the macro. Attach and test the macro.

CHAPTER

FOUR

Dealing with Errors in Macros

- Syntax, run-time, and logical errors

- Troubleshooting

- Using the Debug window

- Visual Basic error-handling code for the Error event

- Avoiding errors in macros

In a broad sense an *error* is anything that deviates from what you want in your application. Errors occur at every stage of application development, from the initial paper and pencil design of the database structure, to creating database objects and expressions, to creating macros and Visual Basic modules to automate tasks and transform your interactive database into an application, to entering data and printing reports, to… The list goes on and on. There is a good chance of error at each step. Errors can be large and obvious or small and subtle. You have to deal with the obvious errors right away. It's the subtle ones that cause the real headaches—the hidden error that you aren't aware of until it springs out at an unexpected moment. The best way to deal with errors is learn how to avoid them in the first place. Knowing the kinds of errors that can—and will—occur, and knowing how to predict when different kinds of errors are likely to occur, is the best way to begin.

In this chapter, I assume that you've used the built-in techniques for avoiding data entry errors, including setting properties that restrict the values that can be entered, such as the DefaultValue, ValidationRule, Required, and InputMask properties. I'll focus instead on the errors that occur in macros.

Kinds of Macro Errors

There are three kinds of macro errors:

- *Syntax errors* occur when you are creating macros and before you try to run them.

- *Run-time errors* occur when a macro tries to execute an action that is impossible to execute.

- *Logical errors* occur when your macros are free of syntax errors, execute all of their actions, and yet fail to produce the result you intended.

Syntax Errors

Syntax errors occur when you are creating a macro in the macrosheet. These errors occur when you violate the rules of Access *syntax*, which is the set of rules governing the spelling of certain words and the arrangement of words, symbols, and operators that you enter into the blanks in the macrosheet. If you spell a macro action incorrectly, a syntax error occurs and Access provides you with the error message

"The text you enter must match an entry in the list."

If you omit a parenthesis in an action argument or a condition, you generate a syntax error and Access displays the error message

"Can't parse expression:"

Access *parses* an expression when it separates the expression into its parts and recognizes the parts as known items that are correctly related according to a set of Access rules.

Access checks your syntax automatically and displays a default error message when it detects a syntax error: however, some syntax errors aren't found until you run the macro. In this case, you may have entered an expression in the macrosheet that Access can parse, but you used the wrong syntax for the situation. For example, if you use the wrong syntax to refer to a control in the `GoToControl` action, or if you forget to use an equal sign in the `FindWhat` argument of the `FindRecord` action, the macro won't run correctly.

Run-Time Errors

Run-time errors occur when some circumstance makes it impossible to execute your macro. For example, if you misspell the name of a control in a macro condition or action argument, syntax checking won't find the error—the error lurks until you try to run the macro. For example, if you have a control named grpTitle and you misspell it as grpTitl in a macro argument, when you try to run the macro Access generates a run-time error and displays the error message

"Invalid reference to field 'grpTitl'"

to let you know that an expression in your macro refers to a field that doesn't exist.

One way to avoid identifier errors like this one is to use the Expression Builder when you create expressions. With the Expression Builder you create expressions by selecting object names from lists instead of typing the names, thus avoiding all misspellings. The Expression Builder is discussed in Chapter 5, "Looking Up Information in Forms."

Here are some examples of situations that result in run-time errors in macros:

- referring to a control on a form that isn't open

- executing a menu command that isn't available

- moving the focus to a control using the control's full name instead of its short name

When it is not possible to execute a macro action, Access displays a default error message and stops the macro. For example, if you use the **OpenForm** action and misspell the form's name, Access displays the default error message shown in Figure 4.1.

FIGURE 4.1:

A typical default error message.

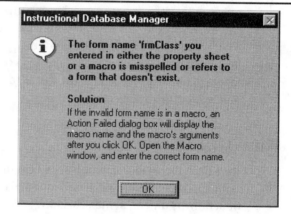

After you acknowledge the error message by clicking the OK button, Access displays the Action Failed dialog box (see Figure 4.2).

The Action Failed Dialog

The Action Failed dialog tells you exactly where the error occurred by providing the name of the macro, the action that caused the error, and the action's arguments. If there is a condition for the action, the dialog displays the condition and whether the condition has the value True or False.

After you click the Halt button you are left with the problem of troubleshooting the error to determine its cause. Often the default error message alerts you to the cause

FIGURE 4.2:

The Action Failed dialog.

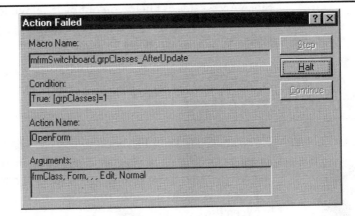

immediately and additional troubleshooting isn't necessary. Once you have determined the cause, you must take whatever steps are required to eliminate the problem. For example, for a simple misspelling error, "fixing the bug" means correcting the spelling error in the macro argument.

Logic Errors

Logic errors occur when the macro action's arguments and conditions are correct and the macro executes without generating a run-time error, but the macro doesn't give you the result you intended. These errors are often the most difficult to understand and correct. Logic errors occur for varied reasons, such as:

- The macro actions are in the wrong sequence.

- Two macros are executed in the wrong order.

- An action has been omitted inadvertently.

- You misunderstood what a particular macro action does (for example, you used `RepaintObject` when the correct action is `Requery`).

- You specified the wrong field or control.

- You used the wrong operator (for example, you used < when you should have used <=).

- You attached the macro to the wrong event.

Since Access doesn't help you out by displaying a default error message or an Action Failed dialog when a logic error occurs, you have to develop a set of troubleshooting tools you can use to sleuth the error.

Troubleshooting

There are several troubleshooting tools available to help you to analyze run-time and logic errors. To be successful at troubleshooting you must thoroughly understand two things: how your macro is supposed to work, and how your macro actually does work. In a sense, troubleshooting is just understanding the difference between the two.

Single-Stepping Macros

You can use the Single Step feature to step through a macro one action at a time. You turn on the Single Step feature by choosing the Run ➤ Single Step command or clicking the Single Step button in the toolbar.

> **TIP**   Add the Single Step button to the Form view toolbar so that you can turn the feature on and off when you are in Form view (see the section "Customizing the Toolbars" in Chapter 1).

With Single Step turned on, the Single Step dialog appears when you start to run a macro (see Figure 4.3).

The dialog displays information about the action that is going to be executed next, including the name of the macro, the current value of the condition, the name of the action, and the settings of the action arguments. The Single Step dialog is similar to the Action Failed dialog, except that the Step and Continue buttons are available. You click the Step button to "step into" and execute the action displayed if the value of the condition is True. If the value of the condition is False, the action isn't executed; instead, Access steps into the next action and displays its Single Step dialog. You click the Continue button to step into the action and turn off the Single Step feature. If you don't click the Continue button, the Single Step feature remains on

FIGURE 4.3:

The Single Step dialog.

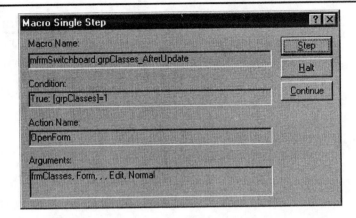

for the rest of the current macro and for all subsequent macros, until you turn it off. In between running macros, you can turn off the Single Step feature by clicking the Single Step button or by choosing (and unchecking) the Run ➤ Single Step command.

You can use the Single Step feature to watch the execution of each action that precedes an error; this information may help you to determine the error's cause. The Single Step feature can help you to observe the interaction of two macros that may have worked as intended when you ran them separately, but don't work correctly when they interact; this information can be useful in deciding that one or the other macro traps the wrong event.

Using Breakpoints

You can use a breakpoint when you want to stop a macro at a certain step and check the current values of controls and properties. You create a breakpoint by entering a dummy name, such as Break, in the Macro Name cell of the row where you want to stop.

You can use the Debug window (discussed below) to actually check current values.

NOTE

You can prevent execution of a specific action in a macro by entering the word "False" without the quotation marks (or the numeral 0, which means the same thing) in the Condition cell in the same row. You can use this technique when you want to run a macro without a particular action.

Printing Macros

You can use the Database Documentor to print out your macros; reviewing an entire macro in print is an excellent way to understand how the macro works.

1. Choose Tools ➤ Analyze ➤ Documentor to start the Documentor (see Figure 4.4). The Print Definition dialog displays the object type and a list of your database objects of that type.

2. Choose Macros from the combo list and then click the Options button. You can choose to include information about macro properties, actions, arguments, and security information (see Figure 4.5).

3. Select the macro objects you want to document, then click OK. Access produces an Object Definition report which you can print. Figure 4.6 shows a portion of the report for the mfrmSwitchboard macro group.

FIGURE 4.4:

The Database Documentor.

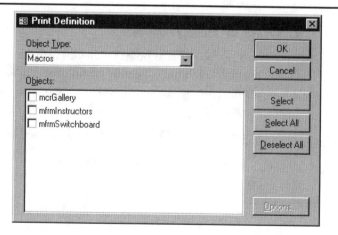

FIGURE 4.5:
The Documentor options.

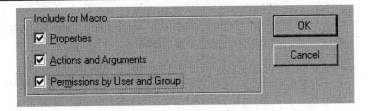

FIGURE 4.6:
The Object Definition report for a macro.

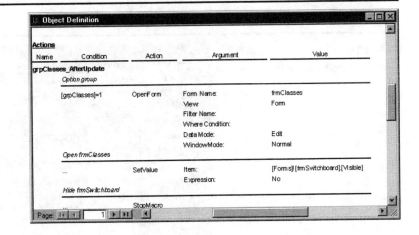

Using the MsgBox Action to Troubleshoot

Use the MsgBox action at critical points in a macro to tell yourself what the macro is doing. You can use a simple message, like "Got to this point", or display the current value of a control or a property. When you want to display a message, enter it into the **Message** argument as either the message itself, for example:

Got to here

or as the text expression

= "Got to here"

When you want to display the value of a control or property you can enter an expression that concatenates the text message and the control or property name, for example:

= "The value in the Address control is" & [Address]

A message box displaying this expression is shown in Figure 4.7.

FIGURE 4.7:

Using the MsgBox action to display a value.

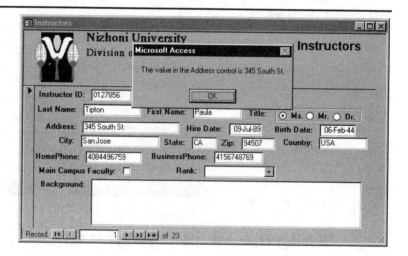

Using the Debug Window to Troubleshoot

Another general troubleshooting tool is the Debug window (see Figure 4.8). You can use the Debug window to display the value of a field, control, or property on a form or report, or to evaluate any valid expression. This information can help you to diagnose the error. You can also use the Debug window to assign values to control and properties. In this way you can change the values and run the macro again to see the result. You can even use the Debug window to run a macro action, a macro, or Visual Basic code.

FIGURE 4.8:
The Debug window.

NOTE There is a toolbar button for the Debug window, displayed by default on the Visual Basic toolbar. For troubleshooting purposes, you can add this button to the Macro and Form view toolbars. You can also open the Debug window by pressing ctrl+G.

Using the Debug Window to Evaluate Expressions

You can display a value in the Debug window by typing a question mark followed by the expression you want Access to evaluate and then pressing the ENTER key.

1. Press CTRL+g.

2. Enter **?2+3** and press ENTER. The value of the expression (5) is displayed in the next line.

3. Enter **?Date()**. The next line displays the current date.

Using the Debug Window to Display Values from Forms and Reports

You can display a value in the Debug window by typing a question mark followed by the name of the field, control or property of a form or report. The form or report must be open and you must use the correct reference to the object or property (called the *qualified reference* or the *full identifier*). In Chapter 5, "Looking Up Information in Other Forms", you learn how to refer to objects and their properties.

1. On the switchboard, click the Add/Edit Class button.

2. Click into the Debug window and enter **?Forms!frmClasses!Fee**. The next line of the Debug window displays the value in the Fee control for the current record.

3. Enter **?Forms!frmClasses.RecordSource**. The Debug window displays the name of the query that provides the records to the frmClasses form.

Using the Debug Window to Run a Macro Action or a Macro

You can run a macro action by typing **DoCmd** followed by a dot and the name of the macro action with the list of arguments. You must enclose all text arguments in quotation marks; use commas to separate multiple arguments. If you omit arguments, Access assumes the default values for the action; you must still use commas to hold the place of the omitted arguments in the argument list unless you are omitting all arguments, or all arguments after the last one you want to specify.

NOTE When you run a macro action this way, you are actually running the corresponding Visual Basic *method*. Nearly all macro actions have equivalent Visual Basic methods. You can get help on the corresponding method by searching online Help for the name of the action and choosing the corresponding method from the topics list.

- Enter the expression **DoCmd.OpenForm "frmRegistration"** and press ENTER. Access opens the form. The **OpenForm** macro action has six arguments, and the corresponding Visual Basic **OpenForm** method has the same six plus an additional argument; however, to open the form with all default values, you can omit all arguments and specify only the name of the form.

You can run a macro in the Debug window by typing **DoCmd.RunMacro** followed by the full name of the macro enclosed in quotation marks, for example:

DoCmd.RunMacro "macrogroupname.macroname"

Using the Debug Window to Assign Values to Forms and Reports

You can assign a value using the Debug window by typing the full identifier reference of the object followed by an equal sign followed by the value. If the value is a text expression, you must enclose the expression in quotation marks.

- Enter the expression **Forms!frmRegistration.Caption = "Hi there!"** and press ENTER. Access immediately changes the Caption property of frmRegistration to the expression you entered.

Handling Run-Time Errors—Macros versus Visual Basic

The result of successful troubleshooting is that you eliminate detectable run-time macro errors and correct logical errors. But even with the most thorough macro testing procedures, the application you develop will probably still have some run-time errors. As examples, standard unavoidable run-time errors occur in the following situations:

- if you enter a name in a combo box that is not in the list and the LimitToList property has been set to Yes

- if you enter a number that would result in an attempt to divide by zero

- if you create or modify a record so that a required field is empty (in this case, the default error message is "Field 'tblInstructors.LName' can't contain a null value")

The Error Code **for an Error**

Each run-time error has an integer value, called an *error code*, that uniquely identifies it. Table 4.1 lists codes for some of the default error messages you may have seen.

When a run-time error occurs, Access displays the default error message and responds with default behavior. For example, when you try to save a new record without entering a value for the primary key: the run-time error with error code 3058 occurs, Access displays the default error message, and responds by cancelling the save operation.

You *handle a run-time error* by interrupting the default response, replacing the default message with a custom error message, and specifying the actions you want Access to take instead of the default behavior. Continuing with the same example, you can handle a 3058 error by displaying a custom message, moving the focus to the primary key control, suppressing the default message, and cancelling the save operation. In order to handle a run-time error that has occurred, you must identify the error by its error code. A key difference between using macros and Visual Basic

TABLE 4.1: Some Error Codes and Messages.

Error Code	Error Message
3058	Index or primary key can't contain a null value
3022	Duplicate value in index, primary key or relationship. Changes were unsuccessful.
3200	Can't delete or change record. Since related records exist in '|', referential integrity rules would be violated.
2427	Object has no value
2237	The text you enter must match an entry in the list
2079	Entry Required!
2105	Can't go to specified record
2107	The value you entered is prohibited by the validation rule set for this field
2110	Can't move to control <name>
2169	The record being edited can't be saved. If you close the form, the changes you've made to the record will be lost. Close anyway?
3051	Couldn't open file '|'
7889	Couldn't find file '|'

is that you can't determine the error code with a macro—this means that you can't handle a run-time error that has already occurred using macro programming.

Using Macro Programming

You can't use a macro to determine the error code after a run-time error has occurred, so you can't prevent Access from executing its default response. When you can't prevent a particular run-time error from occurring, you may be able to create a macro to display a custom message when the error does occur. For example, you can't prevent someone from entering a name that isn't in a combo list, so you can't prevent the run-time error (error code 2237) from occurring, but you can create a macro to display a custom message and trigger the macro with the **NotInList** event when such a name is entered (the custom message this macro displays in response to the **NotInList** event is in addition to the default error message that Access displays in response to the 2237 error).

If a run-time error causes a macro to fail, you can't stop Access from terminating the macro and displaying the Action Failed dialog box. For example, if you run a macro to delete a record and a run-time error occurs because referential integrity prevents you from deleting the record (error code 3200), Access displays the default error message and the action to delete the record fails. In Chapter 8, "Data Entry Operations," you'll learn how to modify this macro to prevent the 3200 error from occurring.

Using Visual Basic Programming

An advantage of using Visual Basic programming is that you can create *error-handling code* to determine the error code when a run-time error occurs, and then interrupt and modify the default response to the error. You handle a run-time error in one of two ways, depending on which part of Access generated the error.

Although we normally think of Access as a single entity, we can also consider Access to be three components: the interface (including programming with macros), the database engine (which handles the processing of data and the storage of the database objects), and Visual Basic (see Appendix A for more information on these components). If the run-time error is generated by a Visual Basic procedure, you handle the error by adding error-handling code to the procedure itself. If the run-time error is generated by the interface or the database engine, the run-time error triggers the **Error** event for the active form or report, and you handle the error by creating a Visual Basic event procedure for the **Error** event.

A Simple Visual Basic Error Handler for the Error Event

A form or report recognizes the **Error** event whenever the interface or the database engine generates a run-time error. You can use the **Error** event to *set traps for specific run-time errors* that may occur and tell Access what to do if one of them does. You create an event procedure for the **Error** event in the form or report module stored with the form or report.

The Form Module

You can open the form module by clicking in the OnError property of the form.

1. In the Database window, select frmStudents and click the Design button.

2. Click in the form's OnError property, then click the Build button to the right of the property box, select Code Builder, and click OK. The form module opens displaying a *code template* for the **Error** event consisting of the first and last lines for the procedure (see Figure 4.9).

Words that Visual Basic uses as part of its language are called *keywords*. In the first line of the code template, the **Private** keyword indicates that the procedure applies only to the form or report with which it is stored and the **Sub** keyword indicates the procedure doesn't return a value (only **Function** procedures return values). The **End Sub** keyword in the last line indicates the end of the procedure. Access names an event procedure for a form using the syntax

Form_eventname

so the error handler for a form is Form_Error. (This is the same syntax that the L/R naming standard uses for naming a macro.)

FIGURE 4.9:

The code template for a form's error-handler procedure.

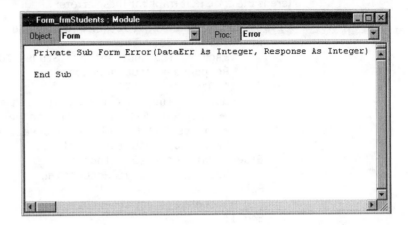

The Form_Error procedure has two arguments:

- **DataErr** is the error code of the run-time error that occurred.

- **Response** is a response code that represents the way you want Access to respond to the run-time error. You use built-in constants to specify the response: to suppress the default error message, you set **Response** to the constant **acDataErrContinue**; to display the default error message, you set **Response** to **acDataErrDisplay**.

You enter Visual Basic code statements between the two lines of the code template. As an example, you can write a simple Visual Basic error handler that traps for three errors:

- the error that occurs when you try to save a record without entering a value in the primary key field (error code 3058)

- the error that occurs when you try to create a new record with a primary key value that has already been used by another record in the table (error code 3022)

- the error that occurs when you enter a value in a combo box that isn't in the list and the LimitToList property has been set to Yes (error code 2237)

Here is the code that traps for these errors:

```
Private Sub Form_Error (DataErr As Integer, Response As Integer)
    If DataErr = 3058 Then
        MsgBox "You must enter a StudentID, please enter it now."
        Response = acDataErrContinue
    ElseIf DataErr = 3022 Then
        MsgBox "There is a student with this StudentID already
        ➥ entered. Either change the value and try again or
        ➥ press ESC to delete this record."
        Response = acDataErrContinue
    ElseIf DataErr = 2237 Then
        Response = acDataErrContinue
    Else
        Response = acDataErrDisplay
    End If
End Sub
```

When the form recognizes the **Error** event, Access runs the Form_Error procedure and sets the **DataErr** argument to the error code of the error that occurred. The procedure compares **DataErr** to specific error codes. The **If** clause compares **DataErr** to 3058. If there is a match, the procedure displays the custom message using the **MsgBox** function (the Visual Basic version of the **MsgBox** macro action). Next, the procedure sets the **Response** argument to **acDataErrContinue** to suppress display of the default error message, and then the procedure ends. If there is no match, the **ElseIf** clauses provide tests for other specific errors. If there is a match with either **ElseIf** clause, the procedure displays the custom message (if there is one), suppresses the default message, and ends. (This example assumes you have created a macro to display a message when the **NotInList** event is triggered and the 2237 error is generated, so the error-handler code for the 2237 error only suppresses the default error message.) If there is no match for the **If** or either **ElseIf** clause, Visual Basic executes the **Else** clause, which sets the **Response** argument to **acDataErrDisplay** to display the default error message for the error that did occur, and then ends the procedure.

Enter the Visual Basic Code

The title bar of the module in Figure 4.9 indicates that the module has been automatically named Form_frmStudents. Access automatically creates a form module to store the *event procedures* triggered by events recognized by the form and its controls. Form modules are analogous to the form macro groups we've been creating.

1. Type in the code from the error handler above.

2. Choose <u>R</u>un ➤ Compile Lo<u>a</u>ded Modules. When you *compile* a module, Access checks for errors and converts your code into a format that will execute faster. If there is an error in your code, Access stops compiling, displays a message and highlights the line with the error.

Handling Conditions with If...Then...Else in Visual Basic

Visual Basic procedures have several ways to handle conditions. The error-handler code in this example uses the `If...Then...Else` structure to execute statements conditionally. You use the `If...Then...Else` structure to define blocks of code that you want Visual Basic to execute if a specified condition is true. In the simple two-alternative case, the Visual Basic syntax analogous to the IIf() function or the macro with two alternatives is

If *condition* Then

   blockTrue

Else

   blockFalse

End If

where `condition` is any expression that evaluates to a numeric value. Visual Basic interprets a zero numeric value as false and any nonzero numeric value as true. If `condition` is true, Visual Basic executes all of the code in `blockTrue`, otherwise Visual Basic executes the code in `blockFalse` (following `Else`), and then executes the code following `End If`.

(continued)

You can test more than one condition by including `ElseIf` clauses, as in this example:

If *condition1* Then

    block1 True

ElseIf *condition2* Then

    block2 True

ElseIf *condition3* Then

    block3 True

Else

    blockFalse

End If

Beginning with *`condition1`*, Visual Basic tests the conditions one by one until it finds a true condition. When it finds a true condition, Visual Basic executes the code in the corresponding block; if none of the conditions is true, Visual Basic executes the code in the block following `Else`; and then executes the code following `End If`.

3. Select all of the lines between the first and last code template lines and copy the code to the clipboard. You'll paste this code into your controls gallery after you test it.

4. Close the module. Notice that the OnError property displays the expression [Event Procedure] to indicate that a procedure has been assigned.

5. Save the form.

6. In the Database window, click the Modules tab. The Modules tab is blank because the form module you just created is stored with the form and is not a separate database object.

Test the Visual Basic Error Handler

1. Switch to Form view and observe the StudentID for the student.

2. Click the New button in the toolbar (or at the bottom of the form).

3. Tab out of the StudentID, enter a Last Name and a First Name and press SHIFT+ENTER to try to save the record. Your custom message appears.

4. Click OK. The default error message has been suppressed.

5. Click in StudentID, enter the same StudentID that appeared in the first record, then press shift+enter to try to save the record. Your custom message appears.

6. Click OK. The default error message does not appear.

7. Press ESC to undo the record.

8. Close the form. You'll use the third condition to test for the error that occurs when you enter a value in a combo box that isn't in the list (error code 2237) in Chapter 7, "Navigating to Controls and Records."

Copy the Visual Basic Error Handler to the Controls Gallery

Copy the error handler to the controls gallery so that it is available for pasting into other forms. You can modify this error handler to test for other error codes and display custom messages appropriate for each form.

1. Click into zsfrmGallery, click into the OnError property, and click the Build button.

2. Select Code Builder and click OK.

3. Press CTRL+V (the error handler that is still on the Clipboard is pasted).

Designing to Avoid Macro Errors

Since you can't use macros to identify error codes after run-time errors have occurred, the best strategy for dealing with run-time errors that cause macros to fail is to avoid them whenever possible. Here is a list of ways to help you to create error-free macros.

Test preconditions in your macros. Run-time errors occur when circumstances make your macro impossible to execute. Often you can avoid errors by creating and testing preconditions. A *precondition* is a condition for an action that you use to test whether running the action would cause a run-time error. As examples:

- if a macro action refers to a control on another form, test to see if that form is open first
- if a macro action requires the value of a control in a calculation, test to see if the value is null first
- if a macro action tries to move the focus to a new record, test to see if the current record is the new record (in which case the **DoMenuItem** action would fail)
- if a macro action saves a record, test to see if the primary key value is not null and is unique

Test for errors and fix them as they appear. When you create a macro, try to anticipate the different ways the user will try to interact with your application. Test your application by trying out different sequences of interactions. For example, click command buttons in different sequences to see if you can deliberately trigger an error.

Use macro flow diagrams. A macro flow diagram is a valuable aid in understanding exactly what went wrong with your macro—for example, whether you are using the wrong event, the wrong macro action, or the wrong sequence of actions.

Use comments. When you troubleshoot a macro, you must understand the purpose of each of its actions. Comments in the macrosheet are essential for seeing the purpose of a macro action at a glance without having to select the row to view the action arguments.

Use a consistent naming convention. When you use a naming convention such as the one in this book, your objects are self-documenting: The object name includes information about the type of the object and its purpose. This information can help you to understand your macros more easily.

Create shorter macros. Long macros are difficult to understand. It is often best to break a long macro into a set of short macros, each with a defined purpose. You can troubleshoot each short macro separately and isolate errors more quickly.

Endnotes

This chapter has introduced you to the kinds of errors that occur, the troubleshooting tools you can use to diagnose the cause of the error, and ways to avoid errors in macros. You've seen that an important difference between macro and Visual Basic programming is that you can't identify the specific run-time error that occurred using macros, but you can using Visual Basic. To work around this limitation of macro programming, we adopt the approach of testing preconditions in macros in order to avoid run-time errors that would cause specific actions to fail.

In addition, you've learned how to write simple Visual Basic error-handling code for the **Error** event recognized by a form or report when the run-time error is generated in the Access interface or by the database engine. As necessary, we'll create Visual Basic error-handling code to suppress default error messages that can't be suppressed with macros, and in Chapter 13, "Closing Out a Session," we'll create Visual Basic error-handling code that tells a macro that an error has occurred so the macro can stop before running the action that would otherwise fail.

On Your Own

In the exercises you'll add Visual Basic error handling code to the frmClasses form. You'll also learn how to discover the error code for an error so that you can trap for that error the next time it occurs.

Adding to the Application

1. Add a Visual Basic Error Handler to frmClasses.

   a. Copy the error handler from zsfrmgallery to the OnError event procedure for the frmClasses form.

b. Modify the first two messages so that they are appropriate for frmClasses.

c. Display a new record, select a Course and try to save the record.

d. Select a Course, enter the schedule number of an existing course (try **13381**) and try to save the record.

e. Create a message for the third error that occurs if you try to enter a program that isn't on the list in the Course combo box. Include the instruction to press the ESC key to undo the entry.

f. Display a new record, type **HIST** into the Course combo list and try to tab out of the control.

Extending the Concepts

1. Determine the Error Code.
You can display the error code for a run-time error in a text box on the active form.

a. Place an unbound text box in the header of the frmInstructors form. Set the Name property to **ErrorCode** and delete the label.

b. Open the event procedure for the Error event of the form and enter the following line of code between the two lines of the code template:

```
ErrorCode = DataErr
```

In Visual Basic you assign a value to a control with the code

```
controlname = value
```

which is analogous to the **SetValue** macro action.

c. Compile and close the module.

d. Enter a last name for a new instructor and try to save the record. Observe the error code and the default message.

e. Enter a first name and try to save the record. Observe the error code and the default message.

f. When you are finished, either delete the ErrorCode text box or set its Visible property to No.

CHAPTER

FIVE

Looking Up Information in Other Forms

- The Screen object

- Understanding control reference syntax

- Synchronizing forms

- Special properties of the subform control

- Building expressions with the Expression Builder

- Using the Modal and PopUp properties to control a form

A primary reason for using a relational database to manage information is that you can minimize the duplication of stored information by storing facts about different subjects in separate tables. If you design a relational database correctly, the only fields that must have duplicated information are the fields that you use to join the tables, while the data in all other fields appears only once. If you change data (such as an address, the spelling of a name, or the fee for a class) you make the change in one place and the changed data is automatically reflected in the queries, forms, and reports. Having data stored in separate tables gives a relational system its power, but makes it more difficult when you want to see and use information from different tables simultaneously. Access provides several ways to use information stored in separate tables. In Chapter 6, "Looking Up Information in Tables and Queries", you learn techniques for displaying information from two tables or queries in the same form. In this chapter you'll learn how to use separate forms to display information from two different tables or queries.

This chapter shows you how a form can refer to itself and its own controls, and look up information in another form; how a main form can look up information from its subform; and how a subform can look up information from its parent main form.

NOTE When you begin this chapter, only the switchboard and the Database window should be displayed. Close any other objects.

An important concept in looking up information is the way Access refers to forms and reports and to their controls. Access uses these basic naming rules:

- Naming the database objects: within each type of database object, names must be unique. Each table, query, form, and so on must have a unique name; but you can use the same name for different types of database objects (except that tables and queries cannot have the same name). For example, there can be a Students table or a Students query, a Students form, a Students report, a Students macro group, and a Students module!

- Naming the objects contained in a database object: within each form or report, names of controls must be unique. While each control on a form or report must have a unique name, you can use the same name for controls on different forms and reports. For example, there can be a control named

CourseID on two different forms. In fact, every one of your forms and every one of your reports can have a control named CourseID. Additionally, every one of your tables and every one of your queries can have a field named Course ID. By default, Access assigns a bound control on a form or report the same name as the field it is bound to. Further, a control on a form or report can even have the same name as the form or report and a field in a table or query can have the same name as the table or query. This means that you can have a control named Students on the Students form as well as a control named Students on the Students report and a field named Students in the Students table or the Students query. Additionally, you could have a macro named Students in the Students macro group.

With all this flexibility in naming objects, how does Access know which object you are referring to? For that matter, how do *you* know which object you are referring to? You can say to someone else "I'm talking about the Students combo box on the Students report" and you will have identified a unique object. Access has its own way of saying the same thing—a set of rules for uniquely identifying an object in your database. In Chapter 2 you learned the Access syntax for referring to a form or form property; in this chapter you learn the syntax for referring to controls on forms and reports.

Referring to the Same Form

Interestingly, Access has a way to uniquely identify controls on the active form or report without using the specific names you've given them. Avoiding specific names is necessary when you create objects that you want to reuse in your application and in other Access applications (if you can reuse objects, you save time since you don't have to start from scratch each time). If you can reuse an error-free macro, you save troubleshooting time. In Chapter 2 you created a Return button and its macro as reusable objects. In this case, the macro is reusable because when you leave the `Close` action arguments blank, the action refers to the active form; thus you can avoid using a specific name (refer to Table 2.5 in Chapter 2).

The Screen Object

You use the *Screen object* to refer to the active form, the active report, the active control or the control that last had the focus. You identify the object by using one of the following identifiers:

Screen.ActiveForm

Screen.ActiveReport

Screen.ActiveControl

Screen.PreviousControl

You can use these identifiers in macro action arguments and conditions to create reusable macros. As an example, we'll create a macro to capitalize a word entered into a control; by using the Screen object instead of the control's name, the macro becomes reusable.

Creating a Macro to Capitalize Names

Although Access has built-in functions to convert letters to lowercase or uppercase, there isn't a built-in function to capitalize the first letter in a word. There is, however, a custom Visual Basic function, named Proper( ), stored in a module in the Orders database. To use this function, or another custom function created in another Access database, you need only import the module containing the function into your own database. You use imported functions as though they were built-in functions.

Importing a Visual Basic Module from Another Database

We'll begin by importing the module named UtilityFunctions from the Orders sample application.

1. Click in the Database window and choose File ➤ Get External Data ➤ Import.

2. Locate the Samples folder (inside the Access folder), select Orders, and click the Import button.

3. Click the Modules tab, select UtilityFunctions, and click OK.

4. In the Database window, click the Modules tab, then click the Design button. The declarations page of the module is displayed.

5. Click the arrow in the combo box on the right with the label Proc: (for procedure). The list displays the function procedures contained in the module (see Figure 5.1).

6. Select Proper. The window displays the Visual Basic code for the Proper( ) function.

7. Close the module.

The Proper( ) function converts the first letter of each word in its argument to uppercase. For example,

Proper(as you like it)

converts its argument to As You Like It. You can use the Proper( ) function to capitalize most, but not all, proper names correctly (Proper( ) converts smith to Smith, but converts mcdonald to Mcdonald rather than McDonald and converts van buren to Van Buren rather than van Buren).

Using the Proper() Function to Capitalize Names

1. Open frmStudents and switch to Design view. The text boxes containing a student's last and first name are named LName and FName, respectively.

FIGURE 5.1:
The custom functions in the UtilityFunctions module of the Orders database.

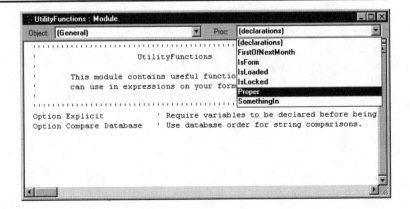

After you change the data in the LName control, you can use the Proper ( ) function to return the changed name with the first letter of each word capitalized. Create a macro that sets the LName control to the value that the Proper ( ) function returns. You run the macro after Access has updated the control to the record buffer; that is, when the text box recognizes the **AfterUpdate** event. At this instant, Access can use the updated value for the argument of the Proper( ) function and can return the capitalized result.

Creating the Macro for a Specific Text Box

First you create a macro called LName_AfterUpdate specifically for the LName control, and then use the Screen object to modify the macro into one that you can reuse for any control on any form or report. Figure 5.2 is the flow diagram for the macro.

1. Open a new macrosheet and save it as **mfrmStudents**

2. Click in the first Macro Name cell and enter **LName_AfterUpdate** as the name of the new macro.

3. Click in the next row, select the **SetValue** action, and set the arguments as follows:

    Item   LName

    Expression   Proper(LName)

    (Note that Access places square brackets around the control names.)

4. Save the macro.

FIGURE 5.2:

Macro flow diagram to capitalize a name.

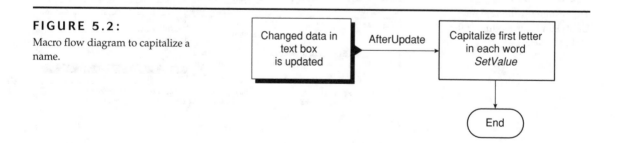

CAUTION　Do not include an equal sign in the `Expression` argument. if you include the equal sign, Access evaluates the expression first and treats the result as the name of a field. For example, if you have typed smith, Access evaluates =Proper (smith) and treats Smith as the name of a field. Since there is no such field, Access can't execute the macro action, displays the default error message "Invalid reference to field 'Smith' " , and stops the macro.

Attach and Test the Macro

1. Select the LName text box, click in the AfterUpdate property, and select the macro mfrmStudents.LName_AfterUpdate.

2. Switch to Form view and click the New button.

3. Enter **144112222** into the Student ID control, then enter **smith** in the Last Name control, and press TAB. In response, the control displays Smith.

Creating a Reusable Macro Using the Screen Object

To make the macro reusable, change its name and action arguments so that they don't refer to the control by name. Use the identifier Screen.ActiveControl in the action arguments to refer to the control, and change the name of the macro to Active-Control_AfterUpdate. You'll store the macro in the mcrGallery macro group.

1. Click in the macrosheet, select and delete the two rows of the LName_AfterUpdate macro, then close the macrosheet.

2. Open the mcrGallery macro group in Design view.

3. Click in a new row, and enter a new macro named **ActiveControl_AfterUpdate**

4. Click in the next row, select the **SetValue** action, and set the arguments as follows:

> **Item**   Screen.ActiveControl
>
> **Expression**   Proper(Screen.ActiveControl)

5. Save the macro.

The macro is shown in Table 5.1.

TABLE 5.1: A reusable macro to capitalize a name.

Macro Name	Action	Action Arguments
ActiveControl_AfterUpdate		
	SetValue	**Item**: Screen.ActiveControl
		Expression: Proper(Screen.ActiveControl)

Attach and Test the Macro

1. Click in frmStudents and switch to Design view.

2. One by one, click in each of the LName, FName, and City text boxes and set the AfterUpdate property to the mcrGallery.ActiveControl_AfterUpdate macro.

3. Save the form, then switch to Form view.

4. Click the New button to display a blank record.

5. Enter the values below. Notice that the Proper( ) function capitalizes the first letter of each word as soon as you tab to the next control.

> **StudentID**   112223333
>
> **LName**   stern
>
> **FName**   beth
>
> **City**   san francisco

Looking Up Related Information on Another Form

Often when you are using a particular form for a task, you need to refer to information on another form. For example, while registering a student in classes using frmRegistration you may need to edit the student's personal information using frmStudents.

1. Click the Register in Classes button on the switchboard.

The frmRegistration form is designed for registering existing students in classes. The student information in the upper part of the main form is locked and disabled, so you can't edit student information with this form. (This is the data entry form for the tlnkClassStudent linking table, and you can change data only in the combo box control. After you select a class using the combo box control and save the record, the values of the Schedule No and the Student ID are stored in the linking table.)

2. In the Database window, double-click frmStudents (the data entry form for student information).

TIP One way to avoid data integrity problems in two tables that have a one-to-many relationship is to use separate forms for data entry into the tables. In the current example, tblStudents is the one table and tlnkClassStudent is the many table. The data entry form for the table on the many side (frmRegistration) displays information from the table on the one side (tblStudents) in controls that are locked in order to impose a sequence for data entry. By requiring records for new students to be entered and saved using a separate form, you easily avoid the problem of trying to register a non-existent (as far as Access is concerned) student with the registration form.

When you work interactively, in order to edit the student's information, you open the frmStudents form and find the corresponding student record. To automate this operation, create a macro that opens frmStudents displaying the record for the same student whose record is displayed in the frmRegistration form; this is called *synchronizing the form*.

Placing a Command Button to Open a Related Form

You'll place a command button on frmRegistration to run the macro that opens and synchronizes frmStudents.

1. Click on frmRegistration and switch to Design view.

2. With the Control Wizards tool deselected, select the Command Button tool; create a button 0.5" wide and 0.25" tall in the form header just to the left of the Return button (placed in Chapter 2).

3. Set the Name property to **cmdReview** and the Caption property to **Re&view**

Creating a Macro to Open a Form with a Related Record

You create a new macrosheet to store the macros for frmRegistration and then create a macro to open and synchronize frmStudents.

1. Open a new macrosheet and save it as **mfrmRegistration**

2. Click in the first Macro Name cell and enter **cmdReview_Click** as the name of the new macro.

3. In the Action cell of the next row, select the `OpenForm` action and set the `Form Name` argument to frmStudents.

You can use the `Where Condition` argument to tell Access which record to display. You want to find the record in the tblStudents table that has the same StudentID as the record that is displayed in frmRegistration, and display this record when the frmStudents form opens. You need to refer to the value of the StudentID field in the table underlying the form you are opening (frmStudents) and to the value of the StudentID control on the open form (frmRegistration).

Referring to Controls on Forms

In Chapter 2 you learned the syntax for referring to forms and reports. In order to refer to a form or report, it must be open, and because Access lets you use the same name for a form and a report, you must tell Access what the object is by specifying the collection name:

Forms![formname]   for a form

Reports![reportname]   for a report

where the exclamation point operator separates the collection name from the name of an object in the collection.

You refer to a property of a form or report as follows:

Forms![formname].[propertyname]   for a form property

Reports![reportname].[propertyname]   for a form property

where the dot operator separates the name of the object from the name of one of its properties.

The properties that you can set in Design view are listed in an object's property sheet. In addition, most objects have properties that you can't set in Design view and aren't listed in the property sheet. A form has a *Form* property which refers to the form itself and a *Controls* collection which contains the form's controls. Similarly, a report has a *Report* property which refers to the report itself and a Controls collection containing the report's controls. The complete syntax for referring to a control on a form or report is:

Forms![formname].Form.Controls![controlname]

for a control on a form

Reports![reportname].Report.Controls![controlname]

for a control on a report

However, the Form property is the *default property* that Access assumes for a form (and the Report property is the default property for a report), which means that you don't have to include it in the identifier. Also, the Controls collection is the *default collection* for a form (and for a report) so you don't have to include the collection name when you refer to a control. Therefore, you can use the expressions:

> *Forms![formname]![controlname]*
>> for a control on a form
>
> *Reports![reportname]![controlname]*
>> for a control on a report

These expressions are called the *full identifier syntax* or the *qualified reference* for a control. For example,

> Forms!frmRegistration!StudentID

refers to the StudentID control on the frmRegistration form.

The full identifier syntax for referring to a property of a control includes the identifier for the control followed by the dot operator followed by the property name, as follows:

> *Forms![formname]![controlname].[propertyname]*
>> for a property of a control on a form
>
> *Reports![reportname]![controlname].[propertyname]*
>> for a property of a control on a report

For example,

> Forms!frmRegistration!StudentID.Enabled

refers to the Enabled property of the StudentID control on the frmRegistration form.

When the form (or report) is the active object, you can often, but not always, use a shorter version called the *unqualified reference*, as follows:

> *[controlname]*   for a control on the active form
>
> *[controlname]*   for a control on the active report

The short syntax for referring to a control property is:

> *[controlname].[propertyname]*
>
>> for a control on the active form
>
> *[controlname].[propertyname]*
>
>> for a control on the active report

As an example, if frmRegistration is the active form, the short syntax for referring to the StudentID control is

> StudentID

and the short syntax for the Enabled property of the StudentID control is

> StudentID.Enabled

As a general rule, you can use either syntax when the control is on the active form or report, but there are situations where one or the other is required. (I'll note these cases when they occur.)

NOTE I am not explicitly including the square brackets in these references. If you avoid using spaces and special characters in names, you save having to type the square brackets because Access enters them automatically when they are needed.

Completing the Where Condition Argument

Returning to the problem of using the `OpenForm` action to open a related form while synchronizing it to the open form, you use the syntax

> *[fieldname]=Forms![formname]![controlname]*

in the `Where Condition` argument. In this expression, *[fieldname]* refers to the field in the underlying table or query of the form you want to open, and *[controlname]* refers to the control on the other form that contains the value you want to match. For example, to open the frmStudents form displaying a record synchronized to the record in the frmRegistration form, use the expression

[StudentID]=Forms![frmRegistration]![StudentID]

Notice that the full syntax is required on the right side of the expression, even though frmRegistration is the active form when the macro executes the **OpenForm** action—this is an example of a case where you must use the full syntax to refer to a control on the active object. Notice also that the short syntax is required on the left-hand side of the expression.

1. Enter the expression **[StudentID] = Forms![frmRegistration]![StudentID]** in the **Where Condition** argument.

2. Save the macro and close the macro window.

Table 5.2 shows the macro and Figure 5.3 depicts the macro flow diagram.

TABLE 5.2: A reusable macro to capitalize a name.

Macro Name	Action	Action Arguments
cmdReview_Click		
	OpenForm	**Form Name**: frmStudents
		Where Condition: [Student ID] = Forms![frmRegistration]![StudentID]

Attach and Test the Macro

1. Click in frmRegistration and select the cmdReview command button.

2. In the property sheet, click the Event tab, then click in the OnClick property, and select mfrmRegistration.cmdReview_Click from the list.

3. Save the form and switch to Form view.

4. Using the navigation buttons at the bottom of the form, select a record and click the Review button. Access displays the frmStudents form with the related record displayed.

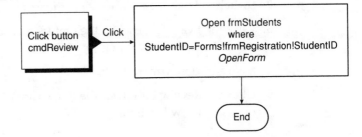

FIGURE 5.3:
The macro flow diagram for a macro
to open a form synchronized to
another form.

There are three modifications to make: first, since frmStudents partially covers the student information in the frmRegistration form, create a macro to move frmStudents when it first opens in order to minimize covering frmRegistration; second, modify the macro that runs when you click the Return button on frmStudents to decide whether to unhide the switchboard when the form closes; and third, modify several form properties of frmStudents to control its behavior.

Creating a Macro to Move a Form

You use the **MoveSize** action to move and resize a database object. When a form opens, it recognizes the **Open** event, so you'll name the new macro Form_Open.

1. Open the macro group mfrmStudents and enter a new macro named **Form_Open**

2. Click in the next row and select the **MoveSize** action (this action moves and resizes the current window). Use the action arguments to specify the new position of the window's upper left corner, measured from the upper left corner of the Access window.

3. Set Right to **2.25"** and Down to **0.5"**

4. Save and close the macro window.

Attach and Test the Macro

1. Activate frmStudents by selecting Students from the list of open objects in the Window menu.

2. Switch to Design view and select the form.

3. Click the Event tab, click in the OnOpen property, and select the macro mfrmStudents.Form_Open.

4. Save and close frmStudents.

5. Click the Review button on the Registration form. The frmStudents form opens in a new location.

The macro Form_Open is triggered indirectly by user action: you click the Review button to open the form. When Access executes the **OpenForm** action, the form recognizes the **Open** event and triggers the macro to move the form.

The relationship between the two macros is shown in Figure 5.4. When a macro flow diagram represents more than one macro, use dashed rectangles, labeled with the names of the macros, to enclose the actions of each macro.

FIGURE 5.4:

A flow diagram for a macro triggering another macro.

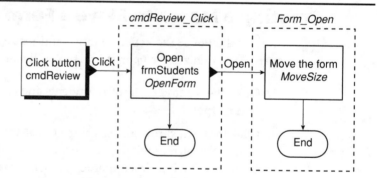

Using the Tag Property to Keep Track of How a Form Is Opened

After reviewing and editing student information, you close the form and return to the registration process. The Return button needs to be modified, because if you click the button now, it closes frmStudents and unhides the switchboard. The problem is that frmStudents can be opened from more than one place: the switchboard or the frmRegistration form. When you open a form directly from the switchboard, the switchboard should be unhidden when you close the form, but when you open a form from another form, the form should simply close without unhiding the switchboard. You can use the Tag property to keep track of which form is used to open another form.

Forms, form sections, reports, report sections, and controls all have a Tag property. The Tag property doesn't affect the object at all; it is available as a space for you to store information. In this case, you can use the Tag property of a form to indicate whether you opened the form from the frmSwitchboard form or from any other form. You can modify the cmdReview_Click macro to set the value of the Tag property of frmStudents to any value except null—for example, to set the value to 1 when frmStudents is opened from the Registration form (see Figure 5.5). (If it is important to remember which form is the opener, you can enter the name of the form enclosed in quotation marks in the Tag property, e.g., "frmRegistration".)

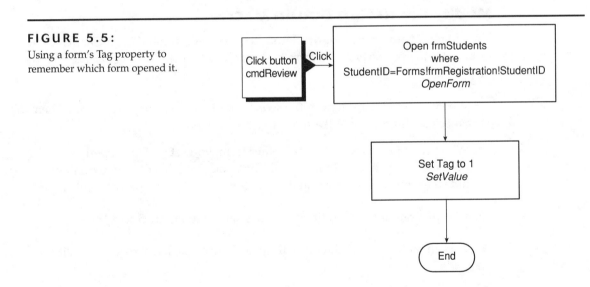

FIGURE 5.5:
Using a form's Tag property to remember which form opened it.

1. Click in mfrmRegistration and modify the macro cmdReview_Click as shown in Table 5.3.

2. Save the macro.

TABLE 5.3: Using the Tag property to remember the opener.

Macro Name	Action	Action Arguments
cmdReview_Click		
	OpenForm	**Form Name**: frmStudents
		Where Condition: [StudentID] = Forms![frmRegistration]![StudentID]
	SetValue	**Item**: Screen.ActiveForm.Tag
		Expression: 1

As soon as Access executes the **OpenForm** action, the opened form becomes the active form, so you can use the Screen.ActiveForm identifier in the **SetValue** action.

Modify the Return Button Macro

You can modify the macro for the Return button (refer to Table 2.5 in Chapter 2) by testing the Tag property of the form to decide whether the switchboard should be unhidden, as follows:

- When you open a form from the switchboard, the Tag property is null; when you close this form you'll also unhide the switchboard.

- When you open a form from any other form, you set its Tag property to a non-null value (like 1). In this case, when you close this form you don't unhide the switchboard, but you do reset the form's Tag property to null.

The flow diagram for the modified macro is shown in Figure 5.6.

1. Click in mcrGallery and modify the cmdReturn_Click macro as shown in Table 5.4.

2. Save the macro.

The macro tests the Tag property of the form. If the Tag is null, the macro closes the form, unhides the switchboard, and stops the macro. If the Tag is not null, the macro resets the form's Tag to null and closes the form. You use the Screen object to refer to the form's Tag property, so that the macro continues to be reusable.

FIGURE 5.6:

Using the Tag property to decide whether to unhide the switchboard.

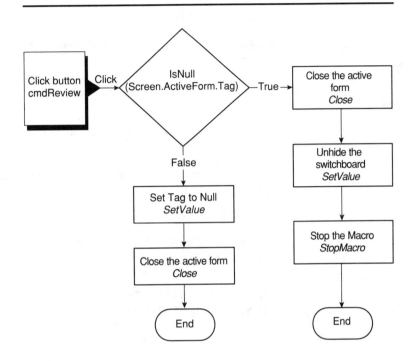

TABLE 5.4: Testing the Tag with the macro cmdReturn_Click

Macro Name	Condition	Action	Action Arguments
cmdReturn_Click			
	IsNull(Screen.ActiveForm.Tag)	`Close`	
	...	`SetValue`	**Item:** Forms!frmSwitch- board.Visible
			Expression: Yes
	...	`StopMacro`	
		`SetValue`	**Item:** Screen.Active- Form.Tag
			Expression: Null
		`Close`	

Test the Macros

Test the macros for the command buttons on the Registration and Students forms to make sure the macros interact as you intend.

1. Click the Review button on the Registration form. The frmStudents form opens.

2. Click the Return button. The Students form closes without unhiding the switchboard.

3. Click the Return button. The Registration form closes and the switchboard appears.

4. Click the Edit/Add Student button. The Students form opens.

5. Click the Return button. The Students form closes and the switchboard reappears.

Setting Properties to Control Form Behavior

There are several properties you can set to control how the user works with the form:

- When you click the Review button on frmRegistration, Access displays the single related record on frmStudents. The record number indicator at the bottom of the window displays "Record 1 of 1". Since there is only one record, you don't need the navigation buttons. You remove them by setting the form's NavigationButtons property to No.

- To reduce the number of ways to close the form, remove the form's default Control box and Close button. (You can still close the form by choosing the File ➤ Close command or pressing CTRL+F4. Chapter 16, "Controlling the User Interface," shows you how to eliminate these two ways to close a form.)

- To prevent minimizing or maximizing the form, remove the Minimize and Maximize buttons.

- To control when the user closes the form, require that the user close frmStudents before returning to work with frmRegistration by setting the Modal and PopUp properties to Yes. A form with a modal property turned on retains the focus until you close the form. You can't click in another window while the modal form is open; however, you can click in menu commands and toolbar buttons. To prevent clicking in the menu commands and toolbars as well, set the PopUp property to Yes. A pop-up form stays on top of other open forms. A *dialog box* is an example of a form with Modal and PopUp properties set to Yes.

1. Set the properties of the frmStudents form as follows:

Property	Setting
NavigationButtons	No
ScrollBars	Neither
PopUp	Yes
Modal	Yes
ControlBox	No
MinMaxButtons	None
CloseButton	No

2. Save and close the form.

3. Click the Review button on frmRegistration. The Students form opens as a dialog box.

4. Click frmRegistration, click a menu, and then click a toolbar button. Access responds with beeps and doesn't let the focus leave frmStudents.

5. Edit the student information.

6. Click the Return button. Notice that the Registration form immediately refreshes and displays the updated information.

7. Click the Return button again. The form closes and the switchboard is displayed.

Summary of the Method

When you are working with a form and want to refer to information in a related form, you can use the method summarized below, "Synchronizing Two Forms by Closing the Related Form."

Synchronizing Two Forms by Closing the Related Form

- Use the `OpenForm` action with the expression *[fieldname]=Forms![formname]![controlname]* in the `Where Condition` argument to open the related form displaying the synchronized record. In this expression, *[fieldname]* refers to the field in the underlying table or query of the form you want to open, and *[controlname]* refers to the control on the other form that contains the value you want to match.

- Make the related form a modal pop-up form to require that the related form be closed before returning to the first form.

Keeping Forms Synchronized

There are situations when you want to leave a related form open so you can view the information in the related form while you return to work in the first form. Each time you move to a different record in the first form, the related form should stay "in sync" by locating and displaying the correct related record.

For example, when you are viewing class information using frmClasses, you may want to view course information as well. The College database contains the review form frmCoursesView for this purpose. (While you could design this interaction to allow the user to edit as well as review the course information, we'll use a simpler interaction that allows review only.)

1. In the Database window, select and open frmCoursesView in Design view.

2. Select the form, click in the property sheet and set the PopUp property to Yes (so the form will remain on top) and the BorderStyle property to Dialog (to eliminate a border). With the PopUp property set to Yes, when you open the form in Form view, you can't to switch to Design view; if you want to go to Design view, you have to close the form and reopen it in Design view.

3. Switch to Form view (see Figure 5.7).

4. Save the form.

FIGURE 5.7:

The pop-up form to review course information.

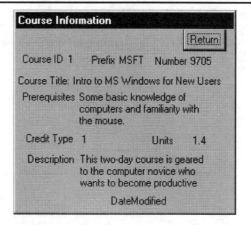

Placing a Command Button to Open and Synchronize a Form

Place a command button (named cmdReviewCourse) on frmClasses, then create a macro that opens frmCoursesView synchronized to frmClasses and sets the Tag property of frmCoursesView to 1. The macro, cmdReviewCourse_Click, has the same actions as shown in Table 5.3, so you can copy and modify the cmdReview_Click macro instead of starting from scratch.

1. Open frmClasses in Design view, and place a command button in the form header; set the Name property to **cmdReviewCourse** and the Caption property to **Re&view Course**

2. Create a new macrosheet named **mfrmClasses** and create a macro named **cmdReviewCourse_Click** as shown in Table 5.5.

3. Save the macro.

4. Attach the macro to the OnClick property of the cmdReviewCourse button on frmClasses.

5. Save the form and switch to Form view.

6. Select a class and click the Review Course button. The corresponding record is displayed in the Courses form.

TABLE 5.5: The Macro cmdReviewCourse_Click

Macro Name	Action	Action Arguments
cmdReviewCourse_Click		
	OpenForm	**Form Name**: frmCoursesView
		Where Condition: [Course ID] = Forms![frmClasses]![Course ID]
	SetValue	**Item**: Screen.ActiveForm.Tag
		Expression: 1

7. Without closing frmCoursesView, click in frmClasses and select a different class. Notice that frmCoursesView does not remain synchronized (see Figure 5.8).

As long as the form frmCoursesView is open, you want to keep it synchronized by always displaying the correct course as you move from class to class.

FIGURE 5.8:

The review form doesn't remain synchronized automatically when you move to a different record.

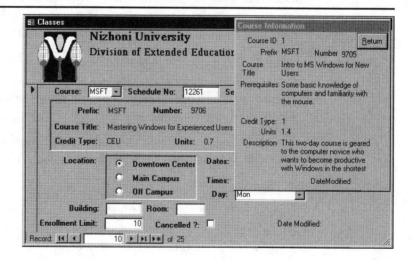

Create a Macro to Keep the Forms Synchronized

When you move to a different class, it becomes the current record and frmClasses recognizes the **Current** event. If frmCoursesView is open when you move to a different class, you can resynchronize frmCoursesView with a macro that uses the same **OpenForm** action; since the form is already open, the **OpenForm** action just recalculates the **Where Condition**. If frmCoursesView isn't open when you move to a different class, you don't take any action. Figure 5.9 shows the macro flow diagram. You can use the IsLoaded( ) function in the UtilityFunctions module you imported earlier to determine if a form is open. Enter the name of the form enclosed in quotation marks as the argument of the IsLoaded( ) function. The IsLoaded( ) function returns the True value if the form is open and displays records and returns the False value otherwise.

1. Click in a new row in the mfrmClasses macro group and name a new macro **Form_Current**

2. Enter the macro as shown in Table 5.6.

3. Save the macro.

FIGURE 5.9:

Resynchronizing a form using the Current event.

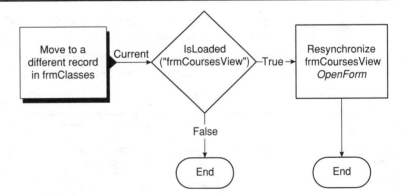

TABLE 5.6: A macro to resynchronize another form.

Macro Name	Condition	Action	Action Arguments
Form_Current			
	IsLoaded("frmCoursesView")	**OpenForm**	**Form Name**: frmCoursesView
			Where Condition: Course ID=Forms! frmClasses!Course ID

Attach and Test the Macro

1. Click in frmClasses, then switch to Design view; click in the form's OnCurrent property, and select the macro mfrmClasses.Form_Current.

2. Save the form and switch to Form view.

3. Click in frmClasses and move to a different record. Access resynchronizes frmCoursesView and displays the correct related record.

Create a Macro to Close the Related Form

When you close frmClasses, you want to close frmCoursesView also (if it is open). You create a new macro, and run it when frmClasses closes and recognizes the **Close** event. This macro, called Form_Close, closes frmCoursesView if the form is open. Figure 5.10 shows the macro flow diagram.

FIGURE 5.10:

A macro to close another form if it is open.

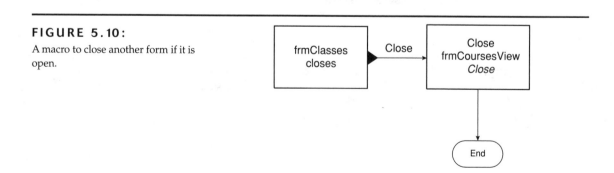

NOTE

It is interesting to note the exceptional behavior of the `Close` action—the `Close` action does not fail and a run-time error does not occur if you specify the name of an object that isn't open or that doesn't exist. This means that it is not necessary to test to determine if a form is open before running the `Close` action.

1. Click in the mfrmClasses macrosheet and create a new macro named **Form_Close**

2. Enter the macro as shown in Table 5.7.

3. Save and close the macro.

TABLE 5.7: A macro to close another form.

Macro Name	Action	Action Arguments
Form_Close		
	Close	**Object Type**: Form
		Object Type: frmCoursesView

Attach and Test the Macro

1. Click in the OnClose property and select mfrmClasses.Form_Close.

2. Save the form and switch to Form view.

3. Click the Review Course button.

4. Click in the Classes form, then click the Return button. Both forms close.

5. Click the Edit/Add Class button on the switchboard and then click the Return button. The form closes.

Summary of the Method

When you are working with a form and want to refer to information on a related form and keep the related form open and synchronized to the first form, use the method summarized below, "Synchronizing Two Forms Using the Current Event."

Synchronizing Two Forms Using the Current Event

- Use the `OpenForm` action with the expression *[fieldname]=Forms![formname]![controlname]* in the `Where Condition` argument to open the related form displaying the synchronized record. In this expression, *[fieldname]* refers to the field in the underlying table or query of the form you want to open, and *[controlname]* refers to the control on the other form that contains the value you want to match.

- Make the related form a pop-up form to keep it on top.

- Use the `Current` event of the first form to trigger a macro that resynchronizes the related form using the same `OpenForm` action *after testing that the related form is open.*

- Use the `Close` event of the first form to trigger a macro to close the related form.

Drilling Down for More Information

As a final example of looking up information on a separate form, we'll examine the "drill-down" technique used in most commercial accounting applications. Often you want to see the detail that supports the calculation of a number—that is, you want to *drill down* into the supporting records.

The tabular form frmEnrollmentSummary contains the current enrollment and enrollment limit for each class; it is a summary form because the current enrollment for a class is the total number of students registered in the class. In this case, drilling down means displaying the frmClassList form corresponding to the selected class in frmEnrollmentSummary.

1. Select Review Enrollments in the switchboard.

2. Switch to Design view and set the following properties to control how the user works with the form. (Record selectors won't be necessary because you'll create a command button to select a record.)

Property	Setting
ControlBox	No
MinMaxButtons	None
CloseButton	No
ScrollBars	Vertical Only
RecordSelectors	No

To give this form drill-down capability, place a button in the Detail section of frmEnrollmentSummary and use the button to run a macro that opens the related record in frmClassList. Since the macro opens frmClassList from a task form rather than the switchboard, the macro sets the form's Tag property to 1 (similar to the cmdReview_Click macro shown in Table 5.3). To make sure the frmClassList form displays the correct related record, you can have the macro set the form's Modal property to Yes in order to require that the related form be closed before you can return to frmEnrollmentSummary and select a different class. The macro flow diagram is shown in Figure 5.11.

Placing the Drill-Down Button

You place a command button in the Detail section.

1. Switch to Design view.

2. With the Control Wizards tool deselected, click the Command Button tool and place a button 0.2" wide and 0.2" tall in the Detail section, to the left of the ScheduleNo control.

3. Set the Name property to **cmdDetail**, the Caption property to + (plus sign), the FontSize to **10** and the FontWeight to **Bold**. The plus sign is a visual cue that more information is available.

FIGURE 5.11:

The flow diagram for the drill-down button.

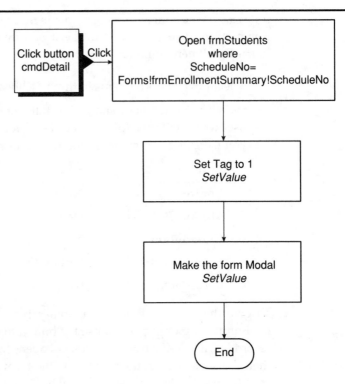

Create the Macro

You create a macro to open frmClassList and synchronize it to the selected record.

1. Open a new macrosheet, save it as **mfrmEnrollmentSummary**, and create a new macro named **cmdDetail_Click**

2. Enter the macro shown in Table 5.8. (You can create the macro by copying and modifying the macro in Table 5.3.)

3. Save and close the macro group.

TABLE 5.8: The drill-down macro.

Macro Name	Action	Action Arguments
cmdDetail_Click		
	OpenForm	**Form Name**: frmClassList
		Where Condition: [ScheduleNo] = Forms![frmEnrollmentSummary]![ScheduleNo]
	SetValue	**Item**: Screen.ActiveForm.Tag
		Expression: 1
	SetValue	**Item**: Screen.ActiveForm.Modal
		Expression: Yes

Attach the Macro and Test the Drill-Down Process

1. Click in the property sheet for cmdDetail, then set the OnClick property to the macro **mfrmEnrollmentSummary.cmdDetail_Click**

2. Save the form and switch to Form view.

3. Select a record by clicking its Detail button. The corresponding Class List opens. With the Modal property set to Yes, you have to close frmClassList before selecting another record in the frmEnrollmentSummary form.

4. Click the Return button. The Class List closes.

5. Click the Return button again. The frmEnrollmentSummary form closes and frmSwitchboard appears.

You can use the techniques in this section whenever you want to display data stored in two related tables or queries. Essentially, the procedure is: create a form based on each table or query, then place a command button on one of the forms and use the button's **Click** event to trigger a macro that opens the second form and synchronizes its records. To make sure the forms display related records, you can use a macro (like the one shown in Table 5.8) that requires that you close the second form before returning to the first, or you can use the **Current** event of the first form to trigger a second macro (like the Form_Current macro shown in Table 5.6) to resynchronize the second form. The form with the command button controls the synchronization, but either form can have the button.

Usually, two related tables or queries have a one-to-many relationship. If the controlling form is on the many side of the relationship, as in the previous examples, clicking the command button displays the single related record. If the controlling form is on the one side, clicking the command button selects several records in the second form. For example, you can place a command button on frmCourses and create macros to open frmClasses as a related form. When you click the button for a course that has several scheduled classes, you can browse through the classes one by one. Alternatively, you can use the command button to open a tabular form based on tblClasses and display all of the related classes at once.

Using the Form/Subform Technique to Display Information in Related Tables

The techniques in the previous section provide ways to display information from two related tables or queries in two separate forms, and use macros to keep the records linked and synchronized. Another way to display related information from two tables or queries is to use the built-in form/subform technique to display the two forms in a single window as though they were one form.

Access uses the subform control as a way to link two forms and keep their records synchronized. One of the forms becomes the main form when you place a subform control on it. You link the second form to the first when you set the SourceObject property of the subform control to the name of the second form; subsequently, you call the second form a *subform*. When you open the main form in Form view, the subform control displays the second form. If you leave blank the two record-linking properties, LinkChildFields and LinkMasterFields, the forms are linked but their records aren't, and you can browse their records independently. After you set the two record-linking properties, the records are linked and remain synchronized. As you browse through the records of the main form, Access displays the synchronized records in the second form. Normally, you create the subform in tabular format, or display its records in Datasheet view, so that more than one related record is displayed in the subform control.

In the form/subform technique, all you need to do is set the subform control properties and Access automatically keeps the forms synchronized. You can use the form/subform technique to display a one-to-many relationship by basing the main form on the one side and the subform on the many side. For example, frmRegistration displays the one-to-many relationship between the tblStudents table and the tlnkClassStudent linking table. The main form is based on tblStudents, while the subform is based on a query that uses the linking table to automatically look up class and course information. You'll learn how to create queries that automatically look up information in other tables in the next chapter.

You can also display a many-to-one relationship using the form/subform technique. For example, you can base the main form on tblClasses and the subform on tblCourses. When you open the form in Form view, the main form displays a class while the subform control displays the related course; as you browse to view different classes, the subform control displays the correct course for each class.

Access has special identifiers for referring to the controls on one form from the other form when the two forms are linked with a subform control. You learn about these identifiers in the next two sections.

Looking Up Information on a Subform

1. Click the Register in Classes button in frmSwitchboard.

2. Note the calculation of the total units displayed at the bottom of the form. Each time you register a student in a class, the total of the units is recalculated and appears at the bottom of the main form.

The Properties of the Subform Control

1. Switch to Design view and click in the subform control.

2. In the property sheet, observe that the Name of the subform control is frmRegistrationSub. The SourceObject property identifies the form that the subform control displays. In this case the Name and the SourceObject properties are identical, but this isn't necessary. The two record-linking properties, LinkMasterFields and LinkChildFields, are both set to StudentID; Access matches records in the main form to records displayed in the subform control using these linking fields.

The subform control has the usual properties that represent the attributes of the control: name, size, visibility, whether the control is locked or enabled, etc., and event properties. In addition to attribute properties, a subform control has linking properties: SourceObject, LinkChildFields, and LinkMasterFields. A subform control also has the Form property—the Form property of a subform control refers to the form displayed within the subform control.

Earlier in this chapter you learned the syntax that Access uses to refer to objects. We extend the discussion to include references to subform controls and controls displayed within a subform control.

To refer to a subform control on a form, use the syntax

Forms![formname]![subformcontrolname]

To refer to the form displayed within the subform control, use the syntax

Forms![formname]![subformcontrolname].Form

To refer to a property of the form displayed within the subform control, use the syntax

Forms![formname]![subformcontrolname].Form.[propertyname]

To refer to a control on the form displayed within a subform control, you could use the Controls collection as follows:

Forms![formname]![subformcontrolname].Form.Controls![controlname]

However, the Controls collection is the default collection for a form so you use the shorter reference:

Forms![formname]![subformcontrolname].Form![controlname]

and to refer to a property of the control, use

Forms![formname]![subformcontrolname].Form![controlname].[property-name]

It is important to note that the Form property is not the default property for the subform control, so you must include it explicitly in references to properties and controls of the form displayed within a subform control.

For example, use

Form!frmRegistration!frmRegistrationSub.Form.RecordSource

to refer to the RecordSource property of the form displayed within the frmRegistrationSub subform control on the frmRegistration form, and use

Forms!frmRegistration!frmRegistrationSub.Form!TotalUnits

to refer to the TotalUnits control displayed within the subform control.

When the form is the active form, the short syntax to refer to a control displayed in a subform control is

[subformcontrolname].Form![controlname]

and the short syntax for one of its properties is

[subformcontrolname].Form![controlname].[propertyname]

In the same example, if frmRegistration is the active form, the short syntax for referring to the enabled property of the TotalUnits control is

frmRegistrationSub.Form!TotalUnits.Enabled

The syntax for referring to controls displayed within subform controls is complicated. The last section of this chapter shows you how to use the Expression Builder to help create these references, but first you need to understand the syntax in order to modify the expressions that the Builder creates.

Observing the Calculation of the Sum on the Subform

1. Click once outside the subform control to deselect it, then double-click the subform control. The form frmRegistrationSub opens in Design view. Notice that the form header contains a hidden calculated control to sum the values in the Units field.

2. Click on the text box in the form header and note the properties shown below. The expression Sum([Units]) determines the sum of the units for all of the records displayed by the form. (In Chapter 3 you modified the original expression, = Sum([Units]), by using the IIf( ) function in order to replace a null value with zero.) When the form is displayed in the subform control, the classes for a single student are displayed and Sum([Units]) is the total units for the student.

Name	TotalUnits
ControlSource	=IIf(IsNull(Sum([Units])),0,Sum([Units]))

3. Notice that the Visible property for both the text box and its label are set to No (the main form displays the total value so you hide the calculation on the subform).

4. Close the form.

5. Click in frmRegistration and switch to Form view. The result of the calculation is displayed in the TotalUnits text box on the main form.

6. Switch to Design view, click on the calculated control at the bottom of the main form, and note the properties

Name	TotalUnits
ControlSource	=[frmRegistrationSub].[Form]![TotalUnits]

Calculate the Total Fees

In a similar way, you'll calculate the total fees for the student and display the result in a calculated control on the main form.

1. Double-click the subform control frmRegistrationSub.

2. In the toolbox, click on the Text Box tool. Click in the form header and drag to place an unbound text box.

3. Click in the property sheet, then select the ControlSource property and enter the expression

    =IIf(IsNull(Sum([Fee])),0,Sum([Fee]))

4. Set the Name property to **TotalFee**, the Format property to Currency, and the DecimalPlaces property to 0.

5. Click in the label, then select the label text, and type **Total Fee**

6. Select both the text box and the label and set their Visible properties to No.

7. Save and close the form.

Display the Sum on the Main Form

You'll place an unbound text box on the main form to display the result of the calculation.

1. Select the Text Box tool and place an unbound text box in the lower part of frmRegistration, to the right of the Total Units controls.

2. Click in the label, select the label text, and type **Total Fee**

3. Click in the text box, then click in the ControlSource property and enter the following expression (to refer to the value in the TotalFee control displayed in the subform control):

    =[frmRegistrationSub].Form![TotalFee]

4. Set the Format property to Currency, the DecimalPlaces property to 0, the Enabled property to No, and the Locked property to Yes.

5. Click on the TotalUnits text box, then click the Format Painter button on the toolbar and click on the TotalFee text box. The formatting is copied from the TotalUnits text box to the TotalFee text box.

6. Save the form and switch to Form view. Observe the calculation of the TotalFee by browsing through a few records (see Figure 5.12).

Looking Up Information on a Main Form

The subform control also has a *Parent* property which refers to the controls on the main form (refer to Appendix A for more information). To refer to a control on the main form when a control within the subform control has the focus, use the syntax

Parent![controlname]

You can also refer to a field in the table or query that underlies the main form using the syntax

Parent![fieldname]

You can use this syntax refer to a field in the table or query even if there is no control on the form bound to the field. As an example, you'll delete the Program control displayed on the main form, and display this information in the subform control instead.

1. Switch to Design view.

2. Select and delete the Program label and text box.

3. Double-click the subform control.

4. Increase the footer of the frmRegistrationSub form to 0.2".

5. Place an unbound text box control in the footer, then click in the Control-Source property and enter the expression

   =Parent!Program

6. Click in the Units control in the Detail section, then click the Format Painter button on the toolbar and click the text box.

7. Select the label and set the Caption property to **Program**

8. Save and close the form.

9. Switch to Form view. Observe that the subform control displays the student's major program (see Figure 5.12).

FIGURE 5.12:

The main form looks up units and fee totals from the subform and the subform looks up the major program from the main form.

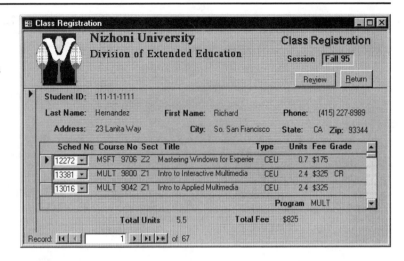

Using the Expression Builder

The expressions for referring to controls on forms and subforms can be very complex. You can use the Expression Builder to help create expressions of any kind, including expressions for query criteria and property settings as well as control references for macro action arguments and conditions. You can summon the Expression Builder whenever the Build button appears next to a property or argument edit box. You can also start the Expression Builder in a macrosheet by clicking in an action argument's edit box or a Condition cell and then clicking the Build button on the toolbar. Figure 5.13 shows the Expression Builder.

The lower pane contains three list boxes. The list box on the left contains folders for all of the tables, queries, forms, and reports in your database. There are also folders for built-in functions, constants, operators, common expressions, and custom Visual Basic functions. The folders for forms and reports contain folders for all of your forms and reports and separate folders for the open forms (in the Loaded Forms folder) and for the open reports (in the Loaded Reports folder). If a form with a subform is open when you start the Expression Builder, Access recognizes the relationship between the form and the subform and shows a folder for the subform within the folder for the form.

FIGURE 5.13:

Using the Expression Builder to create object references.

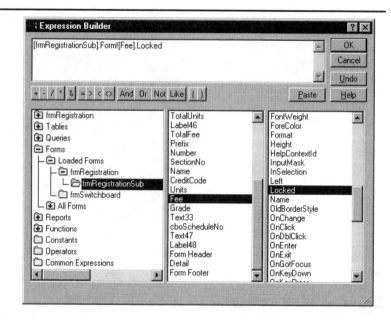

In Figure 5.13, the frmRegistration form was open when the Builder was started. When you select a particular database object in the list box on the left, the list box in the center changes to show the objects contained in the selected database object. If you select a form, the first item in the center list is <Form> representing the form itself, the second item is <Field List> representing the field list for the table or query that underlies the form, and the remaining items are the controls and sections on the form. When you select an item in the center list box, the list box on the right changes to display the properties of the item you selected. After you have made your choices, press the Paste button to paste the *full identifier syntax* of your selection into the edit box at the top of the Builder dialog. Figure 5.13 shows the full identifier for the Locked property of the Fee control on the frmRegistrationSub form. You create expressions in the edit box by pasting selections and editing them using the keyboard and the operator buttons in the Builder dialog.

To see how the Expression Builder works, use it to re-create two of the references needed in this chapter.

Creating the Where Condition Expression

The macro mfrmRegistration.cmdReview_Click opens the Students form and displays the student record related to the record displayed in frmRegistration (see Table 5.3). Use the Expression Builder to create the **Where Expression** argument.

1. With all objects closed except the Database window and frmSwitchboard, click the Add/Edit Students button.

2. Open the mfrmRegistration macrosheet, then click in the row containing the macro cmdReview_Click; click in the **Where Condition** argument and delete the expression.

3. Click the Build button.

4. Double-click the Forms folder, then double-click the Loaded Forms directory. The only forms that should be loaded are frmStudents and frmSwitchboard.

5. Double-click frmStudents.

6. Select StudentID and click the Paste button. The full syntax for the control is pasted in the text box. (From our previous work we know the short syntax is required here, but we'll ignore that for now and make the correction later.) The Expression Builder always uses the full identifier sequence.

7. Click the equal sign button.

8. In the first box, double-click the All Forms folder, then double-click frmRegistration. The center list box displays the objects corresponding to frmRegistration.

9. Select StudentID and click the Paste button.

10. Click OK.

When you click OK in the Expression Builder, the expression in the edit box is copied into the cell that had the focus when you started the Builder. The copied expression replaces whatever was there. In this case, the expression is copied into the **Where Condition** argument.

If you save this macro and click the Review button on frmRegistration, the frmStudents form opens but displays the empty record—this is an indication that **Where Condition** is using the wrong identifier expression. You must correct the expression so that the left side includes the short identifier syntax. The Expression Builder is helpful, but you have to know when the short identifier syntax is required and make the correction.

Modify the Expression in the Expression Builder Edit Box

1. Select and delete the expression [Forms]![frmStudents]! so that the left side of the expression contains only [StudentID].

2. Save and close the macro group.

Creating a Reference to a Control on a Subform

When working with the form frmRegistration, you created a calculated control to sum the total fees on the form frmRegistrationSub and referred to this value in a calculated control on the main form. You can re-create the reference using the Expression Builder.

1. Open frmRegistration and switch to Design view.

2. Select the text box named TotalFee, then click in the ControlSource property and delete the expression.

3. Click the Build button for the ControlSource property edit box. Because the active window is the Design view of frmRegistration, the Expression Builder opens displaying the information about that form; but you want to refer to a control on the form frmRegistrationSub, so you must locate this form in the first list box.

4. Double-click the Forms folder.

5. Double-click the folder for frmRegistration. The subfolder for frmRegistrationSub is displayed.

6. Double-click the folder for frmRegistrationSub, then select the control To-talFee, and click the Paste button. In this case, the expression pasted into the edit box is the correct syntax.

7. Click OK, then click Enter. The expression is copied into the ControlSource property.

8. Switch to Form view to observe the calculation.

CAUTION   The Expression Builder is very useful in creating expressions containing references to forms, reports, and controls, if for no other reason than that it provides a complete listing of your objects and helps to prevent spelling errors. The Builder is also helpful in creating the references, but you have to know when to use the short syntax instead of the full identifier, and you have to make sure that a form with a subform is open before starting the Builder. Also, if you are using the Builder to create an argument for a function such as the IsLoaded() function, you have to know when to enclose the name in quotes. You can't rely on the Expression Builder to create the correct expression—you need to be ready to make corrections.

Endnotes

In this chapter you've learned how to:

- look up information on other forms, including separate related forms, sub-forms, and main forms. You also learned the syntax required to refer to forms, properties, subforms, and controls.

- synchronize two forms and keep them synchronized, as well as some tech-niques for avoiding data integrity problems by allowing changes to only one form at a time.

- avoid macro errors by testing to determine if a form is open before taking action.

- use the Tag property to determine which actions to take.

- use the Expression Builder to help you create control references.

On Your Own

In the exercises you can practice techniques from this chapter by adding lookup capabilities to the instructor appointment form and by adding detail drill-down to the course list. You'll extend the ideas from this chapter by exploring the DSum( ) function, creating a macro to avoid displaying a blank record in a form, and creating a one-to-many-to-many form.

Adding to the Application

1. Look up information on another form.
   When making an instructor appointment, you may want to look up the instructor's information.

   a. Place a Review button on frmAppointments.

   b. Create a new macro group **mfrmAppointments**.

   c. Create a macro **cmdReview_Click** that synchronizes the forms frmAppointments and frmInstructors so that when the macro opens frmInstructors it shows the related record in frmInstructors.

   d. Attach the macro to the OnClick property of the Review button.

   e. Set the properties of frmInstructors to remove the default form controls, including the shortcut menu, navigation buttons, scroll bars, control box, the close button, and the minimize and maximize buttons.

   f. Set the Modal and PopUp properties to Yes to create a dialog box.

2. Drill down from frmCourseList to frmCourses.
   The form frmCourseList provides a list of approved courses. Place detail buttons on this form to drill down to the related form frmCourses so you can edit course information.

    a. Place an uncaptioned button named **cmdDetail** in the Detail section of frmCourseList.

    b. Create a new macro group **mfrmCourseList** and create a macro named **cmdDetail_Click** to open the related record in frmCourses.

    c. Attach the macro to the OnClick property of the button.

3. Look up appointment information from a subform control.
You sum the units that an instructor is assigned and display the total on frmAppointments.

    a. Place a text box in the footer section of frmAppointmentsSub and enter an expression to determine the total units for the instructor. Name the control **TotalUnits** and make it invisible.

    b. Place an unbound text box with name **TotalUnits** on frmAppointments, and set the ControlSource property to refer to the value in the TotalUnits control on the form contained in the subform. Set the enabled property to No and the Locked property to Yes.

    c. Set the BackColor property to light gray, the appearance to normal and the border to clear.

    d. Set the format to Fixed and the DecimalPlaces to **1**

    e. Label the calculation **Total Units**

Extending the Concepts

1. The DSum( ) function
You can use the domain aggregate function DSum( ) to calculate a total on the main form based on the records displayed in a subform by using the data directly from the table or query that underlies the embedded subform, instead of referring to controls in the subform. The DSum( ) function has three arguments. In the simplest case, the first argument is the field whose values you want to sum, the second argument is the name of the table or query containing the records you want to include in the sum, and the third argument is the criteria you use to select the records (see online Help for more information). All three arguments are string expressions and must be enclosed in quotations. For example, you can sum the Units a student is enrolled in and display the sum on frmRegistration by using the function

DSum("Units","qalkClassStudent","StudentID=
Forms!frmRegistration!StudentID")

    a. Open frmRegistration in Design view and place an unbound text box in the bottom of the form, to the left of the Total Units label. (You'll show both calculations on the form.)

    b. Set the ControlSource property using the DSum( ) function above.

    c. Set the Format property to Fixed and the DecimalPlaces property to 1.

    d. Save the form and switch to Form view. The new control looks up the data directly in the qalkClassStudent query underlying the subform, selects only the records for the student, and calculates the sum of the Units field.

2. Test a precondition to avoid displaying a blank record.
Whenever a macro argument involves a form or control that might not exist or the argument uses the value of a control that might be null, there is the possibility of a macro error and you should consider testing a precondition to avoid the error. For example, open frmClasses, click the New button on the toolbar, and then click the Review Course button on the form. If the CourseID is null when the Review Courses button is pressed, Access displays an empty course form. While this is not technically an error, you can avoid displaying a blank form by testing a precondition: IsNull(CourseID). If the condition is true you can display a message, place the insertion point in the CourseID combo box, and stop the macro. If the condition is false, you can open the form displaying the related record.

    a. Draw the macro flow diagram for the cmdReviewCourse_Click macro (refer to Table 5.5).

    b. Modify the flow diagram to test the condition, display a message "You must select a course first", and place the insertion point in the cboCourse control.

    c. Modify the macro.

    d. Save and test the macro.

3. Create a one-to-many-to-many form.

The frmCoursesByProgram form (refer to Figure 1.26 in Chapter 1) displays a program in the main form and a subform that displays the approved courses for the program. The frmClassesByCourse form (refer to Figure 1.27 in Chapter 1) displays a course in its main form and a subform that displays the classes scheduled for the course. You can create a single form that displays the information in both forms. The new form displays a program in its main form, a subform that displays the approved courses for the program, and a second subform that displays the classes scheduled for the current course record in the first subform.

    a. Copy and paste frmCoursesByProgram, and then paste as **frmClasses-ByCourseByProgram**. Open the new form in Design view, change the Caption to **Classes by Course by Program** and increase the width of the form.

    b. Open frmCoursesByProgramSub in Design view and drag CourseID from the field list to the detail section. Delete the label. Save and close the form.

    c. Place an unbound text box in frmClassesByCourseByProgram; set the Name property to CourseID and set the ControlSource to the expression **=frmCoursesByProgramSub.Form!CourseID** to display the CourseID for the current course record in the subform. Switch to Form view to view the result.

    d. Open frmClassesByCourseSub in Design view. Drag CourseID from the field list to the detail section. Delete the label. Save and close the form.

    e. Select the Subform/Subreport tool and create a new subform control on frmClassesByCourseByProgram. Set the SourceObject to frmClassesBy-CourseSub. Set the linking properties to CourseID. The new subform is now synchronized to the CourseID displayed on the main form, but since this control displays the CourseID of the current record in the first subform, the new subform is now synchronized to the first subform. Figure 5.14 shows the form with the CourseID controls shown explicitly.

    f. When you are finished, set the Visible property of all three CourseID controls to No.

FIGURE 5.14:

The one-to-many-to-many frmClassesByCourseByProgram form. The main form contains a control to hold the value of the CourseID for the current course in the first subform. The second subform is linked to this control; the effect is to synchronize the second subform to the current course in the first subform.

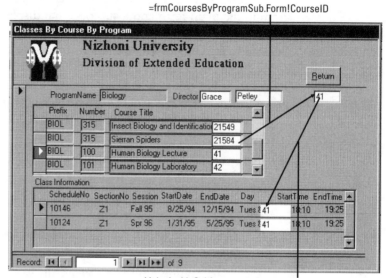

=frmCoursesByProgramSub.Form!CourseID

Linked with Subform control properties

CHAPTER

SIX

Looking Up Information in Tables and Queries

- Lookup fields and the Lookup Wizard

- The Column property of a combo box

- Data type conversion functions

- Point-of-entry inventory system

- Domain aggregate functions

- Queries as SQL statements

- AutoLookup queries

- Data entry for linking tables

In a relational database, the data is stored in different tables. The advantage of this design is that a piece of data needs to be stored only once, but a disadvantage is that you have to design ways to display information from more than one table at once.

In the last chapter you learned two ways to view information displayed in two forms: either the forms are displayed in separate windows and you use macros to link the records and keep them synchronized, or the forms are displayed in a single form window, using the subform control to display a second form within the first form, and you set the properties of the subform control to keep the forms synchronized.

In this chapter you learn ways to view information in two tables or queries using a single form. The first part of the chapter explores two ways to look up information stored in a table or query other than the one that the form is based on: by using a combo box to display a mini-datasheet based on another table or query, and by using the DLookup( ) function. In the second part of the chapter you learn how to base a form on a query that automatically looks up information in a second table.

NOTE When you begin the chapter, only the switchboard and the Database window should be displayed. Close any other objects.

Using a Combo Box to Look Up Information

1. Open a blank form, set the RecordSource property to tblClasses, and then select all of the fields and drag them to the form.

2. Switch to Form view. The controls display the data stored in the table's fields (see Figure 6.1).

The tblClasses table is related to the tblCourses table with CourseID as the matching field in both tables. The form you just created displays the CourseID for the related course, and displays a numerical value for the location where the class is given. The tblClasses table is also related to the tblLocation table, which stores the text equivalents for the numerical values shown in the Location control. The form

FIGURE 6.1:

Viewing the data stored in
tblClasses. The form displays
CourseID as the value used for
matching records in tblCourses.

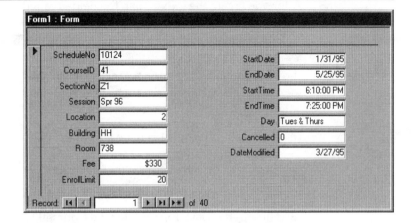

would be more useful if the numerical codes for the course and location were re-
placed (or at least augmented) with the text values stored in the related tables.

When a table is related to another table or query, you can create a field that displays
values looked up from the related table or query. You can create a combo box
lookup list for a table field by setting lookup properties in the table's Design view
(see Figure 6.2); the lookup list can be based on the same table or on another table
or a query, or can display a fixed set of values.

FIGURE 6.2:

Setting the lookup properties to
create a combo box lookup field.

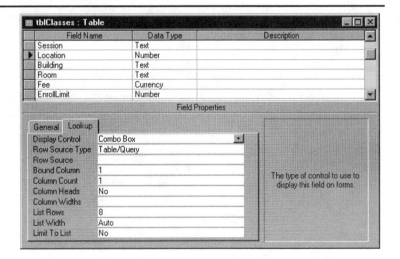

After you create the lookup list, the field is called a *lookup field* and a combo box is displayed in the table's Datasheet view. When you add a lookup field to a form, Access automatically creates a combo box or list box with the properties you set. You can create the lookup field manually or use the Lookup Wizard. Figure 6.3 shows the lookup properties set manually for the Location field; with these settings, the Location field stores the numerical value and displays the corresponding text value looked up in tblLocation.

Use the Lookup Wizard to create a combo lookup list for CourseID.

1. Close the form without saving.

2. In the Database window, open tblClasses in Design view.

3. Click in the Data Type cell for the CourseID field and select Lookup Wizard from the Data Type list. The Lookup Wizard displays the first dialog, which asks for the source of the list values.

4. Accept the default to look up values in a table or query, and click the Next button.

5. Select tblCourses and click the Next button.

6. Select the CourseID, Prefix, Number, Name, CreditCode, and Units fields, and then click the Next button.

FIGURE 6.3:

Creating a lookup field for Location. When you add a lookup field to a form, Access automatically creates a combo or list box with the properties you set.

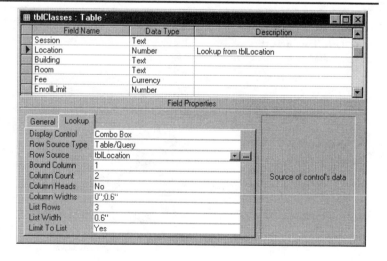

7. Adjust the columns to minimize their widths, clear the Hide Key Column check box, and click the Next button. If you check the Hide Key Column check box, the field displays the value in the first non-key column in the lookup list and Access uses the key column to uniquely identify the rows in the lookup list. If you clear the option, the field displays the value in the key column and the next dialog asks you to choose a field that uniquely identifies the row in the lookup list.

8. Select CourseID and click the Next button.

9. Click Finish. The lookup property sheet displays the Wizard's settings.

> **NOTE**
>
> The Lookup Wizard creates an SQL statement for the RowSource property. You can modify the settings to redesign the lookup. In particular, if you set a column's width to zero, that column isn't displayed in the list, but the information in the list is still "available". The combo list *passes* all of the information in its columns regardless of column width.

10. Switch to Datasheet view, click in a CourseID cell, and click the arrow. The combo list displays the course information as a mini-datasheet based on tblCourses (see Figure 6.4).

FIGURE 6.4:

Using the lookup field to display information from another table or query in a table datasheet.

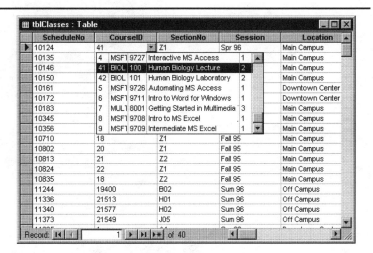

Creating a Form with a Lookup Field

When you create a form based on tblClasses, Access automatically displays a combo box for the lookup field.

1. Create a new form based on tblClasses and add all fields to the form. You can use a Form Wizard or create the form manually.

2. Click in the CourseID control and change the Name property to **cbo-CourseID**. Because the control is a combo box, we'll use the cbo tag.

3. Set the form's Caption property to **Column Lookup** and save the form as **frmClassColumn**. Figure 6.5 shows the form created by using the zsfrmMaster form master (created in Chapter 1).

4. Choose File ➤ Save As and save the form as **frmClassDLookup**. You need this form as the starting point for learning two ways to use the information displayed in the combo list, so create both forms now.

5. Switch to Design view and change the Caption property to **DLookup Function**.

6. Save and close the form.

7. Open frmClassColumn in Design view.

FIGURE 6.5:

Using the lookup field to create a combo box lookup list on a form.

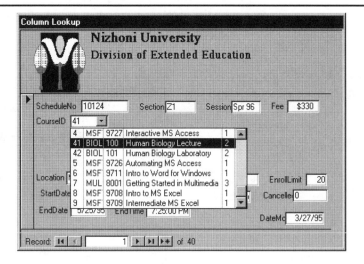

> **NOTE**
>
> When you create a control on a form by dragging from the field list, the control inherits the table properties that are in effect when you create the control; a control created from a lookup field inherits the lookup and field list properties that are in effect when the control is created. Changes that you make in the lookup properties for a field in table Design view affect all new controls you create with the field, but not controls you have previously created.

Using the Column Property of a Combo Box

You can display the value from any column of a combo box (or a list box) in a control on the form—you can display the value in a calculated control or you can use a macro to set the value of a bound or unbound control. In either case, use the Column property of the combo box or list box to refer to a specific column. The Column property is *zero-based*, which means that Column(0) refers to the first column, Column(1) refers to the second column, and so on. For example, the full identifier syntax to refer to the Prefix value in the second column of the combo box list on the frmClassColumn form is

    Forms!frmClassColumn.cboCourseID(1)

Before you select a value in the combo list, the control's value is null and the values in the specific columns are also null.

By default, the values you display in the columns of a combo box list have the Text data type. Before you can use a value as a number in calculations, you need to convert the data type from Text using one of the numeric conversion formulas that follow:

Data conversion function	Converts a string or numeric expression to
CCur	Currency
CDbl	Double
CInt	Integer
CLng	Long
CSng	Single

219

For example, you can convert the data type of the Units value in the sixth column of the combo box list to the Number data type with the single field size as follows:

CSng(Forms!frmClassColumn.cboCourseID(5))

Displaying Lookup Information in a Calculated Control

You can display a value from any column passed by the combo box list in a calculated control by placing an unbound text box on the form and setting its ControlSource property to refer to the column in the combo box.

1. Open the frmClassColumn form in Design view.

2. Place three unbound text boxes on the form.

3. Set the properties of the text boxes and their labels as follows:

Label Caption	Text Box Name	Text Box Control Source
Prefix	Prefix	=cboCourseID.Column(1)
Number	Number	=cboCourseID.Column(2)
Title	Name	=cboCourseID.Column(3)

4. Save the form and switch to Form view (see Figure 6.6).

As you browse through the records, the new text boxes display the information passed using the combo box. Calculated controls are read-only so you can't modify the values.

You can also refer to the value in one or more columns in an expression. For example, you'll delete the first two text boxes you placed and replace them with a single calculated control displaying an expression that concatenates the information in the two columns.

1. Switch to Design view, then select and delete the Prefix and Number text boxes and their labels.

2. Place an unbound text box, set the label's Caption property to **Number**, and set the Name property of the text box to **CourseNo**

FIGURE 6.6:

Displaying lookup information in calculated controls. Use the zero-based Column property of the combo box to refer to a specific column in the list.

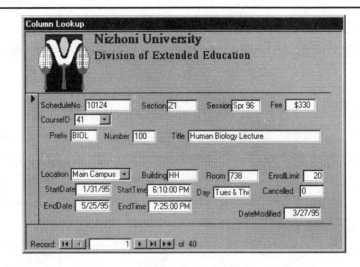

3. Click in the ControlSource property and enter the expression

   =cboCourseID.Column(1)&" "&cboCourseID.Column(2)

4. Save the form and switch to Form view. The form displays the concatenated value.

Displaying Lookup Information by Using a Macro to Set the Value

You can also use the **SetValue** action in a macro to display a value in any column passed by a combo box or list box in either a bound or unbound text box. You update the value by running the macro each time you move to a different record (that is, when the form recognizes the **Current** event).

Create the Macro to Set the Values of the Unbound Text Boxes

As an example, you'll place two more unbound text boxes and create a macro to set their values.

1. Switch to Design view, place two text boxes on the form, and set their properties as follows:

Label Name	Text Box Name
Credit Code	CreditCode
Units	Units

2. Open a new macrosheet and save it as **mfrmClassColumn**

3. Click in the first Macro Name cell and enter **Form_Current** as the name of the new macro.

4. Click in the next row, select the **SetValue** action and set the arguments as follows:

Item	Credit Code
Expression	cboCourseID.Column(4)

5. Click in the next row, select the **SetValue** action and set the arguments as shown below. Because Units is a decimal number that may be used in numerical calculations, you use the CSng() function to convert its data type.

Item	Units
Expression	CSng(cboCourseID.Column(5))

6. Save the macro group.

Attach and Test the Macro

1. Click in the form, then choose Edit ➤ Select Form.

2. In the property sheet, click the Event tab; click in the OnCurrent property and select the macro mfrmClassColumn.Form_Current.

3. Save the form and switch to Form view.

As you browse through the records, each time you move to a different record the macro runs and displays the correct values in the text boxes. Notice, however, that if you change the value in the CourseID combo box, the CreditCode and Units text boxes don't update. If you plan to use the form for data entry you need a macro to update the text boxes after you change the value in the combo box (that is, when the combo box recognizes the **AfterUpdate** event). You can use the Form_Current macro and assign it to the **AfterUpdate** event also, but it is better to copy this macro to create a new macro named cboCourseID_AfterUpdate.

> **TIP**
>
> It is easier to understand and troubleshoot problems if the name for each macro triggered by an event includes the name of the event and name of the object that recognizes the event.

1. Click in mfrmClassColumn, then select the three rows of the Form_Current macro.

2. Copy the macro, then click in a new row and paste the macro.

3. Change the name of the pasted macro to **cboCourseID_AfterUpdate**

4. Save the macro.

5. Click in frmClassColumn and switch to Design view.

6. Click in the combo box, then click in the AfterUpdate property and select mfrmClassColumn.cboCourseID_AfterUpdate.

7. Save the form and switch to Form view.

8. Click the New button and select a CourseID. The macro displays the Credit-Code and Units for the selected course.

9. Change the CourseID. The text boxes display the values for the changed CourseID.

10. Press ESC and close the form.

Using a Macro to Store Lookup Information in a Bound Control

You can use the macro technique to set the value of a bound text box. For example, in the College database the faculty in a program may modify a course and change its number of units. Thus, classes for a course that are scheduled for sessions occurring before and after the change have different unit values. In order to keep track of the unit value for a particular class, you can add a Units field to tblClasses and use a macro to set the value in tblClasses.

> **NOTE**
>
> Even though tblCourses and tblClasses will have a Units field, the fields have different purposes and may store different values. The Units field in tblCourses contains the most recent value, while the Units field in tblClasses contains the value that is in effect for the session. You can use the same concept to track price changes in an orders database.

1. Open tblClasses in Design view and create a new field named **Units** with the Number data type; set the FieldSize property to Single.
2. Save and close the table.
3. Open frmClassColumn in Design view, then select and delete the Units text box.
4. Drag Units from the field list to the form.
5. Save the form and switch to Form view.

As you browse through the classes, each time you switch to a different record the Form_Current macro runs. Since Units is now a bound control, the displayed value is stored in the field.

> **NOTE**
>
> You can't use the calculated control method to store the displayed value in a table. A control can't be both calculated and bound, so you have to use the macro method if you want to pass a value to a form with a combo box and then store the value in a field of the form's underlying table or query.

CAUTION When you use a macro to set the value of a control, you can change the value interactively after the macro sets it. If the control is bound and you change the value after the macro sets it, the changed value, not the passed value, is saved to the table and inconsistent data can result. For example, you could store a class Units value that isn't the same as the current course Units value. When using the macro method to display a value passed by a combo box, you can protect the text box by setting its Enabled property to No and Locked property to Yes. Notice that when a control is disabled and locked, you can't change its value interactively, but a macro (or code) can.

Determining If a Class Is Filled— The Inventory Problem

The inventory problem is an interesting example of using a combo box to pass information. The inventory problem occurs when you are tracking inventory. When an item is requested, you check the current inventory. Each item that is entered on the invoice must be removed from inventory. If you are sold out of the item, you can't add it to the invoice. If your inventory system is designed to check inventory levels at the time you create the invoice, it is called a *point-of-entry inventory system*. The same problem occurs in the College database when a student wants to register for a class: you need to check the current class enrollment, and if the current enrollment equals the enrollment limit for the class, the class is filled and you don't permit the student to register for the class; if there is still room, you register the student in the class. The terminology is different, but the problem and its solution are the same.

In this example, you create a point-of-entry inventory system to track available seats in a class by testing and updating the enrollment when the student requests enrollment.

1. In the switchboard, click the Register in Classes button.
2. Click the arrow in the combo box. The combo list displays the available classes.

When a student wants to register for a class, you select the class using the combo box. The combo box displays three columns, including:

ScheduleNo

Class Prefix, Number, and Section

Course Name

The combo box row source is the qlkpClasses query based on the tblClasses and tblCourses tables. You can create a new query that calculates the current enrollment in each class and use it as the row source for the combo box in order to pass the enrollment information to the registration form.

1. In the Database window, click the Query tab, then copy and paste qryEnrollmentSummary as a new query named **qlkpClassesEnrollment** and double-click it. The qryEnrollmentSummary query was designed as the record source for enrollment summary forms and reports and contains more fields than you need. You can delete the unnecessary fields.

2. Open qlkpClassesEnrollment in Design view, and delete the Canceled, Fee, TotalFee, and ProgramName fields.

3. Clear the Show check box for the Session field. You need to have the Session field in the query to select the classes for the current session, but you don't need to show it in the combo box list.

4. Save and close the query.

5. Click in the Registration form, then switch to Design view and double-click the subform control.

6. Select the combo box and set its properties as follows:

RowSource	qlkpClassesEnrollment
ColumnCount	5
ColumnWidth	0.4; 0.9; 1.5; 0.3; 0.3
ListWidth	3.6

7. Save and close the subform, switch to Form view, and drop down the combo box list. The combo box list displays the current enrollment in the fourth column and the enrollment limit in the fifth column (see Figure 6.7).

FIGURE 6.7:

Using a combo box to display enrollment information on the registration form.

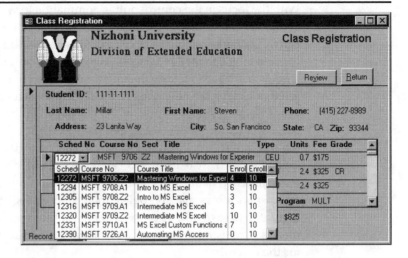

The current enrollment information is now available, but there are no built-in registration limitations: you can register a student in a class even if the class is filled. To prevent this from happening, you can create a macro to compare the current enrollment with the enrollment limit. If the current enrollment is less than the enrollment limit for the class, the registration occurs; otherwise, the macro displays a message that the class is filled and prevents the registration. The macro runs whenever you select a value from the combo box. In order to select the appropriate event to trigger this macro, you need to understand how Access handles changes in controls and records.

Deciding Between the BeforeUpdate and the AfterUpdate Events

In Chapter 2, "Building a User Interface," you saw that Microsoft Access maintains two temporary buffers: a control buffer and a record buffer. When you change the value in the combo box, the control recognizes the **BeforeUpdate** and the **AfterUpdate** events and you can use either event to trigger a macro. The combo box recognizes the **BeforeUpdate** event when Access acknowledges the changed data, but before Access places the changed data in the record buffer. At that instant the focus is in the control buffer and you are restricted to the actions and the commands that apply to the control.

With the focus in the control buffer, commands for working with the record are not available: you cannot undo the record and you cannot save, select, or delete the record. You could use the **BeforeUpdate** event for the combo box to trigger a macro that uses the **CancelEvent** action to cancel the updating of the combo box, but the user would have to take some interactive action to undo the selection if the class is filled or to save the new registration if the class isn't filled. Using the **AfterUpdate** event leads to the more polished result. The combo box recognizes the **AfterUp-date** event after Access places the changed data in the record buffer; at that instant, the commands for working with a record are available, so the macro can undo or save the record. By using the **AfterUpdate** event, you can trigger a macro that compares the current enrollment to the enrollment limit; if the class is filled, the macro can display a message and delete the proposed registration record without having to ask the user to take additional action. If the class isn't filled, the macro can save the class registration record automatically. Figure 6.8 shows the flow diagram for the macro.

The macro needs to execute several of the built-in menu commands. The macro actions grouped by task are shown in Table 2.2 (see also Table B.1 in Appendix B); the table lists several actions equivalent to menu commands, such as the **Save**, **Print-Out**, and **Quit** actions which are equivalent to the File ➤ Save, File ➤ Print (except that the **PrintOut** action doesn't display the Print dialog), and File ➤ Exit menu commands, respectively. Most of the menu commands, however, are not available as separate macro actions but can be duplicated using the **DoMenuItem** macro action.

FIGURE 6.8:

A macro to cancel enrollment if the class is filled. Trigger the macro with the **AfterUpdate** event of the combo box so that the commands to Save or Delete the record are available.

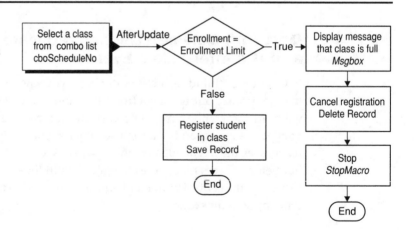

Using the `DoMenuItem` Action

The `DoMenuItem` action is equivalent to selecting a built-in menu command. The menu commands are arranged on menu bars. Each view has its own built-in menu bar which includes only the menu commands appropriate for that view. When you work interactively, the only menu bar and menu commands available are the ones that are appropriate to the current view. When you use the `DoMenuItem` to specify a menu command, you can specify any menu command from any menu bar; however, you must be careful to select only menu commands that are appropriate to the view that will be current when the macro runs. If you specify a menu command that isn't appropriate to the current view when the macro runs, Access can't execute the `DoMenuItem` action and the macro action fails.

You specify the menu command by setting the action arguments. Begin with the first argument; as you set each argument, the combo lists for the subsequent arguments change to display the appropriate choices.

`DoMenuItem` argument	Description
`Menu Bar`	Select the view that will be the current view when the macro runs.
`Menu Name`	Select the menu name that contains the menu command.
`Command`	Select the command you want to run.
`Subcommand`	Select the subcommand if one is required. For example, the Filter command in Form view requires that you select a subcommand such as Filter By Form.

Even if a menu command is listed for a menu bar, the command may not always be available and may appear to be grayed out at different times as you work with the object. For example, in the Form view menu bar, the availability of the Undo commands in the Edit menu changes as you work with the form. When you first open a form in Form view, the command Edit ➤ Can't Undo is

(continued)

grayed out and unavailable. When you click in a control and type a character, the command Edit ➤ Undo Typing is available. When you tab out of the control, the command Edit ➤ Undo Current Field/Record is available. When you save the record, the command Edit ➤ Undo Saved Record is available until you begin editing another record. When you begin editing another record, the cycle begins again and Edit ➤ Undo Typing is available. If you try to run one of these Undo commands at a moment when it isn't available, the `DoMenuItem` action fails.

Creating the Macro

You create a macro to permit registration in a class only if there are spaces available.

1. Open a new macrosheet and save it as **mfrmRegistrationSub**

2. Click in the first Macro Name cell and name the new macro **cboScheduleNo_AfterUpdate**

3. Enter the macro shown in Table 6.1. Because the enrollments are integers, the macro uses the CInt( ) function to convert the text data type to integer data type.

4. Save the macro.

Attach and Test the Macro

1. Switch to Design view and double-click the subform control.

2. Select the combo box, then click in the AfterUpdate property and select the macro mfrmRegistrationSub.cboScheduleNo_AfterUpdate.

3. Save and close the subform, then switch to Form view.

4. Click in a new class record and select a class that is not filled. The class is added and the record is saved automatically (but notice that the combo box list does not automatically update to reflect the student you just added to the class).

TABLE 6.1: The sample table for the Programming Series.

Macro Name	Condition	Action	Action Arguments
cboScheduleNo_ AfterUpdate			
	CInt(cboScheduleNo. Column(3)) = CInt(cboScheduleNo. Column(4))	**MsgBox**	**Message**: This class is filled. You won't be able to register the student in this class.
	...	**DoMenuItem**	**Menu Bar**: Form
			Menu Name: Edit
			Command: Delete Record
	...	**StopMacro**	
		DoMenuItem	**Menu Bar**: Form
			Menu Name: Records
			Command: Save Record

5. Click in a new class record and select a class that is filled. After displaying your message, Access displays the default confirmation dialog box (see Figure 6.9). This dialog message is confusing because the user isn't aware of the status of the buffers.

6. Click OK.

Modify the Macro to Suppress Warnings and Screen Updates

You can modify the macro to suppress the default confirmation message using the **SetWarnings** action. Also, whenever a macro has more than a few actions you can suppress the screen updates that occur after Access executes each action. You an use the **Echo** action to turn off screen updating while the macro runs (turning off screen updating results in faster execution because Access doesn't take the time to redraw the screen after each action).

FIGURE 6.9:

The default confirmation dialog box.

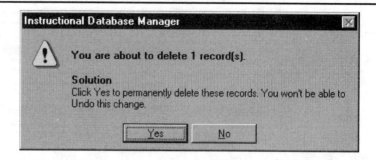

1. Click in the macrosheet, then insert two rows just below the row with the macro's name; select the **Echo** action as the first action of the macro, and set the **Echo On** argument to No.

2. Click in the next row and select the **SetWarnings** action. The **Warnings On** argument is No by default so all system messages are suppressed while the macro runs. When the macro is finished, Access automatically turns the display of system messages on. (You can't use the **SetWarnings** action to suppress error messages or system dialogs that require user input.)

3. Save the macro.

4. Click in a new class record and select a class that is filled. Access displays the custom message.

5. Click OK. Access removes the selected class from the display.

Create a Macro to Requery the Combo Box

The ScheduleNo combo box doesn't update automatically after you register a student. You can create a macro to requery the combo box after you have registered a student in a class and the record has been saved. The subform recognizes the **AfterUpdate** event after data in an existing record has been changed and saved, or when data has been entered into a new record and saved.

1. In the mfrmRegistrationSub macro group, click in the Macro Name cell of a new row, and enter the new macro name **Form_AfterUpdate**

TABLE 6.2: The sample table for the Programming Series.

Macro Name	Action	Action Arguments
Form_AfterUpdate		
	Requery	**Control Name**: cboScheduleNo

2. Enter the macro shown in Table 6.2.

3. Save the macro.

The Form_AfterUpdate macro is triggered whenever a changed or new record is saved, which means whenever the cboScheduleNo_AfterUpdate macro runs and a student is actually registered in a class. Figure 6.10 shows the relationship between this macro and the cboScheduleNo_AfterUpdate macro.

Attach and Test the Macro

1. Switch to Design view and double-click the frmRegistrationSub subform control.

2. Click in the AfterUpdate event and select the macro mfrmRegistration-Sub.Form_AfterUpdate.

3. Save and close the subform, then switch to Form view for frmRegistration.

4. Click in a new class record and select a class that isn't filled. Note the current enrollment.

5. Click in a new class record and drop down the combo list. Note that the list has been updated.

6. Click in the class record you entered in step 4 and choose Edit ➤ Delete Record.

7. Click in a new class record and drop down the combo list. Note that the list has not been updated to reflect the class you deleted in step 6. The subform does not recognize the **AfterUpdate** event when an existing record is deleted, so we'll have to deal separately with deleting a class registration.

FIGURE 6.10:

Macro flow diagram for the macro that runs when the combo box is updated and the macro that runs when the subform is updated.

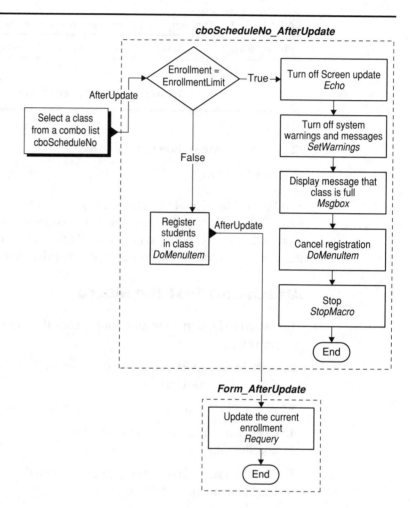

Triggering the Requery When a Record Is Deleted

You can create another macro to requery the combo box whenever you delete a class. When you take a step to delete an existing record, the following sequence occurs:

The form recognizes the **Delete** event.

Access removes the record from the tables and places the record in the deletion buffer.

The form recognizes the **BeforeDelConfirm** event.

Access displays the dialog box asking for confirmation.

The form recognizes the **AfterDelConfirm** event after you respond to the dialog box and after the record is actually deleted from the table and from the deletion buffer, or after you respond to the dialog and cancel the deletion.

Because you want to requery the combo box after the record is actually deleted, you use the **AfterDelConfirm** event to trigger the macro.

Create a New Macro for the AfterDelConfirm **Event**

The new macro is identical to the Form_AfterUpdate macro shown in Table 6.2; you need only copy and paste to create the new macro Form_ AfterDelConfirm.

1. Click in the mfrmRegistrationSub macrosheet and select the two rows containing the Form_AfterUpdate macro.

2. Copy the macro, then click in a new row and paste the macro.

3. Click in the Macro Name cell and change the name of the new macro to **Form_AfterDelConfirm**

4. Save and close the macro.

Attach and Test the Macro

1. Click in frmRegistration and switch to Design view.

2. Double-click the subform control, then click in the AfterDelConfirm property and select the mfrmRegistrationSub.Form_AfterDelConfirm macro.

3. Save and close the form.

4. Switch to Form view for frmRegistration.

5. Select a class that is not filled and note the value of the current enrollment.

6. Select another student and then select the same class. Observe that the current enrollment displayed in the ScheduleNo combo box updates to reflect the addition.

7. Press SHIFT+ENTER to save the current record.

8. Choose the Edit ➤ Select Record command or click the record selector for the record you just saved.

9. Press DELETE or choose the Edit ➤ Delete Record command. The delete confirmation dialog box is displayed.

10. Click Yes to delete the record.

11. Click in the ScheduleNo combo box of the same record and drop down the combo list. The current enrollment has been updated to reflect the deletion.

Summary of the Point-of-Entry Inventory Method

To demonstrate the generality of the method, I'll summarize the point-of-entry inventory system in terms of an order entry database application. The method depends on a "smart" combo box that you use to add or change an item for an order and that passes the current inventory levels to the orders form. The system relies on three macros:

1. The macro triggered when you select an item either adds the item to the order form or displays a message and rejects the request, depending on a test of the current inventory level.

2. The macro triggered when you select a new item, or change an existing item and save the result, recalculates the current inventory levels.

3. The macro triggered when you delete an item from the order recalculates the current inventory levels.

Using the DLookup( ) Function

The DLookup( ) function is another way to look up information in a table or query. We'll consider the data entry form for classes. When you schedule a new class, you base the class on an approved course. When you specify the course, you want the data entry form to look up and display the course information from tblCourses. As an alternative to passing the data from tblCourses to the form using a combo box, you can use the DLookup( ) function to look up each fact directly from the tblCourses table.

Domain Aggregate Functions

The DLookup() function is an example of a *domain aggregate function*—a built-in Access function that you can use to perform calculations based on the values in a field of a table or query. You can specify criteria to select the set of records in the table or query that you want to use for the calculation. The selection criteria is optional; if you don't specify additional criteria then all of the records in the table or query are used. The table or query is called the *domain*. You must also specify the field that you want the function to work with (instead of specifying a field, you can specify an expression that performs a calculation on values in a field). Once the domain and criteria are specified and the particular field is selected, the function performs a calculation on the values in the field and returns the result of the calculation. The domain aggregate functions are:

- **DLookup()**—returns the value in the specified field
- **DMin()**, **DMax()**—returns the minimum or maximum value in the specified field
- **DFirst()**, **DLast()**—returns the value in the specified field from the first or last physical record
- **DAvg()**—returns the arithmetical average of the values in the specified field
- **DSum()**—returns the sum of the values in the specified field
- **DStDev()**, **DStDevP()**—returns the standard deviation or population standard deviation for the specified field
- **DVar()**, **DVarP()**—returns the variance or population variance for the specified field
- **DCount()**—returns the number of records with non-null values in the specified field

The Syntax for the DLookup( ) Function

Use the DLookup( ) function to retrieve the value in a particular field in a table or query; you can use the DLookup( ) function in

- a query—in a calculated field expression in a Field cell, to specify criteria in a Criteria cell, or in an expression in the Update To cell in an update query

- a macro—in a condition or an action argument

- a module

- a form or report—in a calculated control

In particular, you can use the DLookup( ) function in a form or report when you want to display a value from a table or query that isn't in the record source of the form or report. The DLookup( ) function takes three arguments. In the simplest case, the first argument is the name of the field in the table or query that holds the data you want to look up; the second argument is the name of the table or query; and the third argument is the criteria you want to use to select the record. Each of the arguments must be enclosed in quotation marks, as follows:

DLookup("[fieldname]", "[tablename] or [queryname]", "criteria")

For more information on this function, search for DLookup in online Help.

When you use the DLookup( ) function on a form to look up a table or query value that corresponds to the record displayed in the form, the expression to locate the first record in the table or query that corresponds to the record displayed in the form is

[fieldname]=Forms![formname]![controlname]

where *[fieldname]* refers to the field in the table or query, and *[controlname]* refers to the control (on the form) that displays the record. For example, when the frmClassDLookup form displays a class, you can use the expression

CourseID = Forms!frmClassDLookup!CourseID

in the criteria argument to find records in another table or query that correspond to the course number for the displayed class.

The syntax for the DLookup() function that looks up a table or query value that is synchronized to the record displayed in a form is

DLookup("[lookupfieldname]","[tablename] **or** *[queryname]","[fieldname]= Forms![formname]![controlname]")*

where *[lookupfieldname]* is the name of the field with the value you want to get, *[fieldname]* refers to the field in the table or query that you use to synchronize the table or query to the form, and *[controlname]* refers to the control on the form that displays the value you are using to synchronize. For example, to look up the value of Units in tblCourses for the course corresponding to the class displayed on the form frmClassDLookup, the DLookup( ) function is

DLookup("Units","tblCourses","CourseID = Forms!frmClassDLookup!CourseID")

Create the Text Boxes to Hold the Lookup Values

Place unbound text boxes on the form to hold the lookup values.

1. In the Database window, open frmClassDLookup in Design view.

2. Place three unbound text boxes on the form.

3. Set the properties of the text boxes and their labels as follows:

Label Caption	Text Box Name	Text Box ControlSource
Prefix	Prefix	=DLookup("Prefix","tbl-Courses","CourseID=Forms!frmClassDLookup!CourseID")
Number	Number	=DLookup("Number","tbl-Courses","CourseID= Forms!frmClassDLookup! CourseID")
Title	Name	=DLookup("Name","tbl-Courses","CourseID= Forms!frmClassDLookup! CourseID')

4. Save the form and switch to Form view.

5. Browse through the records and observe the lookup of the values directly from the tblCourses table.

Updating the LookUp Interactively

The lookup values do not update automatically when you select a different course in the combo box.

1. Click the New button and enter **1000** as the ScheduleNo for the new class.

2. Select a course from the combo box. The corresponding course information is displayed in the text boxes.

3. Select a different course from the combo box. Notice that if you change the course, the text boxes do not update automatically. You can manually recalculate the text boxes by pressing the F9 key.

4. Press the F9 key. Pressing F9 recalculates all of the calculated fields on the form.

You can automate the recalculation by creating a macro that uses either the **Send-Keys** action to send the F9 keystroke or the **Requery** action to specify any one of the controls to be recalculated. When several calculated controls are based on the same table or query using the same criteria expression, recalculating any one recalculates the others. Run the macro when you change the value in cboCourseID (that is, when the combo box recognizes the **AfterUpdate** event).

Create a Macro to Recalculate the DLookup( ) Function

Create a macro to automate the update of the lookup values.

1. Create a new macrosheet and save it as **mfrmClassesDLookup**

2. Click in the first Macro Name cell and name the new macro **cboCourseID_AfterUpdate**

3. Click in the next row, select the **Requery** action, and set the `Control Name` argument to **Prefix**

4. Save the macro.

Attach and Test the Macro

1. Click in frmClassesDlookup and switch to Design view.

2. Click in the combo box, then click in the AfterUpdate property, and select mfrmClassesDLookup.cboCourseID_AfterUpdate.

3. Save the form and switch to Form view.

4. Click in the combo box and select a different course. The text boxes display the course information for the course you selected.

If you open the frmClassColumn form (created in the first section of the chapter) in Form view and browse through the records in both forms, you'll notice that the DLookup( ) function is noticeably slower to display its values than the lookups that are based on the Column property of the combo box.

Figure 6.11 shows all three views of a simple query that is based on one table; Figure 6.12 shows the same views of a more complex query that is based on two related tables.

NOTE The domain aggregate functions are actually SQL statements in a different format. You can think of a domain aggregate function as a query that returns a single value. The criteria argument is equivalent to an SQL WHERE clause without the word WHERE. Every time you use one of these functions, you run a query as an SQL statement. Before running an SQL statement, Access must analyze the query to determine the optimal way to execute it. As a result, the domain aggregate functions may be slower than other alternatives.

FIGURE 6.11:

Design, SQL, and Datasheet views
for a simple query based on one
table.

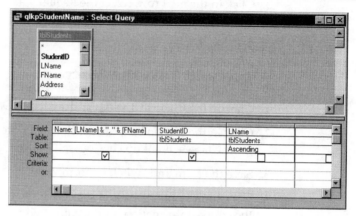

Design view

SELECT DISTINCTROW [LName] & ", " & [FName]
AS Name, tblStudents.StudentID
FROM tblStudents
ORDER BY tblStudents.LName;

Sql view

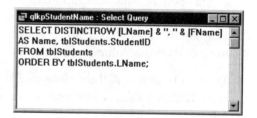

Datasheet view

FIGURE 6.12:

Design, SQL, and Datasheet views for a query based on two tables with an inner join. The result of qlkpClasses includes a record for a course only if there are related classes and includes a record for a class only if there is a related course.

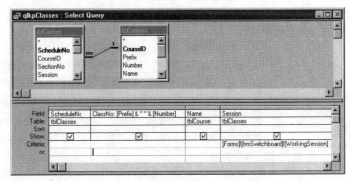

Design view

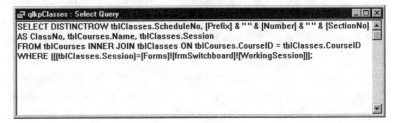

SELECT DISTINCTROW tblClasses.ScheduleNo, [Prefix] & "" & [Number] & "" & [SectionNo] AS ClassNo, tblCourses.Name, tblClasses.Session
FROM tblCourses INNER JOIN tblClasses ON tblCourses.CourseID = tblClasses.CourseID
WHERE (((tblClasses.Session)=[Forms]![frmSwitchboard]![WorkingSession]));

Sql view

ScheduleNo	ClassNo	Course Title	Session
14103	MSFT 9705 Z5	Intro to MS Windows for New Users	Fall 95
12261	MSFT 9706 A1	Mastering Windows for Experienced Users	Fall 95
12272	MSFT 9706 Z2	Mastering Windows for Experienced Users	Fall 95
12412	MSFT 9727 A1	Interactive MS Access	Fall 95
12390	MSFT 9726 A1	Automating MS Access	Fall 95
12401	MSFT 9726 Z2	Automating MS Access	Fall 95
12294	MSFT 9708 A1	Intro to MS Excel	Fall 95
12305	MSFT 9708 Z2	Intro to MS Excel	Fall 95
12316	MSFT 9709 A1	Intermediate MS Excel	Fall 95
12320	MSFT 9709 Z2	Intermediate MS Excel	Fall 95
12331	MSFT 9710 A1	MS Excel Custom Functions and Macros	Fall 95
12876	MULT 9026 A1	Overview of Multimedia	Fall 95
13381	MULT 9800 Z1	Intro to Interactive Multimedia	Fall 95
13016	MULT 9042 Z1	Intro to Applied Multimedia	Fall 95

Record: 11 of 25

Datasheet view

Queries as SQL Statements

There are two ways that you can create queries in Microsoft Access: you can use the design grid in query Design view to create the query graphically, or you can use SQL view to create a query using Structured Query Language or SQL (pronounced ess-cue-ell or sequel) as an *SQL statement*. SQL is the standard database language used by Microsoft Access and every other major database application. You use SQL to write a statement that describes the set of data that you want to retrieve. SQL is designed to be software independent; in theory, it doesn't matter which software application you are using to actually retrieve the data. In practice, there are several dialects of SQL that are not completely interchangeable. You can use either SQL view or Design view to create and edit most kinds of queries. When you create a query in the design grid, Access creates the equivalent SQL statement. You can observe the SQL statement for a query by choosing <u>V</u>iew ➤ S<u>Q</u>L or by selecting SQL View from the Query View button (on the toolbar when you are in Design view). Figure 6.11 shows all three views for qlkpStudentName, a simple query based on one table. Figure 6.12 shows the view for qlkpClasses, a more complex query based on two tables.

An SQL statement includes special SQL keywords shown in uppercase in the SQL views. Here are the most important SQL keywords:

- **SELECT** is the first word in any query that you use to select data from tables.

- **DISTINCTROW** eliminates duplicate records in the result.

- **AS** specifies the *alias* that you want to use for the field name that precedes the alias.

- **FROM** specifies the tables or queries that contain the fields you want in the result.

- **WHERE** specifies the criteria that you want to use to select records. **WHERE** is followed by a *search condition*; the result includes only records for which the search condition is true.

(continued)

- **JOIN** specifies the link between records in different tables or queries. **JOIN** is used with the keywords **INNER, LEFT**, and **RIGHT** to specify the type of link.

- **ORDER BY** specifies the sort order of the result.

- **GROUP BY** specifies the field that you want to use to form groups from the rows selected. The query returns one record for each unique value in the specified field.

Every SQL statement must end with a semicolon.

While every query you create in the design grid has a corresponding SQL statement, there are four queries that you can create only as SQL statements in SQL view and that have no Design view equivalents. They are called SQL queries (or *SQL specific* queries). The four SQL queries are:

- **union queries**—used to combine the results of two or more select queries into a single result when each of the select queries has the same number of columns and corresponding fields have the same data type.

- **data definition queries**—used to create, modify, or delete a table or create or delete an index on a table.

- **subqueries**—used when a query depends on the result of another query.

- **pass-through queries**—used to send commands that retrieve records or change data directly to an SQL database server.

After you create a query in Design or SQL view there are two ways to use it: you can save it as a *stored* query listed in the Database window and enter the name of the query wherever you need to use it, or you can enter the SQL statement directly. The wizards enter SQL statements automatically: when you use a Form or Report Wizard, the wizard expresses the RecordSource property as an SQL statement instead of a stored query; when you use the Control or Lookup Wizard to create combo boxes and list boxes, the wizard expresses the RowSource property as an SQL statement.

(continued)

While you can use either a stored query or an SQL statement, there are performance considerations. When you store a query as a database object, Access analyzes the query and stores an optimized version. When you run the stored query, you are running an optimized version. If you change the query, Access analyzes it again the next time you run it and stores the newly optimized version. On the other hand, every time you run an SQL statement, Access analyzes the statement and determines the optimal way to execute it. Since the analysis and optimization take time, the SQL statement usually executes more slowly than the equivalent stored query. In most cases, using a stored query instead of an SQL statement gives the best performance.

Using an AutoLookup Query to Look Up Information

Another way to display fields from two related tables in a form is to create a query based on the tables and use the query as the record source for the form. You can even design the query as an *AutoLookup query* that automatically fills in some of the fields when you enter a value in the join field. For example, you can create a query based on tblClasses and tblCourses joined by the values of the CourseID; if you design the query with AutoLookup, you can enter the value of a CourseID and the query automatically displays the course information.

Observing AutoLookup in a Query

The College database contains several queries with AutoLookup and uses the qalk tag to name a query with this capability.

1. In the Database window, double-click qalkCourseClass0.

2. Click the New button (grouped with the navigation buttons).

3. Click in the CourseID cell, type **16**, and press TAB. Observe the course information is looked up automatically and entered into the appropriate cells.

AutoLookup works in queries when the four conditions shown in "The AutoLookup Conditions" (below) are met.

The AutoLookup Conditions

Auto Lookup works in a query when these four consitions are met:

- Two tables in the query have a one-to-many relationship.

- The join field on the one side of the relationship has a unique index (that is, the Indexed property is set to Yes(No Duplicates)).

- The query includes the join field from the 'many' side of the relationship.

- The value you enter in the join field in the query must already exist in the join field of the 'one' side.

1. Press ESC to undo the partially entered record.

2. Switch to Design view.

3. If the Table Names row is not displayed, select View ➤ Table Names to display the row.

NOTE To display the Table Names row in all subsequent queries, select Tools ➤ Options, then click the Tables/Queries tab, check the Show Table Names checkbox, and click OK.

There is a one-to-many relationship between tblCourses (the 'one' table) and tblClasses (the 'many' table) with CourseID as the join field. CourseID is a unique index for tblCourses (and is the primary key for the table). In the design grid, notice that the join field comes from the 'many' table, tblClasses. When you enter the value of a CourseID for an existing course, Access automatically displays the course information because all four AutoLookup conditions in "The AutoLookUp Conditions", above are met.

Observing AutoLookup Behavior

If the query contains the join field from the 'one' table instead, the query won't have the AutoLookup capability; further, you can't even add a new record.

1. Click in the Table cell below the CourseID Field cell, and change the value to tblCourses.

2. Switch to Datasheet view, then click the New button.

3. Click in the Course ID cell, enter **16**, and press TAB. The additional course information isn't displayed—AutoLookup doesn't occur.

4. Click in ScheduleNo and try to enter a new schedule number, say **21456**. Access won't let you enter a new schedule number. The status bar reports the message "Can't add record(s); join key of table 'tblClasses' not in recordset."

By design, you can only add a new record to a query based on tables in a one-to-many relationship if the join field from the many side is included in the query.

5. Press ESC to undo the partial record and switch to Design view.

6. Click in the Table cell below the CourseID Field cell and change the value back to tblClasses.

7. Save and close the query.

When you design a query with AutoLookup you can use a name that reflects this capability as follows:

   qalk[one side][many side]

where qalk is the tag for the AutoLookup capability and *[one side]* and *[many side]* are name segments chosen to reflect the two tables in the one-to-many relationship. In this case, the qalkCourseClass0 query automatically displays course information as soon as you enter a value for CourseID in a record that contains class and course fields. This query is the record source for the frmClasses form used for data entry of class information. The College database includes several examples of AutoLookup queries: when registering a student in a class using frmRegistration, qalkClassStudent automatically displays class information as soon as you enter a ScheduleNo (tblClasses is the 'one' table and tlnkClassStudent is the 'many' table);

and when appointing an instructor to a class using frmAppointments, qalkClass-Instructor automatically displays class information as soon as you enter a ScheduleNo (tblClass is the 'one' table and tlnkClassInstructor is the 'many' table).

Observing the AutoLookup Feature in a Form

If you want to use AutoLookup in a form, base the form on an AutoLookup query and display the join field from the many side in a control on the form.

1. In the switchboard, select the Edit/Add Class button. The frmClasses form is designed for scheduling a new class based on an existing course. To schedule a new class you pick a course using the Course combo box.

2. Click the arrow in the Course combo box. The list displays the prefix, course number, and title for the courses in tblCourses, sorted by prefix and course number.

3. Click on the New button (grouped with the navigation buttons).

4. From the Course combo list, select the course MSFT 9708 Intro to MS Excel. When you select a course, the combo box stores the value of the CourseID in the control. Because CourseID is the join field for the AutoLookup query, Access looks up and displays the corresponding course information.

5. Enter the new class information:

Item	Entry	Item	Entry
Schedule No	14092	End Date	
Section No	Z3	Start Time	9:00
Session	Fall 94	End Time	17:00
Location	Downtown Center	Day	Sat
Start Date	10/29/94	Enrollment Limit	10

6. Save the record.

Using AutoLookup Queries with Many-to-Many Relationships

AutoLookup queries are particularly useful for creating data entry forms for tables in a many-to-many relationship. Whenever two tables have a many-to-many relationship, such as tblStudents and tblClasses, you must create a linking table to resolve the relationship into a pair of one-to-many relationships—the linking table stores the details of the relationship. For example, each record in tlnkClassStudent corresponds to a particular student enrolled in a particular class. Figure 6.13 shows the three tables (with the linking table sorted by StudentID) to demonstrate the one-to-many relationship between tblStudents and tlnkClassStudent.

Normally, you create separate data entry forms for the two base tables, tblStudents and tblClasses, and enter data directly into these tables. But how can you create a record in the linking table (i.e., a record with values for StudentID and ScheduleNo) to reflect a student registered in a class? You can create a data entry form for the linking table as a form/subform, with the subform based on an AutoLookup query for the one-to-many relationship between one of the base tables and the linking table, and the main form based on the *other* base table, as follows:

1. Create an AutoLookup query for the one-to-many relationship between one of the base tables and the linking table; include both of the primary key fields from the link table and include your choice of fields from the base table, but do not include the primary key of the base table. You use an AutoLookup query to display information from the base table. For example, qalkClassStudent (based on tblClasses and tlnkClassStudent) is an AutoLookup query that automatically displays class information as soon as you enter a value for ScheduleNo. This query includes the join field ScheduleNo from the linking table. Figure 6.14 shows the design of the query. (This query also includes tblCourses and tblCreditType in order to display course information.)

2. Create a tabular subform based on the AutoLookup query, with a control for the join field. Do not include a control for the other primary key field of the linking table. For example, frmRegistrationSub has a combo box control for ScheduleNo that provides a list of the available classes (see Figure 6.15). By design, when you select a class, Access stores the ScheduleNo and displays class information. This form does not have a control for StudentID, however, since the value of StudentID is entered automatically when you link the subform to the main form.

FIGURE 6.13:

The pair of one-to-many relationships between the base tables and their linking table.

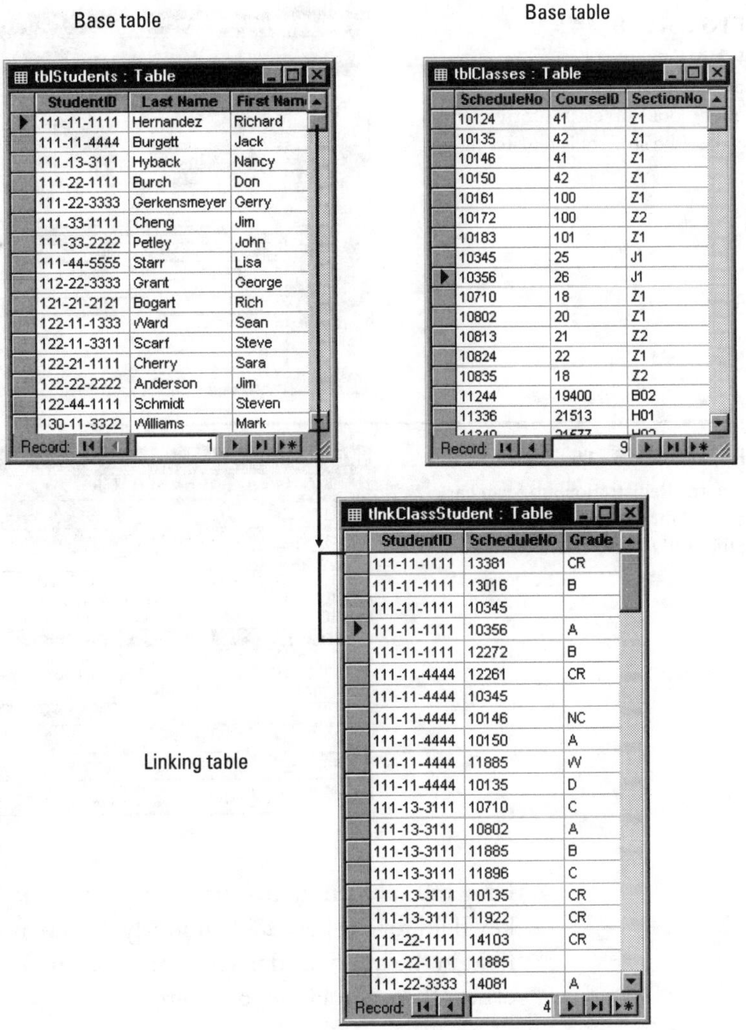

Base table

Base table

tblStudents : Table		
StudentID	**Last Name**	**First Nam**
▶ 111-11-1111	Hernandez	Richard
111-11-4444	Burgett	Jack
111-13-3111	Hyback	Nancy
111-22-1111	Burch	Don
111-22-3333	Gerkensmeyer	Gerry
111-33-1111	Cheng	Jim
111-33-2222	Petley	John
111-44-5555	Starr	Lisa
112-22-3333	Grant	George
121-21-2121	Bogart	Rich
122-11-1333	Ward	Sean
122-11-3311	Scarf	Steve
122-21-1111	Cherry	Sara
122-22-2222	Anderson	Jim
122-44-1111	Schmidt	Steven
130-11-3322	Williams	Mark

Record: 1

tblClasses : Table		
ScheduleNo	**CourseID**	**SectionNo**
10124	41	Z1
10135	42	Z1
10146	41	Z1
10150	42	Z1
10161	100	Z1
10172	100	Z2
10183	101	Z1
10345	25	J1
▶ 10356	26	J1
10710	18	Z1
10802	20	Z1
10813	21	Z2
10824	22	Z1
10835	18	Z2
11244	19400	B02
11336	21513	H01
11240	21577	H02

Record: 9

Linking table

tlnkClassStudent : Table		
StudentID	**ScheduleNo**	**Grade**
111-11-1111	13381	CR
111-11-1111	13016	B
111-11-1111	10345	
▶ 111-11-1111	10356	A
111-11-1111	12272	B
111-11-4444	12261	CR
111-11-4444	10345	
111-11-4444	10146	NC
111-11-4444	10150	A
111-11-4444	11885	W
111-11-4444	10135	D
111-13-3111	10710	C
111-13-3111	10802	A
111-13-3111	11885	B
111-13-3111	11896	C
111-13-3111	10135	CR
111-13-3111	11922	CR
111-22-1111	14103	CR
111-22-1111	11885	
111-22-3333	14081	A

Record: 4

3. Create a main form that uses the other base table as its record source. Include a control for the table's primary key. In this example, frmRegistration is the main form and has a control for StudentID.

FIGURE 6.14:

When you enter a schedule number, the qalkClassStudent AutoLookup query looks up class information for a class the student is registering in.

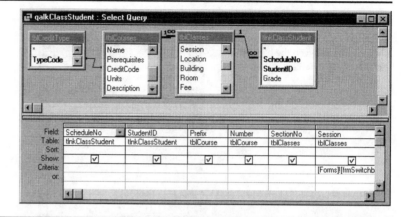

FIGURE 6.15:

The frmRegistrationSub form has a control for ScheduleNo but not for StudentID.

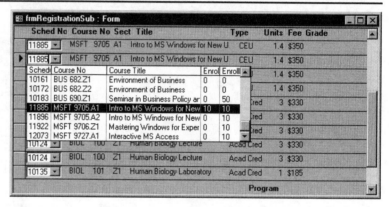

4. Drag the subform to the main form and link the forms, using the primary key field for the base table underlying the main form and the corresponding field in the query underlying the subform. In this example, the subform properties (shown in Figure 6.16) are:

SourceObject	frmRegistrationSub
LinkChildFields	StudentID
LinkMasterFields	StudentID

5. Switch to Form view and display a student who hasn't registered in any classes. The main form displays student information and the subform displays only the blank record.

FIGURE 6.16:
The linking properties for the subform control.

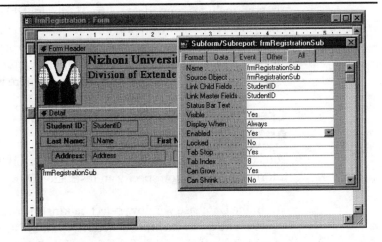

How the Process Works

You register a student in a class by selecting a class from the combo list and then entering a value for ScheduleNo in a record of the subform. When you save the record, Access uses the form/subform linkage to retrieve the value of StudentID displayed in the main form and enters this value for the StudentID field in the subform record. When you save the record in the subform, you have saved a record (with this StudentID value and the selected ScheduleNo value) in the linking table.

If you've enforced referential integrity for the relationships between the linking table and the two base tables, you can't add a record to the linking table until the "parent" records have been entered into both of the base tables. In this example, you can't register a student in a class until the student has been entered in tblStudents and the class has been scheduled in tblClasses. The simplest way to preserve the order of data entry required by referential integrity is to lock all of the data controls on the main form and on the subform—except the controls for the linking table fields in the subform. That way, the only data controls you can change with the form/subform are the linking table controls in the subform.

Creating a Data Entry Form for a Linking Table

As an example, create a data entry form for the tlnkClassInstructor linking table for the many-to-many relationship between instructors and classes. The College database already includes one data entry form for this table: the frmAppointments form/subform displays instructor information in the main form and is designed for appointing an instructor to teach classes (refer to Figure 1.9 in Chapter 1). You'll create another form/subform that displays class information in the main form—then you can use the new form to appoint one or more instructors to teach the class.

Creating the Subform Based on an AutoLookup Query

You create a subform based on the qalkInstructorClass query to look up instructor information when you specify an InstructorID.

1. In the Database window, select qalkInstructorClass and click the Design button. The query includes ScheduleNo and InstructorID from tlnkClassInstructor and includes other fields from tblInstructors; therefore, the query automatically looks up instructor information when you specify an InstructorID. (The query also includes tblClasses in order to include the Session field in the query, so that only classes from the current working session are available.)

2. Select the zsfrmMasterSubform subform master, then copy and paste the form as **frmAppointmentsbyClassSub**

3. Open frmAppointmentsbyClassSub in Design view, and set the RecordSource property to qalkInstructorClass.

4. From the toolbox, select the Combo Box tool and drag it to the Detail section; set its properties shown below. This combo box displays instructor name information and stores the InstructorID.

Name	cboInstructorID
ControlSource	InstructorID
RowSource	qlkpInstructorName
ColumnCount	2
ColumnWidths	0.75; 1
BoundColumn	1
ListWidth	2

5. Drag the FName and the LName fields to the Detail section.

6. Resize and move the controls as necessary so that the form is three inches wide (see Figure 6.17).

7. Save and close the form.

FIGURE 6.17:

The subform with a combo box to display the list of available instructors.

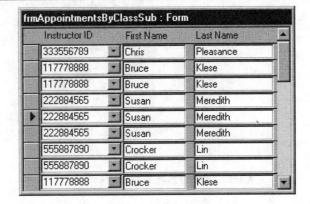

Creating the Main Form

You create a main form to display class information, basing it on the qalkCourse-Class0 query in order to display course information for the class. (In this example, both the main form and the subform are based on AutoLookup queries.)

1. In the Database window, select the form master zsfrmMaster, then copy and paste it as **frmAppointmentsByClass**

2. Open frmAppointmentsByClass in Design view and set the RecordSource property to qalkCourseClass0.

3. In the field list, select the ScheduleNo, Prefix, Number, Name, and SectionNo fields and drag them to the Detail section of the form; select the Session field and drag it to the Header section of the form.

4. Select all of the data controls and set their Enabled properties to No and their Locked properties to Yes.

5. Resize and arrange the controls as shown in Figure 6.18.

FIGURE 6.18:

The main form with controls that are disabled and locked.

Linking the Forms

Use the Subform/Subreport Wizard to create the link between the form and subform.

1. In the toolbox, click the Control Wizards tool, then click the Subform tool, and then click in the form below the Prefix control. The Subform/Subreport Wizard is summoned.

2. Select the frmAppointmentsByClassSub form and click the Next button.

3. Click the Define My Own option. (The list box isn't wide enough to display the full choice. In fact, the first choice is the correct link.)

4. Select ScheduleNo for both form and subform, and click Next.

5. Enter **Instructors:** and click Finish.

6. Switch to Form view and browse through the records (see Figure 6.19).

Enter a New Record in the Linking Table

Test the method by appointing an instructor.

1. In the Database window, double-click the table tlnkClassInstructor. Note the number of records in the table.

FIGURE 6.19:
The data entry form for the linking table tlnkClassInstructor.

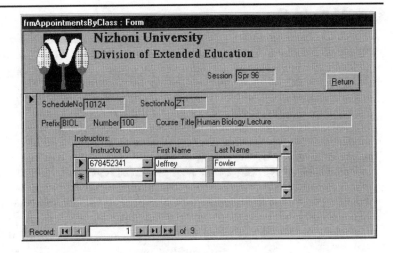

2. Select a class, then click in the combo box in the subform and select an instructor. Note the ScheduleNo and the InstructorID.

3. Click in the table and press SHIFT+F9 to update the table. Note that the number of records increases by one.

4. Locate the record you just added.

Endnotes

This chapter has shown you how to display information from more than one table or query in a single form by

- passing data from another table or query using a combo box, and using the Column property to display and use values displayed in any combo box column.

- using the DLookup( ) function to display and use a value from a related table or query.

- combining related tables into a query using the AutoLookup capability, so they automatically display information from the "one side" of the relationship.

On Your Own

In the exercise, you create a query with AutoLookup that looks up program information when you select a course. You explore the domain aggregate function DCount( ) when you create a macro procedure that prevents duplicate registration and avoids the default error message "Duplicate value in index, primary key or relationship. Changes were unsuccessful."

Adding to the Application

1. Create an AutoLookup query to look up program information for a course.

    a. Open (in Datasheet view) and examine the records in the tables tblPrograms and tblCourses.

    b. Create a new query based on the tables tblPrograms and tblCourses. From tblPrograms, drag the ProgramName and DirectorLName fields, and from tblCourses, drag the Prefix, Number, and Name fields to the design grid. Switch to Datasheet view and observe that there is a row for each record in tblCourses but that there are no rows for those programs that do not yet have courses in tblCourses (because the default join is an inner join).

    c. To include rows in the query result for all programs, whether or not they have courses, change the join to an outer join by clicking the join line and selecting the second option.

    d. Switch to Datasheet view and begin entering a new record by typing **cine** into the Prefix cell. As you tab out of the cell, note that the program name and director are filled in automatically. The query has the AutoLookup property. Press the ESC key to undo.

    e. Switch to Design view. Drag ProgramID from tblPrograms to the design grid and delete the Prefix column. Switch to Datasheet view and type **cine** into the ProgramID field in a new record. This time the program information is not looked up automatically—the query has lost the AutoLookup property because the matching field is now from the 'one' side.

    f. Press the ESC key to undo. Replace the ProgramID field with the Prefix field to return the AutoLookup feature. Save the query as **qalkProgram-Course.**

CHAPTER

SEVEN

Navigating to Controls and Records

- Automating mouse and keystroke actions for going to a control

- Physical and logical navigation techniques

- Finding records

- Sending keystrokes

- Reusable controls and macros for logical navigation

- Visual Basic error handler to suppress default messages

When you work interactively, you use keystrokes, menu commands, and the mouse to move among controls, between records, and from one Database window object to another. You can make your application easier to use by using macros to automate navigation.

> **NOTE** When you begin this chapter, only the switchboard and the Database window should be displayed. Close any other objects.

Moving to a Control

You can create macros for moving to specific controls on forms and subforms and within records.

Moving to a Specific Control on the Active Form

When working interactively, you move to a specific control on the active form by using the mouse to click the control; you can use the `GoToControl` macro action to automate this mouse action.

Use the `GoToControl` action to move the focus to a control on the active form or to a field in the active table or query. In the `Control Name` argument, enter the name of the control or field (using the short syntax).

> **NOTE** You must use the short syntax in the `Control Name` argument to refer to the field or control for the `GoToControl` action. If you use the full identifier syntax, Access displays an error message (see Figure 7.1) and the action fails.

FIGURE 7.1:

FIGURE 7.1:

The default error message appears when you use the full identifier in the `GoToControl` action—you must use the short syntax in the `Control Name` argument.

Create a Macro Using the GoToControl Action

Create a macro to move the focus to a control on a form.

1. In the Database window, double-click frmCoursesByProgram (you created this form in Chapter 1).

2. Open a new macrosheet and save it as **mcrTest**. You'll use this macrosheet to store some example macros.

3. Create a macro named **ToControl**.

4. In the next row, select the `GoToControl` action and enter **DirectorLName** in the `Control Name` argument.

5. Save the macro.

6. Click in frmCoursesByProgram, then choose <u>T</u>ools ➤ <u>M</u>acro or click the Run Macro button on the toolbar (added in Chapter 2); select mcrTest.ToControl, and then click OK. The focus moves to the specified control.

Moving to a Specific Control on a Subform of the Active Form

When working interactively, you move the focus to a specific control on a subform by clicking the control. Automating this single mouse action requires two macro actions: first, you must move the focus to the subform control (using a `GoToControl` action), and then you move the focus to the control (using a second `GoToControl` action).

1. Click in the macrosheet, and create a macro named **MoveToSubformControl**

2. In the next row, select the `GoToControl` action and enter **frmCoursesByProgramSub** in the `Control Name` argument.

3. In the next row, select the `GoToControl` action and enter **Number** in the `Control Name` argument.

4. Save the macro.

5. Click in frmCoursesByProgram, then click the Run Macro button on the toolbar; select mcrTest.ToSubformControl, and click OK. The focus moves to the specified control on the subform.

NOTE   You can test the effect of trying to move to the control without moving to the subform control first: enter the value False in the Condition cell of the first `GoToControl` action and try to run the MoveToSubformControl macro. When you are finished testing, delete the False condition.

Moving to a Specific Control on Another Open Form

When working interactively, you take two steps to move to a specific control on an open form that isn't active: first you click in the form to activate it, and then you click in the control. To automate this process, you use two macro actions: first use the `SelectObject` action to activate the open form, and then use the `GoToControl` action to move to the control.

1. Click in the mcrTest macrosheet and create a new macro named **ToOtherFormControl**

2. Click in the next row, then select the `SelectObject` action and set the arguments as follows:

`Object Type`	Form
`Object Name`	frmCoursesByProgram

3. Click in the next row, then select the `GoToControl` action and enter **DirectorLName** for the `Control Name` argument.

4. Save the macro.

5. Click in the switchboard, then click the Run Macro button on the toolbar; select mcrTest.ToOtherFormControl, and click OK. The focus moves from the switchboard to the form, then to the specified control.

Moving to a Control on a Subform of Another Form

Moving to a specific control on a subform that's on another open form requires three actions: use the `SelectObject` action to activate the form, then use the `GoToControl` action to move to the subform control, and finally use the `GoToControl` action to move to the control.

1. Click in the macrosheet and create a new macro named **ToOtherFormSubformControl**

2. Click in the next row, then select `SelectObject` and set the arguments as follows:

    Object Type   Form

    Object Name   frmCoursesByProgram

3. Copy the two rows of the ToSubformControl macro, and paste them as the next two rows of the ToOtherFormControl macro.

4. Save the macro.

5. Click in the switchboard, then click the Run Macro button on the toolbar; select mcrTest.ToOtherFormSubformControl, and click OK. The focus moves from the switchboard to the form, and then to the specified control in the subform.

Moving Within a Record

When you work interactively you can use the keyboard (instead of the mouse) to move the focus among the controls of the active form. The navigation keystrokes (for moving in tab order) are:

- TAB— to the next control

- SHIFT+TAB—to the previous control

- HOME—to the first control

- END—to the last control

Using SendKeys

Use the **SendKeys** action to send keystrokes to Access or to another active Windows application. The action arguments are:

- **Keystrokes**—Enter the characters (up to 256) that you want to send. If a key represents a character that is displayed when you press the key, then enter the character (for example, to send v, enter v as the **Keystrokes** argument). If a key represents a character that isn't displayed when you press the key, such as TAB, ENTER, or a function key, you must enter a code in the **Keystrokes** argument (search the **SendKeys** Statement in online Help for a complete list of the **SendKeys** codes).

- **Wait**—Enter Yes to pause the macro until the keystrokes have been processed; otherwise enter No.

Here are examples of some of the keystrokes and their codes:

Keystroke	SendKeys Code	Keystroke	SendKeys Code
TAB	{tab}	ENTER	{enter} or ~
HOME	{home}	END	{end}
PAGE UP	{pgup}	PAGE DOWN	{pgdn}
SHIFT	+	CTRL	
ALT	%	Function key, Fn (for example, F2)	{Fn} (for example, {F2})

To automate a menu command that requires you to enter additional information before the command can be carried out, you can use the **Sendkeys** action together with the **DoMenuItem** action. For example, the File ➤ Save As menu command requires you to enter a new name if you are saving the

(continued)

object in the same database. When a menu command requires additional information (such as a new name), Access displays a dialog and suspends execution of the macro action until you enter the information and close the dialog. You can use **SendKeys** to send the keystrokes containing the information to the dialog. Place the **SendKeys** action before the **DoMenuItem** action in the macro.

You can even use **SendKeys** to send the access keys of the menu command itself; for example, to send the keystrokes for the File ➤ Save As command, you can use the **SendKeys** action with **%FA** as the **Keystrokes** argument. You should avoid doing so, however, because the location of a particular menu command or its access key may change in future versions of Access. If a menu command has a corresponding macro action, the best approach is use the macro action; for example, to save a file under a new name, use the **Save** action instead of either **SendKeys** or **DoMenuItem**.

Creating a Macro to Send Keystrokes

You can use the **SendKeys** action to duplicate the keystrokes to move the focus among the controls of the active form.

1. Click in the macrosheet.

2. Click in the row following the last row of the ToOtherFormSubformControl macro, then select the **SendKeys** action and enter these arguments:

Keystrokes	{tab}
Wait	Yes

3. Save the macro.

4. Click in the switchboard, then click the Run Macro button on the toolbar; select mcrTest.ToOtherFormSubformControl, and click OK. The focus moves from the switchboard to the form, then to the Number control in the subform, and finally to the next control.

Physical Navigation among Records

When you work interactively, you can navigate among records according to their physical location within the recordset; this is called *physical navigation*. The record you navigate to becomes the *current record*—the record you modify with subsequent mouse or keyboard actions.

You can use keystroke combinations, or the default navigation buttons (in the lower left corner of datasheets, forms, and reports), or the Edit ➤ Go To command to move to the first, previous, next, or last record in a set. Each of these physical navigation methods can be automated with macros.

Automating Keystroke Navigation

You can duplicate the keystroke combinations for physical navigation among records by using the **SendKeys** action in a macro; Table 7.1 shows the corresponding **Keystrokes** arguments.

Moving to the Last Record in a Subform

As an example, we'll modify the ToOtherFormSubformControl macro to move the focus to the last control of the last record in the subform.

1. Click in the mcrTest macrosheet.

2. Click in the row following the last row of the ToOtherFormSubformControl macro, then select the **SendKeys** action and set the arguments as follows:

    Keystrokes   ^{end}

    Wait   Yes

3. Save the macro.

4. Click in the switchboard, then click the Run Macro button on the toolbar; select mcrTest.ToOtherFormSubformControl, and click OK. The focus moves

TABLE 7.1: The Keystrokes argument for the SendKeys action for moving among records.

To move the focus to	Keystrokes argument
the first control of the first record	^{home}
the last control of the last record	^{end}
the next record	^{pgdn}
the previous record	^{pgup}

from the switchboard to the form, then to the Number control in the first record of the subform, then to the Name control of the same record, and finally to the last control of the last record in the subform.

Automating the Default Navigation Buttons and Menu Commands

You can use the GoToRecord action to duplicate mouse clicks that select a default navigation button or the Edit ➤ Go To command.

Move to a Record on the Active Form

If the active form has a subform, there are two sets of records you can move among: the records for the main form and the records for the subform. The result of the GoToRecord action depends on whether the focus is in the main form or in the subform control when you initiate the action.

1. Click in the Macro Name cell of a new row of the mcrTest macrosheet and name the new macro **ToLastRecord**

2. Click in the next row, then select the GoToRecord action and set the Record argument to Last. When you leave the Object Type argument blank, the GoToRecord action makes the specified record in the active object the current record.

3. Save the macro.

4. Click in frmCoursesByProgram, then click a control on the main form; click the Run Macro button, then select mcrTest.ToLastRecord and click OK. The last program in the set of records underlying the main form becomes the current record.

5. Click a control in the first record displayed in the subform, then click the Run Macro button; select mcrTest.ToLastRecord and click OK. The last record in the subform becomes the current record.

Moving to a Record on a Subform of the Active Form

If the focus is in the main form of the active form, and you want to move to a record on the subform, you move the focus to the subform control using the `GoToControl` action and then move to the record using the `GoToRecord` action.

1. In the mcrTest macrosheet, click in the Macro Name cell of a new row and name the new macro **ToLastSubformRecord**

2. Click in the next row, then select the `GoToControl` action and set the `Control Name` argument to **frmCoursesByProgramSub**

3. Click in the next row, then select the `GoToRecord` action and set the `Record` argument to **Last**

4. Save the macro.

5. Click in frmCoursesByProgram, then click a control on the main form; click the Run Macro button, then select mcrTest.ToLastSubformRecord and click OK. The last subform record becomes the current record.

Moving to a Record on Another Open Form

To select a record on another open form as the current record, use the `GoToRecord` action. Use the `Object Type` and `Object Name` arguments to specify the database object that contains the record that you want to select. The `GoToRecord` action does not activate the database object; you can even select a record on a hidden form as the current record.

As an example, you'll hide a form, then move to a record on the hidden form and edit the record.

1. In the mcrTest macrosheet, click in the Macro Name cell of a new row and name the new macro **ToHiddenRecord**

2. Click in the next row, then select the `GoToRecord` action and set the arguments as follows:

`Object Type`	Form
`Object Name`	frmCoursesByProgram
`Record`	Last

3. Click in the next row, then select the `SetValue` action and set the arguments as shown below. (You must use the full identifier for the control name because the hidden form is not the active form.)

`Item`	Forms!frmCoursesByProgram!DirectorLName
`Expression`	"hiddenname"

4. Save the macro.

5. Click in frmCoursesByProgram, then choose <u>W</u>indow ➤ <u>H</u>ide.

6. Click the Run Macro button on the toolbar, then select mcrTest.ToHiddenRecord, and click OK.

7. Choose <u>W</u>indow ➤ <u>U</u>nhide, then select Courses By Program and click OK. The last program record is displayed with hiddenname entered as the director's last name.

8. Press ESC.

9. Close frmCoursesByProgram.

10. Close the mcrTest macrosheet.

Tabbing to the Next Record

By default you can move to the next record by tabbing out of the last control of the previous record; however, you can use the new Cycle property of a form to control tabbing. Set the Cycle property to CurrentRecord to prevent tabbing out of the record; then, if the focus is in the last control of the form's tab order when you press TAB, the focus moves to the first control in the same record. Set the Cycle property to CurrentPage to repeatedly cycle through the controls in a page for the same record, or use the default setting, AllRecords, to allow tabbing to the next record or to the next page of the same record.

Logical Navigation among Records

Working interactively, you can move to a specific record (if you happen to know its position number in the recordset) by entering its number in the record number box at the bottom of the window and pressing ENTER. Normally, you don't know the record's position number; that number changes each time you use a different sort order and may also change when you add a record to the recordset.

A more meaningful way to navigate to a specific record is to use the data in the record instead of its physical location within a recordset; this is called *logical navigation*. You can find a specific record interactively by choosing the Edit ➤ Find command or by clicking the Find button on the toolbar, then entering search criteria in the Find dialog box and navigating directly to the first record that matches the criteria. If you want to search for a matching value in a particular control, you click in the control and then display the Find dialog box.

Finding a Specific Record

First, we'll review how to find a specific record interactively, then we'll automate the process.

Finding a Specific Record Interactively

As an example, try finding a specific course in frmCourses interactively.

1. In the switchboard, select the Edit/Add Course option button.

2. Click in the CourseID control, then select the Edit ➤ Find command. The Find In Field dialog box is displayed (see Figure 7.2). You enter the value you want Access to search for and set the various find options (in this example, you'll find the course with a CourseID value of 12).

FIGURE 7.2:
Finding a specific record
interactively.

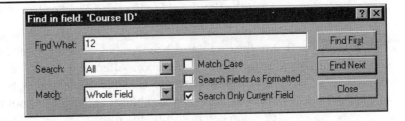

3. Enter **12** in the Find What text box.

4. Click the Find First button. Access locates the record that has a CourseID of 12.

Automating the Search Process

You can automate the search process by placing a combo box on the form to display
the course prefix, number, title, and CourseID, and creating a macro to find the record that corresponds to the CourseID value you selected in the combo list. The
macro *synchronizes the form to the combo box*.

1. Switch to Design view.

2. With the Control Wizards tool deselected, select the Combo Box tool and
   place an unbound combo box in the form header. The combo box must be unbound because you are using the combo box control as a temporary con-
   tainer to hold the search value of CourseID. You synchronize the form to this
   value.

3. Select the combo box, click in the RowSource property, and click the Build
   button. The Query Builder opens with the Show Table dialog box. You'll use
   the Query Builder to create an SQL statement that selects information for the
   combo list from tblCourses.

4. In the Show Table dialog box, select tblCourses and click OK.

5. Click in the first Field cell of the design grid, press SHIFT+F2 to open the
   Zoom box, and enter the expression below. (The fields are concatenated so
   that the pick list is compact.)

   Course: [Prefix]&" "&[Number]&" "&[Name]

6. From the field list, drag CourseID to the second Field cell in the design grid.

7. Drag the Prefix field to the third Field cell and the Number field to the fourth Field cell in the grid.

8. For the Prefix and Number fields, select Ascending from the Sort cell list and clear the Show check box. Alternatively, you can sort on the calculated column with the concatenated name expression, but it may be faster to sort on the separate Prefix and Number fields (without having to calculate the expression before sorting the records) when the table contains a very large number of records. Figure 7.3 shows the query.

FIGURE 7.3:

Using the Query Builder to create an SQL statement.

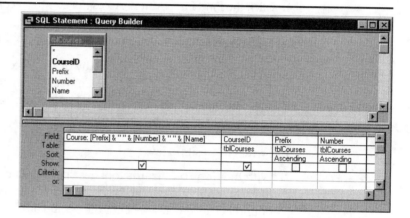

9. Switch to Datasheet view. The Datasheet displays the course information as it will appear in the combo list.

10. Close the Datasheet and save the changes.

11. Switch to SQL view. Figure 7.4 shows the SQL statement that the Builder pastes as the RowSource of the combo box; note the use of the AS keyword between the concatenated expression and its alias, Course.

Setting the Combo Box Properties

You'll set the remaining combo box properties to be sure that the combo box is unbound and holds the CourseID value.

FIGURE 7.4:

The SQL statement that the Query Builder pastes as the RowSource property of the combo box.

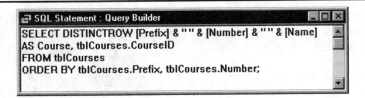

SQL Statement : Query Builder

```
SELECT DISTINCTROW [Prefix] & " " & [Number] & " " & [Name]
AS Course, tblCourses.CourseID
FROM tblCourses
ORDER BY tblCourses.Prefix, tblCourses.Number;
```

1. In the property sheet, set the combo box properties as shown below. (Notice that the RowSource property displays the SQL statement you just created.)

Property	Setting
Name	cboFind
ControlSource	
ColumnCount	2
ColumnWidths	1.75;0.3
BoundColumn	2
ListWidth	2.3

2. Select the label, then set the Name property to **lblFind** and set the Caption property to **Lookup**. You label the pick-list combo box as Lookup to direct the user to use this combo box to look up a course.

3. Select the label, set the ForeColor property to red and click the Bold button on the toolbar. These additional visual cues direct the user to the Lookup pick list.

4. Switch to Form view and click the arrow of the combo box, or place the cursor in the combo box control and press ALT+↓ to open the pick list (see Figure 7.5). When you select a value in the list, the value is displayed in the combo box, but the corresponding record is not selected because you haven't created the macro to find the corresponding record.

Creating a Reusable Macro to Find a Record

You create a macro to find the record that matches the value in the combo box. You want the macro to run when you select a different value for the combo box and the

FIGURE 7.5:

Using a pick-list combo box to select a record.

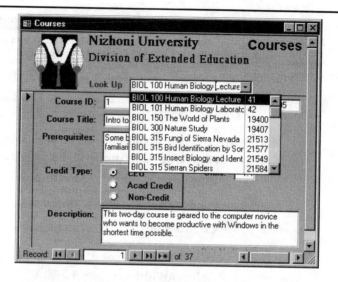

combo box recognizes the **AfterUpdate** event. The macro moves the focus to the control that you want to search (in this case the CourseID control) to limit the search to the values in that control. If you don't move the focus to a specific control, Access can search any of the controls on the form looking for the value you picked; when Access finds the value in the cboFind combo box itself, the search ends without finding the matching record. After moving the focus to the search control, the macro uses the **FindRecord** action to find the first record that has a value in the CourseID field that matches the value in the combo box.

Searching for a specific record is a basic database operation that you want to have available in many of the forms in the application. You'll design the search technique so that you can use it on other forms without having to modify it for each form. The macro must move the focus to the control that contains the primary key value—by default, this control has the same name as the primary key field in the underlying table, so the control has a different name for each form. You can make the search technique reusable by renaming this control as PrimaryID on any form that will use the search technique.

Figure 7.6 shows the macro flow diagram for the search technique.

FIGURE 7.6:

The macro flow diagram for finding a record.

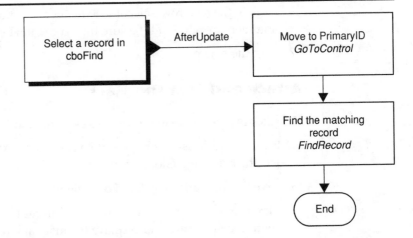

Renaming the control doesn't affect any other macros that refer to the field; for example, if a field and the control bound to it are named CourseID, then [CourseID] refers to both the control and the field. If you change the control name to PrimaryID, then [CourseID] still refers to the field and [PrimaryID] refers to the control bound to the field—both refer to the same field.

1. Click in frmCourses and switch to Design view.

2. Click in the CourseID text box and change the Name property to **PrimaryID**

3. In the Database window, click the Macro tab, then select mcrGallery and click the Design button.

4. Click in the Macro Name cell of a new row and name the new macro **cboFind_AfterUpdate**

5. Click in the next row, select the `GoToControl` action, and set the `Control Name` argument to **PrimaryID**

6. Click in the next row, select the **FindRecord** action, and set the **Find What** argument to **=cboFind** (be sure the expression begins with the equal sign).

7. Save the macro.

Attach and Test the Macro

1. Click in frmClasses and switch to Design view.

2. Select the pick-list combo box, then click in the AfterUpdate property and select the macro mcrGlobal.cboFind_AfterUpdate.

3. Save the form and switch to Form view.

4. Pick a course from the pick list. Access places the cursor in the PrimaryID control, then locates and displays the matching record.

Modify the Macro

You can make several modifications to improve the macro.

- If you change the value in the combo box by backspacing over an entry, the value is null; if you then trigger the macro by tabbing out of the control after changing its value to null, Access displays the error message shown in Figure 7.7 and the **FindRecord** action fails. You can avoid this error by testing the combo box for a null value. If the value is null, you stop the macro.

- After the macro finds the record with the matching value, it can return the focus to the pick-list combo box (because that is where you left it and where you expect it to be after the search).

- After the record has been found, the macro can set the combo box value to Null to prepare it for the next search.

- You can avoid the screen flickering as the macro runs by using the **Echo** action to turn off screen updating.

The flow diagram for the modified macro is shown in Figure 7.8.

1. Click in mcrGallery and modify the cboFind_AfterUpdate macro as shown in Table 7.2.

2. Save the macro.

FIGURE 7.7:

The error message if the combo box is null when you trigger the cboFind_AfterUpdate macro.

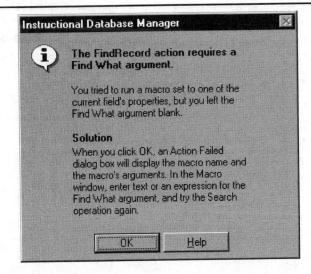

Instructional Database Manager

ⓘ **The FindRecord action requires a Find What argument.**

You tried to run a macro set to one of the current field's properties, but you left the Find What argument blank.

Solution
When you click OK, an Action Failed dialog box will display the macro name and the macro's arguments. In the Macro window, enter text or an expression for the Find What argument, and try the Search operation again.

[OK] [Help]

TABLE 7.2: Automate the search for a record by using a combo box.

Macro Name	Condition	Action	Action Arguments
cboFind_After-Update			
	IsNull(cboFind)	StopMacro	
		Echo	Echo On: No
		GoToControl	Control Name: PrimaryID
		FindRecord	Find What: =cboFind
		GoToControl	Control Name: cboFind
		SetValue	Item: cboFind
			Expression: Null

Retest the Macro

You'll test the modifications.

1. Click in the form.

2. Pick a course from the combo list. Access places the cursor in the PrimaryID control, locates and displays the matching record, and returns the insertion point to the pick-list combo box.

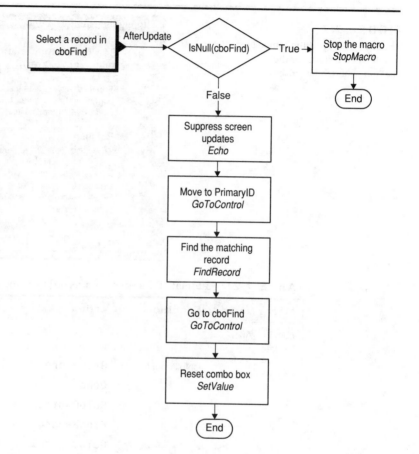

3. Click in the combo box and type **biol**; then select and delete the entire expression in the combo box and press ENTER. The macro stops.

4. Click in the combo box, type **zzz**, and press ENTER. Access displays the default error message shown in Figure 7.9.

When the Value Is Not in the Combo List

You can create a macro that displays a custom error message when the value you enter is not in the combo box list and the LimitToList property is set to Yes, and run the macro when the combo box recognizes the **NotInList** event. A combo box

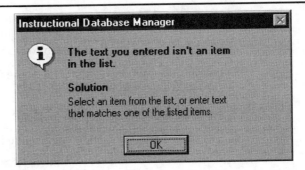

FIGURE 7.9:
The default error message that is displayed when you enter a value not in the combo list.

recognizes the **NotInList** event when you enter a value that isn't in the list and then try to move to move to another control or press the ENTER key.

Creating a Macro to Display a Custom Message

We'll create a macro to display a custom message and undo the entry when you enter a value that isn't in the combo box list.

1. In the error message dialog box, click the OK button.

2. Open a new macrosheet and save it as **mfrmCourses**

3. Click in the Macro Name cell of the first row and enter **cboFind_NotInList**

4. Click in the next row, select the **MsgBox** action and type this message:

    The course you entered isn't in the list of approved courses.
    Review the list to select an approved course.

5. In the next row, select the **DoMenuItem** action and enter the arguments:

Menu Bar	Form
Menu Name	Edit
Command	Undo

6. Save the macro.

Attach and Test the Macro

1. Click in frmCourses and switch to Design view.

2. Select the combo box, then click in the OnNotInList property and select mfrmCourses.cboFind_NotInList.

3. Save the form.

4. Switch to Form view and type a name in the combo box that isn't in the list. Your custom message is displayed (see Figure 7.10).

5. Click OK. The default error message is displayed (see Figure 7.9).

6. After clicking OK, the combo box list is dropped down.

You can't suppress the default error message using only macros. The **NotInList** event occurs as soon as the combo box recognizes the entry is not in the list (and before the control recognizes the **BeforeUpdate** event). You can't cancel the default behavior following the **NotInList** event (see Chapter 2 for a list of events for which you can cancel the default behavior using the **CancelEvent** action) and you can't suppress a default error message using the **SetWarnings** action. You can, however, use the Visual Basic error handler you created in Chapter 4, "Dealing with Errors in Macros," to suppress the default error message.

FIGURE 7.10:

Display a custom message for the combo box.

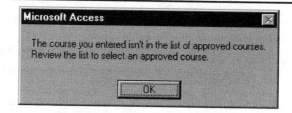

Using a Visual Basic Error Handler to Suppress a Default Message

Table 4.1 indicates that the error code is 2237 for the run-time error generated when you enter a value that is not in the combo list and the LimitToList property has been set to Yes.

1. Click in the form, then click in the On Error property; click the Build button, select Code Builder, and click OK.

2. At the insertion point between the lines of the code template, enter the code shown below (which suppresses the default error message):

```
If DataErr = 2237 Then
    Response = acDataErrContinue
Else
    Response = acDataErrDisplay
End If
```

3. Choose Run ➤ Compile Loaded Modules, then close the module.

4. Save the form and switch to Form view.

Test the Error Handler

1. Enter a course that isn't in the list (try **zzz**) and press ENTER. The custom message is displayed (see Figure 7.10).

2. Click OK. The default error message does not appear.

Returning to the Previous Record

After finding a particular record, you may want to undo the search and return to the previously displayed record. In order to undo the search, you need to know which record was displayed last. You can keep track of the previous record by holding the value of its primary key in an unbound, hidden text box, called PreviousID, in the header section of the form. You'll modify the cboFind_AfterUpdate macro to set the value of this text box to the value of the primary key of the current record at the beginning of the macro. To return to the previous record, place a command button (named cmdPrevious) in the form's header, and create a macro which uses the value held in the PreviousID text box to find and display the previous record.

Modify the Combo Box Macro

Modify the combo box macro to keep track of the previous record.

1. Click in the macrosheet and insert a new row in the cboFind_AfterUpdate macro, just after the row with the **Echo** action.

2. Select the **SetValue** macro action, and set the arguments as follows:

Item	PreviousID
Expression	PrimaryID

Create a Hidden Text Box

Create a hidden text box to hold the primary key value of the previous record.

1. Click in frmCourses and switch to Design view.

2. Place an unbound text box in the header section; set the Name property of the text box to **PreviousID** and the Caption property of the label to **PreviousID**

3. Select the text box and label, and set their Visible properties to No (see Figure 7.11).

Create a Command Button and Macro

Create the command button and macro that will display the previous record.

1. Place a button named cmdPrevious in the header section (just to the left of the Return button) and set the Caption property to **Pre&vious**

FIGURE 7.11:

Using a hidden unbound text box to hold the primary key value of the previous record.

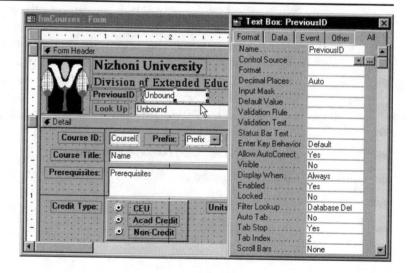

2. Click in the macro sheet, then click in a new row and name the new macro **cmdPrevious_Click**

3. Enter the macro shown in Table 7.3.

4. Save the macro.

TABLE 7.3: The macro to return to the previous record.

Macro Name	Action	Action Arguments
cmdPrevious_Click		
	GoToControl	Control Name: PrimaryID
	FindRecord	Find What: =PreviousID
	GoToControl	Control Name: cboFind

Attach and Test the Macro

1. Click in frmCourses, then select the cmdPrevious command button and set its OnClick property to mcrGallery.cmdPrevious_Click.

2. Save the form and switch to Form view.

3. Use the combo box to select a course. Note the course you selected.

4. Use the combo box to select another course, and then click the Previous button. The previous course is displayed.

5. Close frmCourses, then reopen the form in Form view.

6. Without selecting a course, click the Previous button. Access displays the error message shown in Figure 7.7 and the Action Failed dialog box shown in Figure 7.12.

The problem is that when the form first opens, there is no value stored in the PreviousID text box. If you click the Previous button before selecting a course, the **FindRecord** action fails because nothing has been entered in the Find What argument. A simple resolution is to test the value in the PreviousID text box, terminate the macro if the value is null and continue otherwise.

FIGURE 7.12:

The Action Failed dialog box is displayed when you click the Previous button before selecting a course.

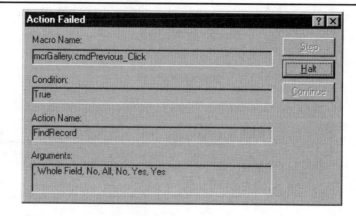

Modify the Macro to Test for a Null Value in the PreviousID Control Value

We'll modify the cmdPrevious_Click macro to test the value in the PreviousID control and terminate if the value is null.

1. Click in the macrosheet and insert a new first row in the cmdPrevious_Click macro.

2. Enter the condition **IsNull(PreviousID)**

3. In the same row, select the **StopMacro** action.

4. Save the macro.

Test the Macro

We'll test the modified macro.

1. Click in frmCourses.

2. Click the Previous button. The macro doesn't fail.

The modified macros for logical navigation are shown in Table 7.4.

TABLE 7.4: The logical navigation macros, to find a record and to return to the previous record.

Macro Name	Condition	Action	Action Arguments
cboFind_AfterUpdate			
	IsNull(cboFind)	StopMacro	
		Echo	Echo On: No
		SetValue	Item: PreviousID
			Expression: PrimaryID
		GoToControl	Control Name: PrimaryID
		FindRecord	Find What: =cboFind
		GoToControl	Control Name: cboFind
		SetValue	Item: cboFind
			Expression: Null
cmdPrevious_Click			
	IsNull(PreviousID)	StopMacro	
		Echo	Echo On: No
		GoToControl	Control Name: PrimaryID
		FindRecord	Find What: =PreviousID
		GoToControl	Control Name: cboFind

Remove Navigation Buttons from a Form with Logical Navigation

The default navigation buttons at the bottom of the form allow you to move back and forth through the records and display a new record. In data entry operations, you don't really need physical navigation; instead, you need to navigate in a logical manner: you locate and edit an existing record, locate and display another existing record, perhaps return to the previous record you just edited, and display a new blank record for data entry. Once you've provided for the logical navigation between records, the default navigation buttons for physical navigation are no longer necessary. (In Chapter 8, "Data Entry Operations," you'll place a command button on the form to display a blank record.)

1. Switch to Design view, select the form, and set the NavigationButtons property to No.

2. Save the form and switch to Form view.

NOTE

If you want to provide physical navigation as well as logical navigation, you have to create a custom set of command buttons that update the value held in the PreviousID text box, so that clicking the Previous command button displays the previous record regardless of whether that record was selected logically or physically. The default navigation buttons do not update the PreviousID text box, so leaving them on a form with logical navigation gives inconsistent behavior.

Placing Logical Navigation Controls in the Controls Gallery

The techniques for finding a record and then undoing the find depend on four controls:

- cboFind combo box

- cmdPrevious command button

- PreviousID text box

- PrimaryID text box control, bound to the primary key field of the table or query that underlies the form

The macros for the logical navigation techniques are stored in the macro gallery mcrGallery and refer only to these four controls, so you can reuse these techniques on any form as long as the control that is bound to the primary key field is named PrimaryID. For efficiency, you can store the logical navigation controls in the controls gallery, zsfrmGallery, along with instructions for their use.

1. Switch to Design view, then select the cboFind combo box and its label, the cmdPrevious button, and the PreviousID text box and its label; and copy the selection to the clipboard.

2. Open zsfrmGallery in Design view, then paste the contents of the clipboard and move the selection 1" to the right and 2" down.

3. Click in the combo box, then click in the RowSource property and delete it (you have to reset the RowSource property when you use the control in another form).

4. Select the Label tool, create a label 2" tall and 3" wide above the controls, and enter the following instructions:

> **To implement logical navigation to find records:**
>
> **1. Copy the combo box, text box, their labels, and the command button to the header of the form.**
>
> **2. Change the name of the control to be searched to PrimaryID. This control must be bound to the primary key field for the table or query that provides the records for the form.**
>
> **3. Set the RowSource property of the combo box to the lookup query, or create an SQL statement to provide the rows for the combo box. Set the ColumnCount, ColumnWidth, and ListWidth properties as appropriate. Set the BoundColumn property to the column that contains the value for the search.**
>
> **4. Make sure the macros cboFind_AfterUpdate and cmdPrevious_Click are in the mcrGallery macro group.**
>
> **5. Remove the default navigation buttons from the form.**

5. In the toolbar, select the Rectangle tool and draw a rectangle that encloses the controls and the instruction label (as in Figure 7.13).

Adding Logical Navigation to Another Form

You can now simply copy the logical navigation controls from the controls gallery, paste them into another data entry form and make the required changes. As an example, you add the logical navigation capability to frmStudents.

1. In the Database window, select frmStudents and click the Design button.

2. Click in the zsfrmGallery form.

FIGURE 7.13:

Storing the reusable controls for logical navigation in zsfrmGallery.

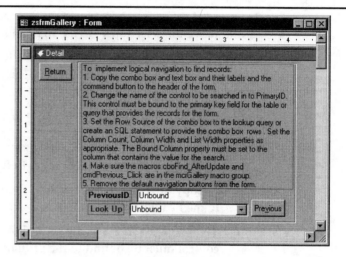

3. Select and copy the set of logical navigation controls.

4. Click in the header of frmStudents, paste the controls, and rearrange them as necessary.

5. Select the StudentID control and change its Name property to **PrimaryID** (StudentID is the control you will be searching).

6. Select the cboFind combo box and set its properties as follows:

RowSource	qlkpStudentName
ColumnWidths	1.25; 0.75
ListWidth	2.25
BoundColumn	2

7. Save the form and switch to Form view (see Figure 7.14).

8. Use the combo box to select a student; select another student and then click the Previous button. The record of the first student you selected is displayed.

9. Click the Return button.

When frmStudents is opened from frmRegistration by clicking the Review button, the logical navigation controls are not appropriate because only the synchronized record on frmStudents should be available for review and editing.

FIGURE 7.14:
Giving logical navigation capability to frmStudents.

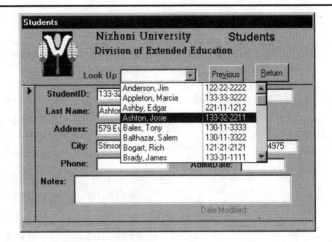

Modify the cmdReview_Click Macro to Hide the Logical Navigation Controls

You'll modify the cmdReview_Click macro (refer to Table 5.3) to hide the logical navigation controls on frmStudents when it is opened from frmRegistration.

1. Open the mfrmRegistration macro sheet.

2. Modify the cmdReview_Click macro as shown in Table 7.5. Note that when you hide a control its label is hidden, too, so you don't need to hide the label with a separate **SetValue** action.

3. Save the macro.

Test the Macro

We'll test the modified macro.

1. In the switchboard, click the Register in Classes option button.

2. Use the navigation buttons to select a student, then click the Review button. The frmStudents form opens displaying the synchronized record. The logical navigation buttons are hidden.

TABLE 7.5: Modify the cmdReview_Click macro to hide the logical navigation controls.

Macro Name	Actions	Action Arguments
cmdReview_Click		
	OpenForm	**Form Name**: frmStudents
		Where Condition: [StudentID] = Forms![frmRegistration]i[StudentID]
	SetValue	**Item**: Screen.ActiveForm.Tag
		Expression: 1
	SetValue	**Item**: Forms!frmStudents!cboFind.Visible
		Expression: No
	SetValue	**Item**: Forms!frmStudents!cmdPrevious.Visible
		Expression: No

3. Click the Return button to close frmStudents, then click the Return button on frmRegistration.

4. In the switchboard, click the Add/Edit Student option button. The frmStudents form opens with the logical navigation buttons displayed.

Adding the Visual Basic Error Handler

In Chapter 4, "Dealing with Errors in Macros," we added a Visual Basic error handler to frmStudents. You can modify the event procedure to display a custom message if you enter a value that is not in the combo list (and error 2237 is generated).

1. Enter the value **999889999** in the lookup combo box, and then tab out. The combo list drops, but there is no other response to indicate that the value you entered is not in the list of existing students.

2. Switch to Form view, click in the OnError property, and click the Build button. The form module opens displaying the error handler. Notice that if error 2237 is generated, the procedure suppresses the default error message. You'll modify the event procedure to display a custom message.

3. Click at the end of the line

```
ElseIf DataErr = 2237
```

Then press ENTER and enter the new lines

```
MsgBox "The student you entered isn't in the list of students.
➥Review the list to select a student or press ESC to undo your
➥entry."
```

4. Choose Run ➤ Compile Loaded Modules and close the module.

5. Save the form and switch to Form view.

6. Test the form's logical navigation capability.

Endnotes

This chapter has shown you how to automate and control navigation among controls and records by using

- the **GoToControl** macro action

- the **GoToRecord** macro action

- the Cycle property of a form

- a custom lookup combo box automated with a macro to find a record

- a command button to display the previous record

You created reusable controls and macros for logical navigation among records and stored the controls in the controls gallery. The macros you created test preconditions to avoid errors.

You used Visual Basic error-handling event procedures to deal with the run-time errors that occur when you enter a value in a combo box that is not in the list. Visual Basic is necessary because you can't avoid or suppress default error message by using only macros.

On Your Own

In the exercises, you'll create a macro to make sure the frmRegistration form always shows the first class a student is registered in as the current record, and you'll add logical navigation to two other forms. You'll explore two kinds of custom VCR buttons for physical navigation between records: first using macros, and then using the Command Button Wizard.

Adding to the Application

1. Move to the first record in the Registration subform.

   a. Create a macro to move to the first record in the subform when the frmRegistration form first opens, and again each time you move to another student's record. Use the **Current** event to trigger the macro.

2. Use a pick list to find a Class List.
   Add the logical navigation capability to the frmClassList form.

   a. Copy the logical navigation controls from zsfrmGallery to the form and make the changes listed in the instructions.

   b. Create a pick-list query (named **qryClassName**) based on tblCourses and tblClasses. In the first Field cell concatenate Prefix, Number, SectionNo and Name, and then rename the field **ClassName**. Drag ScheduleNo to the second Field cell. Sort in Ascending order on the first field.

   c. You want the query to select only the classes for the session that you are working with (that is, the value displayed in the WorkingSession text box on the switchboard). Drag Session to the design grid and enter the following expression into the Criteria cell:

   Forms!frmSwitchboard!WorkingSession

   d. Add the Visual Basic error handler, and modify it to display a custom message.

   e. Remove the default navigation buttons.

3. Add logical navigation to frmInstructors.

   Using what you learned in the section "Adding Logical Navigation to Another Form,"

   a. Add logical navigation to frmInstructors.
   b. Paste the error-handling event procedure from zsfrmGallery, and modify the code for all three errors as appropriate to frmInstructors.

Extending the Concepts

1. Custom VCR buttons

   a. Place a set of four custom VCR buttons in the footer of frmCourses with Name properties **cmdFirst**, **cmdBack**, **cmdNext**, and **cmdLast**. Click the Build button for the Picture properties and select appropriate VCR pictures.

   b. In mcrGallery, create a macro for each button that synchronizes the button to the logical navigation controls (by updating the PreviousID text box with the value displayed in the PrimaryID text box) and then moves to another record using the appropriate `GoToRecord` action.

   c. Test the custom VCR buttons and their interaction with the logical navigation controls.

   d. Copy the VCR buttons to the controls gallery (zsfrmGallery).

   e. Create an instruction label as follows:

   > **To add physical navigation to a form by using the three logical navigation controls:**
   >
   > **1. Copy the set of VCR buttons to the form.**
   >
   > **2. Make sure these macros are in mcrGallery: cmdFirst_Click, cmdBack_Click, cmdNext_Click, and cmdlast_Click.**
   >
   > **3. Set the NavigationButtons property of the form to No.**

2. Custom VCR buttons using the Command Button Wizard

   a. With the Control Wizards tool selected, you'll follow the dialogs of the wizard to create a set of four custom VCR buttons in the footer of frmCourses, with Name properties **cmdFirstVB**, **cmdBackVB**, **cmdNextVB**, and **cmdLastVB**. For each button, in the first dialog of the Command Button wizard, select the Record Navigation category and the appropriate command. In the next dialog, select the blue arrows (to distinguish the buttons from those you placed in the previous exercise).

   b. Modify the event procedures to synchronize the buttons with the logical navigation controls. For each of the buttons:

   • Click the Build button for the OnClick property. The event procedure is displayed. The line beginning DoCmd runs the **GoToRecord** macro action.

   • In the line *before* the DoCmd line, enter the following statement to update the value of the PreviousID control to the value in the PrimaryID control: **PreviousID = PrimaryID**

   • Choose Run ➤ Compile Loaded Modules and close the module.

   c. Test the custom VCR buttons and their interaction with the logical navigation controls.

CHAPTER

EIGHT

Data Entry Operations

- Preconditions for avoiding macro errors

- Changing the timing of validation testing

- The DCount( ) function

- The MsgBox( ) function

- Reusable data entry controls and macros

- Run-time form properties

In this chapter you learn how to automate data entry operations. For several of these tasks, you can create automation controls as reusable objects, linked to reusable macros, that you can paste directly to other data entry forms. Reusability depends on the primary key control having the same Name property (in this case, PrimaryID) on all data entry forms, so that the macro can always use the same reference for this control; you'll change the primary key control's Name property on each data entry form.

In addition, whether the automated operation is reusable or not, you'll use the Screen object to avoid referring to specific forms and controls (in order to minimize changes when you use the operation on another form).

The routine data entry operations include:

- adding new records
- editing data and entering new data
- validating data
- reversing changes made during editing
- saving records
- deleting records

NOTE When you begin the chapter, only the switchboard and the Database window should be displayed. Close any other objects.

Using Macros to Validate Data

Typically, you create a data entry form with combo boxes, list boxes, option groups, and check boxes to aid in fast and accurate data entry. In addition to using these special controls to improve accuracy, you can protect your data with validation rules that specify requirements for the data you enter. Access provides opportunities to validate data by setting ValidationRule properties, and to display custom messages when the rules are not satisfied by setting the ValidationText properties. You can create validation rules and messages when you set field and table properties in table design and when you set control properties in form design, as follows:

- For an individual field, set a validation rule by setting the ValidationRule property in the field properties list in the table's Design view. Access tests a field's ValidationRule property when you try to tab out of the field. A field validation rule cannot contain references to other fields. If the validation rule is satisfied, Access updates the field to the record buffer; otherwise, Access doesn't update the field, displays the message you set in the ValidationText property if there is one (or a default message if there isn't), and prevents you from tabbing out of the field until you either undo the entry or enter a value that satisfies the rule (refer to Chapter 2 for more information on the update process).

- For a record in a table, set a validation rule by setting the ValidationRule property in the table's property sheet in the table's Design view. A record validation rule can refer to other fields in the same record. Access tests the ValidationRule property for the record when you try to save the record. If you have enforced referential integrity, Access tests these rules at the same time. If the validation rule for the record is satisfied, Access updates the record to the table; otherwise, Access doesn't update the record, displays your custom message (or a default message), and prevents you from saving the record until you either undo the record or enter values that satisfy the validation rule. Figure 8.1 shows the ValidationRule property in the field properties list and in the table properties sheet.

- For an individual control displayed in a form, set a validation rule by setting the ValidationRule property in the control's property sheet in form Design view. A control's validation rule can refer to other fields in the table, to fields and controls in other forms, or to the results of calculations with domain aggregate functions. Access tests the control's validation rule when you try to tab out of the control. If the control's validation rule is satisfied, Access updates the control to the record buffer; otherwise, Access doesn't update the control, displays your custom message (or a default message), and prevents you from tabbing out of the control until you undo the value or enter valid data. Figure 8.2 shows the ValidationRule property in a control's property sheet.

FIGURE 8.1:

The ValidationRule property in the field properties list and in the table properties sheet.

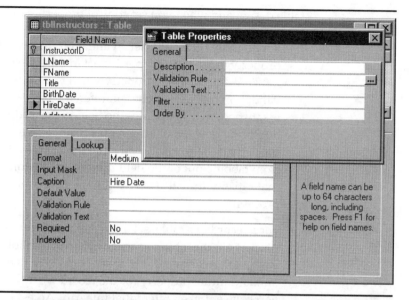

FIGURE 8.2:

The Validation Rule property in a control's property sheet.

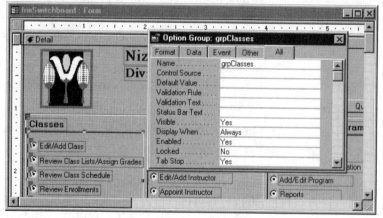

When you set validation rules in a form as well as in its underlying table, Access enforces both sets of rules. A validation rule that you set for a control at form level overrides any validation rules you may have set at the table level. Validation rules for controls and fields are enforced in the following order:

1. The control's ValidationRule property as set in the control's property sheet

2. The field's ValidationRule property as set in the field's property sheet

3. The record's ValidationRule property as set in the table's property sheet

You can use macros to set more complicated validation rules. For example, you can use macros when you want to

- display different messages depending on the value entered

- use more than one validation rule to validate a record

- change the timing of the validation

The order of validation depends on which event triggers the validation macro. As an example, a macro triggered by the `BeforeUpdate` event of a control is executed before the control's ValidationRule property is enforced.

In this section you use a macro to change the timing of the test for uniqueness of the primary key value, By default, Access tests for uniqueness when you try to save the record—you'll create a macro to perform the test as soon as you enter a value in the primary key control instead.

NOTE   This book assumes the primary key for a table is a single field unless the table is a linking table. You have to modify the techniques when the primary key is more than one field.

Checking for Duplicate Primary Key Values

When you design a data table, you specify how the primary key is entered. You can:

- automatically assign sequential numbers by using an AutoNumber field as the primary key,

- create your own expressions to assign unique values automatically, or

- permit the primary key to be entered as part of data entry.

No matter how the value is entered, Access checks for duplicate values when you try to save the record.

1. In the switchboard, click the Edit/Add Course option button.

2. On the toolbar, click the New Record button, then enter the following data:

Course ID	8
Prefix	CINE
Number	876
Name	Films of the '70s
CreditCode	Acad Credit
Units	3

3. Choose the Records ➤ Save Record command or press SHIFT+ENTER. Access displays the default error message shown in Figure 8.3.

4. Click OK and then press the ESC key.

You can create a macro that tests for uniqueness when Access acknowledges that the data in the control has been changed, but before updating the control (that is, when the control recognizes the BeforeUpdate event).

Using DCount() to Test for Uniqueness

You can check for uniqueness by using the DCount() function to determine if there is another record in the table having a primary key value that matches the value entered in the control. Use the syntax

DCount("*","[tablename]","[fieldname]=Forms![formname]![controlname]")

where fieldname is the name of the matching field in the table and controlname is the name of the control on the open form that displays the value you want to match.

FIGURE 8.3:

The default error message that is displayed when you try to save a record with the same primary key value as another record in the table.

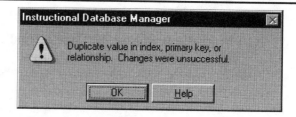

Enclose each argument of the DCount( ) function in quotation marks. Use the asterisk in the first argument to count all of the records. In this example, the expression

DCount("*","tblCourses","CourseID=Screen.ActiveForm.PrimaryID")

counts the number of records in the tblCourses table whose CourseID field has the same value as that displayed in the PrimaryID control on the active form. If there is another record with the same primary key value, the DCount( ) function has the value 1; in this case, the macro displays a custom message and cancels the updating. If there isn't another record, the DCount( ) function has the value 0, the macro terminates, and Access updates the control. Figure 8.4 is the flow diagram for the macro.

Create the Macro

You'll create a macro that tests for uniqueness of the primary key value as soon as you enter a primary key value for a new course and try to tab out of the control.

1. Open a new macrosheet and save it as mfrmCourses

2. Click in a new row and name the new macro PrimaryID_BeforeUpdate

3. Enter the macro shown in Table 8.1.

4. Save the macro.

FIGURE 8.4:

The flow diagram for the macro to test for uniqueness of the primary key value.

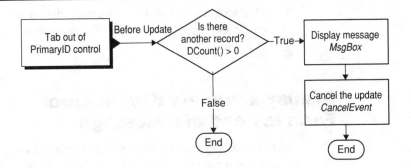

TABLE 8.1: A macro to validate the uniqueness of the primary key value when you try to update the primary key control.

Macro Name	Condition	Action	Action Arguments
PrimaryID_BeforeUpdate			
	DCount("*","tblCourses","CourseID=Screen.ActiveForm.PrimaryID")>0	MsgBox	**Message**: There is another record with this ID. You must enter a unique ID for this record or press the Esc key to undo the record.
	...	CancelEvent	

Notice the macro uses the `CancelEvent` action to cancel the updating of the control. (Refer to Chapter 2 for more information on cancelling the default behavior following an event.)

Attach and Test the Macro

1. Click in the form, then click in the BeforeUpdate property, and select the macro mfrmCourses.PrimaryID_BeforeUpdate.

2. Save the form and switch to Form view.

3. In the toolbar, click the New button, then enter 8 in the Course ID and press TAB. Access displays the custom message (see Figure 8.5).

4. Click OK.

Display a Primary Key Violation Form Instead of a Message

Instead of displaying a message that there is another record with the same primary key value entered previously in the table, it is more helpful to display the previous record itself. With the previous record displayed, you can determine whether the record you are trying to enter duplicates a record already in the table or the record only needs a

FIGURE 8.5:

Displaying a custom message before cancelling the update.

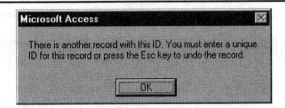

different primary key value before it can be saved. The College database contains a form for reviewing course information, called frmCoursesView, that you can use to display the record with the duplicate primary key.

Modify the Macro

You modify the macro to open frmCoursesView and display the synchronized record. Use the SetValue action to change the form's Caption property to Primary Key Violation. You also set the form's Tag property to 1 (or any non-null value) so that the form's Return button closes the form without unhiding the switchboard (see the section "Using the Tag Property to Keep Track of How a Form is Opened" in Chapter 5).

1. Click in mfrmCourses, then click in the MsgBox action of the PrimaryID_ BeforeUpdate macro.

2. Modify the macro as shown in Table 8.2.

3. Save the macro.

Test the Macro

1. Click in frmCourses, then switch to Form view.

2. Click the New button, enter 8 for the CourseID and then try to tab out of the control. Access displays the Primary Key Violation form (see Figure 8.6).

3. Click the Return button, then press ESC twice to undo the control and the record.

4. Click the Return button again. The frmCourses form closes.

TABLE 8.2: A macro to validate the uniqueness of the primary key value and display a primary key violation form.

Macro Name	Condition	Action	Action Arguments
PrimaryID_ BeforeUpdate			
	DCount("*","tblCourses","CourseID= Screen.ActiveForm.PrimaryID")>0	OpenForm	**Form Name**: frmCoursesView
			Where Condition: CourseID = Screen.ActiveForm.PrimaryID
	...	SetValue	**Item**: Screen.ActiveForm.Caption
			Expression: "Primary Key Violation"
	...	SetValue	**Item**: Screen.ActiveForm.Tag
			Expression: 1
	...	CancelEvent	

FIGURE 8.6:

Displaying the record that has the duplicate primary key instead of a message. Avoid data inconsistencies by displaying a read-only form.

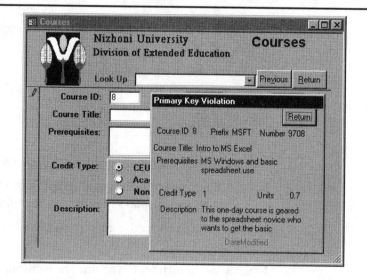

Adding New Records

You can automate a set of standard operations that all simple data entry forms need. You begin with operations for

- adding a new record
- undoing changes
- saving a record

In each case, you analyze the interactive process, then create a command button and design a macro to automate the process. In designing the macro you'll anticipate macro errors and standard run-time errors, and include tests of preconditions in order to avoid these errors.

Creating Command Buttons for Data Entry Operations

Create a set of command buttons for the data entry operations.

1. In the switchboard, click the Edit/Add Course option button.

2. Switch to Design view.

3. With the Control Wizards tool deselected, select the Command Button tool, then click in the form header and draw a button 0.5" wide and 0.2" tall.

4. Choose the Edit ➤ Duplicate command twice.

5. Align the top edges of the three new buttons.

6. Select all three new buttons and the cmdPrevious and cmdReturn buttons, then choose Format ➤ Align ➤ Top to align their top edges; choose Format ➤ Horizontal Spacing ➤ Decrease, and then move the aligned button group to the lower right corner of the header section.

7. One by one, click in each of the three new buttons and set a Name and Caption property for each as follows:

Name	Caption
cmdNew	&New
cmdUndo	&Undo
cmeSave	&Save

Analyze and Automate the Process

When you work interactively, you can add a new record by selecting the Edit ➤ Go To ➤ New command or by clicking the New button (either on the toolbar or grouped with the default navigation buttons on the form).

1. Select the Edit ➤ Go To ➤ New command. A new blank record is displayed.

2. Select the Edit ➤ Go To ➤ New command again. Since a new record is the current record, the New command is not available.

You could use the DoMenuItem action to issue the Edit ➤ Go To ➤ New menu command, but a better solution is to use the GoToRecord action to move to a new record.

> **NOTE**
>
> The problem with the DoMenuItem action is that the action fails if the current record happens to be the new record (and the New subcommand isn't available). You could avoid the action failure by testing the value of the form's NewRecord property to determine if the current record is the new record before issuing the command. The NewRecord property is not listed in the form's property sheet because you can't set this property in Design view. Access sets the NewRecord property when the application runs, and you can only observe its value. If the current record is new, the NewRecord property has the value True; otherwise, the NewRecord property has the value False. We'll use the GoToRecord action instead, because this action doesn't fail when the current record is new.

Create the Macro

You can create a macro that uses the GoToRecord action to go to a new record (see Figure 8.7).

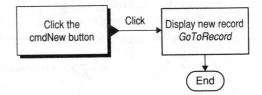

FIGURE 8.7:
The macro flow diagram to display a new record.

1. Switch to Design view, click the cmdReturn button, and then click the Build button on the toolbar. The mcrGallery macrosheet opens.

2. Click in an empty row and name the new macro cmdNew_Click

3. Enter the macro shown in Table 8.3.

4. Save the macro.

5. Click in frmCourses, then click in the New command button.

6. Click in the OnClick property, then select mcrGlobal.cmdNew_Click, and save the form.

7. Switch to Form view; using the default navigation buttons, go to the first record and then click the form's New button. A new record is displayed.

8. Click the New button again. There is no response to additional clicks of the New button because the `GoToRecord` action doesn't fail when the current record is the new record.

TABLE 8.3: A macro to display a new record.

Macro Name	Action	Action Arguments
cmdNew_Click		
	GoToRecord	**Record:** New

Undoing Changes

After you make changes to a control, you can undo the changes interactively by selecting either the Edit ➤ Undo Typing command (if the focus has not left the control) or by selecting the Edit ➤ Undo Current Field/Record command (if the focus has left the control but you have not moved to another record). If you have not made any changes to the record, neither Undo command is available.

Take a look at how the Undo commands respond to changes in focus:

1. With the new record displayed, click the Edit menu. Notice the Can't Undo command is grayed out and unavailable.

2. Using the default navigation buttons, move to another record and click the Edit menu. Notice the Can't Undo command is still grayed out.

3. Click in the Number field, change the number, then click the Edit menu. Notice the Undo Typing command is available.

4. Tab to the next control and click the Edit menu. Notice the UndoCurrent-Field/Record command is available.

Design the Macro to Test the Dirty Property

You can create a macro with a DoMenuItem action to issue an Undo command. Since one of the Undo commands is available only when you have actually made a change to the record, you need a way to test whether the current record has been changed before issuing the command. You can use the form's Dirty property (yes, it is actually called the Dirty property!). The Dirty property has the value True if the current record has been modified since it was last saved, and False otherwise. The Dirty property is not listed in the form's property sheet because you can't set this property. Access controls the value of the Dirty property and you can only observe the value.

If the Dirty property is True, the record has been changed and the macro reverses the change. If the Dirty property is False, the macro terminates. Figure 8.8 shows the flow diagram for the macro.

1. Click in mcrGallery and name the new macro cmdUndo_Click

2. Enter the macro shown in Table 8.4.

3. Save the macro.

FIGURE 8.8:

The flow diagram to test for changes in a form before issuing a command to undo them.

TABLE 8.4: A macro to undo a change. This macro determines if the record has been changed before issuing the command.

Macro Name	Condition	Action	Action Arguments
cmdUndo_Click			
	Screen.ActiveForm .Dirty	DoMenuItem	**Menu Bar**: Form
			Menu Name: Edit
			Command: Undo

Attach and Test the Macro

1. Click in the form and switch to Design view.

2. Click the Undo button, then click in the OnClick property, and select the macro mcrGallery.cmdUndo_Click.

3. Switch to Form view.

4. Use the lookup combo box to select an existing record, then click in the Number control and make a change.

5. Click the Undo button. The change is reversed.

6. Click in the Number control, make a change and tab to the next control.

7. Click the Undo button. The change is reversed.

8. Select another existing record and click the Undo button. There is no response.

9. Click the New button and then click the Undo button. There is no response.

Saving Changes

When you work interactively with a form, there are several ways you can save changes to a record, including:

- choosing Records ➤ Save Record

- choosing File ➤ Close to close the form

- pressing SHIFT+ENTER

- pressing CTRL+F4 to close the form

- moving the focus to a different or new record

You can also initiate saving a record by using the custom controls you've placed on the form, including:

- clicking the Return button on the form

- clicking the New button on the form

- selecting another record using the lookup combo box

Create the Macro

You can create a macro with a `DoMenuItem` action to issue the Records ➤ Save Record command.

1. Click in mcrGallery, then click in a new row and name a new macro cmdSave_Click

2. Enter the macro shown in Table 8.5.

3. Save the macro.

TABLE 8.5: The macro to save a record.

Macro Name	Action	Action Arguments
cmdSave_Click		
	DoMenuItem	Menu Bar: Form
		Menu Name: Records
		Command: SaveRecord

Attach and Test the Macro

1. Click in frmCourses and select the Save button.

2. Click in the OnClick property and select the macro mcrGlobal-.cmdSave_Click.

3. Switch to Form view.

4. Edit a record and click the form's Save button.

Validating Changes to a Record

When you make changes to a record, Access tests the changes against the validation rules and the referential integrity rules. If the changes satisfy the rules, Access saves the current record; otherwise, Access displays an error message and doesn't save the record. For example, if the value in the primary key is null when you try to save the record by any of the save methods, Access displays a default error message and won't save the record. Interestingly, the DoMenuItem action to issue the Records ➤ Save Record command doesn't fail.

1. Click the form's New button.

2. Enter the following new course information:

Prefix	Bus
Number	474
Course Title	International Business

3. Click the form's Save button. Access displays the default error message:

Index or primary key can't contain a null value

Design a Macro to Validate the Record

Although the macro doesn't fail when the validation rules aren't satisfied, you can create a macro to replace the default error messages with custom messages. You can create a macro to test the validation rules when Access acknowledges that the record has been changed and before updating the record to the table (that is, when the form recognizes the `BeforeUpdate` event). The macro can test all of the validation rules. If the data is valid, the macro terminates. If the data in the record isn't valid, the macro displays a different message for each error and cancels the updating. When you initiate saving the record by running another macro (such as by clicking the New button or selecting another record with the lookup combo box) you need to stop execution of the other macro when you cancel the update; otherwise, the other macro may fail. You can use the `StopAllMacros` action to stop execution. As an example, you create a macro to test the primary key value for null. Figure 8.9 shows the macro flow diagram.

FIGURE 8.9:

Macro flow diagram to test a validation rule before updating a record.

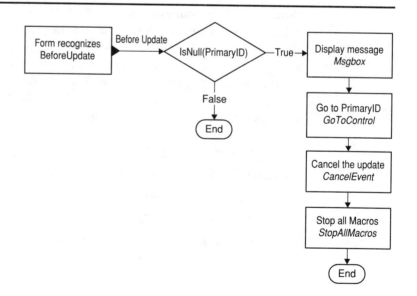

1. Click in a new row in the mcrGallery macrosheet, and create a new macro named Form_BeforeUpdate

2. Enter the macro shown in Table 8.6.

TABLE 8.6: The macro to test a validation rule before updating the record.

Macro Name	Condition	Action	Action Arguments
Form_BeforeUpdate			
	IsNull(PrimaryID)	MsgBox	**Message**: You must enter a unique ID value for this record.
	...	GoToControl	**Control Name**: PrimaryID
	...	CancelEvent	
	...	StopAllMacros	

Attach and Test the Macro

1. Click in frmCourses, then switch to Design view and set the form's Before-Update property to mcrGallery.Form_BeforeUpdate.

2. Save the form and switch to Form view.

3. Click the New button on the form, then enter a prefix, number, and course title.

4. One by one, do each of the operations listed below. In each case, the custom message is displayed, the insertion point is placed in the PrimaryID control, and there is no further response.

   - Click the New button on the form.
   - Click the Save button on the form.
   - Select a course in the lookup combo box.
   - Choose Records ➤ Save Record, or press SHIFT+ENTER.
   - Tab out of the record.

5. Press CTRL+F4. The custom message is displayed.

6. Click OK. The form closes.

7. Open the form and enter a prefix, number and course title.

8. Click the Return button on the form. In this case, after the custom message is displayed, Access displays the additional default message shown in Figure 8.10.

This message occurs because the cmdReturn_Click macro initiates the Close action before executing the Form_BeforeUpdate macro, or before default testing of the record validation rules. Access is aware that the Close action was issued and that the current record violates one of the record validation rules. Access displays the message in Figure 8.10 to give you the choice to close the form without saving the changes or to cancel the command to close the form. This message may be confusing to a novice using your application, so you can choose to suppress it.

Modify the Visual Basic Error Handler to Suppress the Message

You can't suppress the message shown in Figure 8.10 using the SetWarnings action (which turns off most system warnings and messages) because the message requires input; however, you can suppress the message by modifying the Visual Basic error handler for the form's Error event. You add two lines of code to suppress this message (error code 2169).

FIGURE 8.10:
The default message that is displayed when you try to close the data entry form using the Return button.

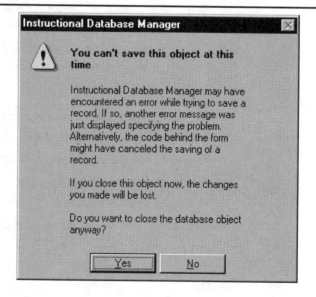

1. Click the form's Undo button.

2. Switch to Design view and select the form.

3. Click in the OnError property and then click the Build button.

4. Modify the event procedure by inserting the two new rows (shown in bold) as follows:

```
Private Sub Form_Error(DataErr As Integer, Response As Integer)
    If DataErr = 2237 Then
        Response = acDataErrContinue
    ElseIf DataErr = 2169 Then
        Response = acDataErrContinue
    Else
        Response = acDataErrDisplay
    End If
End Sub
```

5. Choose Run ➤ Compile Loaded Modules.

6. Close the module.

7. Switch to Form view.

Test the Error Handler

This modification has the effect of accepting the default Yes button in the error message, so if you click the Return button on the form and the record validation rules are not satisfied, the form closes without saving the changes to the record.

1. Click the New button on the form, then enter a prefix, number, and course title.

2. Click the Return button on the form. The custom validation message is displayed.

3. Click OK. This time the additional default message (see Figure 8.10) isn't displayed. The form closes.

Date-Stamp a Changed Record

You can create a macro that saves the current date when you edit a record. Include a DateModified field with a Date/Time data type in each data table to keep track of the last edit date. It isn't necessary to place a control the data entry form: you can use a macro to set the value of a field whether or not the form has a control bound to the field. Use the syntax:

Forms!formname!fieldname

to refer directly to a field in the underlying table or query. If you do place a DateModified control on a data entry form, set its Enabled property to No and its Locked property to Yes, set the TabStop property to No, and set the visual cues to indicate the control can't be changed. In the College database, a DateModified control has been placed on each of the data entry forms: frmCourses, frmStudents, frmInstructors, frmClasses, and frmPrograms. In these forms the DateModified control and its label have light gray backgrounds and dark gray font colors, and both controls "float" on the form with clear borders.

You can create a macro that uses the built-in Now( ) function to set the value of the DateModified control to the current date and time. Run the macro when Access acknowledges that the record has been changed, but before the changes are updated to the table (that is, when the form recognizes the `BeforeUpdate` event). Modify the Form_BeforeUpdate macro you created in the last section.

1. Click in mcrGallery, then click in the row following the last row of the Form_BeforeUpdate macro.

2. Select the `SetValue` action, and set its arguments as follows:

    `Item`   DateModified

    `Expression`   Now( )

3. Save the macro.

4. Switch to Form view, then make a change in a control and click the form's Save button. The DateModified control displays the current date and time.

Saving a New Record

When you save a new record on a data entry form that has a lookup combo box, Access doesn't automatically run the query that provides the records for the combo box list.

1. Click the New button, and add the following new course:

CourseID	30	**Prefix**	CINE
Number	325	**Course Title**	Masters of Suspense
Credit Type	Acad Credit	**Units**	1

2. Click the form's Save button. The record is saved.

3. Click the arrow of the combo box. Observe that the new record does not appear in the list.

Requery the Combo Box Interactively

When you work interactively, you requery the combo box by choosing Records ➤ Refresh or by pressing the F9 key.

1. Click in the form and press F9.

2. Click the arrow of the combo box. The new course appears in the combo box list.

Design a Macro to Requery the Combo Box

You can create a macro that requeries the combo box using the Requery action, and run the macro just after the new record is saved (that is, when the form recognizes the AfterInsert event).

1. Select the Window menu and choose mcrGallery:Macro; click in a new macro row and name the new macro Form_AfterInsert

2. Click in the next row, select the Requery action, and set the Control Name argument to cboFind

3. Save the macro.

Attach and Test the Macro

1. Click in frmCourses and switch to Design view.

2. Click in the AfterInsert property and select the macro mcrGallery.Form _AfterInsert.

3. Save the form and switch to Form view.

4. Click the form's New button and enter the new course:

CourseID	31	**Prefix**	CINE
Number	355	**Title**	Screenwriting
Credit Type	Acad Cred	**Units**	3

5. Click the form's Save button.

6. Click the arrow of the combo box. The new course appears in the list.

Place the Data Entry Command Buttons in the Controls Gallery

In the previous sections of this chapter you created a set of three buttons (cmdNew, cmdUndo, and cmdSave) and associated macros to carry out the data entry operations that all of the data entry forms in the College database need. You'll copy the three buttons to the control gallery, zsfrmGallery, and provide instructions on how to use them.

1. Switch to Design view, then select the New, Undo, and Save buttons and copy the button set to the clipboard.

2. Click in zsfrmGallery; in the toolbar, select the Page Break tool, then click in the form and on the 2.5" mark on the vertical ruler.

3. Paste the contents of the clipboard, then drag the three buttons to the 4.5" mark on the vertical ruler.

4. In the toolbar, select the Label tool; create a label above the buttons, 2.5" tall and 3.5" wide, and enter the instructions:

> To implement data entry operations for a form:
>
> 1. Copy the three buttons to the header or footer of the form.
>
> 2. Change the name of the control bound to the primary key of the underlying table or query to PrimaryID. (You can hide this control, but it must

be on the form because the Form_BeforeUpdate macro refer to it.)

3. Make sure the corresponding macros for the buttons (cmdNew_Click, cmdUndo_Click, and cmdSave_Click) and the Form_BeforeUpdate and Form_AfterInsert macros are in the mcrGallery macro group and that the macro group is stored in the database.

4. Set the form's BeforeUpdate property to mcrGallery.Form_BeforeUpdate. If the data entry table doesn't have a field named DateModified, delete the last row of the Form_BeforeUpdate macro that date-stamps the record.

5. Set the form's AfterInsert property to mcrGallery.Form_AfterInsert.

5. Select the Rectangle tool and draw a rectangle that encloses the label and the three buttons.

6. Save the form. Figure 8.11 shows the second page of the control gallery. Press PAGE UP or PAGE DOWN to view the pages of the control gallery.

FIGURE 8.11:

Storing the data entry command buttons in the control gallery.

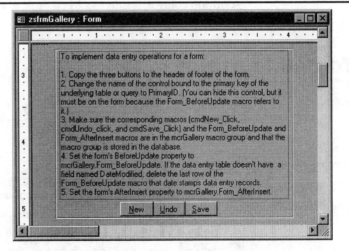

Prevent Tabbing Out of a Record

When you tab through a form in Form view, the insertion point moves from one control to another according to the tab order that you specified, or the default tab order if you didn't specify one. When you tab out of the last control in the tab order, Access automatically tries to save the current record and then move to the next record. As the application designer you can decide whether you want to be able to tab out of a record or whether you want the last tab to place the insertion point back into the first control in the tab order. You can prevent tabbing out by setting the form's Cycle property to Current Record.

1. Click in frmCourses and switch to Design view.

2. Click in the Cycle property and set its value to Current Record.

3. Save the form and switch to Form view.

4. Tab through the controls. Notice that when the focus moves out of the Description control, it moves directly to the PrimaryID control.

To Delete or Not to Delete?

When working interactively, you can delete a record by choosing Edit ➤ Delete Record or by selecting the record and pressing DELETE. In designing the application you can decide whether you want to allow record deletions from a particular table.

WARNING   Once you delete a record the information is gone. As you design your application, think carefully about whether or not to permit deletions. In many cases the database must provide a complete audit trail for all entries, so you don't permit any record deletions.

Not to Delete

In the College database, tblCourses contains course information about each course the college has approved. After a course is approved, the faculty in the program can schedule classes for the course. The tblCourses table exists as a record of all courses that have been approved. The approval status may change or the course may become obsolete, but the record of the course as an approved course must remain. To prevent deletions you can use the form's AllowDeletions property. When you set the AllowDeletions property to No, the Edit ➤ Delete Record command is grayed out; if you select the record and press delete, the system beeps and the record is not deleted. Each of the data tables in the College database includes data required for the college's complete historical records, so record deletions shouldn't be permitted in any of the data entry forms.

To Delete

If you want to allow record deletion, you can automate the interactive process by creating a macro with the DoMenuItem action to issue the Edit ➤ Delete Record command, and run the macro when you click a command button.

Create a Command Button and Macro

For the sake of this example, we'll allow records to be deleted from tblCourses by changing the AllowDeletions property back to Yes.

1. Switch to Design view and set the AllowDeletions property to Yes.

2. Select the Command Button tool, and draw a button 0.5" wide and 0.2" tall in the form header.

3. Set the Name property to cmdDelete and the Caption to &Delete

4. Open the mfrmCourses macrosheet, then click in a new row and enter the macro cmdDelete_Click.

5. Click in the next row , select the DoMenuItem action and set the arguments as follows:

Menu Bar	Form
Menu Name	Edit
Command	Delete Record

6. Save the macro.

7. Click in frmCourses, click in the OnClick property and choose mfrmCourses.cmdDelete_Click.

8. Save the form.

9. Switch to Form view and click the Delete button. Access displays the default error message shown in Figure 8.12.

10. Click OK. Access displays the Action Failed dialog box.

Access recognizes that tblCourses has related records in other tables. The database schema in Chapter 1 indicates that tblClourses is the 'one' table in a one-to-many relationship with the tblClasses table. Some sleuthing in the Relationships window reveals that the Cascade Delete Related Records option is not selected; this means Access permits you to delete a record from the 'one' table only if there are no related records. In this example, if there are no classes scheduled for a course, you can delete the course, but if there are any classes scheduled for the course, you cannot delete it. The default error message indicates that there is at least one class scheduled.

FIGURE 8.12:
Default error message displayed when you try to delete a record that has related records in another table and the Cascade Delete Related Records option is not checked.

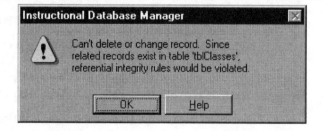

Handling the Macro Error When There Are Related Records

You can avoid macro failure by testing to determine if there are related records. You can use the DCount( ) function to count the number of related records in the related table. The syntax is:

DCount("*","tblRelated","fieldname=Forms!formname!controlname") where tblRelated is the name of the related table, fieldname is the name of the matching field in the related table, and controlname is the name of the control on the open form that displays the value you want to match. In this example, you use the DCount( ) function to create the test condition:

DCount("*","tblClasses","CourseID=Screen.ActiveForm.PrimaryID")=0

If the condition is true, there are no related records in tblClasses and the macro deletes the course. If the condition is false, there are related classes in tblClasses, the macro displays a message and terminates. Note that using the DCount( ) function to test for related records requires that you refer explicitly to a specific field and a specific table by name; this explicit reference prevents the macro from being reusable.

1. Click in mfrmCourses, then click in the first row of the cmdDelete macro and enter the macro shown in Table 8.7.

2. Save the macro.

TABLE 8.7: The macro to delete a record when the Cascade Delete Related Records option is not selected. If there are no related records in a related table, the macro issues the command to delete the record.

Macro Name	Condition	Action	Action Arguments
cmdDelete_Click			
	DCount("*","tblClasses","CourseID=Screen.ActiveForm.PrimaryID")=0	DoMenuItem	**Menu Bar**: Form
			Menu Name: Edit
			Command: Delete Record
	...	StopMacro	
		MsgBox	**Message**: You can't delete this record because records in another table depend on it.

Attach and Test the Macro

1. Click in frmCourses and switch to Design view.

2. Select the cmdDelete button and set its OnClick property to mfrmCourses.cmdDelete_Click.

3. Switch to Form view and click the Delete button. Your custom message is displayed and the macro error is avoided.

4. Using the lookup combo box, select the course CINE 325 Masters of Suspense, and click the Delete button on the form. Access displays the delete confirmation box.

5. Click No.

Modify the Macro to Suppress the Confirmation Box and Screen Updates

You can choose to suppress the default confirmation box by starting the macro with the SetWarnings action. You can also include the Echo action to suppress screen updates while the macro runs.

1. Click in the macrosheet and insert two rows just after the row containing the macro name cmdDelete_Click.

2. In the first inserted row, select the Echo action and set the Echo On argument to No.

3. In the second inserted row, select the SetWarnings action.

4. Save the macro.

5. Click in frmCourses and click the Delete button on the form. The record is deleted without the confirmation box.

Other Ways to Delete a Record

The technique you've created automates the deletion operation by using a command button. If you try to delete a record by choosing Edit ➤ Delete Record or by selecting the record and pressing DELETE (and the record has related records in another table), Access displays the default error message in Figure 8.12. In Chapter 15, "Controlling the User Interface," you learn how to create custom menus and how to disable the DELETE key so that the alternate ways to delete a record are not available. Nevertheless, when these alternatives are available, you can still avoid the default message by creating a macro that tests for related records. If there are related records, the macro displays a custom message and cancels the deletion; otherwise, the macro terminates and the deletion proceeds. Run the macro when Access recognizes that a delete has been initiated, but before deleting the record (that is, when the form recognizes the Delete event).

1. Click in mfrmCourses, then click in a new row and name the new macro Form_Delete

2. Enter the macro shown in Table 8.8.

3. Save the macro.

TABLE 8.8: The macro to test for records in a related table before deleting a record.

Macro Name	Condition	Action	Action Arguments
Form_Delete			
	DCount("*","tblClasses","CourseID= Screen.ActiveForm.PrimaryID")=0	**StopMacro**	
		MsgBox	**Message**: You can't delete this record since records in another table depend on it.
		CancelEvent	

Attach and Test the Macro

1. Click in frmCourses and switch to Design view.

2. Click in the OnDelete property and choose mfrmCourses.Form_Delete.

3. Save the form and switch to Form view.

4. Choose the Edit ➤ Delete Record command. Access displays the delete confirmation dialog. This time you'll leave the confirmation dialog to make sure the user wants to delete the record.

A drawback to this design is that when you click the Delete button to trigger the cmdDelete_Click macro, the form recognizes the `Delete` event and the Form_Delete macro runs, too—this means that the custom message box is displayed twice when there are related records. Controlling the interface with custom menus and a disabled DELETE key eliminates the need for the Form_Delete macro, so we won't try to polish the design.

Cascading a Delete

Sometimes you want to allow a record that has related records to be deleted. If you elect the Cascade Delete Related Records option, then when you try to delete the record, Access displays the message shown in Figure 8.13.

You can replace this message with a custom message that indicates the number of related records that will be deleted if the operation continues and asks for confirmation. You can use the DCount( ) function to count the number of related records. You could display the record count using the `MsgBox` action, but the `MsgBox` action has a single OK button and doesn't allow you to make a choice. Instead, you can use the built-in MsgBox( )function to create a dialog.

The MsgBox( ) function displays a set of buttons and returns a value that indicates which button you selected. You can use the simplified syntax:

MsgBox(message, buttons, title)

where the first argument is a string expression for the prompt you want to display; the third argument (optional) is a string expression for the title of the dialog box;

FIGURE 8.13:
The default message displayed when you try to delete a record that has related records and Cascade Delete Related Records is checked.

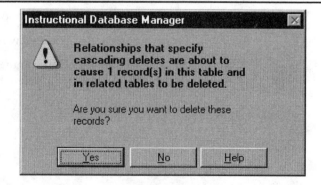

and the second argument is a numeric expression that you can use to specify the number of buttons, which button is the default, the type of icon displayed, and the mode of the dialog box window. Each of these options has an integer code. The buttons argument is the sum of the integers corresponding to the options you select. For example, to display Yes and No buttons with Yes as the default and the information message icon, the buttons argument is 4+64 or, using the built-in constants, vbYesNo+vbInformation. If you click the Yes button, the function has the value 6 and if you choose the No button the function has the value 7. (Search MsgBox( ) function in online Help for more information.)

Using the Message Box Function to Collect User Input

The **MsgBox** macro action is a way to display a warning or an informational message. The action results in a dialog box that displays the custom text, title, and icon you have chosen. The dialog box has a single OK button that you must press to continue.

The **MsgBox( )** function is a built-in function that displays a dialog box containing a custom message and title and a set of buttons that you can choose. You can display any of the following sets of buttons:

Button Sets	Button Sets	Button Sets	Button Set Type	Constant
OK			0	vbOKOnly
OK	Cancel		1	vbOKCancel
Abort	Retry	Ignore	2	vbAbortRetryIgnore
Yes	No	Cancel	3	vbYesNoCancel
Yes	No		4	vbYesNo
Retry	Cancel		5	vbRetryCancel

(continued)

You indicate the button set type by specifying the Button Set Type number or the built-in constant. The **MsgBox( )** function returns a value depending on which button the user selects, as follows:

MsgBox( ) Function Value	Constant	Button Chosen
1	vbOK	OK
2	vbCancel	Cancel
3	vbAbort	Abort
4	vbRetry	Retry
5	vbIgnore	Ignore
6	vbYes	Yes
7	vbNo	No

The MsgBox() function has five arguments. The first three arguments are:

- **Prompt**—this is the string expression you want displayed as a message in the dialog box.

- **Buttons**—this is a numerical expression that allows you to customize the design of the dialog box by specifying four numerical codes as follows: the type and number of buttons you want to display (including one or more of the following: OK, Cancel, Yes, No, Abort, and Retry) by specifying the **Button Set Type** number; the icon you want to display, if any (by specifying an **Icon Type** number); which button is to be the default button if you display more than one (by specifying a **Default Type** number); and the mode of the message box (by specifying a **Modal Type** number). The Buttons argument is the sum of the four codes which can be expressed using numbers or built-in constants:

Buttons = Button Set Type + Icon Type + Default Type + Modal Type

(continued)

The Buttons argument is optional: if you omit this argument, an OK button is displayed and there is no icon.

- **Title**—this is the string expression you want displayed in the title bar of the dialog box. This argument is optional; if you omit this argument, the default title Microsoft Access is displayed.

The fourth and fifth arguments allow you to identify context sensitive help for the message box.

For reference, the Icon Type settings and their built-in constants are

Icon Displayed	Icon Type	Constant
Critical Message	16	vbCritical
Warning Query	32	vbQuestion
Warning Message	48	vbExclamation
Information	64	vbInformation

The Default Type settings and their built-in constants are

Default Button	Default Type	Constant
First button	0	vbDefaultButton1
Second button	256	vbDefaultButton2
Third button	512	vbDefaultButton3

and the Modal Type settings and built-in constants are

Mode	Modal Type	Constant
Respond before continuing work in Microsoft Access	0	vbApplicationModal
Respond before continuing in any application	4096	vbSystemModal

In the College database, a class is cancelled if the enrollment is too low. If you don't need a record of which students were registered and which instructors were appointed to teach the class, you can elect the Cascade Delete Related Records option for the relationships between tblClasses and the linking tables tlnkClassStudent and tlnkClassInstructor. In this example, you create a message box for each relationship displaying the number of related records in the related table. You can create a message for the MsgBox( ) function by concatenating the DCount( ) function with text expressions. For example, you can count the records in tlnkClassStudent for the current class and create the following message:

> "There are " & DCount("*","tlnkClassStudent","ScheduleNo=Screen.Active-Form.ScheduleNo")& "students registered in this class. If you delete the class, registration information will be deleted also. Do you wish to delete the class?"

Similarly, you can count the records in tlnkClassInstructor for the current class and create the message:

> "There are " & DCount("*","tlnkClassInstructor","ScheduleNo=Screen.ActiveForm.ScheduleNo")& "instructors appointed to teach this class. If you delete the class, appointment information will be deleted also. Do you wish to delete the class?"

Using the MsgBox( ) Function as a Condition in a Macro

When you include the MsgBox( ) function in the Condition cell of a macro, Access displays the dialog box and waits until you choose a button. When you choose a button, the function returns the corresponding value; Access evaluates the condition and then continues to execute the macro. In this example, the condition

> MsgBox("There are " & DCount("*","tlnkClassStudent",
> "ScheduleNo=Screen.ActiveForm.ScheduleNo")& "students registered in this class. If you delete the class, registration information will be deleted also. Do you wish to delete the class?",4+64)=6

is True if you choose the Yes button and False if you choose the No button.

You can create a new macro that allows the deletion of records that have related records. The macro uses the MsgBox( ) function to display the numbers of records in related tables that would be deleted and to provide the choice to continue or cancel the deletion. You place a command button (cmdDeleteCascade) to run the macro (cmdDeleteCascade_Click). If you click the Yes buttons for both message boxes, the macro deletes the current record and the related records in the linking tables; otherwise, the macro terminates without deleting records. Figure 8.14 shows the flow diagram for the macro.

FIGURE 8.14:

Macro flow diagram for the command button to determine the number of related records in related tables and allow the choice to delete.

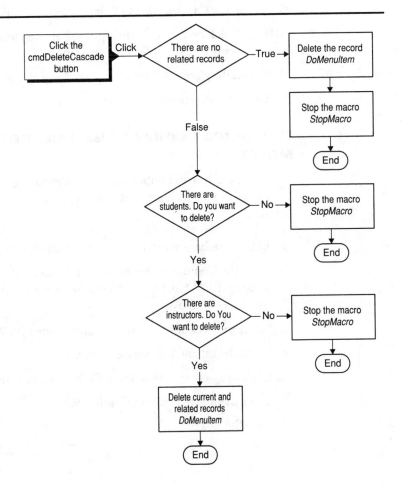

Select the Cascade Option for the Relationships

For carrying out this example, you'll elect the Cascade Delete Related Records option for the relationships between tblClasses and the two linking tables.

1. Choose Tools ➤ Relationships. The Relationships window is displayed.
2. Right-click the relationship line between tblClasses and tlnkClassStudent, and select Edit Relationship.
3. Check the Cascade Delete Related Records check box and click OK.
4. Right-click on the relationship line between tblClasses and tlnkClass-Instructor and select Edit Relationship.
5. Check the Cascade Delete Related Records check box and click OK.
6. Close the Relationships window.

Create the Command Button and Its Macro

You create a command button and its macro to determine how many related records exist, and provide a choice to delete the record and the related records or cancel the deletion.

1. In the Database window, select frmClasses and click the Design button.
2. Click the Command Button tool and place a button in the form header, 0.5" wide and 0.2" tall. Set the Name property to cmdDeleteCascade and the Caption to &Delete All
3. Select the ScheduleNo text box and change the Name property to PrimaryID
4. Open the mfrmClasses macro group.
5. Click in a new row and name the new macro cmdDeleteCascade_Click
6. Enter the macro shown in Table 8.9.
7. Save the macro.

TABLE 8.9: The macro to delete a record when the Cascade Delete Related Records option is selected. The macro displays message boxes with the numbers of records in related tables, and offers a choice to delete the record and all related records or stop without deleting.

Macro Name	Condition	Action	Action Arguments
cmdDelete-Cascade_Click	DCount("*","tlnkClassStudent","ScheduleNo= Screen.ActiveForm.PrimaryID") = 0 and DCount("*","tlnkClassInstructor","ScheduleNo =Screen.ActiveForm.PrimaryID") = 0	**DoMenuItem**	
			Menu Bar: Form
			Menu Name: Edit
			Command: Delete Record
	...	StopMacro	
	MsgBox("There are "& DCount("*","tlnkClassStudent","ScheduleNo =Screen.ActiveForm.PrimaryID")& " students registered. Do you want to delete all?",4+64)=7	**StopMacro**	
	MsgBox("There are "& DCount("*","tlnkClassInstructor","ScheduleNo =Screen.ActiveForm.PrimaryID")& " instructors appointed. Do you want to delete all?",4+64)=7	**StopMacro**	
		DoMenuItem	
			Menu Bar: Form
			Menu Name: Edit
	.		**Command**: Delete Record

Create the Form_Delete Macro

If your interface allows you to initiate a record deletion by choosing the Edit ➤ Delete Record command or by pressing DELETE, you need a second macro, Form_Delete, that runs whenever the deletion is initiated. This macro displays the same message boxes. If you click the Yes buttons for both message boxes, the macro allows the deletion to proceed. Figure 8.15 shows the macro flow diagram for the macro.

FIGURE 8.15:

Macro flow diagram to determine the number of related records in related tables and allow the choice to delete.

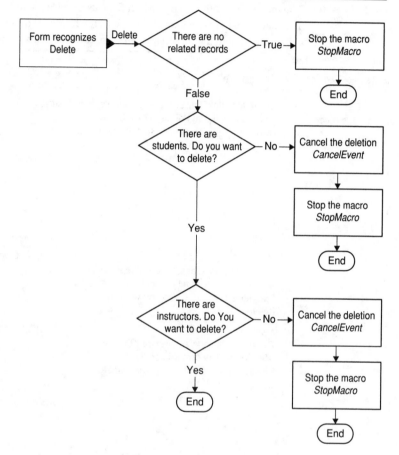

1. Click in a new row and name the new macro Form_Delete

2. Enter the macro shown in Table 8.10.

3. Save the macro.

Attach and Test the Macros

1. Click in frmClasses and switch to Design view.

2. Select the cmdDeleteCascade button, then click in the OnClick property and choose mfrmClasses.cmdDeleteCascade_Click.

TABLE 8.10: The macro to allow or prevent deletion of a record and its related records when the Cascade Delete Related Records option is selected. The macro displays the numbers of records in related tables that would be deleted, and provides the choice to continue or

Macro Name	Condition	Action	Action Arguments
Form_Delete			
	DCount("*","tlnkClassStudent","ScheduleNo= Screen.ActiveForm.PrimaryID") = 0 and DCount("*","tlnkClassInstructor","ScheduleN o=Screen.ActiveForm.PrimaryID") = 0	StopMacro	
	MsgBox("There are "& DCount("*","tlnkClassStudent","ScheduleNo =Screen.ActiveForm.PrimaryID")& " students registered. Do you want to delete all?",68)=7	CancelEvent	
	...	StopMacro	
	MsgBox("There are "& DCount("*","tlnkClassInstructor","ScheduleNo =Screen.ActiveForm.PrimaryID")& " instructors appointed. Do you want to delete all?",68)=7	CancelEvent	
	...	StopMacro	

3. Select the form, then click in the OnDelete property and choose mfrmClasses.Form_Delete.

4. Save the form and switch to Form view.

5. Click the Delete All button. The first message, indicating the number of students registered, is displayed.

6. Click the Yes button. The second message, indicating the number of instructors appointed, is displayed. If you click the Yes button, the class and the corresponding records in tlnkClassStudent and tlnkClassInstructor are removed from the tables and placed in the deletion buffer; if you also click Yes in the default delete confirmation dialog, the records are actually deleted. If you click the No button the deletion is cancelled.

7. Click the No button.

8. Choose Edit ➤ Delete Record. The first message box is displayed.

9. Click Yes. The second message box is displayed.

10. Click Yes. The default confirmation dialog is displayed.

11. Click Yes to delete the class and the related records.

A drawback to this design is that when you click the Delete button to trigger the cmdDeleteCascade_Click macro, the form recognizes the Delete event and the Form_Delete macro runs, too—this means that the message boxes are displayed twice. Controlling the interface with custom menus and a disabled DELETE key (see Chapter 15, "Controlling the User Interface") eliminates the need for the Form_Delete macro, so we won't try to polish the design.

NOTE The macros you created to automate record deletion use the DCount( ) function to count records in related tables. Because the arguments of the DCount( ) function refer to specific fields in specific tables, these macros must be modified for each data entry form. Therefore, you won't store the controls and macros in the galleries.

Automating Another Data Entry Form

You can automate another data entry form with the controls and macros you've created in this chapter. You can copy the data entry controls from the controls gallery, paste them into other data entry forms, make the changes required, and then assign the various macros to the appropriate form and control events. As an example, you'll provide the frmStudents form with the capabilities you've learned about in this chapter.

Add a Check for Uniqueness of the Primary Key

Copy the macro that checks for uniqueness of the primary key to the frmCourses form, and modify the condition for frmStudents.

1. In the Database window, select mfrmCourses and click the Design button.

2. Select the rows of the macro PrimaryID_BeforeUpdate, copy, and close the macrosheet.

3. In the Database window, select the mfrmStudents macro group and click the Design button.

4. Click in a new row and paste the copied rows.

5. Click in the Condition cell containing DCount() and change the expression to:

   DCount("*","tblStudents","StudentID=Screen.ActiveForm
   .PrimaryID")>0

6. Change the action to MsgBox and enter the Message argument:

   There is another record with this ID value. You must enter a unique ID value or undo.

7. Delete the next two rows that have the SetValue action. You are displaying a message and not opening another form, so these actions are not needed.

8. Save the macro.

9. In the Database window, select frmStudents and click the Design button.

10. Select the PrimaryID control, then click in the BeforeUpdate property and select mfrmStudents.PrimaryID_BeforeUpdate.

11. Save the form.

Adding the Data Entry Operations

You add the data entry operations to frmStudents.

1. Click in the form's AllowDeletions property and set the property to No. This prevents any record deletions. The college wants a permanent record of anyone who has ever enrolled in a class.

2. Click in the form's Cycle property and set the property to Current Record. This prevents tabbing out of the record.

3. Click in the form's BeforeUpdate property and select mcrGallery.Form_BeforeUpdate. This macro tests the primary key value for null and date-stamps the record.

4. Click in the form's AfterInsert property and select mcrGallery.Form_AfterInsert. This macro requeries the lookup combo box after you add a new record.

5. Click in the form's OnError property and insert these two lines of code before the `Else` statement:

```
ElseIf DataErr = 2169 Then
    Response = acDataErrContinue
```

This code suppresses the default error message (see Figure 8.10) that is displayed if you click the Return button when the current record violates one of the record validation rules.

6. Click in zsfrmGallery, then select the New, Undo, and Save buttons and copy the selection to the clipboard.

7. Click in the header of frmStudents, then paste the copied buttons and realign the controls as shown in Figure 8.16.

8. Save the form.

9. Test the data entry buttons.

10. Close the form.

The frmStudents data entry form can now check for uniqueness of the primary key, display a new record, test the primary key value for null, undo and save changes to the current record, date-stamp the changes, prevent deletions of records, and close the form.

Modify the Macro That Opens frmStudents from frmRegistration

When you open frmStudents from the switchboard, it functions as a data entry form so all of the data entry controls should be visible; however, when you open frmStudents from the Class Registration form by clicking the Review button on that form, its purpose is to review or edit the displayed record. You'll hide the New button by modifying the macro attached to the Review button on frmRegistration.

1. In the Database window, select mfrmRegistration and click the Design button.

FIGURE 8.16:
The frmStudents form with data entry controls.

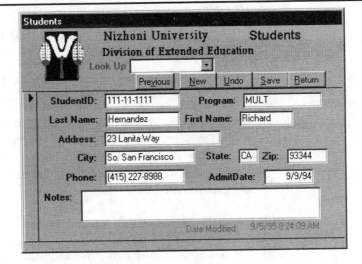

2. Click in the row following the last row of the cmdReview_Click macro, then choose the `SetValue` action and set the arguments as follows:

   `Item`   Forms!frmStudents!cmdNew.Visible

   `Expression`   No

3. Save and close the macrosheet.

4. In the switchboard, click the Register in Classes option button and then click the Review button. The Students form opens with the New button hidden.

5. Click the Return button to close frmStudents.

6. Click the Return button to close frmRegistration.

Endnotes

This chapter has shown you how to provide a data entry form with the following capabilities:

- Test the primary key control for uniqueness of the entered value. (Use a macro similar to those in Table 8.1 or 8.2.)

- Date-stamp a record if any changes have been made.

- Use custom buttons to display a new record, undo changes, and save the record. (The macros for these operations are shown in Tables 8.3, 8.4, 8.5, and 8.6.)

- Suppress the display of a default message if you click the Return button and the changes to the current record don't satisfy the validation rules.

- If you decide to permit deletions, use a custom button to delete a record subject to the referential integrity rules you've set for the relationship. (Tables 8.7 and 8.8 show macros to automate deletion when the Cascade Delete Related Records option is not selected, and Tables 8.9 and 8.10 show the corresponding macros when the option is selected.)

In creating these macros you learned how to:

- avoid macro failure by creating and testing conditions before trying to execute an action.

- use the MsgBox( ) function in a macro condition to create a two-way dialog with the user.

- use the DCount( ) function to count records and use this information to make decisions in a macro.

On Your Own

In the exercises, you add data entry capabilities to another data entry form and explore using the Command Button Wizard to create buttons for the several of the data entry operations. Also, you learn a technique for automatically filling a new record with data from the previous record.

Adding to the Application

1. Add data entry capabilities to frmInstructors.

   a. Using what you learned in the section "Automating Another Data Entry Form," add data entry capabilities to frmInstructors.

Extending the Concepts

1. Fill a new record with data from the previous record automatically.

When you are creating new records and the new records have fields with the same values as the previous record, you can speed data entry by having the fields in the new record filled in automatically. In this exercise you use a technique based on queries and macros for entering data into tblClasses: you enter the new record into a temporary table; when you save the new record, a macro appends the record to the data table and updates the record in the temporary table to set to null those fields that you don't want filled in automatically.

a. In the Database window, copy tblClasses and paste it (structure only) as tblClassesTemp. Remove the primary key index for the ScheduleNo field.

b. Using AutoForm, create a new data entry form based on tblClassesTemp and save as frmClassesTemp

c. Place a command button in the header of frmClassesTemp; set the Name property to cmdNew and the Caption property to &New

d. Create a new query based on tblClassesTemp; use the asterisk method to select all the fields and drag to the first Field cell of the query. Change it to an append query, and enter tblClasses as the name of the table to append the data to. Save the query as qappClassesTemp

e. Create a second query based on tblClassesTemp. Drag ScheduleNo to the design grid; change it to an update query, and enter Null in the Update To cell. Save the query as qupdClassesTemp

f. Create a new macro group mfrmClassesTemp and create the macro shown in Table 8.11. The macro tests to determine if the data table already has a record with the same primary key as the record displayed in frmClassesTemp.

g. Attach the macro to the Click event of cmdNew.

h. To test the technique, enter data for a new record and click the New button. If the value of ScheduleNo is new, the record is saved to tblClasses, and frmClassesTemp displays a new record with all fields (except ScheduleNo) filled in with values from the previous record.

TABLE 8.11: The macro to automatically fill a new record with data from a previous record.

Macro Name	Condition	Action	Action Arguments
cmdNew_Click			
	DCount("*","tblClasses","ScheduleNo= Forms!frmClassesTemp!ScheduleNo")	MsgBox	**Message**: There is already a class with thie schedule no. You won't be able to add this record.
	...	StopMacro	
		SetWarnings	**Warnings On**: No
		DoMenuItem	**Menu Bar**: Form
			Menu Name: Records
			Command: Save Record
		OpenQuery	**Query Name**: qappClassesTemp
		OpenQuery	**Query Name**: qupdClassesTemp

2. Use the Command Button Wizard to create New, Undo, and Save buttons.

    a. With the Control Wizards tool selected, place a set of three data entry buttons in the footer of frmCourses; give them Name properties of cmdNewVB, cmdUndoVB, and cmdSaveVB. In the first dialog of the Command Button Wizard, select the Record Operations category and then select Add New Record, Undo Record, and Save Record, respectively. In the next dialog, select an appropriate picture for each button.

    b. Switch to Form view to test the buttons.

    c. Click the New button and then click the New button again. Note that the default message (stating that the command is not available) is not displayed, so you don't have to modify the event procedure.

    d. Click the Save button. There is no response.

    e. Click the Undo button. The default message is displayed. You can suppress the default error message by modifying the event procedure.

f. Switch to Design view, and click the Build button for the OnClick property of the Undo button. Scroll down to the default error-handling code that the wizard has built into the event procedure:

```
Err_cmdUndoVB_Click:
MsgBox Err.Description
Resume Exit_cmdUndoVB_Click
```

When a run-time error occurs in the event procedure, Visual Basic jumps to this section of the procedure, runs the `MsgBox` function to display the default error message, and runs the `Resume` statement to return to the event procedure code at the line with the label Exit_cmdUndoVB_Click:. Visual Basic jumps back to this label and runs the `Exit Sub` statement to exit the procedure. You can delete the `MsgBox Err.Description` statement to suppress the default message.

g. Modify the code by deleting the `MsgBox` function and test the Undo button.

CHAPTER

NINE

Advanced Techniques for Data Entry

- Hiding and unhiding controls

- Entering data in two open forms

- Refreshing versus requerying

- Macro loops

In this chapter we look at several complex design issues for data entry forms, including:

- Controlling how you can work with a form by hiding and unhiding the logical navigation and data entry controls to provide different capabilities.

- The problems that arise when two data entry forms are open at the same time. With two data entry forms open, you need to make sure that both forms display the most current information. Also, you need to control the interaction between the forms to preserve the order of data entry required for referential integrity.

- A technique to allow a single form to function as both a review-only form and a data entry form. The technique gives a single form both sets of capabilities by dynamically changing control properties to hide and show command buttons, lock and unlock data controls, and change visual cues.

NOTE When you begin this chapter, only the switchboard and the Database window should be displayed. Close any other objects. This chapter assumes you have worked through Chapters 5, 7, and 8, and have made the changes to the switchboard, frmRegistration, and frmStudents.

Operations for Review-Data Entry Forms

In the College database, you use the frmRegistration form/subform to register students in classes (frmRegistration is the data entry form for the linking table tlnkClassStudent). The main form displays student information in controls that are locked and disabled to protect the data from inadvertent changes. The subform contains a single data control for the schedule number of the class in which you are registering the student. After you select the class from the combo list, the subform displays class information in locked, disabled controls.

Adding Logical Navigation

When a student wants to register, you need to find the student's registration record quickly. You add the logical navigation capability you developed in Chapter 7, "Navigating to Controls and Records," to the registration form.

1. In the switchboard, click the Register in Class option button and switch to Design view.

2. Select the StudentID control and change the Name property to **PrimaryID**. The reusability of the logical navigation technique depends on the primary key control having the name PrimaryID.

3. Click in zsfrmGallery, select the logical navigation controls on the first page of the form, and copy the set of controls to the clipboard.

4. Click in the form header, paste the controls, and realign as shown in Figure 9.1.

5. Select the cboFind combo box and set the following properties:

RowSource	qlkpStudentName
ColumnWidths	1; 0.5
BoundColumn	2
ListWidth	2

6. Select the form and set the NavigationButtons property to No.

7. Save the form.

FIGURE 9.1:

Adding logical navigation to frmRegistration.

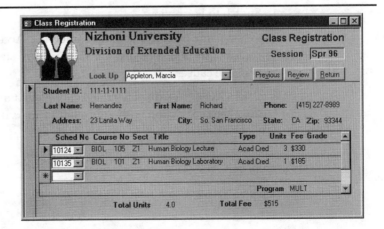

Adding a Visual Basic Error Handler

Add a Visual Basic error handler to display a custom message if you enter a value that is not in the combo list and an error with error code 2237 is generated (refer to Table 4.1).

1. Click in the OnError property, then click the Build button; select Code Builder and click OK.

2. Between the lines of the code template, enter the following code:

```
If DataErr = 2237 Then
    MsgBox "The student you entered isn't in the list of
➥students. Review the list to select a student or press
➥ESC to undo your entry and click the New button to
➥add a new student."
    Response = acDataErrContinue
Else
    Response = acDataErrDisplay
End If
```

3. Choose Run ➤ Compile Loaded Modules, and then close the module.

4. Save the form and switch to Form view.

Test the Lookup Combo Box

Test the logical navigation controls by trying to look up a student using the combo box.

1. Switch to Form view.

2. Pick a name from the Lookup combo list. Access displays the default error message shown in Figure 9.2. The message states the problem and suggests possible causes.

3. Click OK. Access displays the Action Failed dialog box indicating that the GoToControl action with argument PrimaryID can't be executed.

FIGURE 9.2:

The default error message when the `GoToControl` action fails.

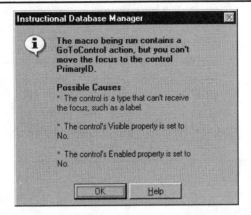

Handling a Failed Macro

When a macro action fails, you click the HALT button, return to the macro window, and try to resolve the problem. In this case, the default error message in Figure 9.2 and the Action Failed dialog box indicate that the problem is with the PrimaryID control.

1. Click the HALT button.
2. Switch to Design view and click the PrimaryID text box. Observe that the control's Enabled property is No and its Locked property is No.

When a control is disabled it can't have the focus, so a `GoToControl` action to move the focus to the control fails. The solution is to change the macro so that it enables the PrimaryID control before moving the focus to the control, and then after finding the record the macro returns the control to its disabled state.

Modify the Macro to Enable and Disable the Control

Both of the macros for logical navigation, cboFind_AfterUpdate and cmdPrevious, move the focus to the PrimaryID control and require the same modification if they are to work when the control is disabled. Because we want the logical navigation controls to be reusable, we design the modification so that the new macros are still reusable. One solution is to modify these macros so that they test whether the PrimaryID control is enabled. If the control is enabled, each macro continues as originally designed; otherwise, the macro executes a modified set of macro actions that enable the PrimaryID control, then find the record, and finally disable the control. To modify the search technique, you create a new macro named Find that includes all of the actions of the cboFind_AfterUpdate macro (refer to Table 7.4) and run Find as a called macro in the modified cboFind_AfterUpdate macro. Figure 9.3 shows the flow diagram for the modified search technique.

FIGURE 9.3:

Modifying the cboFind_After-Update macro to run whether or not the PrimaryID control can have the focus.

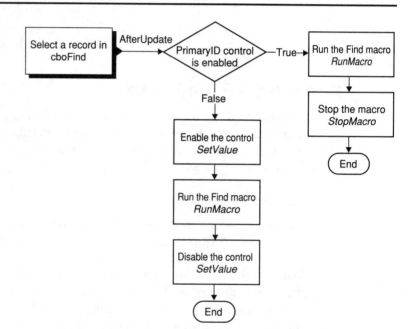

To modify the technique for undoing the search, you create a new macro named Previous that includes all of the actions of the cmdPrevious_Click macro (refer to Table 7.4 in Chapter 7) and run Previous as a called macro in the modified cmdPrevious_Click macro. Figure 9.4 shows the flow diagram for the modified technique to undo the search.

FIGURE 9.4:

Modifying the cmdPrevious_Click macro to run whether or not the PrimaryID control can have the focus.

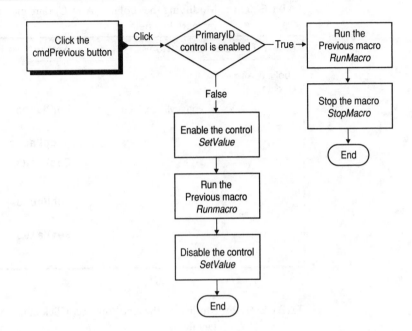

Modify the Macros

1. Click in mcrGallery, click in the Macro Name cell for the cboFind_AfterUpdate macro, and change the name to **Find**. You'll run the Find macro as a called macro.

2. Click in a new row and name the new macro **cboFind_AfterUpdate**

3. Enter the macro shown in Table 9.1.

4. Click in the Macro name cell for the cmdPrevious_Click macro and change the name to **Previous**

5. Click in a new row, name the new macro **cmdPrevious_Click**, and then enter the macro shown in Table 9.2.

6. Save the macro group.

TABLE 9.1: Modifying the cboFind_AfterUpdate macro to handle a disabled primary key field.

Macro Name	Condition	Action	Action Arguments
cboFind_After-Update			
	PrimaryID.Enabled = Yes	RunMacro	Macro Name: mcrGallery.Find
	...	StopMacro	
		SetValue	Item: PrimaryID.Enabled
			Expression: Yes
		RunMacro	Macro Name: mcrGallery.Find
		SetValue	Item: PrimaryID.Enabled
			Expression: No

TABLE 9.2: Modifying the cmdPrevious_Click macro to handle a disabled primary key field.

Macro Name	Condition	Action	Action Arguments
cmdPrevious_Click			
	PrimaryID.Enabled = Yes	RunMacro	Macro Name: mcrGallery.Previous
	...	StopMacro	
		SetValue	Item: PrimaryID.Enabled
			Expression: Yes
		RunMacro	Macro Name: mcrGallery.Previous
		SetValue	Item: PrimaryID.Enabled
			Expression: No

Test the Modified Macros

1. Click in frmRegistration and pick a name from the lookup combo box. The macro execution is successful.

2. Select another name, then click the Previous button. The record for the previous student is displayed.

Edit an Existing Student Record

While registering a student, you may need to edit information in the student's record; if the student is new, you may need to add a new record. In either case, you need to open the second form, frmStudents.

- Click the Review button. The student's data entry form appears (see Figure 9.5).

FIGURE 9.5:

The Students form displays only command buttons to undo, save, and close the form when you open it from the Class Registration form. The logical navigation controls and the command button to display a new record are hidden.

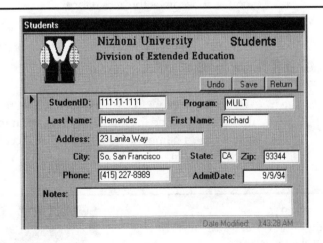

In Chapter 7, "Navigating to Controls and Records," you added logical navigation controls to this form, but you also modified the macro for the Review button on the Class Registration form to hide these controls when frmStudents is opened while registering a student in classes. In Chapter 8, "Data Entry Operations," you added standard data entry capabilities to this form, and you modified the Review button on the Class Registration form to hide the New button when you open frmStudents while registering a student. When you open frmStudents directly from the switchboard, the form's full capabilities are displayed.

Observing the Automatic Update of Edited Data

Edit the student record.

1. Change the spelling of the first name and click the Return button. Notice that the changed spelling is displayed automatically in frmRegistration.

2. Locate the same student again in the combo box. Notice that the changed spelling is also displayed in the combo box list.

When you edit data, Access automatically updates the data in the active window. This is called *refreshing* the displayed records. In this example, when you change data using frmStudents, Access updates the data displayed in frmRegistration as soon as it becomes the active form.

Add a New Student

When a student wants to register, you use the lookup combo box and either select the name from the list, or start typing the name. But a new student isn't in the list; if you type a name that isn't in the list, Access displays the custom error message (see Figure 9.6).

FIGURE 9.6:
The custom message displayed with the Visual Basic error handler.

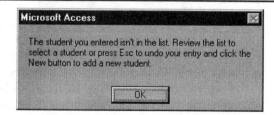

Display a New Data Entry Record

You'll create a macro to open frmStudents displaying a new blank record. When you are entering a new student you need only editing capabilities and you don't need either the New button or the logical navigation controls; therefore, you can create the macro by copying the macro for the Review button and then modifying the copied macro to open frmStudents in data entry mode.

1. Switch to Design view for frmRegistration.

2. With the Control Wizards tool deselected, select the Command Button tool; click in the form header (between the combo box and the Review button), and create a button 0.5" wide and 0.2" tall; set the Name property to **cmdNew** and the Caption property to **&New**

3. Click in mfrmRegistration, select all rows of the cmdReview_Click macro, and copy to the clipboard.

4. Select a new row and paste the copied rows.

5. Change the name of the pasted macro to **cmdNew_Click**

6. Select the **OpenForm** action and set the **Data Mode** argument to Add. With the **Data Mode** set to Add, you can add new records but you can't edit existing records.

7. Save the macro.

Attach and Test the Macro

1. Click in frmRegistration, then click the New button; click in the OnClick property, and select mfrmRegistration.cmdNew_Click.

2. Save the form and switch to Form view.

3. Click the New button. Access opens a new record in frmStudents.

4. Enter a new student:

StudentID	132112222	**City**	San Francisco
Last Name	Dondick	**State**	CA
First Name	Lisa	**Zip**	94135
Address	123 Noriega St.		

5. Click the Return button. The new record is saved.

6. Click the arrow on the lookup combo box. The new student does not appear in the pick list.

Refresh Does Not Display New Records

When you edit an existing record, Access automatically refreshes (updates), but refresh does not display *new* records. In order to display new records, you must requery the controls and the form. When working interactively, you requery a control by pressing F9 and you requery the form by pressing SHIFT+F9; separate actions are needed because Access can requery only one object at a time.

Requery the Combo Box and the Form Interactively

You'll go through the requery process interactively and then create a macro to automate it.

1. With the insertion point in the combo box, press F9.

2. Click the arrow of the combo box. The new student appears in the combo list.

3. Select the new student. The new student's record is not displayed.

4. Press SHIFT+F9 and select the new student again using the combo box. The new student's record is displayed.

Creating a Macro to Requery a Form and Its Controls

You create a macro that requeries frmRegistration and its cboFind combo box just after the new record is saved (that is, when the frmStudents form recognizes the **AfterInsert** event). If you display the property sheet for frmStudents, you can see that the form's **AfterInsert** event is already triggering the mcrGallery.Form_AfterInsert macro, which requeries the lookup combo box on frmStudents as part of the logical navigation technique added in Chapter 7. Since an event can trigger only one macro, you replace this macro with a new macro that includes the actions of the original macro as well as the new actions. The new macro, mfrmStudents.Form_AfterInsert, is triggered by an event on one form (frmStudents) but takes action on another form (frmRegistration).

Because you can only requery an active object, the macro must activate the frmRegistration form before it can execute the requeries. But before you can activate a form, it must be open. During the registration process, frmRegistration is open; however, if you've opened frmStudents directly from the switchboard to enter or edit student information, frmRegistration isn't open. You can determine if frmRegistration is open by using the IsLoaded( ) function. If frmRegistration is not open, the macro terminates; otherwise, the macro selects frmRegistration and executes the requeries. Figure 9.7 shows the macro flow diagram.

1. In the Database window, select mfrmStudents and click the Design button.

2. Click in a new row and name the new macro **Form_AfterInsert**

3. Enter the macro shown in Table 9.3. The macro requeries the cboFind combo box on frmStudents, and then takes action on frmRegistration. Leave the **Control Name** argument blank in the third **Requery** action; when no control is specified, Access requeries the active object.

4. Save the macro.

FIGURE 9.7:

The macro flow diagram for Form_AfterInsert. The macro determines if another form is open before taking action on it.

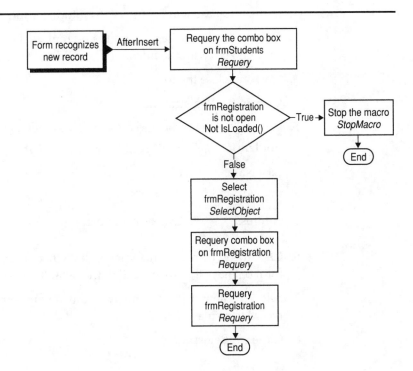

357

TABLE 9.3: A macro to select another form and requery the form and its control.

Macro Name	Condition	Action	Action Arguments
Form_AfterInsert			
		Requery	Control Name: cboFind
	Not IsLoaded("frm-Registration")	StopMacro	
		SelectObject	Object Type: Form
			Object Name: frmRegistration
		Requery	Control Name: cboFind
		Requery	

Attach and Test the Macro

1. In the Database window, select frmStudents and click the Design button.

2. Click in the AfterInsert property and replace the mcrGallery.Form_After-Insert macro with the mfrmStudents.Form_AfterInsert macro.

3. Save and close the form.

4. Click in frmRegistration.

5. Click the New button and enter a new student:

StudentID	130112222	**City**	Half Moon Bay
Last Name	Moll	**State**	CA
First Name	Leo	**Zip**	94075
Address	13 Seadrift Drive		

6. Click the Return button. Observe that when frmRegistration is requeried, the form displays the first record in the default sort order.

7. Select the new student name from the lookup combo box. The new student's record is displayed.

8. Close frmRegistration.

Giving Multiple Capabilities to a Form

Sometimes you want to use the same form for both review and data entry. In order to protect the data from casual changes, you can provide a single form with two modes and change the control properties to provide the look and feel appropriate to each mode.

You'll set the properties so that the form opens in review mode. In review mode:

- the New, Undo, and Save command buttons are hidden

- the data entry controls are locked to prevent changes

- the background color of the data entry control matches the form's background (to provide the visual cue that the controls can't be changed)

- an Edit button is displayed in the form header

In review mode, the logical navigation controls let you find and review records. Figure 9.8 shows frmCourses in review mode.

When you click the Edit button, the form switches to edit mode. In edit mode:

- the New, Undo, and Save command buttons are unhidden

- the logical navigation controls and the Edit button are hidden

FIGURE 9.8:

The frmCourses form in review mode. The form displays logical navigation controls and an Edit button to switch to edit mode.

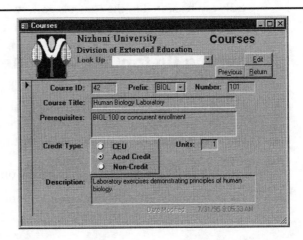

- the data entry controls are unlocked

- the background color of the data entry controls is changed to white (to provide the visual cue that the controls can be changed)

In edit mode you can edit the displayed record or add a new record. Figure 9.9 shows frmCourses in edit mode. When you click the Save button, the form changes back to review mode.

FIGURE 9.9:

The frmCourses form in edit mode. The form displays the command buttons for editing.

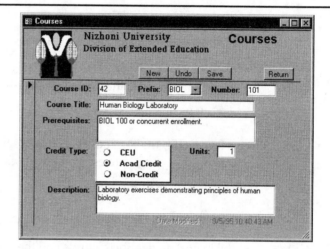

You can create the necessary controls and macros in reusable form so that the controls can be stored in the controls gallery and used in other forms. As an example, you'll provide the frmCourses form with dual mode capability.

Setting Up frmCourses in Review Mode

First, you'll remove the Delete button (placed in Chapter 8 to demonstrate automating the deletion operation), and change the form's AllowDeletions property to No. Then, you'll set control properties so that the form opens in review mode.

1. In the Database window, select frmCourses and click the Design button.

2. Select and delete the cmdDelete command button, and then set the form's AllowDeletions property to No.

3. Save the form and switch to Form view. This form has controls for both logical navigation and data entry: you can look up a specific course, add a new course, undo changes to a record, save the record, review related program information, and close the form. The data entry controls have the standard data entry look: sunken with a white background.

4. Switch to Design view, then choose the Command Button tool; click in the form header and place a button (0.5" wide and 0.2" tall) above the Return button; set the Name property to **cmdEdit** and the Caption property to **&Edit**

5. Select the data controls in the Detail section, including all text boxes, the combo box, and the option group; set their Locked properties to Yes.

6. Click in the BackColor property, then click the property's Build button and set the color to light gray.

7. Select the New, Undo, and Save command buttons in the header and set their Visible properties to No.

8. Save the form and switch to Form view. The form is now in review mode (see Figure 9.8).

Create a Macro to Hide and Unhide Controls

You'll create a macro for the Edit button that unhides the Add, Undo, and Save buttons and hides the logical navigation controls and the Edit button itself.

1. In the Database window, select mcrGallery and click the Design button.

2. Click in a new row and name the new macro **cmdEdit_Click**

3. Enter the macro shown in Table 9.4. The macro moves the focus to the PrimaryID control before hiding the Edit button because you can't hide a control that has the focus.

4. Save the macro.

Attach and Test the Macro

1. Click in frmCourses and switch to Design view.

TABLE 9.4: The cmdEdit_Click macro hides and unhides controls.

Macro Name	Action	Action Arguments
cmdEdit_Click		
	SetValue	**Item**: cmdSave.Visible
		Expression: Yes
	SetValue	**Item**: cmdNew.Visible
		Expression: Yes
	SetValue	**Item**: cmdUndo.Visible
		Expression: Yes
	GoToControl	**Control Name**: PrimaryID
	SetValue	**Item**: cmdPrevious.Visible
		Expression: No
	SetValue	**Item**: cmdEdit.Visible
		Expression: No

2. Select the Edit button, then click in the Click property and choose mcrGallery.cmdEdit_Click. The form has the command buttons appropriate to edit mode, but the data entry controls are still locked.

Creating a Loop Macro to Toggle the Data Control Properties

You could create macro actions to set the BackColor and Locked properties for each of the specific data entry control on the form. For example, for the Fee control you could create two macro actions with arguments as follows:

Action	Action Arguments	Comment
SetValue	**Item**: Fee.BackColor	Set the BackColor of Fee to white
	Expression: 16777215	
SetValue	**Item**: Fee.Locked	Unlock the Fee control
	Expression: No	

You would need a similar pair of actions for each of the data controls on the form. For frmClasses there are nine data entry controls, so a total of eighteen macro actions would be required! That is a lot of work but the task would be accomplished... for this form only. The real problem with this approach is that the macro would not be reusable. Other data entry forms have controls with different names and differing numbers of data controls. To be reusable, the technique must not depend on the specific names of the data controls nor require that you know beforehand how many controls there are. Instead, you create a reusable macro that selects the first data control, then changes the control's properties by referring to it using Screen.ActiveControl instead of by name:

Action	Action Arguments	Comment
SetValue	Item: Screen.ActiveControl.BackColor	Set the BackColor of the active control to white
	Expression: 16777215	
SetValue	Item: Screen.ActiveControl.Locked	Unlock the active control
	Expression: No	

After setting properties, the macro tabs to the next control (which then becomes the active control). The macro repeats these actions for the second control (that is, changes its properties and tabs to the next control). You want the macro to repeat these actions until all of the data controls have been changed. You can repeat actions by using the RunMacro action.

Macro Loops

The RunMacro action provides two ways to repeat actions:

- by running another macro for a specified number of times (a *counted loop*)

- by running another macro until a given condition becomes true or false (a *tested loop*)

The **RunMacro** action has three arguments:

- **Macro Name** is the name of the macro you want to run (the *called macro*).

- **Repeat Count** is the number of times you want the macro to run.

- **Repeat Expression** is an expression that evaluates to True or False. The called macro continues to repeat until the expression is False.

Using either of the **Repeat** arguments to run a macro repeatedly is an example of a *loop structure*. A loop structure requires two macros: one macro (the *calling macro*) to call for the loop and another macro (the *called macro*) containing the actions you want to repeat. We'll look at a simple example of each kind of loop.

Create a Simple Loop to Run a Specific Number of Times

As an example of a counted loop, you create a macro that calls another macro four times using the **Repeat Count** argument. The called macro displays a message box.

1. Open a new blank form in Design view.

2. Save the form as **frmLoop** and set the Caption property to **Loop Examples**

3. Select the Command Button tool, click in the form and create a button 1" wide and 0.2" tall; set the Name property to **cmdLoopCount** and set the Caption property to **Loop&Count**

4. Open a new macrosheet and save it as **mfrmLoop**

5. Click in the Macro Name cell of the first row and name the macro **cmdLoopCount_Click**. This is the calling macro.

6. Click in the next row, select the **RunMacro** action, and set the arguments as follows:

Macro Name	mfrmLoop.LoopCount
Repeat Count	4

7. Click in a new row and create a new macro with name **LoopCount**. This is the called macro.

8. Click in the next row, select the **MsgBox** action, and set the **Message** argument to the expression **= "Loop"**. The **Message** argument can be a set of characters (for example, Loop), or an expression preceded by an equal sign (for example, ="Loop").

9. Save the macro.

Attach the Macro and Run the Loop

1. Click in the form, then select the command button; select the OnClick property, and select mfrmLoop.cmdLoopCount_Click.

2. Switch to Form view.

3. Click the button. A message box with the message Loop is displayed (see Figure 9.10).

FIGURE 9.10:

The message displayed by the called macro.

4. Click OK. The message box is displayed again. Each time you click OK, the message box is displayed again until it has been displayed four times.

When you enter a number in the **Repeat Count** argument, Access automatically sets up an *implicit counter* to keep track of the number of passes through the loop, and stops execution after completing the specified number of passes. You can represent these macros with the macro flow diagram shown in Figure 9.11.

In the flow diagram, the operation box for the **RunMacro** action contains a dotted condition diamond to represent the testing of the implicit counter. Unless you keep track of how many message boxes have been displayed, you can't tell which pass Access is executing. You can have Access tell you which pass it is executing by defining an *explicit counter* and displaying the value of the counter as each pass is executed. Set the counter to 1 in the calling macro before the **RunMacro** action, and

FIGURE 9.11:

The macro flow diagram for a loop to display a message four times. When you specify a number in the **Repeat Count** argument, Access sets up an implicit counter to keep track of the loops.

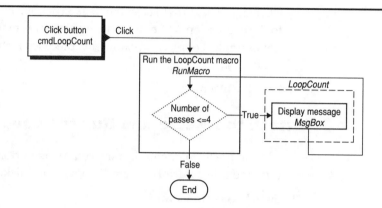

modify the message to display the value of the counter. At the end of each pass you increase the counter by 1 before returning to the calling macro. Hold the value of the counter in an unbound text box on the form. You can use either loop structure to specify that the macro is to run 4 times: by using a counted loop (with the **Repeat Count** argument set to 4), or by using a tested loop with the **Repeat Expression** argument set to the expression

Counter <= 4

The result is the same: the macro runs for 4 circuits and displays identical sets of message boxes. Figure 9.12 shows the flow diagram for the tested loop.

FIGURE 9.12:

The macro flow diagram for a tested loop. The macro uses an explicit counter to keep track of the loops.

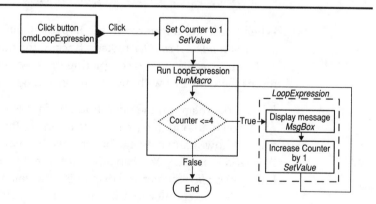

Creating a Tested Loop with a Counter

Create a text box to hold the value of the counter, and a macro that uses the counter to keep track of how many times the loop is run.

1. Click in the form and switch to Design view.

2. Copy and paste the command button to create a duplicate command button.

3. Select the new button, change the Name property to **cmdLoopExpression**, the Caption property to **Loop&Expression**, and the OnClick property to mfrmLoop.cmdLoopExpression_Click.

4. Select the Text Box tool, then click in the form and place an unbound text box above the new command button; set the Name property to **Counter**, and set the Enabled property to No.

5. Select and delete the text box label.

6. Click in the macro sheet, then click in a new row and name the new macro **cmdLoopExpression_Click**. This is the calling macro.

7. Enter the macros shown in Table 9.5. LoopExpression is the called macro for the tested loop. The **SetValue** action in the LoopExpression macro increases the counter by 1 at the end of each circuit.

8. Save the macro.

Run the Loop

1. Click in the form and switch to Form view.

2. Click the button. A message box displaying Counter = 1 is displayed and the value in the text box control is 1 (see Figure 9.13).

FIGURE 9.13:
The message displayed by the tested loop with a counter.

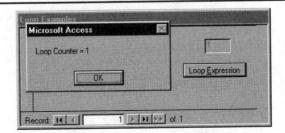

TABLE 9.5: Macros for a Tested Loop with a Counter.

Macro Name	Action	Action Arguments
cmdLoopExpression_Click		
	SetValue	**Item**: Counter
		Expression: 1
	RunMacro	**Macro Name**: mfrmLoop.LoopExpression
		Repeat Expression: Counter ≤ 4
LoopExpression		
	MsgBox	**Message**: ="Loop Counter ="&[Counter]
	SetValue	**Item**: Counter
		Expression: Counter + 1

When you click OK, the called macro increments the counter; the first circuit is now finished. Access returns to the calling macro, evaluates the **Repeat Expression** argument with the current value of the counter (Counter = 2), determines that the expression Counter ≤ 4 is true, and executes the next circuit. After two more repetitions, the message box displays the message Loop Counter = 4; when you click OK, the called macro increments the counter to 5; the fourth circuit is now finished. Access returns to the calling macro, evaluates the **Repeat Expression** with the current value of the counter, determines that the expression Counter ≤ 4 is false, and terminates the calling macro.

1. Click OK four times. The value in the Counter text box is 5 and the loop terminates because the **Repeat Expression** is false.

2. Close frmLoop and mfrmLoop.

In this example you used an explicit counter in the **RepeatExpression** argument to control the loop; however, the expression that you use for the argument can be based on a value in a control, a property of a control, or the value returned from a function.

Design the Macro to Loop through the Data Controls

We'll design a loop macro to loop through the data controls on any data entry form. By the term *data control*, I mean a control in the Detail section that you can tab into. You can determine how many data controls there are using the TabIndex property. When you create controls on a form, Access assigns a tab order to each control that you can tab into. The TabIndex property of a control indicates the control's place in the tab order; the TabIndex starts with 0 for the first control and takes consecutive integer values for the subsequent controls. A new control is placed last in the tab order. As you add or remove controls, or change the tab order, Access automatically reassigns the TabIndex so that the value of the TabIndex always indicates a control's place in the tab order. Since the TabIndex starts with 0, the value of the TabIndex of the last data control in the tab order is one less than the total number of data controls. To determine the total number of data controls for any form, you can place an unbound text box, named LastTab, in the Detail section to mark the end of the data controls. The number of data controls equals the TabIndex of this text box (because the LastTab text box is the last control placed, it is last in the tab order).

When you tab through the controls in the Detail section, eventually you tab into the last data control. Your next tab moves the focus to the LastTab text box and you are finished. You create a loop macro that duplicates tabbing through the data controls. With the focus in a control, the macro tests the condition

Screen.ActiveControl.TabIndex < LastTab.TabIndex

If this condition is true, the active control is a data control and the loop repeats; if this condition is false, the active control must be the LastTab text box and the loop doesn't run again.

You can create a macro named Unlock that sets the BackColor property of the active control to white, and the Locked property of the active control to No, then tabs to the next control. The cmdEdit_Click macro moves the focus to the first data control in the Detail section, hides and unhides the navigation controls and command buttons in the header section (to display edit mode), and then calls Unlock. After Unlock runs, Access returns to cmdEdit_Click and tests the **Repeat Expression** condition. If the condition is true, Access runs Unlock; otherwise, Access runs the next action in cmdEdit_Click and moves the focus back to the first data control. Figure 9.14 shows the macro loop.

FIGURE 9.14:

The flow diagram for the loop macro. The Unlock macro unlocks a data control and tabs to the next control. The calling macro runs Unlock as long as the focus has been moved to a data control.

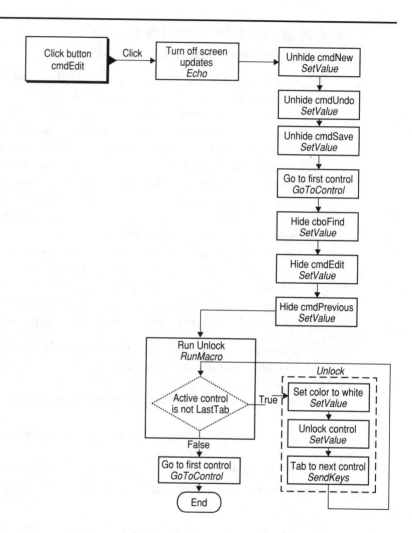

Implementing the Loop Macro Design

Place the unbound LastTab text box on the form to mark the end of the data controls.

1. Click in frmCourses and switch to Design view.

2. Select the Text Box tool and place an unbound text box in the Detail section.

3. Select and delete the text box label.

4. Select the text box and set the Name property to **LastTab**. The text box shouldn't appear in Form view, so you need to hide it. Since you can't tab into a control that has its Visible property set to No, you hide this text box either by hiding it under another control (by placing it on top of the Description control and choosing Format ➤ Send to Back) or by making it transparent.

5. Set the BackStyle and the BorderStyle properties to Transparent.

Create the Macros

Create the macros to unlock the data controls.

1. Click in mcrGallery, then click in the row following the last row of the macro cmdEdit_Click; choose the **RunMacro** action, and set the arguments as follows:

Macro Name	mcrGallery.Unlock
Repeat Expression	Screen.ActiveControl.TabIndex <LastTab.TabIndex

2. Click in the next row, then select the **GoToControl** action and set the **Control Name** argument to **PrimaryID**

3. Click in a new row and name the new macro **Unlock**

4. Enter the macro shown in Table 9.6.

5. Save the macro.

Test the Loop Macro

Test the macro that switches the form to edit mode.

1. Switch to Form view and click the Edit button. When execution stops, the data controls are unlocked and have a white background color, and the insertion point is in the primary key control. You can avoid seeing the individual loops and allow the loops to execute faster by using the **Echo** action to turn off screen updating while the macro runs.

2. Click in mcrGallery and insert a new first row in macro cmdEdit_Click.

3. Select the **Echo** action and set the **Echo On** argument to No.

4. Save the macro.

TABLE 9.6: The macro that changes the form to edit mode and calls the UnLock macro to unlock the controls.

Macro Name	Action	Action Arguments
Unlock		
	SetValue	
		Item:Screen.ActiveControl.BackColor
		Expression:16777215
	SetValue	
		Item:Screen.ActiveControl.Locked
		Expression:No
	SendKeys	
		Keystrokes:{tab}
		Wait:yes

5. Click in frmCourses, switch to Design view and then switch back to Form view. This resets the form to review mode.

6. Click the Edit button. The form changes to edit mode.

The modified cmdEdit_Click macro is shown in Table 9.7.

Designing the Return to Review Mode

After you edit the record or add a new record, the form presents two choices: you can click the Return button to close the form, or you can click the Save button to save the record. You can replace the Save button with a new command button named cmdSaveEdit and create a new macro for the button that not only saves the record but also returns the form to review mode.

Create a Button to Save the Record and Switch to Review Mode

Create a button to save the changes and switch back to review mode.

TABLE 9.7: The Unlock macro unlocks a control, changes its back color and then tabs to the next control.

Macro Name	Action	Action Arguments
cmdEdit_Click		
	Echo	**Echo On**: No
	SetValue	**Item**: cmdNew.Visible
		Expression: Yes
	SetValue	**Item**: cmdUndo.Visible
		Expression: Yes
	SetValue	**Item**: cmdSave.Visible
		Expression: Yes
	GoToControl	**Control Name**: PrimaryID
	SetValue	**Item**: cboFind.Visible
		Expression: No
	SetValue	**Item**: cmdPrevious.Visible
		Expression: No
	SetValue	**Item**: cmdEdit.Visible
		Expression: No
	RunMacro	**Macro Name**: mcrGallery.Unlock
		Repeat Expression: Screen.ActiveControl.TabIndex<Last-Tab.TabIndex
	GoToControl	**Control Name**: PrimaryID

1. Click in frmCourses, then switch to Design view and select the Save button.

2. Click in the property sheet and change the Name property to **cmdSaveEdit** and the Caption property to **&SaveEdit**

3. Click in the OnClick property and enter **mcrGallery.cmdSaveEdit_Click**

4. Click in mcrGallery; in cmdEdit_Click, click in the row with the **SetValue** action that unhides the Save button, and change its **Item** argument to **cmdSaveEdit.Visible**. You modify the cmdEdit_Click macro so that it unhides the new button.

The cmdSaveEdit_Click macro saves the record, moves the focus to the first data control, hides and unhides the header controls as appropriate to switch the form to review mode, and then loops through the data controls while calling another macro named Lock. The Lock macro locks the active control, sets its back color to light gray and tabs to the next control. Figure 9.15 shows the cmdSaveEdit_Click and Lock macros.

Create the Macros

Create the macros to save the record and switch back to review mode.

1. Click in a new row in mcrGallery and name the new macro **cmdSaveEdit_Click**

FIGURE 9.15:

The flow diagram for the macro to save the record, change the form to review mode, and loop through the data controls to lock them using the Lock macro.

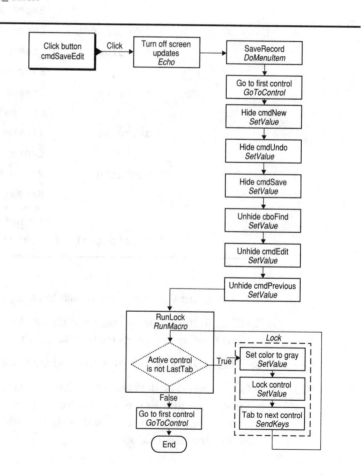

2. Enter the macro shown in Table 9.8.

3. Click in a new row and name the new macro **Lock**

4. Enter the macro shown in Table 9.9.

5. Save the macrosheet.

Test the Macro

1. Click in frmCourses and switch to Form view.

2. Click the Edit button. The form switches to edit mode: data controls become white and are unlocked, the data entry command buttons are displayed, and logical navigation controls are hidden.

3. Click the SaveEdit button. The form switches back to review mode: data controls become light gray and are locked, the data entry command buttons are hidden, and logical navigation controls are displayed.

Placing the Mode-Change Controls in the Controls Gallery

You can place copies of the three mode-change controls in the controls gallery and create an instruction label for the use of the controls.

1. Select the cmdEdit and cmdSaveEdit command buttons and the LastTab text box, and copy to the clipboard.

2. Click in zsfrmGallery, paste the copied controls, and drag the controls down to the 7.25" mark.

3. In the toolbar, select the Page Break tool and place a page break at about 5.5".

4. Move and align the controls.

5. Select the Label tool, then click in the form and create a label 3" wide and 1.5" tall. Enter these instructions:

> **To change the mode of a form between review and data entry**
>
> **1. Copy the cmdEdit and cmdEditSave buttons to the header. The cboFind, lblFind, cmdUndo, cmdNew, and cmdReturn controls must be in the header also.**

TABLE 9.8: The macro that saves the record, changes the form to review mode, and calls the Lock macro to lock the controls.

Macro Name	Action	Action Arguments
cmdSaveEdit_Click		
	Echo	**Echo On**: No
	DoMenuItem	**Menu Bar**: Form
		Menu Name: Records
		Command: Save Record
	GoToControl	**Control Name**: PrimaryID
	SetValue	**Item**: cmdNew.Visible
		Expression: No
	SetValue	**Item**: cmdUndo.Visible
		Expression: No
	SetValue	**Item**: cmdSaveEdit.Visible
		Expression: No
	SetValue	**Item**: cboFind.Visible
		Expression: Yes
	SetValue	**Item**: cmdPrevious.Visible
		Expression: Yes
	SetValue	**Item**: cmdEdit.Visible
		Expression: Yes
	RunMacro	**Macro Name**: mcrGallery.Lock
		Repeat Expression: Screen.ActiveControl.TabIndex< LastTab.TabIndex
	GoToControl	**Control Name**: PrimaryID

2. Copy the LastTab text box to the detail section. (In the tab order, the LastTab text box must follow the last data control in the detail section.)

3. The cmdEdit_Click, cmdSaveEdit_Click, Unlock, and Lock macros must be in mcrGallery.

4. The primary key control must be named PrimaryID.

TABLE 9.9: The Lock macro locks a control, changes its back color and then tabs to the next control.

Macro Name	Action	Action Arguments
Lock		
	`SetValue`	**Item**:Screen.ActiveControl.BackColor
		Expression:12632256
	`SetValue`	**Item**:Screen.ActiveControl.Locked
		Expression:Yes
	`SendKeys`	**Keystrokes**:(tab)
		Wait:Yes

6. Select the Rectangle tool, then draw a rectangle to enclose the instruction label and the three controls (see Figure 9.16).

7. Save the form.

FIGURE 9.16:

Storing the controls to toggle between review and data entry mode in the control gallery.

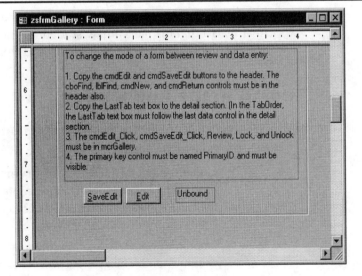

Endnotes

This chapter has shown you how to incorporate several complex design features into data entry forms. You learned to control how the user works with two data entry forms that are open at the same time, by ensuring that:

- each form displays the current data.
- the order of data entry is preserved by locking data controls.
- navigation or data entry capabilities are provided by hiding and unhiding controls.

You learned how to create a macro loop structure for repetitive operations, and then used the technique to loop through the data controls on a form in order to toggle back and forth between review and data entry modes.

On Your Own

In the exercises, you add logical navigation to the Instructor Appointments form and then add a command button to add a new instructor. Also, you design and create a macro that displays a new student in the Class Registration form automatically after you have added the student and closed the Students form.

Adding to the Application

1. Add logical navigation to frmAppointments.

   a. Change the Name property of the InstructorID control to **PrimaryID**.

   b. Create a pick-list query named **qryInstructorName** based on tblInstructors. In the first Field cell, concatenate LName and FName and rename the field **Name**. Drag InstructorID to the second Field cell. Sort in Ascending order on the first field.

   c. Copy the logical navigation controls from zsfrmGallery, and set the cboFind combo box properties.

   d. Add the Visual Basic error handler to the form, and modify the message that Access displays when you enter an instructor who is not in the combo list.

2. Add a new instructor.

   a. To add a new instructor, you first place a command button with caption **&New** and name **cmdNew** on frmAppointments. Next you create a macro that will be triggered by the `Click` event of the button: open mfrmAppointments and create a new macro named **cmdNew_Click** with the single **OpenForm** action, which you will use to open frmInstructors in the Add Data Mode. Attach this macro to the New button.

   b. Test your work by clicking the New button, adding a new instructor, and clicking the Return button. Notice that while the pick list does update to include the new instructor, you can't actually use the pick list to display the corresponding appointment record. You still need to requery frmAppointments itself.

   c. Create a macro to requery the Instructor Appointments (frmAppointments). Open mfrmInstructors and create a new macro Form_AfterInsert. You must first select frmAppointments using the `SelectObject` action, and then use the `Requery` action (first to requery the lookup combo box, and then to requery frmAppointments). Since you want the macro to run only when a new record is added, trigger the macro with the `AfterInsert` event for the frmInstructors form.

Extending the Concepts

1. Display the new student in frmRegistration.

   a. Modify the mfrmStudents.Form_AfterInsert macro so that, when you close frmStudents after adding a new student, the new student's record is displayed in frmRegistration. Do this by adding actions to find the record on frmRegistration with PrimaryID that matches the value of StudentID on frmStudents. Hint: You need to enable the PrimaryID control on frmRegistration, move the focus to the control, run the `FindRecord` action, move the focus to the lookup combo box, and disable the control.

   b. Insert the `Echo` action at the beginning of the macro to suppress screen updating.

CHAPTER

TEN

Working with a Group of Records

- OrderBy and OrderByOn properties

- Filter queries

- Query By Form

- Union queries

- Multi-criteria selection of records

- Synchronizing two combo boxes

In the previous three chapters you've learned techniques for working with a single record, including finding a specific record, automating data entry operations, and designing special purpose forms for data entry and review.

This chapter focuses on working with groups of records. You'll learn how to automate two standard database operations: sorting and selecting groups of records. You'll learn how to sort records by using a macro to set a form's sorting properties. You'll learn how to use a form to collect your selection criteria, pass the values to a filter query (called Query By Form), and then use the filter query to retrieve the specific records. We'll also use the Query By Form technique to improve the performance of the form/subform combination and to synchronize two combo boxes.

> **NOTE**   When you begin this chapter, only the switchboard and the Database window should be displayed. Close any other objects.

Sorting Records

When working interactively, you can easily sort a group of records displayed in a form by the values in a single field. To sort by the values in a single field in ascending or descending order, you click in the control and then click the Sort Ascending or Sort Descending button in the toolbar (or choose Records ➤ Sort ➤ Ascending or Records ➤ Sort ➤ Descending). To remove the sort, you choose Records ➤ Remove Filter/Sort.

Sorting by a Single Field Interactively

As an example, sort the Class Schedule by course title.

1. In the switchboard, click the Review Class Schedule option button. The Sort toolbar buttons and menu command are not available because all of the controls on the form are disabled.

2. Switch to Form view, then select all of the controls in the detail section and set the Enabled property to Yes.

3. Click the title of any course and then click the Sort Ascending button. The records are sorted by course title (in ascending order).

4. Choose the Records ➤ Remove Filter/Sort command. The sort is removed and the records are displayed in their original order.

5. Click the course number of any course. The Sort buttons are disabled because the Course No control is a calculated control.

Automate the Sort Process

You can automate and improve the interactive sort process using the OrderBy property. You can use a form's OrderBy property to sort by a single field, or create a complex sort by several fields with some fields in ascending and others in descending order. The OrderBy property is a string expression that consists of the name of the field or fields you want to sort, arranged in the order of the sort and separated by commas; to sort a field in descending order, you type **DESC** after the name of the field. You can create a macro to set the OrderBy property, and apply the sort by setting the OrderByOn property to True.

Create a Macro to Set the OrderBy Property

As an example, you'll create a macro to sort the Class Schedule records by prefix and then by course title in descending order.

1. Switch to Design view; select all of the controls in the detail section and set their Enabled properties to No, and then switch back to Form view. The controls don't need to be enabled when you use the OrderBy property for the sort.

2. Create a new macrosheet and save as **mfrmClassSchedule**

3. Click in the first Macro Name cell and name the macro **Sort**. We'll use the Debug window to run this macro instead of triggering it with an event.

4. In the next row, select the **SetValue** action and set the arguments as follows:

Item	Forms!frmClassSchedule.OrderBy
Expression	"Prefix, Name DESC"

5. In the next row, select the **SetValue** action and set the arguments as follows:

Item	Forms!frmClassSchedule.OrderByOn
Expression	True

6. Save the macro.

Test the Macro Using the Debug Window

We'll use the Debug window to run the macro.

1. Press CTRL+G. The Debug window opens.

2. Enter the following:

```
DoCmd.RunMacro "mfrmClassSchedule.Sort"
```

3. Press ENTER. The records are displayed, sorted first by prefix in ascending order and then by course name in descending order.

4. Close the Debug window.

Sort by Any Column

When records are displayed in a tabular form, you can automate sorting the records by specific columns by placing a transparent command button over the label of each column you want to sort by, and creating a macro to sort the records by a field in the column. Also, instead of using a transparent button, you can replace the column label with a (non-transparent) command button.

1. Switch to Design view, then select the Command Button tool; in the form header, draw a button the size of the Course Title label, and place the button on top of the Course Title label (so the Course Title label is hidden).

2. Set the Name to **cmdName** and the Transparent property to Yes.

3. Click in the ControlTipText property and type **Click to sort by Course Title**

4. Click in the macrosheet, then click in an empty row and name the new macro **cmdName_Click**

5. Enter the macro shown in Table 10.1.

6. Save the macro.

TABLE 10.1: A macro to sort records by setting the OrderBy and OrderByOn properties.

Macro Name	Action	Action Arguments
cmdName_Click		
	SetValue	**Item**: Screen.ActiveForm.OrderBy
		Expression: "Name"
	SetValue	**Item**: Screen.ActiveForm.OrderByOn
		Expression: True

Attach and Test the Macro

1. Click in the form, then select the button; click in the OnClick property and select mfrmClassSchedule.cmdName_Click.

2. Switch to Form view and click the Course Title label. The records are sorted by Course Title.

Automate the Removal of the Sort

You can automate the removal of the sort by placing a command button in the form header and creating a macro to remove the sort.

1. Switch to Design view, then select the Command Button tool; in the form header, draw a button 1" wide and 0.2" tall.

2. Set the Name property to **cmdUnsort** and the Caption property to **&Unsort**

3. Click in mfrmClassSchedule, then click in a new row and name the new macro **cmdUnsort_Click**

4. Enter the macro shown in Table 10.2.

5. Save the macro.

TABLE 10.2: A macro to remove a sort by setting the OrderByOn property.

Macro Name	Action	Action Arguments
cmdUnsort_Click		
	SetValue	Item: Screen.ActiveForm.OrderByOn
		Expression: False

Attach and Test the Macro

1. Click in frmClassSchedule, then select the Unsort button; click in the OnClick property and select the macro mfrmClassSchedule.cmdUnsort_Click.

2. Switch to Form view.

3. Click the Unsort button. The records are displayed in the original sort order.

Repeat for All Columns on the Form

This is the general procedure for sorting by a column—use it to set up sorting by each column on the form:

1. Place a transparent button over the label.

2. Create a macro to set and apply the sort order.

3. Assign the macro to the OnClick property of the button.

Display an Instruction Label for the Sort Procedure

Since the sort capability is hidden, you can provide an instruction label in the form header.

1. Switch to Design view, then select the Label tool; in the form header, draw a label and enter the expression **Click a heading to sort. Click the Unsort button to undo the sort.**

2. Save the form and switch to Form view (see Figure 10.1).

Finding a Group of Records by Using Query By Form

A basic database operation is selecting a group of records that meet one or more selection criteria. For example, in the College database, the frmClassSchedule form contains class information for all of the classes offered in a session—you may want to display a schedule for the classes in one department; you may want to review all classes offered on the Main Campus, or all classes offered on Tuesdays; or you may want to look at classes in one department that are offered on Tuesdays. When working interactively, you select a specific group of records by creating and applying a filter. Microsoft Access provides several ways to create filters, including Filter By Form and Filter By Selection. This section describes another technique called Query By Form that you can use to provide a simple interface for selecting a group of records.

Selecting a Group of Records Interactively

You'll select the classes for the Cinema department.

1. Choose Records ➤ Filter ➤ Advanced Filter/Sort. The Filter design window opens and displays the field list for the qalkCourseClass query and the field used for the last sort in the design grid.

2. Choose Edit ➤ Clear Grid.

3. From the field list, drag the Prefix field to the first Field cell in the filter grid.

4. Type **cine** into the Criteria cell (see Figure 10.2).

FIGURE 10.2:
Using the Filter design window to create a filter.

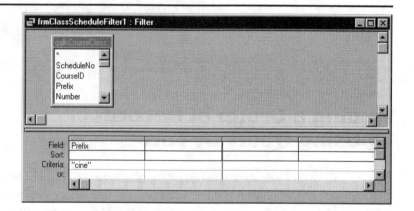

5. Click the Apply Filter button on the toolbar. The filter window closes and the selected records are displayed. Access indicates the number of filtered records in the lower left corner of the form.

Save the Filter as a Query

1. Choose Records ➤ Filter ➤ Advanced Filter/Sort.

2. Choose File ➤ Save As Query, and save as the filter as **qfltCourseClass**

3. Close the filter.

Automate the Selection Process

To automate the selection process, you place a combo box containing the prefix values in the header of the frmClassSchedule form, and then modify the qfltCourse-Class query to use the value selected in the combo box as the criteria for the prefix field. You create a macro that uses the `ApplyFilter` action to run the filter query and display the filtered records, and you run the macro when the value in the combo box is changed (that is, when the combo box recognizes the `AfterUpdate` event).

Place a Selection Combo Box on the Form

The tblPrograms table contains a list of the available course prefixes; the ProgramID is the prefix for the courses in the program.

1. Click in frmClassSchedule.

2. Click the Control Wizards tool to select it, then click the Combo Box tool.

3. In the form header, create an unbound combo box just above the Course Title label. When you release the mouse button, the Combo Box Wizard is summoned.

4. Click the Next button. You want the combo box to look up the values in tblPrograms.

5. Select tblPrograms and click the Next button.

6. Double-click the ProgramID and ProgramName fields, then click the Next button.

7. Clear the Hide Key Column checkbox, double-click the right edge of each column heading, and then click the Next button.

8. Be sure that the "Remember the value for later use" option button is selected, then click the Next button. When you use a combo box to select a group of records, you must be sure that the combo box is *unbound*—you use the combo box control to temporarily hold the selected value of the prefix so that you can use it in selecting records; you are not storing the value in the database.

9. Type **Program** as the label and click the Finish button.

Set the Combo Box Properties

Next, you name the combo box, and set its properties to provide visual cues and to restrict the values in the combo box to those in the list.

1. Select the combo box and set the Name property to **cboPrefix**

2. Select the label, then click the Build button for the ForeColor property and select red, and set the FontWeight property to Bold. These are additional visual cues to emphasize the purpose of the combo box.

3. Click in the LimitToList property and select Yes. This restricts you to selecting values from the list.

4. Switch to Form view and click the arrow on the combo box. When you select a value from the list and release the mouse button, the value is displayed in the combo box, but the corresponding group of records is not selected because you haven't created the macro that sets the criteria in the filter query.

5. Save the form.

Set the Filter Query Criteria

Modify the filter query to use the value selected in the combo box as the criteria for the query's prefix field.

1. In the Database window, select the qfltCourseClass query and click the Design button.

2. Click in the Criteria cell below Prefix. You can modify the expression in the Criteria cell so that the cell gets its value from the combo box on the form. When you design a parameter query to take its criteria values from a form, you are using *Query By Form (QBF)*.

3. Click SHIFT+F2 to open the Zoom box, and enter the full identifier of the combo box (or click the toolbar Build button and use the Expression Builder to construct the expression):

   Forms!frmClassSchedule!cboPrefix

4. Save the query.

Create a Macro to Apply the Filter

You can use the `ApplyFilter` action to restrict or sort the records in a table or in the record source of a form or report. The `ApplyFilter` action has two arguments:

Action Argument	Description
Filter Name	The name of the query (or filter saved as a query) that restricts or sorts the records.
Where Condition	An expression that restricts the records (maximum length is 256 characters).

If you are using a query to restrict the records, you can enter the name of the query as the **Filter Name** argument or you can enter the query's SQL WHERE clause (without the word WHERE) in the **Where Condition** argument (whichever argument you specify for the query, the query's SQL WHERE clause must satisfy the maximum length requirement of 256 characters).

NOTE   If you specify the name of a query whose SQL WHERE clause exceeds 256 characters as the `Filter Name` argument, the `ApplyFilter` action doesn't select the specified records—the entire recordset is displayed instead. The action does not fail and there is no default error message to indicate a problem.

1. Click in mfrmClassSchedule, then click in a new row and name the new macro **cboPrefix_AfterUpdate**

2. Click in the next row, then select the `ApplyFilter` action and set the **Filter Name** argument to **qfltCourseClass**

3. Save the macro.

Attach and Test the Macro

1. Click in frmClassSchedule, then select the combo box; click in the OnClick property and select the cboPrefix_AfterUpdate macro.

2. Open frmClassSchedule in Form view. All records are displayed.

3. Select a prefix from the combo box. The selected records are displayed; Access displays the number of filtered records in the lower left corner of the form (see Figure 10.3).

4. Click the Course Title. The selection is sorted by course title.

5. Click the Unsort button. The selection is returned to its original sort order.

6. Choose Records ➤ Remove Filter/Sort. The filter is removed and all records are displayed.

FIGURE 10.3:

Using a selection combo box to select records. The value selected in the combo box provides criteria for a filter query.

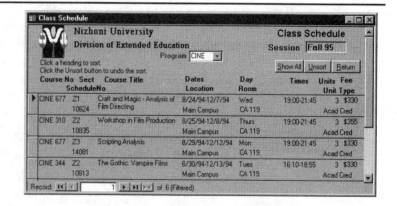

Automate the Removal of the Filter

You can automate the removal of the filter by placing a command button in the form header and creating a macro to remove the filter.

1. Switch to Design view, then select the Command Button tool; in the form header, draw a button 1" wide and 0.2"tall.

2. Set the Name property to **cmdShowAll** and the Caption property to **&Show All**

3. Click in mfrmClassSchedule, then click in a new row and name the new macro **cmdShowAll_Click**

4. Click in the next row and select the **ShowAllRecords** action. The **ShowAll-Records** action removes the sort and requeries the records.

5. Save the macro.

Attach and Test the Macro

1. Click in frmClassSchedule, then select the Show All button; click in the On-Click property, and select the macro mfrmClassSchedule.cmdShowAll_Click.

2. Switch to Form view (see Figure 10.3).

3. Click the Show All button. The filter is removed and all the records are displayed, but the combo box continues to display the value selected.

Set the Combo Box to Null

After you click the Show All button to remove the filter, the combo box should be null to indicate all records are displayed. Modify the macro that removes the filter so that it also sets the combo box to null.

1. Click in mfrmClassSchedule, then click in the row following the last row of the cmdShowAll_Click macro; select the **SetValue** action and set its arguments as follows:

Item	cboPrefix
Expression	Null

2. Save the macro.

3. Click in frmClassSchedule and click the Show All button. The combo box is null and all the records are displayed.

Using Multiple Criteria to Select a Group of Records

Often you want to use more than one selection criteria. For example, you may want to find all classes with a specific prefix that are given at a specified location. You can place a selection combo box in the form header for each field you want to use to select records, modify the filter query to include the additional criteria, create a macro to apply the filter for each new combo box, and finally, modify the macro that removes the filter so that it also sets the combo boxes to null.

Create a Second Selection Combo Box

As an example, you create a second combo box for the location where the class is given.

1. Switch to Design view.

2. With the Control Wizards tool deselected, select the Combo Box tool; in the form header, create a new combo box just below the Prefix combo box.

3. Set the new combo box properties as follows:

Name	cboLocation
RowSourceType	Value List
RowSource	Downtown Center; Main Campus; Off Campus
ColumnWidths	1.5
LimitToList	Yes

4. Select the label and set the Caption property to Location

Modify the Filter Query

Modify the filter query so that it selects classes given at the location selected in the Location combo box.

1. Click in qfltCourseClass, then drag Location to the second Field cell.

2. Click in the Criteria cell and enter the expression **Forms!frmClass-Schedule!cboLocation** (or click the Build button on the toolbar to use the Expression Builder).

3. Save and close the query.

Create and Attach the Macro

Create a macro for the Location combo box by pasting and modifying the macro for the Prefix combo box.

1. Select both rows of the cboPrefix_AfterUpdate macro and copy them, then click in a new row and paste the copied rows.

2. Change the name of the pasted macro **to cboLocation_AfterUpdate**

3. Save the macro.

4. Click in frmClassSchedule, then click in the Location combo box; click in the OnClick property and select mfrmClassSchedule.cboLocation_AfterUpdate

Modify the Macro that Removes the Filter

Modify the macro that removes the filter so that it also sets the Location combo box to null.

1. Click in the row below the last row of the macro cmdShowAll_Click, then select the `SetValue` action and set its arguments as follows:

`Item`	cboLocation
`Expression`	Null

2. Save the macro.

Test the Multi-Criteria Selection Process

1. Click in frmClassSchedule and switch to Form view.

2. Click in the Prefix combo box and select the cinema prefix. No records are displayed.

3. Click in the Location combo box and select the Main Campus. The cinema classes at the Main Campus are displayed.

Modify the Query Criteria to Return Records for All Values of an Empty Combo Box

As currently designed, the filter query requires that you make selections for both combo boxes. If the combo box for a field is null, the query looks for records with a null value in that field; finding no such records, the query displays none. Instead, the query should return records for all values in a field with a null combo box value. You can return all records for a combo box whose value is null by changing the criteria to include a test for null. For example, for the Prefix combo box, use the expression:

> Forms!frmClassSchedule!cboPrefix
> Or Forms!frmClassSchedule!cboPrefix Is Null

If the value in cboPrefix is null, this expression evaluates to True and the query returns records with all values for Prefix.

1. Click in qfltCourseClass.

2. In the Criteria cell for the Prefix field, replace the criteria with the expression

   > Forms!frmClassSchedule!cboPrefix
   > Or Forms!frmClassSchedule!cboPrefix Is Null

3. In the Criteria cell for the Location field, replace the criteria with the expression

   > Forms!frmClassSchedule!cboLocation
   > Or Forms!frmClassSchedule!cboLocation Is Null

4. Save and close the query.

Retest the Multi-Criteria Selection Process

1. Click the Show All button. All records are displayed and all combo boxes are blank.

2. Select Downtown Center from the Location combo box. The records for all of the classes at that location are selected.

3. Select MSFT from the Prefix combo box. Only the records for the MSFT classes at the Downtown Center are selected.

Adding a Null Row to a Selection Combo List

Your multiple criteria selection process works, but there is an additional refinement you can make. After you select a value for one of the combo boxes, you should be able to reset the value of this combo box to null. For example, after you select classes with the prefix MSFT at the Downtown Center, you should be able to view all of the classes at the Downtown Center by simply selecting a null row in the Prefix combo box, or view all the MSFT classes at all locations by selecting a null row in the Location combo box.

Adding a Null Row to the Location Value List

Because the row source for the Location combo box is a value list, you can add a null row directly to the list.

1. Switch to Design view and select the Location combo box.

2. Click in the RowSource property, then place the insertion point at the beginning of the expression and type a semicolon. When you begin the list with a semicolon, the first row in the list is the null row. The expression becomes:

     ;Downtown Center;Main Campus;Off Campus

3. Change the ListRows property to 4.

Adding a Null Row by Using a Union Query

Displaying a null row in a combo box list when the row source is a query is much more difficult. In order to display a null row you have to create a second query consisting of rows with all null values, and then combine the two queries using a special query called a *union query*. An additional complication is that union queries can't be created in the Query design window and are created in SQL view instead.

We'll begin by examining the row source for the combo box list. Each row in the Prefix combo box list contains the ProgramID and ProgramName fields from the tblPrograms table. Because you used the Combo Box Wizard to build the Prefix combo box, the RowSource property is expressed as an SQL statement. Take a look at the SQL statement that the Combo Box Wizard created:

- Select the Prefix combo box, then click in the RowSource property and press SHIFT+F2. The SQL statement is

  SELECT DISTINCTROW tblPrograms.[ProgramID], tblPrograms.[ProgramName] FROM [tblPrograms];

You can learn more about creating SQL statements by searching SQL in the online Help.

Create an Empty List

To add a null row to this list, you create a second list consisting of rows with null values and then combine the two lists into a single list that displays one null row and the rows with the program values. First, create the empty list.

1. Select the entire SQL statement and copy it to the clipboard. You'll need this statement later when you combine the two lists.

2. Modify the expression as shown below to create an SQL statement that displays two null fields in each row. Figure 10.4 shows the query design view that corresponds to this SQL statement.

   SELECT Null AS Program ID, Null AS ProgramName FROM tblPrograms;

FIGURE 10.4:

The Design view for a query that returns null rows.

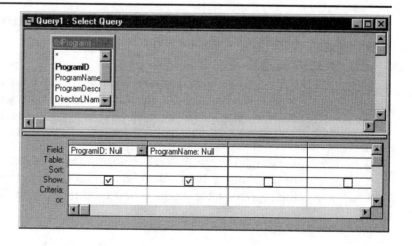

3. Switch to Form view and click the arrow for the Prefix combo box. An empty list is displayed (see Figure 10.5); if you select a row in the empty list, all class prefixes are returned.

FIGURE 10.5:

Using null values to display an empty list.

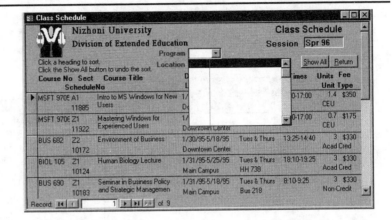

You now have two SQL statements: the first produces a list of the values in the ProgramID and ProgramName fields (this is the SQL statement that you copied to the clipboard), while the second produces a list with null values in these fields. You can combine the two lists using a special query called a union query. You construct a union query by entering the expression for the SQL statement (without the final semicolon) that you want first in the combined list, then the UNION operator, then the expression for the SQL statement that you want second in the combined list. The final statement must end with a semicolon.

Create the Combined List as a Union Query

Create the union query.

1. Switch to Design view, then select the Prefix combo box; click in the RowSource property and press SHIFT+F2. To display the null row first in the list, use the displayed expression as the first SQL statement.

Union Queries

Use a union query when you want to create a single query that contains rows from two select queries. The two select queries must have the same number of fields, and the fields must be in the same order. Corresponding fields don't need to have the same names, but they must have compatible data types.

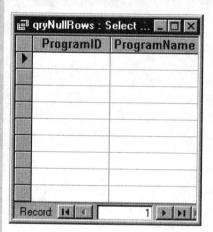

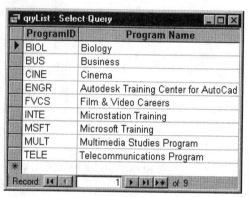

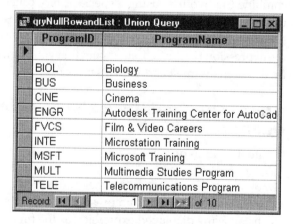

(continued)

You create a union query in SQL view by using the UNION operator to combine the SQL statements for each select query. The operator uses the field names from the first SELECT statement.

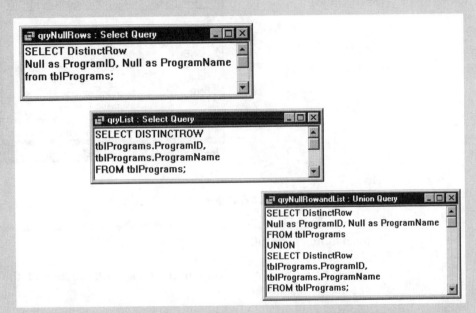

The UNION operator eliminates duplicate rows; use the UNION ALL operator if you want to return duplicate records. If you want to sort the rows, use a single ORDER BY at the end of the last SELECT statement; the field names that you use in the sort must come from the first SELECT statement.

2. Delete the semicolon, then enter the word **UNION** and paste the contents of the clipboard (the SQL statement you copied earlier). The final expression for the RowSource property is:

Select Null As Program ID, Null As ProgramName From tblPrograms
UNION Select tblPrograms.[ProgramID], tblPrograms.[ProgramName]
From [tblPrograms];

The Datasheet view for this union query is shown in Figure 10.6.

3. Switch back to Form view and click the drop-down arrow for the Prefix combo box. The first row is the null row.

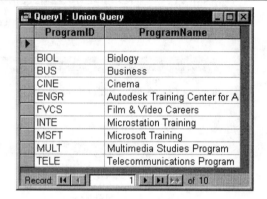

Test the Modification

With each combo box displaying a null row, the multiple criteria selection process is much more powerful.

1. Select a prefix from the Program combo list. All classes with the selected prefix are displayed.

2. Select a location from the Location combo list. Only classes for the selected prefix offered at the selected location are displayed.

3. Select the null row in the Program combo list. All classes for the selected location are displayed.

4. Select the null row in the Location combo list. All classes are displayed.

Using Query By Form to Improve Form/Subform Performance

The Query By Form concept is a general one: whenever the criteria for a query comes from a form, the query is using Query By Form. You can use this concept to improve the performance of a form/subform. When you open a form that contains a subform control, the following sequence occurs:

1. Access opens the form contained in the subform control and loads the records of its underlying table or query.

2. Access opens the main form and loads the first record of its underlying table or query.

3. Access uses the linking properties to filter the records for the form that is contained in the subform control, and displays those records related to the record in the main form.

You can avoid the initial loading of all of the records for the subform if the record source for this form is a query by using Query By Form to set criteria for the linking fields. For each of the fields that is used to link the subform to the main form, set the query criteria to select only records that match the value in the linking field of the current main form record.

Set Query Criteria for the Linking Fields

The Class Registration forms, frmRegistration and frmRegistrationSub, are linked on the StudentID field, and the record source for the subform is the qalkClassStudent query. You can shorten the form's opening time by setting criteria for the StudentID field in the query.

1. In the Switchboard, click the Register in Class option button.

2. Switch to Design view and double-click the subform control.

3. Click in the RecordSource property for frmRegistrationSub, then click the Build button. The underlying query, qalkClassStudent, opens in Design view.

4. In the Criteria cell for StudentID, enter the expression **Forms!frmRegistration!StudentID**

5. Save and close the query.

6. Save and close the subform.

7. Close the main form.

With these changes, the following sequence occurs when you open the frmRegistration form:

- Access opens the subform first, but before loading any records, notes the criteria in the query.

- Access opens the main form and loads the first main form record.

- Access uses the criteria from the main form record to filter the subform records, and loads only the filtered records.

This technique avoids the initial loading of the full set of subform records, so the form/subform takes less time to display its records.

Handling Multiple Sessions, One at a Time

The College database was designed to allow you to work with more than one session. For example, while the Spr 96 session is going on, you can begin planning for the next few sessions by creating classes for Sum 96 and Fall 96; toward the end of the Spr 96 session, you can begin registering students for the future sessions. The session you are currently working with is called the *working session*. The database uses the Query By Form concept to select the records for the working session.

Observing the Working Session

Let's take a look at how the database selects records for the working session.

1. With the Switchboard active, switch to Design view and observe that the RecordSource property is the tblSessions table and the Name of the text box is WorkingSession. The value displayed in the switchboard's WorkingSession control provides query criteria for all of the queries that involve classes.

2. Open qalkClassInstructor in Design view and observe the Criteria cell in the Session column. The Criteria cell contains the expression below. This query

(like each of the other queries involving class data) has a Session column with the same criteria, so all are using Query By Form to select records.

[Forms]!frmSwitchboard]![WorkingSession]

3. Close the query.

All College database forms and reports that involve classes are based on queries with this selection criteria. The result is that after you specify a working session, only the records for that session are available.

Changing the Working Session

You can change the working session by placing a combo box with a list of the available sessions in the switchboard and creating a macro to synchronize the switchboard to the value you select in the combo box.

Create a Combo Box

Create a combo box to display the names of the available sessions.

1. Switch to Design view.

2. Select the WorkingSession text box and set its Enabled property to Yes.

3. With the Control Wizards tool deselected, click the Combo Box tool and place a combo box next to the WorkingSession text box.

4. Delete the combo box label.

5. Select the combo box and set the properties as shown below. You set the default value of the combo box to the value in the WorkingSession text box, so that the combo box won't display a null value when you first open the application and display the switchboard.

Name	cboWorkingSession
RowSource	tblSessions
LimitToList	Yes
DefaultValue	=WorkingSession

Create the Macro

You create a macro that synchronizes the switchboard form to the value selected in the combo box as soon as Access detects the change (that is, as soon as the combo box recognizes the **AfterUpdate** event). You use the **FindRecord** action to synchronize the form's record source to the combo box value (refer to Chapter 7, "Navigating to Controls and Records").

1. Open the mfrmSwitchboard macro group.
2. Click in an empty row and name the new macro **cboWorkingSession_AfterUpdate**
3. Enter the macro shown in Table 10.3.
4. Save and close the macro.

TABLE 10.3: The macro to synchronize the switchboard to the combo box.

Macro Name	Action	Action Arguments
cboWorkingSession _AfterUpdate		
	Echo	Echo On: No
	GoToControl	Control Name: WorkingSession
	FindRecord	Find What: =cboWorkingSession
	GoToControl	Control Name: **cboWorkingSession**

Attach and Test the Macro

1. Click in frmSwitchboard, then select the combo box; click in the AfterUpdate property and select the macro mfrmSwitchboard.cboWorkingSession_AfterUpdate.
2. Switch to Form view and select Fall 95. Both the text box and the combo box display Fall 95 (see Figure 10.7).

With the combo box displaying the selected session, the form no longer needs to display the text box. Because Access can't move the focus to a control that has its

FIGURE 10.7:
Use a combo box to select the working session.

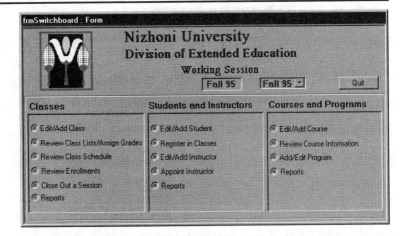

With the combo box displaying the selected session, the form no longer needs to display the text box. Because Access can't move the focus to a control that has its Visible property set to No, you need another technique to hide the text box. One solution is to make the text box transparent by setting its appearance properties and the font color to match the form.

Set the Text Box Properties

1. Switch to Design view, then click in the WorkingSession text box and set its properties as follows:

SpecialEffect	Flat
BorderStyle	Transparent
BackColor	12632256
ForeColor	12632256

2. Move the text box to the left, and move the combo box below the Working Session label.

3. Save the form.

Retest the Macro

1. Switch to Form view and select Fall 95. Only the combo box is displayed (see Figure 10.8).

2. Click the Review Class Schedule option button. The record in tblSessions is Fall 95 and the frmClassSchedule form displays the classes for Fall 95.

3. Click the Return button on the form.

4. Select Spr 96 and click the Review Class Schedule option button. The form displays the classes for Spr 96.

5. Click the Return button on the form.

FIGURE 10.8:

You can hide the text box by making it transparent.

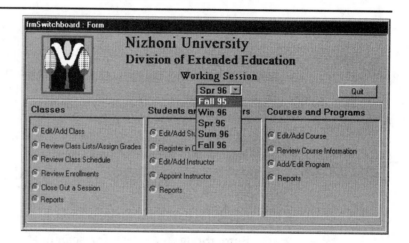

Synchronizing Two Combo Boxes

When the list displayed in a combo box is long, you can use two combo boxes instead of one, and design the pair so that the contents displayed by the second combo box depend on the value you select in the first—that is, *the second combo box is synchronized to the first.* For example, in the College database, the list of classes is typically several hundred in length, so you can use one combo box to select the class prefix and a second combo box to display the classes for that prefix.

1. Open frmClasses in Design view.

2. With the Control Wizards tool deselected, click the Combo Box tool and place a combo box in the form header.

3. Set the label of the combo box to **Prefix** and set the properties of the combo box as follows:

Name	cboPrefix
RowSource	tblPrograms
ColumnCount	1
ColumnWidth	0.4
BoundColumn	1
ListWidth	0.65

4. Switch to Form view and click the combo box arrow. The combo box displays the course prefixes.

5. Click in zsfrmGallery and copy the logical navigation controls.

6. Click in frmClasses, and paste the copied set of controls into the header.

7. Rearrange the controls.

8. Select the lblFind label and change the Caption property to **Find Class**

9. Click in the ScheduleNo text box and make sure the Name property is PrimaryID

Creating the Row Source for the Second Combo Box

You design the interaction of the two combo boxes such that the Find Class combo box displays the classes that correspond to the prefix selected in the Prefix combo box. If you haven't selected a value in the Prefix combo box, the Find Class combo list displays all of the classes for the current session.

1. In the Database window, double-click qlkpClasses. The query displays the classes for the current session. You can modify a copy of this query to create a query for the Find Class combo box that synchronizes it to the Prefix combo box.

2. Choose File➤Save As, then enter **qlkpClassSynchro** in the dialog and click OK.

3. Switch to Design view. The query uses Query By Form to obtain the session value from the switchboard. Note the expression in the Session criteria cell:

Forms!frmSwitchboard!WorkingSession

To further restrict the selection of classes to only those whose prefix matches the value selected in the cboPrefix combo box, you'll add the Prefix field to the design grid and enter the following expression in the Criteria cell for the field:

**Forms!frmClassSchedule!cboPrefix
Or Forms!frmClassSchedule!cboPrefix Is Null**

If you haven't selected a value in the Prefix combo box, the value of cboPrefix is null and this expression evaluates to True. As a result, the query selects records with all prefixes and the second combo box displays all of the classes for the session. If a prefix has been selected, this expression returns the value in the Prefix combo box and the second combo box displays only classes with this prefix for the session.

1. Drag the Prefix field to the design grid.

2. Click in the Criteria cell for Prefix, then open the Zoom box and enter the expression

**Forms!frmClassSchedule!cboPrefix
Or Forms!frmClassSchedule!cboPrefix Is Null**

3. Save the query.

Setting the Properties of the Find Class Combo Box

Next, you set the properties of the Find Class combo box to display the classes selected by the qlkpClassSynchro query.

1. Click the Find Class combo box and set its properties as follows:

RowSource	qlkpClassSynchro
ColumnCount	3
ColumnWidths	0.4;0.8;1.2

| BoundColumn | 1 |
| ListWidth | 2.75 |

Setting the Form Properties

Since frmClasses has logical navigation controls, you'll remove the default navigation buttons. You can also set the other form properties to control the form's behavior.

1. Select the form and set the following properties:

ViewsAllowed	Form
NavigationButtons	No
ControlBox	No
MinMaxButtons	None
CloseButton	No
ScrollBars	Neither
Cycle	Current Record

2. Set the BeforeUpdate property to mcrGallery.Form_BeforeUpdate. (You created this macro in Chapter 8, "Data Entry Operations," to test the primary key value for null and date-stamp the record if the record has been changed.)

Creating a Macro to Synchronize the Second Combo Box

When you select a different value in the Prefix combo box, the Find Class combo box doesn't update automatically, so you need to rerun the query for the Find Class combo box. You can create a macro that requeries the Find Class combo box and then puts the insertion point in the Find Class combo box, ready for you to select a class—you run the macro when the value in the Prefix combo box is changed and the combo box recognizes the `AfterUpdate` event.

1. In the Database window, select the mfrmClasses macro group and click the Design button.

2. Click in a new row and name the new macro **cboPrefix_AfterUpdate**

3. In the next row, select the **Requery** action and set the **Control Name** argument to **cboFind**

4. In the next row, select the **GoToControl** action and set the **Control Name** argument to **cboFind**

5. Save the macrosheet.

Attach and Test the Macro

1. Click in frmClasses and select cboPrefix; click in the AfterUpdate property and select mfrmClasses.cboPrefix_AfterUpdate.

2. Switch to Form view, and without selecting a prefix, drop the Find Class combo list. All of the classes for the current session are displayed.

3. Select a class from the Find Class combo box. The class is displayed in the form.

4. Select a prefix from the Prefix combo box and drop the Find Class combo list. Only the classes for the selected prefix and the current session are displayed (see Figure 10.9).

5. Select a class from the Find Class combo box. The class is displayed in the form.

FIGURE 10.9:

Using synchronized combo boxes.

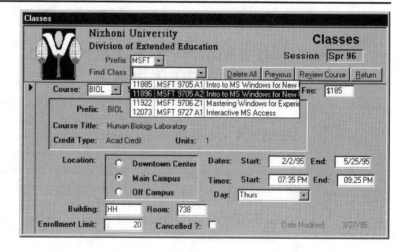

Requerying the Combo Box for a New Record

When you *edit* a class using frmClasses, the Find Class combo box list updates automatically; however, when you *add* a new class, you have to requery the combo box. You can use the Form_AfterInsert macro you created in Chapter 8, "Data Entry Operations," to requery the combo box.

1. Click in the form and switch to Design view.

2. Click in the form's AfterInsert property and select mcrGallery_AfterInsert.

3. Save the form.

Endnotes

This chapter has focused on sorting records using the OrderBy properties and selecting groups of records using filter queries that obtain their criteria from a form (Query By Form). The form holding the criteria values can be the same form that displays the records, as in the case of combo boxes placed in the header of the form itself. Or, the form holding the criteria values can be a separate form, as in the case of the switchboard holding the Session value used by the queries that provide records for a single session. You learned how to use the Query By Form concept, to improve the performance of the form/subform combination, and to synchronize combo boxes.

In the next chapter you explore the use of a custom dialog box to collect criteria from the user for the selection of report records. The custom dialog box also uses the Query By Form concept to pass selection criteria to a filter query.

On Your Own

In the exercises, you'll add a selection combo box to select courses in the Course List form, and then continue the first exercise by exploring how to use wildcards to select courses. In the final exercise, you modify the class registration process by using the DCount( ) function to avoid duplicate registration in a class and avoid the default error message "Duplicate value in index, primary key or relationship. Changes were unsuccessful."

Adding to the Application

1. Selecting groups of courses.

    In this exercise you use a selection combo box based on a union query to select courses with a specified prefix in frmCourseList. When the combo list includes a null row to select all the records, you don't need a separate command button to show all the records.

    a. Copy the cboPrefix combo box and its label from frmClassSchedule to the header of frmCourseList.

    b. Create a filter query by copying and pasting qryCourses as qfltCourseList. In the Criteria cell for Prefix, enter the expression:

    > **Forms!frmCourseList!cboPrefix**
    > **Or Forms!frmCourseList!cboPrefix Is Null**

    This criteria returns all matching records for the specified field, or if the criteria is null, returns all records.

    c. Create a new macrosheet named **mfrmCourseList**, and a new macro named cboPrefix_AfterUpdate. Select the **ApplyFilter** action and set the **FilterName** argument to **qfltCourseList**. Click in the AfterUpdate property of cboPrefix and change the property to mfrmCourseList.cboPrefix _AfterUpdate

Extending the Concepts

1. Query using a wildcard.

    In this exercise you select classes in frmCourseList by using a selection combo box that is based on a union query (to display a null row), and design the combo box and the filter query so that you can query using a wildcard. You select classes by prefix, but if you enter "b" in the combo box, all prefixes beginning with "b" are returned, including Biol and Bus.

    a. Carry out the steps of exercise 1, "Selecting groups of courses."

    b. In the combo box property sheet, set the Auto Expand property to No and the Limit To List property to No. With these properties set to No, you can enter any string of characters.

      c. In the qfltCourseList query, change the criteria to

        Like " | Forms!frmCourseList!cboPrefix | *"
        Or Forms!frmCourseList!cboPrefix Is Null

      You use vertical bars (| |) and quotation marks ("") to refer to the value of a control. The first part of the criteria expression looks for values that begin with the string you enter in the combo box.

      d. Test the search process by entering the letter **b** in the combo box and pressing Enter; all classes with the prefixes Biol and Bus are returned. Type in the letter **h** and press Enter; no classes are returned.

2. Use the DCount( ) function to prevent duplicate registration in a class.

If you try to register a student in a class that the student is already registered in, Access displays the error message "Duplicate value in index, primary key or relationship. Changes were unsuccessful." After acknowledging the message you have to undo the current record yourself. Instead, you can modify the cboScheduleNo_AfterUpdate macro to determine if the student is already registered in the class and automate the undo. If the student is already registered in the class, there must be a record in tlnkClassStudent for the registration.

      a. Create a query named **qryClassStudent** based on tlnkClassStudent; have it use Query By Form to select the record that has the same StudentID as displayed on frmRegistration and the same ScheduleNo as displayed in the ScheduleNo combo box on the subform.

      b. Use the DCount( ) function to count the number of records in the query: DCount("*","qryClassStudent"). If the number is zero, you register the student, but if the number is 1 the student is already registered.

      c. Modify cboScheduleNo_AfterUpdate as follows: insert four rows before the last **DoMenuItem** action; test the condition DCount("*","qryClassStudent")<>0; provide a message if the condition is true; undo the selection by using the **SendKeys** action to send the ESC key (wait for processing) to escape out of the control buffer to the record buffer and then using the **DoMenuItem** action to undo the current record; finally, stop the macro. If the DCount( ) function returns 0 the macro simply saves the record.

      d. Save and test the macro.

CHAPTER

ELEVEN

Finding Records to Print

- Synchronizing a report to a form

- Displaying data values in a message box

- Dialog box form masters

- Custom dialog boxes

- Mini-switchboards for reports

- The `NoData` event

The written reports you generate are important products of your application. In the College database, students want written verification of the classes they are registered in, faculty want printed class schedules for review and publication by each program, and management wants printed enrollment summary reports for making scheduling decisions.

This chapter shows you how to automate the selection of records for reports and the printing of reports. You learn how to generate a report, for a single record or a group of records, when the records for the report are displayed in a form. You also learn a technique that uses a custom dialog box to collect selection criteria from the user when the report isn't based on records displayed in a form.

> **NOTE** When you begin this chapter, only the switchboard and the Database window should be displayed. Close any other objects. This chapter assumes you have worked through Chapter 10 and have made the changes to frmClassSchedule.

Printing an Individual Report Based on the Current Form

After you register a student in classes using the frmRegistration form, you can print out the student's program to give to the student as verification.

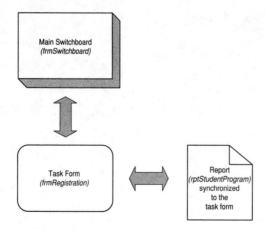

1. In the switchboard, click the Register in Classes option button.

2. Using the lookup combo box, select the student Cameron Shaw. (If this student isn't registered in any classes, register him in a few classes now.) While you could print the frmRegistration form itself, the College database contains a report for this purpose.

3. In the Database window, click the Report tab; double-click rptStudentProgram to open the report in Print Preview. The report opens and displays the verification report for another student.

You need to find and print the report for the student you just registered. You can create a macro that *synchronizes the report to the form*, and run the macro from a command button on the frmRegistration form.

Design a Macro to Synchronize the Report to the Form

The macro determines if the student is registered in any classes by testing the value in TotalFee control. If this value equals zero, the student has not registered in any classes; the macro displays a message and stops. If this value is positive, the macro finds the report record corresponding to the student and displays the synchronized rptStudentProgram report in Print Preview. Use the **OpenReport** action to open a report; to synchronize the report to the record displayed in an open form, use the syntax

[fieldname]=Forms![formname]![controlname]

or, when the form is the active form, you can use the syntax

[fieldname]=Screen.ActiveForm.[controlname]

in the **Where Condition** argument. In this expression, *[fieldname]* refers to the field in the underlying table or query of the report you want to open, and *[controlname]* refers to the control on the form that contains the value you want to match (see section "Looking Up Related Information in Another Form" in Chapter 5). Figure 11.1 shows the flow diagram for the macro.

FIGURE 11.1:

The flow diagram for a macro that synchronizes a report to the active form after determining if there are records in the report.

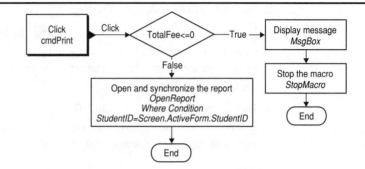

Display Current Data in the Message

To include the student's name in the message box, create the **Message** argument for the **MsgBox** action as a string expression that concatenates the current values in the name text boxes with message text, as follows:

=[FName]&" "&[LName]&" isn't registered in any classes. A Program Varifi-cation Report won't be printed."

Create the Command Button and the Macro

You'll create a command button on frmRegistration that opens and synchronizes rptStudentProgram.

1. Close rptStudentProgram, click in frmRegistration, and switch to Design view.

2. Make sure the Control Wizards button is deselected, then select the Command Button tool and create a button in the header, 0.5" wide and 0.2" tall, to the left of the New button.

3. Set the Name property to **cmdPrint** and the Caption property to **&Print**

4. In the Database window, select the mfrmRegistration macro group and click the Design button.

5. Click in the Macro Name cell of a new row, and name the new macro **cmdPrint_Click**

6. Enter the macro shown in Table 11.1.

7. Save and close the macrosheet.

TABLE 11.1: The macro to synchronize a report to a form after determining if there are records in the subreport.

Macro Name	Condition	Action	Action Arguments
cmdPrint_Click			
	TotalFee ≤0	**MsgBox**	**Message**: =[FName]&" "&[LName]&" isn't registered in any classes. A Program Verification Report won't be printed."
	...	**StopMacro**	
		OpenReport	**Form Name**: rptStudentProgram
			Where Condition: [StudentID] = Screen.ActiveForm.[StudentID]

Attach and Test the Macro

1. Click in frmRegistration, then select the Print button; click in the OnClick property, and select the mfrmRegistration.cmdPrint_Click macro.

2. Save the form and switch to Form view.

3. With the registration form for Cameron Shaw displayed, click the Print button. The Program Verification Report for this student is displayed in Print Preview.

4. Close the report.

5. Select a student without classes, for example Lisa Dondick, and then click the Print button. Access displays your message (see Figure 11.2).

6. Click the Return button on the frmRegistration form.

FIGURE 11.2:

The custom message displayed when a student isn't registered in classes.

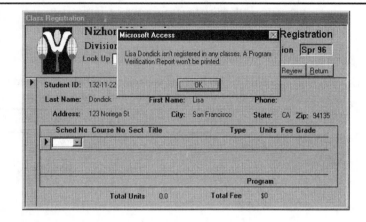

Printing a Group of Records Based on the Current Form

After reviewing the class schedule for a program, you can print out the class schedule for that program.

1. In the switchboard, click the Review Class Schedule option button.

2. Using the program selection combo box, select the prefix BUS. The form displays the business classes.

3. In the Database window, double-click the rptClassSchedule report to open it in Print Preview. The report displays all of the classes (not just those for the prefix BUS).

Design the Macro to Synchronize the Report to the Form

Because the frmClassSchedule form and the rptClassSchedule report are based on the same query, you can synchronize the report to the form by applying the same filter query to the report that you used to select records for the form. You can automate the process by placing a Print button in the form header and creating a macro that applies the filter when the report is opened. You can use the **NoData** event to determine if there are any classes for the selected program at the selected location—the

NoData event occurs when Access recognizes that the record source for the report has no records. If the record set is empty, the report recognizes the **NoData** event immediately following its **Open** event and before its **Activate** event. You'll use the **NoData** event to trigger another macro, one that displays a message and then executes the **CancelEvent** action to cancel the subsequent steps that Access would take to format and print the report with no records. The macro determines whether one or both combo boxes have null values, and displays different messages depending on which combo box combination you've selected:

- both a program and a location

- a program but not a location

- a location but not a program

- neither a program nor a location

You create messages that refer to the selected program and location by concatenating the combo box values with message text.

The flow diagram for the cmdPrint_Click macro (that runs when you click the Print button) and the Report_NoData macro (that is triggered when the record set is empty) is shown in Figure 11.3.

Create the Command Button and the Macro

You'll place a Print button on frmClassSchedule and then create a macro to open and synchronize rptClassSchedule by applying the form's filter to the report.

1. Close rptClassSchedule, then click in frmClassSchedule and switch to Design view.

2. Click the Command Button tool, and create a button in the header, 0.5" wide and 0.2" tall.

3. Set the Name property to **cmdPrint** and the Caption property to **&Print**

4. In the Database window, select the macro group mfrmClassSchedule and click the Design button.

5. Click in the Macro Name cell of a new row and name the new macro **cmdPrint_Click**

FIGURE 11.3:

The flow diagram for a macro that selects records for a report by applying a filter, and a macro to stop the print process and display different messages when there are no records.

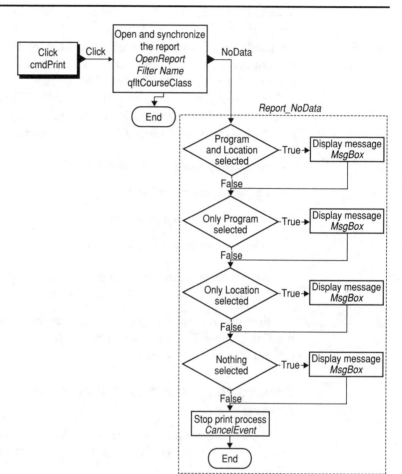

6. In the next row, select the **OpenReport** action; set the **Report Name** argument to **rptClassSchedule** and the **Filter Name** argument to **qfltCourse-Class**

7. Save and close the macrosheet.

Create the Macro for the NoData Event

You'll create a macro that displays a message and then cancels the printing operation when there are no records.

1. Open a new macrosheet and save it as **mrptClassSchedule**

2. Click in the Macro Name cell of the first row, and name the new macro Report_NoData

3. Enter the macro shown in Table 11.2.

4. Save and close the macrosheet.

Attach and Test the Macros

1. Set the OnClick property to mfrmClassSchedule.cmdPrint_Click.

2. Save the form and switch to Form view.

3. Select the BIOL program and the Main Campus location, then click the Print button. The report for these classes is displayed.

4. Switch to Design view of the report, then click in the NoData event, and select the mrptClassSchedule.Report_NoData macro.

5. Save and close the report.

6. Select the ENGR program and the Off Campus location, then click the Print button. Access displays the message that there are no classes (see Figure 11.4).

TABLE 11.2: The macro triggered by the **NoData** event displays a message box and cancels the printing process.

Macro Name	Condition	Action	Action Arguments
Report_NoData			
	Not IsNull(Forms!frmClass-Schedule!cboPrefix) And Not IsNull(Forms!frmClass-Schedule!cboLocation)	**MsgBox**	**Message:** ="There are no classes in the " &[Forms!frmClass-Schedule!cboPrefix]& " program at the " &[Forms!frmClass-Schedule!cboLocation]& " location."

TABLE 11.2: The macro triggered by the **NoData** event displays a message box and cancels the printing process. *(continued)*

Macro Name	Condition	Action	Action Arguments
Report_NoData	Not IsNull(Forms!frmClass-Schedule!cboPrefix) And IsNull(Forms!frmClass-Schedule!cboLocation)	**MsgBox**	**Message:** ="There are no classes in the " &[Forms!frmClass-Schedule!cboPrefix]& " program."
	IsNull(FormsifrmClass-ScheduleicboPrefix) And Not IsNull(Forms!frmClass-Schedule!cboLocation)	**MsgBox**	**Message:** ="There are no classes at the " &[Forms!frmClass-Schedule!cboLocation]& " location."
	IsNull(Forms!frmClass-Schedule!cboPrefix) And IsNull(Forms!frmClass-Schedule!cboLocation)	**MsgBox**	**Message:** There are no classes scheduled for this session.
		CancelEvent	

7. Click OK, and make several other selections to display the messages.

8. Select the Business program and the Downtown Center location. The report for these classes is displayed.

9. Close rptClassSchedule.

10. Click the Return button on the frmClassSchedule form.

FIGURE 11.4:

The message that is displayed when there are no classes in the selected program at the selected location.

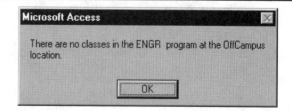

Using a Custom Dialog Box to Select Records

Instead of using a form to select and display the records that you want to print, you can create a custom dialog box to collect selection criteria from the user and use these values as criteria for a filter query that selects the records for the report.

TIP The custom dialog box technique is useful for routine reports when there is no need to view the records in a form before printing the reports; the performance of your application improves because using the custom dialog box eliminates the time to display the form.

In the College database, the production of class lists is a routine operation.

1. In the Database window, double-click rptClassList to open it in Print Preview. The Class List report displays class information, instructor names, and a list of students enrolled. There is a separate page for each class.

You can create a dialog box that provides choices for the program and location, and then print only the class list reports corresponding to the selection. You'll create a custom dialog box to select records for all class lists for:

- a specified location
- one prefix and all locations
- one prefix and one location
- all locations

Create a Filter for the Report

When you are working with a form, you can create a filter while the form is in Form view, because the filter commands (Advanced Filter/Sort, Apply Filter/Sort, and Remove Filter/Sort) are available; however, the filter commands are not available for a report, so you work with the report's underlying record source to create the filter.

A filter query must include all of the tables that contain fields in the report or form that you are applying the filter to and all of the fields in the report or form. When you create the filter query, either drag all of the fields in the report's (or form's) field list to the design grid, or set the query's OutputAllFields property to Yes to show all of the fields in the query's data source. With the OutputAllFields property set to Yes, the only fields that must be shown in the filter query's design grid are the ones you are using to sort by or specify criteria for. (When you save a filter as a query, the OutputAllFields is automatically set to Yes.)

Create a Filter Query Based on the Report's Record Source

After determining the report's record source, you create a filter query to specify criteria for the Prefix and Location fields.

1. Switch to Design view and choose Edit ➤ Select Report. The record source for the main report is the qalkCourseClass query.

2. Close the report.

3. In the Database window, select the query qalkCourseClass.

4. In the toolbar, click the arrow on the New Object button, and then select the New Query button.

5. With Design View selected, click OK. The query design window opens with the field list for qalkCourseClass in the upper pane.

6. Choose the View ➤ Properties command (or right-click in the upper pane and select the Properties command).

7. Click in the OutputAllFields property and choose Yes. With the OutputAll-Fields property set to Yes, the datasheet includes all of the query fields (regardless of which fields are displayed in the design grid). In this example, you'll use the Prefix and Location fields to collect the user's choices.

8. Select the Prefix and Location fields and drag them to the design grid. The selection criteria for these fields will come from the custom dialog box that you create next.

9. Save the query as **qfltClassLists**

Creating a Form Master for a Custom Dialog Box

Design a custom dialog form master that you can use to create custom dialog boxes in the application.

1. In the Database window, select zsfrmMaster, then copy and paste it as **zsfdlgMaster**. (The fdlg tag indicates that the form is a dialog box.)

2. Select zsfdlgMaster and click the Design button.

3. Select all of the controls in the header, then cut and paste the selected controls into the detail section.

4. Choose <u>V</u>iew ➤ Form <u>H</u>eader/Footer, and delete the header and footer sections.

5. Drag the lower right corner of the form to make it 4" wide and 2" tall.

Setting Custom Dialog Box Form Properties

Set the form properties so that the form has the look and feel of a standard Windows dialog box, with one exception: while you are developing the application, let the PopUp property remain at the default No value so that you can switch between Design and Form view and use the menus and toolbars. When you are finished with the development stage, you can set the PopUp property to Yes to prevent access to the menus and toolbars.

1. Set the Form properties to the custom dialog box property settings shown below.

Property	Setting	Property	Setting
DefaultView	Single Form	**BorderStyle**	Dialog
ShortcutMenu	No	**Modal**	Yes
ScrollBars	Neither	**ControlBox**	No
RecordSelectors	No	**MinMaxButton**	None
NavigationButtons	No	**CloseButton**	No
AutoCenter	Yes	**ViewsAllowed**	Form

2. Switch to Form view.

3. Choose <u>W</u>indow ➤ Si<u>z</u>e to Fit Form (see Figure 11.5).

4. Save the form.

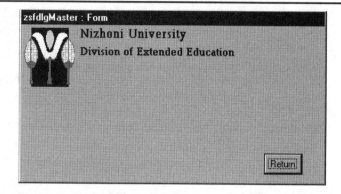

Creating the Class Reports Dialog Box as a Mini-Switchboard

In addition to a custom dialog box that you'll use to collect selection criteria for the class list report, you'll create another custom dialog box that provides a summary of the reports for classes that are available in the application. You'll use this dialog box, named fdlgClassReports, as a *mini-switchboard* to the reports for classes. (I'll refer to frmSwitchboard as the *main switchboard* to prevent confusion.) We'll design the navigation so that

- You open the fdlgClassReports mini-switchboard by clicking the Reports option button in the Classes option group on the main switchboard. As a mini-switchboard, fdlgClassReports displays an option group with a choice of reports.

- You click an option button on the fdlgClassReports mini-switchboard to open either a selected report directly or another dialog box that collects selection criteria for a report. (In this chapter we'll create fdlgClassLists as a dialog box to collect selection criteria for the Class Lists report.)

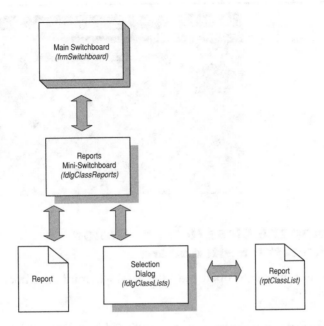

1. Choose File ➤ Save As and save the form as **fdlgClassLists** (later you'll use this dialog box to collect selection criteria for the Class Lists report).

2. Choose File ➤ Save As and save the form as **fdlgClassReports**

3. Switch to Design view.

4. Set the Caption property to **Class Reports**

5. Select the Option Group tool and create an option group 2″ wide and 1.2″ tall.

6. Set the Name property to **grpClassReports**

7. Select the Option Button tool and create an option button in the option group.

8. Set the label's Caption property to **Class Lists**

9. Save the form. Figure 11.6 shows the fdlgClassReports in Form view.

10. Close the form.

FIGURE 11.6:

The dialog box for the Class Reports.

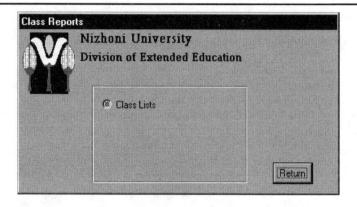

Opening the Class Reports Dialog Box from the Switchboard

You create a macro to open the fdlgClassLists mini-switchboard from the main switchboard.

1. In the Database window, select mfrmSwitchboard and click the Design button.

2. In the grpClasses_AfterUpdate macro, select the row with the `SetValue` action that hides the main switchboard, and click the Insert Row button in the toolbar.

3. Click in the Condition cell of the inserted row and enter the condition **grpClasses = 6** (the Reports option button in the classes option group has the value 6).

4. Select the `OpenForm` action and set its `Form Name` argument to **fdlgClassReports**

5. Save and close the macrosheet.

6. Click in the main switchboard, and click the Reports button in the Classes group. The main switchboard is hidden and the fdlgClassReports mini-switchboard opens.

Opening the Class Lists Dialog Box

Create a macro that closes the mini-switchboard and opens the selected report or report dialog box when you click an option button. This macro will be attached to the option group on the fdlgClassReports mini-switchboard.

1. Open a new macrosheet and save it as **mfdlgClassReports**

2. Click in the first Macro Name cell and name the new macro **grpClassReports_AfterUpdate**

3. Enter the macro shown in Table 11.3.

4. Save the macro.

TABLE 11.3: Macro to close the mini-switchboard and open a report or report dialog box.

Macro Name	Condition	Action	Action Arguments
grpClassReports_ AfterUpdate			
	grpClassReports = 1	OpenForm	Form Name: fdlgClassLists
	...	Close	Object Type: Form
			Object Name: fdlgClassReports

Attach and Test the Macro

1. Click in fdlgClassReports and then switch to Design view.

2. Select the option group, then set its AfterUpdate property to mfdlgClassReports.grpClassReports_AfterUpdate.

3. Save the form and switch to Form view.

4. Click the Class Lists option button. The fdlgClassLists dialog box opens and the fdlgClassReports mini-switchboard closes.

Creating the Multi-Selection Class List Dialog Box

You'll place unbound list boxes for program and class location on the dialog box. You design both list boxes to display an empty first row using the techniques you learned in Chapter 10, "Working with a Group of Records." When you choose the null value for a list box, the filter query returns records with all values for that list box. You can use the RowSource expressions for the combo boxes for the frmClassSchedule form you created in Chapter 10.

1. Switch to Design view.
2. Set the Caption property to **Class List Selection**

Place a List Box for Class Prefix

Create a class prefix list box that has the same row source as the class prefix combo box you created in Chapter 10 (for the Class Schedule form).

1. Click the Review Class Schedule option button in the switchboard, then switch to Design view.
2. Click the Prefix combo box, then click in the RowSource property; select the expression and copy to the clipboard. The RowSource expression is the SQL statement for the union query that displays the null row followed by rows with the course prefixes.
3. With the Control Wizards tool deselected, select the List Box tool; draw a list box, 0.6" wide and 1" tall, in the upper left of the fdlgClassLists form.
4. Set the list box Name property to **lstPrefix**, then click in the RowSource property and paste the expression you copied in step 2.
5. Set the label's Caption property to **Program** and move the label so that it is centered above the list box.

Place a List Box for Class Location

Create a class location list box that has the same row source as the class location combo box on the Class Schedule form.

1. Click in frmClassSchedule, then click the Location combo box; click in the RowSource property and copy its expression to the clipboard. The RowSource expression is the null value followed by a list of locations.
2. With the Control Wizards tool deselected, select the List Box tool; draw a list box in the form, 1" wide and 0.5" tall, to the right of the Program list box.

3. Set the list box properties as follows:

Name	lstLocation
Row SourceType	Value List

4. Click in the RowSource property and paste the expression you copied in step 1.

5. Set the label's Caption property to **Class Location** and move the label so that it is centered above the list box.

Place Command Buttons on the Dialog Box

Place two additional command buttons to provide a choice: display the report in Print Preview or print the report directly.

1. Select the Command Button tool and create a button in the form, 0.5" wide and 0.2" tall.

2. With the command button selected, choose <u>E</u>dit ➤ Dup<u>l</u>icate.

3. Set the following properties for the two buttons:

Name	Caption
cmdPreview	Print Pre&view
cmdPrint	&Print

4. Save the form.

5. Switch to Form view, choose <u>W</u>indow ➤ Si<u>z</u>e to Fit, and then choose <u>F</u>ile ➤ <u>S</u>ave (see Figure 11.7).

Setting Criteria for the Filter Query

The selection criteria expressions for the qfltClassLists filter query are based on the values you select in the list boxes. If you don't select a class prefix, or if you select the null value, the filter query returns classes with all prefixes. If you don't select a location, or if you select the null value, the filter query returns classes in all locations. The criteria expressions are similar to those you created in Chapter 10, "Working with a Group of Records," to select records depending on the values in two combo boxes.

FIGURE 11.7:

The custom dialog box to collect selection criteria.

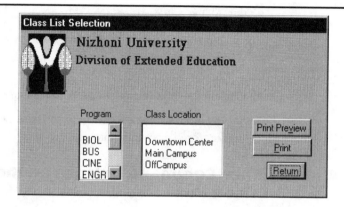

1. Click in the qfltClassLists query, then click in the Criteria cell below Prefix and enter the expression

   Forms!fdlgClassLists!lstPrefix Or Forms!fdlgClassLists!lstPrefix Is Null

2. Click in the Criteria cell below Location and enter the expression

   Forms!fdlgClassLists!!lstLocation Or Forms!fdlgClassLists!lstLocation Is Null

3. Save the query.

Create the Macros for the Buttons on the Dialog Box

The fdlgClassLists dialog box collects criteria for selecting one set of class lists to print. When you click the Print Preview button, a macro hides the dialog box, opens the rptClassList report, and applies the filter query to the report's underlying query. The dialog box must remain open in order to provide the selection criteria to the filter query, so you hide rather than close it. When you close the report window, another macro triggered by the report's **Close** event unhides the dialog box. Figure 11.8 shows the macro for the Print Preview button.

The macro for the Print button doesn't display the report, so the macro opens the rptClassList report without hiding the dialog box and then applies the filter query to the report's underlying query. Figure 11.9 shows the macro for the Print button.

FIGURE 11.8:

The flow diagram for the cmdPreview_Click macro.

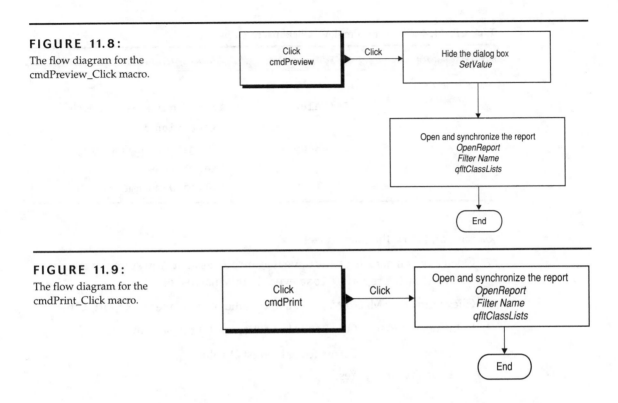

FIGURE 11.9:

The flow diagram for the cmdPrint_Click macro.

1. Open a new macrosheet and save it as **mfdlgClassLists**. You store the macros for the cmdPreview and cmdPrint buttons in this macrosheet.

2. Click in the first Macro Name cell and name the new macro **cmdPreview_Click**

3. Enter the macro shown in Table 11.4.

4. Click in the Macro Name cell of a new row and name the new macro **cmdPrint_Click**

5. Click in the next row, then select the **OpenReport** action and set its arguments as follows:

Report Name	rptClassList
View	Print
Filter Name	qfltClassLists

TABLE 11.4: The cmdPreview_Click macro.

Macro Name	Action	Action Arguments
cmdPreview_Click		
	SetValue	**Item:** Screen.ActiveForm.Visible
		Expression: No
	OpenReport	**Report Name:** rptClassList
		View: Print Preview
		Filter Name: qfltClassLists

6. Save and close the macrosheet.

7. Open a new macrosheet and save it as **mrptClassList**. You store the macro triggered by the report's **Close** event in this macrosheet.

8. Click in the first Macro Name cell and name the new macro **Report_Close**

9. In the next row, select the **SetValue** action and set the arguments:

Item	Forms!fdlgClassLists.Visible
Expression	Yes

10. Save and close the macrosheet.

Attach and Test the Macros

1. In the Database window, select fdlgClassLists and click the Design button.

2. Select the Print Preview button and set its OnClick property to mfdlgClassLists.cmdPreview_Click.

3. Select the Print button and set its OnClick property to mfdlgClassLists.cmdPrint_Click.

4. Save the form and switch to Form view.

5. Select a Prefix from the first list box, then click the Print Preview button. The report opens in Print Preview with the selected classes.

6. Switch to Design view and set the report's OnClose property to mrptClassList.Report_Close.

7. Save the report and switch to Report Preview.

8. Close the report. The fdlgClassLists dialog box is unhidden.

9. Make no list box selections and click the Print Preview button. The report opens in Print Preview with all classes.

10. Close the report.

11. Select the MSFT prefix and the Off Campus location, then click the Print Preview button. There no classes and the report is generated displaying #Error in place of class controls.

Create a Macro For the NoData Event

You can use the **NoData** event, recognized by the rptClassList report when there are no classes, to trigger a macro that displays a message and cancels the printing process.

1. Open the mrptClassList macrosheet.

2. Click in a new row and name the macro **Report_NoData**

3. In the next row, select the **MsgBox** action and set the **Message** argument to: **There are no classes at this location.**

4. In the next row, select the **CancelEvent** action.

5. Save and close the macrosheet.

Attach and Test the Macro

1. Click in the rptClassList report and switch to Design view.

2. Click in the **NoData** event and select the mrptClassList.Report_NoData macro.

3. Save and close the report.

4. Select the MSFT prefix and the Off Campus location, then click the Print Preview button. The message is displayed, the printing process is cancelled and the dialog is unhidden.

Creating an Instruction Label

You can provide onscreen help by displaying an instruction label for the fdlgClassLists selection dialog box.

1. Switch to Design view.

2. Select the Label tool and click in the form above the list box labels (you may need to move the list boxes and their labels down).

3. Enter the following instructions in the label:

    To print all classes make no selections. To print one class prefix and/or one location, make selections from one or both lists.

4. Adjust the size of the label.

5. Save the form and switch to Form view (see Figure 11.10).

6. Click the Return button on the form.

FIGURE 11.10:

The Class List Selection dialog box with instructions.

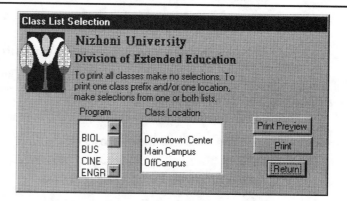

EndNotes

In this chapter you've learned how to automate the selection of records and printing of reports. There are two basic techniques for selecting records for a report:

- When you use a form to select and display the records, you can synchronize the report to the form using macros. When the form displays a single record, you open the report with the **OpenReport** action and specify the **Where Condition** argument. When the form displays several records, you open the report and specify the **Filter Name** argument as the same filter query that selects records for the form.

- When you use a custom dialog box to select records, you use a filter query that obtains selection criteria directly from the dialog box. After selecting the criteria, you open the report using the **OpenReport** action and use the filter query in the **Filter Name** argument. This technique eliminates the time needed to open a separate form.

You used the **NoData** event to trigger a macro that cancels the printing process when the recordset for the report is empty.

You added a custom dialog form master to the set of masters, and used the master to create a mini-switchboard (to navigate to the classes reports) and a dialog box (to collect report criteria for one of the reports).

On Your Own

In the exercises, you can add to the application by automating the process of printing an individual class list and a set of courses.

Adding to the Application

1. Print a Class List based on a current form.

   a. Place a Print button in the Form Header of frmClassList.

   b. Following the steps below, create a macro to find and preview the class list report (rptClassList) corresponding to the selected class displayed in frmClassList. You only want to print a report if there are students registered.

   c. Create a new macro named **cmdPrint_Click** in the macro group mfrmClassList.

   d. Develop a condition to test the value in the TotalEnroll text box. If this value is zero, display the message:

      There are no students registered in this class.

      A Class List will not be printed.

   and stop the macro.

If the value is positive, select the **OpenReport** action using the **Where Condition**:

ScheduleNo = Forms!frmClassList!ScheduleNo

   e. Save the macro and attach it to the Print button.

2. Print a group of courses based on a current form.

In this exercise, you place a Print button on frmCourseList that allows you to print the selected courses using the combo box on the form. (You must complete the exercise "Selecting groups of courses" in Chapter 10 before doing this exercise.)

   a. Place a Print button named **cmdPrint** in the header of frmCourseList.

   b. Create a new macro named **cmdPrint_Click** in the macro group mfrmCourseList. Select the **OpenReport** action to open rptCourseList and set the **Filter Name** argument to **qfltCourseList**

   c. Switch frmCourseList to Form view and test your work.

   d. Modify the macro to count the number of records in the filter query and display a message instead of the report when there are no courses.

CHAPTER

TWELVE

Handling External Data

- Separating program and data files

- Using a mini-switchboard to manage importing data

- Modifying and appending records by using action queries

- Using the Find Unmatched Query Wizard

- Using string manipulation functions

- Using the `Transfer...` actions to import data files

- Setting error flags in a Visual Basic procedure

One of the strengths of Access is its ability to use data from files created in spreadsheet, word processing, and other database applications. Access provides two ways to use such data: linking to the external file in order to use the data created in the native format of another application and importing the data from the external file into your Access database. In this chapter you'll learn how to split your Access database into two files and link your own data file as an external data file. You'll also learn how to automate the process of importing and modifying data created in spreadsheet and word processing applications.

Separating Data and Program Files

When you create a database, Access stores all of the tables, queries, forms, reports, macros, and modules in a single file. There are advantages and disadvantages to this arrangement. If you are working with the application on your own workstation, the principal advantage is performance: all the database objects are in one file so Access doesn't have to take time to find an object in another file. There are disadvantages, however, if you are creating the application for others to use or if the application is employed in a multi-user situation.

If you are creating a custom application for others, you will probably update the application occasionally to fix errors and add new features. When you give others the modified file, the data in the two files will be different, because in most cases the users will have added new data or changed the data in the original file; therefore, someone will have to delete the data in the modified file and append the data from the old file to the modified file. (Also, Microsoft Access for Windows 95 has a new replication feature that you can use to keep files in sync.)

A better solution is to separate the application into two files: a *program file* that contains the queries, forms, reports, macros, modules, and perhaps a few unchanging lookup tables (such as zip code tables); and a *data file* that contains the data tables. You link the data tables as external data tables. In this scenario, you modify the program file. When you are ready to use the new program file, you link the data tables to the modified program file and discard the old program file. As long as you don't change the structure of the data tables, this method allows for easier "upgrades."

If you are creating a custom application for a multi-user environment, you can optimize performance by splitting the file, then storing the data file on one computer (the file server) and placing copies of the program file on each of the computers sharing the data. If you don't split the application and instead place the single application file on one computer, then each time another user wants to use the application, each query, form, report, etc., is sent over the network cable. With the split-file arrangement, only the requested data is sent over the network.

NOTE When you begin this chapter, only the switchboard and the Database window should be displayed. Close any other objects.

Using the Database Splitter Wizard to Separate the Data

You can use the Database Splitter Wizard to split the application file. The wizard creates a new empty database file and moves all of the tables to the new file while preserving field and table properties and table relationships. Then the wizard deletes the tables from the application file and creates links from the application file (which is now the program file) to the data tables (see Figure 12.1).

1. Close the College database and make a backup copy.

2. Open the College database, then press F11 to display the Database window, and close the switchboard.

3. Choose Tools ➤ Add-ins ➤ Database Splitter, and click the Split Database button.

4. Enter **Colldata** as the name of the new database, and click the Split button. The Status Bar messages indicate that Access exports the tables to the new database and then attaches (links) the tables. The message for a successful split is displayed when the operation is complete.

5. Click OK. The Database window displays the linked status of the tables using the linked table icon as shown in Figure 12.2.

After splitting, you work with the application by opening the program file (often called the *front-end* database); changes to the data are stored in the data file (the *back-end* database).

FIGURE 12.1:

Split the application into two files: a program file, and a data file with linked tables.

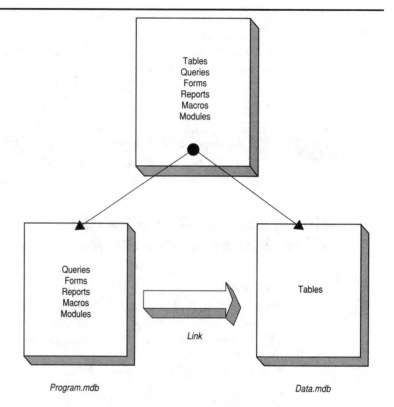

FIGURE 12.2:

The Database window for the split application. The icons indicate that the tables are linked.

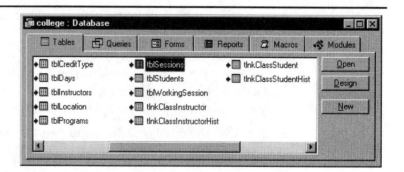

Refreshing the Links Interactively

The Wizard creates link information that includes the specific path of the data file. If you move the data file or the program file to a new path, Access doesn't reestablish, or *refresh*, links to the tables automatically.

1. Close the College database.

2. Move the Colldata data file to a different folder and reopen the College database. Access displays an error message indicating that the colldata.mdb file couldn't be found.

3. Click OK, then open the database again by selecting the College database from the list of recently opened files in the File menu. This time the College database opens and displays the Database window. If you try to open any database object that is bound to a table in any view other than Design view, Access displays the same default error message. When you click OK to acknowledge the error, the object may or may not open (forms and reports open with error symbols in place of the data controls, but tables and queries do not).

Using the Linked Table Manager

To use the program file you must re-establish the links to the data file tables. You can refresh the table links interactively using the Linked Table Manager.

1. Choose Tools ➤ Add-ins ➤ Linked Table Manager. The Linked Table Manager dialog opens (see Figure 12.3).

2. Click the Select All button, then click OK. Access displays a dialog in which you specify the new location of the moved data file (see Figure 12.4).

3. Locate and select the moved data file, then click Open. Access re-establishes the table links and displays a message to indicate success.

You can automate the process of refreshing table links, but the automation requires Visual Basic programming and cannot be accomplished with macros alone.

FIGURE 12.3:

The Linked Table Manager.

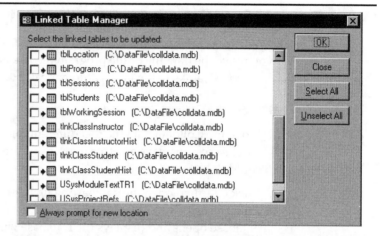

FIGURE 12.4:

Specify the location of the moved data file in the Select New Location dialog box.

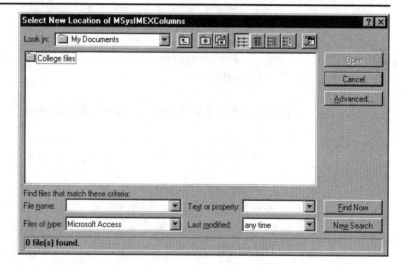

NOTE The Solutions sample application that is provided with Access includes an example of a custom function you can use to refresh your application's table links. You can find other versions of custom functions for refreshing links on the MSACCESS forum on CompuServe.

Importing Spreadsheet Data

Often the data you need in your application has been created using another computer database management program or a spreadsheet or word processing program. In many cases, you import the data and have to modify it before you can use it in your application. This section shows you how to automate the process of importing and modifying a Microsoft Excel spreadsheet file. The next section shows you how to work with a text file.

In the College database, there are several off-campus locations where classes are offered. One of the off-campus sites is a biological field station in a remote setting. Students at this location register for classes using a flat-file database manager. This class registration data is sent periodically, by electronic mail, as a Microsoft Excel spreadsheet file named Offsite.xls. An example of the spreadsheet data is the grade report for several Summer 96 classes, shown in Figure 12.5.

Each row represents a student registration in a particular class. Students who register at an off-campus site may be existing students or new students.

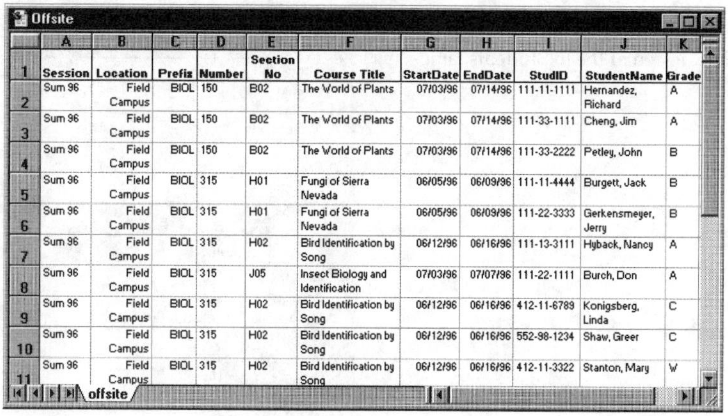

FIGURE 12.5:

A grade report from an off-campus site, created as a Microsoft Excel spreadsheet file.

	A	B	C	D	E	F	G	H	I	J	K
1	Session	Location	Prefix	Number	Section No	Course Title	StartDate	EndDate	StudID	StudentName	Grade
2	Sum 96	Field Campus	BIOL	150	B02	The World of Plants	07/03/96	07/14/96	111-11-1111	Hernandez, Richard	A
3	Sum 96	Field Campus	BIOL	150	B02	The World of Plants	07/03/96	07/14/96	111-33-1111	Cheng, Jim	A
4	Sum 96	Field Campus	BIOL	150	B02	The World of Plants	07/03/96	07/14/96	111-33-2222	Petley, John	B
5	Sum 96	Field Campus	BIOL	315	H01	Fungi of Sierra Nevada	06/05/96	06/09/96	111-11-4444	Burgett, Jack	B
6	Sum 96	Field Campus	BIOL	315	H01	Fungi of Sierra Nevada	06/05/96	06/09/96	111-22-3333	Gerkensmeyer, Jerry	B
7	Sum 96	Field Campus	BIOL	315	H02	Bird Identification by Song	06/12/96	06/16/96	111-13-3111	Hyback, Nancy	A
8	Sum 96	Field Campus	BIOL	315	J05	Insect Biology and Identification	07/03/96	07/07/96	111-22-1111	Burch, Don	A
9	Sum 96	Field Campus	BIOL	315	H02	Bird Identification by Song	06/12/96	06/16/96	412-11-6789	Konigsberg, Linda	C
10	Sum 96	Field Campus	BIOL	315	H02	Bird Identification by Song	06/12/96	06/16/96	552-98-1234	Shaw, Greer	C
11	Sum 96	Field Campus	BIOL	315	H02	Bird Identification by Song	06/12/96	06/16/96	412-11-3322	Stanton, Mary	W

449

Analyzing the Spreadsheet Data

The first step in working with data created in another program is to analyze the data from the perspective of the structure of your database application. In this example, the spreadsheet file includes two kinds of data:

- new student data that needs to be modified and appended to the tblStudents table

- student grade data that needs to be appended to the tlnkClassStudent linking table

The Table Structure of tblStudents

We'll study the structure of tblStudents to determine what modifications are needed for the imported data.

1. In the Database window, select the tblStudents table and click the Design button. Figure 12.6 shows the Design view of the table.

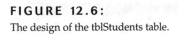

FIGURE 12.6:

The design of the tblStudents table.

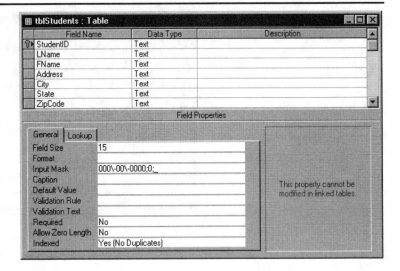

In the tblStudents table, the primary key is StudentID. The next two fields are the student's last name and first name, respectively. The spreadsheet file includes the StudentID, but gives the student's first and last names in a single column in concatenated form:

LastName, FirstName

You'll have to decompose each concatenated name into its last name and first name parts before you can append the student information to tblStudents.

The Table Structure of tlnkClassStudent

Similarly, let's look at the structure of the table that stores the grade data, tlnkClassStudent.

1. In the Database window, select the tlnkClassStudent table and click the Design button. When you open a linked table in Design view, Access displays a message reminding you that the table is linked and that some properties can't be modified.

2. Click Yes. Figure 12.7 shows the Design view of the table.

FIGURE 12.7:
The design of the tlnkClassStudent table.

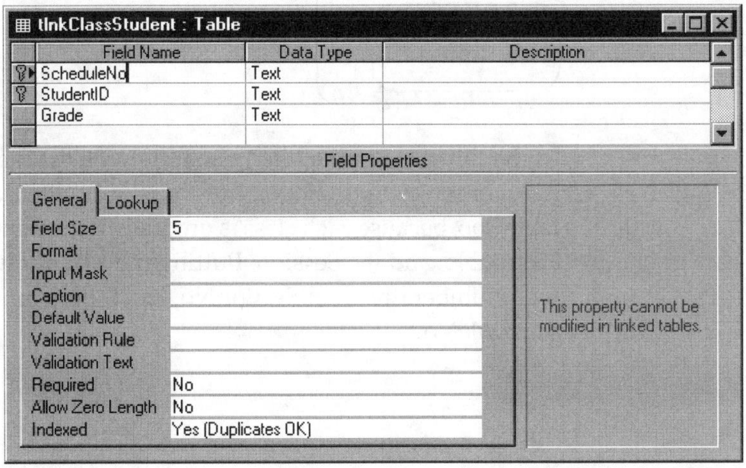

In the tlnkClassStudent linking table, the primary key is the pair of fields StudentID and ScheduleNo. The spreadsheet file does not include the ScheduleNo field explicitly, but a little sleuthing in the table structures for tblCourses and tblClasses provides the solution.

1. In the Database window, open tblCourses and tblClasses in Design view.

In the tblCourses table, the primary key is the CourseID field, which is the unique course number set by the college when a course is approved; however, there is an *alternate primary key* that could be used to uniquely identify courses. A glance at tblCourses in Datasheet view reveals that the college permits two courses to have the same Prefix and Number, but that no two courses can have the same Prefix, Number, and Name; therefore, an alternate primary key is the trio of fields: Prefix, Number, and Name. Since the spreadsheet file includes these three fields, you can determine the CourseID for each record.

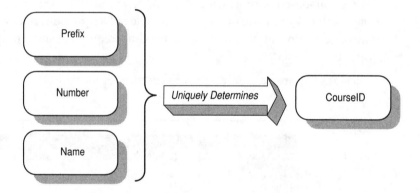

In the tblClasses table, the primary key is the ScheduleNo field (the unique class number set by the college). But there is an alternate primary key possible for this table, too, because each class is uniquely determined if you know the CourseID, the SectionNo, and the Session. Putting the two deductions together, if you know Prefix, Number, Name, SectionNo, and Session, then you can determine the ScheduleNo.

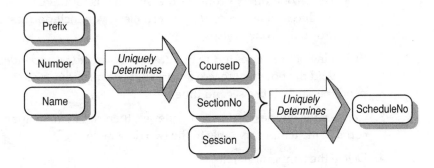

The spreadsheet file contains these five fields, so the ScheduleNo can be uniquely determined.

Strategy for Modifying the Spreadsheet Data

Normally, you can choose to modify external data by using either the program used to create the data or by using Access. In this example, you can modify the spreadsheet in Excel and import directly into the two Access tables or you can import the spreadsheet file and modify the imported table in Access. Since we are going to automate the entire process, we'll import and modify the data in Access. Here are the general steps:

1. Import the spreadsheet file as a new temporary table in the program file. (You modify the imported data in the program file and append the modified data to tables in the data file.)

2. Create queries to modify and test the data. The spreadsheet contains information that must be appended to two tables. Since a query can add records to only one table, you create a separate query for each table.

   - The first query converts the student's name into the separate name fields for tblStudents, and produces records for existing and new students. You include a test to determine if a record is for an existing student or a new student because Access generates a run-time error if you try to append a record for an existing student (that is, a record with a duplicate primary key value).

- The second query produces the three fields for tlnkClassStudent, and produces all new records. Nevertheless, you include a test for new records in this query also.

  By having both queries test to be sure the records to be appended are new, you avoid the potential macro failure that occurs if you try to import and append the same data a second time.

3. Convert the queries into append queries, then run them to append the records in the temporary table to the two data tables.

4. Delete the temporary table.

Importing the Spreadsheet File Interactively

First we'll go through the steps for importing a spreadsheet file interactively, and then we'll automate the process.

1. Close all open tables.

2. Choose File ➤ Get External Data ➤ Import, then select Microsoft Excel from the Files Of Type list, and select Offsite (see Figure 12.8). (Depending on the options you chose when you installed Access, you may see a message instructing you to run the Access Setup program again before working with an Excel file. Follow the directions before continuing.)

3. Click the Import button. Access displays the first dialog of the Import Spreadsheet wizard (see Figure 12.9). In this dialog, you can specify the portion of the spreadsheet file you want to import.

4. Click the Next button. Check the First Row Contains Column Headings check box (see Figure 12.10).

5. Click Next. Use this dialog to specify and modify information for each field (see Figure 12.11).

6. Click Next. You can specify a primary key for the imported table in this dialog (see Figure 12.12), but you don't need a primary key for this temporary table.

FIGURE 12.8:
The Import dialog box.

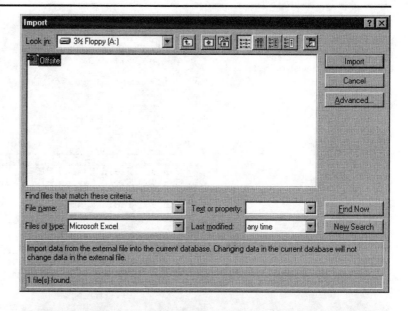

FIGURE 12.9:
The Import Spreadsheet wizard.

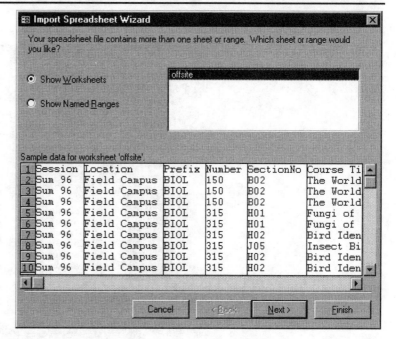

FIGURE 12.10:

Specify that the first row of the spreadsheet contains column headings (field names) for the table.

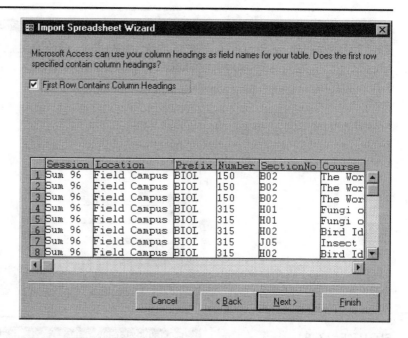

FIGURE 12.11:

Specify the primary key information.

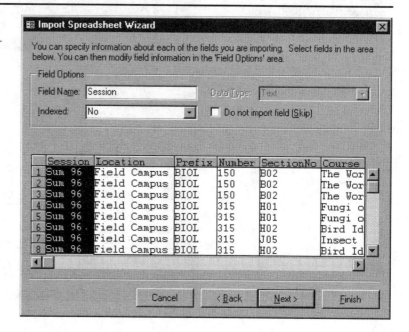

FIGURE 12.12:

Specify the primary key information.

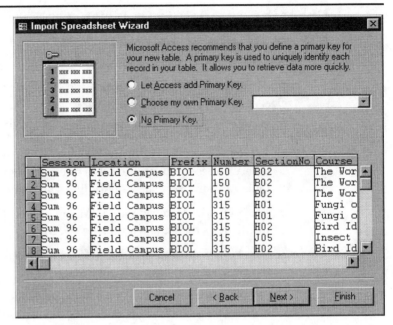

7. Select the No Primary Key option and click Next. Use the next dialog to specify the name for the import table.

8. Enter **tblOffsite** as the name for the import table. You can elect to run the Table Analyzer Wizard in this dialog, but we have already analyzed the table and don't need the wizard's help.

9. Click Finish. Access imports the data into the tblOffsite table in the program file.

10. Click OK, then select tblOffsite in the Database window, and click the Design button. The wizard has created fields and assigned data types for each spreadsheet column. Access recognized the two date fields and assigned them the Date/Time data type, and assigned Text as the default data type for the other fields.

11. Switch to Datasheet view. The import table contains the data from the spreadsheet file.

Creating a Find Unmatched Query to Select Only the New Records

You'll create a query to append new student information to tblStudents. The query selects the new students, decomposes the name field into first name and last name fields, and then appends the records to tblStudents.

1. In the toolbar, click the arrow on the New Object button and select New Query. Access displays the list of query wizards. Use the Find Unmatched Query Wizard to create a query that selects the new students.

2. Select Find Unmatched Query Wizard and click OK. Use the dialog to select tblOffsite as the table with the new records.

3. Select tblOffsite and click Next. Use the dialog to select tblStudents as the table with the existing students.

4. Select tblStudents and click Next. Use the dialog to specify the matching fields. In this example the matching fields have different names, so the wizard can't suggest candidates for the match.

5. In tblOffsite, select StudID; in tblStudents, select StudentID; click the double arrow, and then click Next. Use the dialog to select the fields for the query.

6. Select the StudID and StudentName fields and click Next.

7. Click Finish. Access creates the query and displays the records for the new students.

Understanding the Find Unmatched Query

We'll study the query that the wizard has built because we'll need to create a similar query from scratch later.

1. Switch to Design view. The wizard has created an outer join between the two tables, with the join arrow pointing from tblOffsite to tblStudents.

2. Right-click on the join line and select the Join Properties command from the shortcut menu. The Join Properties dialog box indicates that the query includes all students from tblOffsite and those students from tblStudents with matching StudentID values (see Figure 12.13). The wizard has also placed the

StudentID field from tblStudents in the design grid with Is Null as the criteria expression. To understand the effect of the Is Null criteria, delete it temporarily.

3. Click into the criteria cell for StudentID; delete the Is Null expression, check the Show check box, and then switch to Datasheet view. The datasheet displays the outer join: all rows of tblOffsite are included, whether the students are existing students or new students (see Figure 12.14). The seven rows with values in both StudID and StudentID fields are existing students, while the three rows with blanks in the StudentID column are the new students.

FIGURE 12.13:

Using the Find Unmatched Query Wizard to select new students.

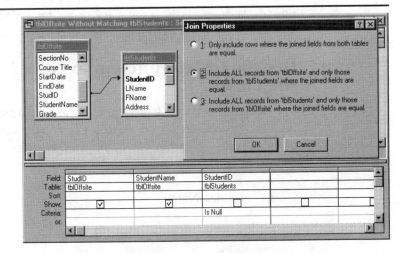

FIGURE 12.14:

The result of the outer join. Existing students are matched with records in tblStudents. New students have no matching records in tblStudents, so their StudentID column is null.

StudID	StudentName	StudentID
111-11-1111	Hernandez, Richard	111-11-1111
111-33-1111	Cheng, Jim	111-33-1111
111-33-2222	Petley, John	111-33-2222
111-11-4444	Burgett, Jack	111-11-4444
111-22-3333	Gerkensmeyer, Jerry	111-22-3333
111-13-3111	Hyback, Nancy	111-13-3111
111-22-1111	Burch, Don	111-22-1111
412-11-6789	Konigsberg, Linda	
552-98-1234	Shaw, Greer	
412-11-3322	Stanton, Mary	

tblOffsite Without Matching tblStudents : Sele...

Record: 1 of 10

When you set the criteria for the StudentID column to Is Null, the query selects only the new students.

4. Switch to Design view; in the StudentID column, clear the Show check box and set the criteria to Is Null.

Using the String Manipulation Functions to Modify Data

You'll use several built-in string manipulation functions to decompose the Student-Name field. Think of StudentName as a string of characters. The character that defines the last name is the comma: if you can determine where the comma is, you can specify the last name as the characters to the left of the comma.

Use the InStr() Function to Locate the Comma

In its simplest form, the InStr() function takes two arguments: the first argument is the string expression you are searching *in*, and the second argument is the string expression you are searching *for*. In this case, search *in* the StudentName string *for* the comma by using the expression

InStr(StudentName,",")

1. Switch to Design view, then click in the next empty field cell and enter the expression:

   Comma:InStr(StudentName,",")

2. Switch to Datasheet view. The position of the comma is correctly determined (see Figure 12.15).

Use the Left() Function to Select the Characters in the Last Name

The number of characters in the last name is the number of characters to the left of the comma, or (Comma − 1). You can use the Left() function to select a specified number of characters starting from the left end of the string. The Left() function

FIGURE 12.15:

Using the InStr() function to determine the location of the comma.

takes two arguments: the first argument is the string expression, and the second argument is the number of characters you want to select, starting from the left end of the string. In this case, the expression is

Left(StudentName,Comma – 1)

1. Switch to Design view, then click in the next empty field cell and enter the expression:

   LName: Left(StudentName,Comma – 1)

2. Switch to Datasheet view. The expression correctly returns the last name.

Use the Right() Function to Select the Characters of the First Name

To return the first name, use the Right() function to select a specified number of characters starting from the right end of the string. The Right() function takes two arguments: the first argument is the string expression, and the second argument is the number of characters you want to take, starting from the right end of the string. The position of the comma is Comma and the position of the space is (Comma + 1), so the sum of the number of characters in the last name, comma, and space is (Comma + 1); the rest of the characters are the first name. In other words, the number of characters in the first name is equal to the difference between the total number of characters in StudentName and (Comma + 1). You can use the Len() function to determine the number of characters in a string. Therefore,

Len(StudentName) – (Comma + 1)

returns the number of characters in the first name.

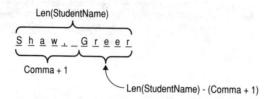

To select the characters in the first name, use the expression

Right(StudentName,Len(StudentName)–(Comma + 1))

1. Switch to Design view, then click in the next empty field cell and enter the expression:

   FName: Right(StudentName,Len(StudentName)–(Comma + 1))

2. Switch to Datasheet view. The expression correctly returns the first name of each student (see Figure 12.16).

FIGURE 12.16:
Using the string manipulation functions to decompose a full name into last name and first name.

StudID	StudentName	Comma	LName	FName
412-11-6789	Konigsberg, Linda	11	Konigsberg	Linda
552-98-1234	Shaw, Greer	5	Shaw	Greer
412-11-3322	Stanton, Mary	8	Stanton	Mary

tblOffsite Without Matching tblStudents : Select Query

Record: 1 of 3

All that remains is to tidy up the calculations by substituting the expression for Comma into the expressions for LName and FName.

1. Switch to Design view, then click in the Comma field cell; select the expression to the right of the colon, and copy to the clipboard.

2. Click in the LName field, select the [Comma], and paste the copied expression. The expression should read:

   LName: Left(StudentName,(InStr(StudentName,",") - 1))

3. Click in the FName field, select the [Comma], and paste the copied expression again. The expression should read:

FName: Right(StudentName,Len(StudentName)–(InStr(StudentName,",") + 1))

4. Switch to Design view; delete the StudentName and Comma fields from the design grid, and move the StudentID field (with the Is Null criteria) to the right of the LName and FName fields.

5. Switch to Datasheet view. The fields are now correct and in position for appending to tblStudents.

Changing the Query to an Append Query

Convert the query into an append query to append the new student data to tblStudents.

1. Switch to Design view, then click the arrow on the Query Type button in the toolbar and choose Append.

2. In the Append dialog box, select tblStudents from the Table Name list, and click OK. The append query includes the Append To row, which indicates the field in tblStudents that the query field will be appended to. Since the StudentID query field is present only to select the new students and is not to be appended, you'll cut the expression in the Append To cell for StudentID and paste it into the Append To cell for StudID.

3. In the StudentID field with the Is Null criteria, click in the Append To cell, select the contents, and cut to the clipboard; then click in the Append To cell under the StudID field and paste the copied information.

4. Save the query as **qappStudentsImport**

5. In the Database window, select and delete the query 'tblOffsite' Without Matching 'tblStudents'.

6. Close the query.

Since append queries actually change the tables, you won't run the append queries interactively.

Creating a Query Using Alternate Primary Keys

You create a query to display the three fields that you'll append to tlnkClassStudent: ScheduleNo, StudentID, and Grade. Because the imported data in tblOffsite doesn't include the ScheduleNo field explicitly, you use alternate primary keys and create the query based on tblOffsite, tblCourses (to uniquely determine the CourseID based on data in tblOffsite), and tblClasses (to uniquely determine the ScheduleNo based on data in tblOffsite and the CourseID).

1. Select the tblOffsite table, then click the arrow on the New Object button in the toolbar; select New Query, then select Design View in the New Query dialog box and click OK. A query window opens with the field list for the tblOffsite table.

2. In the toolbar, click the Show Table button, then add the tblCourses and tblClasses tables and click the Close button. Access displays the relationship join line between tblCourses and tblClasses, but you'll have to create the join lines between tblOffsite and tblCourses and between tblOffsite and tblClasses.

3. Drag the following fields between tables to create new join lines between tblOffsite and tblCourses:

   - drag Prefix from tblOffsite to Prefix in tblCourses
   - drag Number from tblOffsite to Number in tblCourses
   - drag Course Title from tblOffsite to Name in tblCourses

   The tblOffsite and tblCourses tables are joined.

4. From tblOffsite, drag Prefix, Number, and Course Title to the design grid; from tblCourses, drag CourseID to the design grid; then switch to Datasheet view. Observe that the CourseID is uniquely defined.

5. Switch back to design view, and create the joins between tblOffsite and tblClasses:

   - drag Session from tblOffsite to Session in tblClasses
   - drag SectionNo from tblOffsite to SectionNo in tblClasses

   The tblOffsite and tblClasses tables are joined. The tblOffsite table is now joined to tblCourses and tblClasses by the five fields in tblOffsite that uniquely determine the ScheduleNo.

6. From tblOffsite, drag StudID, Grade, Session, and SectionNo to the design grid; from tblClasses, drag ScheduleNo to the design grid; then switch to Datasheet view. The classes are displayed, along with the CourseID and ScheduleNo corresponding to each class (see Figure 12.17). Now that you have observed how the query is built, you can delete all fields from the grid except the three fields that you'll append to the linking table.

7. In the design grid, delete the Session, Prefix, Number, SectionNo, Course-Title, and CourseID fields.

8. Switch to Datasheet view. The result is exactly the data required for the tlnkClassStudent linking table (see Figure 12.18).

9. Save the query as **qryClassStudentImport**

FIGURE 12.17:

Use a query to join five fields from the imported table to fields in tblCourses and tblClasses, in order to uniquely determine the ScheduleNo.

	Session	Prefix	Num	Sect	Course Title	StudID	Grade	Course ID	ScheduleNo
▶	Sum 96	BIOL	150	B02	The World of Plants	111-11-1111	A	19400	11244
	Sum 96	BIOL	150	B02	The World of Plants	111-11-1111	A	19400	34
	Sum 96	BIOL	150	B02	The World of Plants	111-33-1111	A	19400	11244
	Sum 96	BIOL	150	B02	The World of Plants	111-33-1111	A	19400	34
	Sum 96	BIOL	150	B02	The World of Plants	111-33-2222	B	19400	11244
	Sum 96	BIOL	150	B02	The World of Plants	111-33-2222	B	19400	34
	Sum 96	BIOL	315	H01	Fungi of Sierra Nevada	111-11-4444	B	21513	11336
	Sum 96	BIOL	315	H01	Fungi of Sierra Nevada	111-22-3333	B	21513	11336
	Sum 96	BIOL	315	H02	Bird Identification by S<	111-13-3111	A	21577	11340
	Sum 96	BIOL	315	J05	Insect Biology and Iden	111-22-1111	A	21549	11373
	Sum 96	BIOL	315	H02	Bird Identification by S<	412-11-6789	C	21577	11340
	Sum 96	BIOL	315	H02	Bird Identification by S<	552-98-1234	C	21577	11340
	Sum 96	BIOL	315	H02	Bird Identification by S<	412-11-3322	W	21577	11340

FIGURE 12.18:

The records to be appended to tlnkClassStudent.

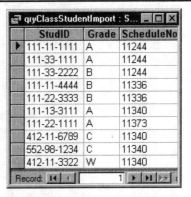

	StudID	Grade	ScheduleNo
▶	111-11-1111	A	11244
	111-33-1111	A	11244
	111-33-2222	B	11244
	111-11-4444	B	11336
	111-22-3333	B	11336
	111-13-3111	A	11340
	111-22-1111	A	11373
	412-11-6789	C	11340
	552-98-1234	C	11340
	412-11-3322	W	11340

Record: |◀| ◀ | 1 | ▶ |▶| |▶*|

Modifying a Find Unmatched Query for Two Matching Fields

You could convert this query to an append query and use it to append the records to tlnkClassStudent. If all of the records are new there will be no problem, but if any of the records have already been added to the table, the duplicate records will generate run-time errors when you try to append them. To avoid errors, you'll test the records for "newness" by creating a Find Unmatched Query (similar to the query you used for the append query for tblStudents).

1. In the toolbar, click the arrow on New Object button; select New Query, then select Find Unmatched Query Wizard and click OK. You will specify the qryClassStudentImport query, as it is the query that contains the records that have no related records in the table or query that you will specify in the next dialog.

2. Select Queries, then select qryClassStudentImport and click Next. You will use this dialog to specify the tlnkClassStudent table as the table with related records.

3. Select tlnkClassStudent and click Next. You use the next dialog to specify the matching fields (see Figure 12.19). When you use the wizard, you can specify only one join field in each table or query; in our case there are two matching fields—we can continue to use the wizard but we'll have to modify the result.

FIGURE 12.19:

You can specify only one matching field using the Find Unmatched Query Wizard.

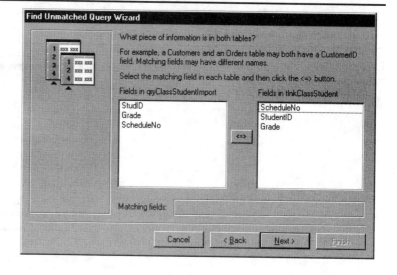

4. Select ScheduleNo in each list, then click the double arrow and click Next. Use this dialog to specify the fields you want in the query results.

5. Click the double arrow to display all of the fields, then click Next. Use this dialog to name the new query. We'll accept the default name.

6. Click Finish.

7. Switch to Design view. Figure 12.20 shows the query created by the wizard. We'll modify the query to include the second matching field.

8. Drag the StudID field in qryClassStudentImport to the StudentID field in tlnkClassStudent.

9. Right-click the join line and select Join Properties from the shortcut menu.

10. Select the second option and click OK.

11. Drag StudentID from tlnkClassStudent to the design grid, then clear the Show check box and enter **Is Null** in the Criteria cell. Figure 12.21 shows the final version of the query to select new records to append to tlnkClassStudent.

FIGURE 12.20:

The query produced by the Find Unmatched Query Wizard. When you use the wizard, you can specify only one join field.

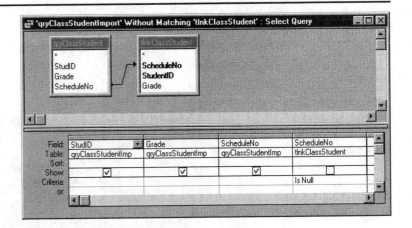

Convert the Query to an Append Query

Convert this query to an append query that appends the new records to tlnkClassStudent.

FIGURE 12.21:

The query to select new (unmatched) records when there are two matching fields.

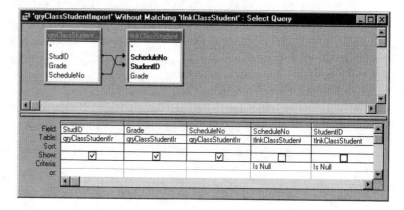

1. Choose Query ➤ Append, then select tlnkClassStudent from the Table Name list in the Append dialog, and click OK. You modify the entries in the Append To row so that the fields from the tblOffsite table are appended.

2. In the ScheduleNo field from tlnkClassStudent, delete the expression in the Append To row; then select the Append To expression in the StudentID field, and cut and paste the expression into the Append To cell for the StudID field.

3. Save the query as **qappClassStudentImport**. Figure 12.22 shows the design of the append query.

FIGURE 12.22:

The query to append new records to tlnkClassStudent.

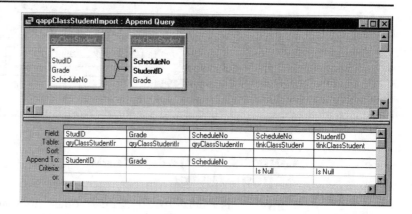

4. Close the qappClassStudentImport query.

5. In the Database window, select and delete the query 'tblOffsite' Without Matching 'tlnkClassStudent'.

6. In the Database window, select and delete the tblOffsite table.

Automating the Import Process

You are now ready to automate the process of importing and modifying the spreadsheet file. You've analyzed the data, and created two append queries that modify the data and append records to two data tables. In automating the process, you need to consider how the process fits into your database design.

Create a Mini-Switchboard for Importing Data

In the College database there are several kinds of imported data, so you'll create a dialog box named fdlgImport and use it as a mini-switchboard that displays the import choices in an option group. You branch to the fdlgImport mini-switchboard by clicking the Import Data option button in main switchboard.

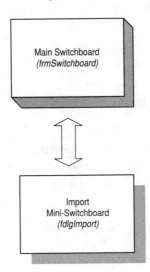

In this chapter you deal with two kinds of imported data: registration data (in the spreadsheet file of this section), and student information (in a text file in the next section). You prepare for both processes now.

Create the Mini-Switchboard as a Custom Dialog Box

You use the dialog box form master you created in Chapter 11 to create the mini-switchboard. You'll create an option group, with option buttons for importing both spreadsheet and text file data.

1. In the Database window, select zsfdlgMaster, then copy and paste it as **fdlgImport** and set its Caption property to **Import Data**

2. Open fdlgImport in Design view. Make sure the form's PopUp property is No so that you have access to the menus and toolbars (we'll make the form pop-up when we are finished designing it).

3. Click the Option Group tool, and create an option group (2" wide and 1.5" tall) in fdlgImport.

4. Set the option group Name property to **grpImport** and delete the label.

5. Click the Option button tool and create two option buttons in the grpImport option group; set the Caption property of the first to **Import Off Campus Registration** and the second to **Import Student Information**

6. Save the form and switch to Form view. Figure 12.23 shows the mini-switchboard for importing data.

7. Click the Return button on the form.

Opening the Import Mini-Switchboard from the Main Switchboard

The Import Data option button is in the Students and Instructors option group on the main switchboard, and has the option value 5. You modify the macro for this option group to open the fdlgImport mini-switchboard.

1. Click in mfrmSwitchboard.

FIGURE 12.23:
The mini-switchboard for
importing data.

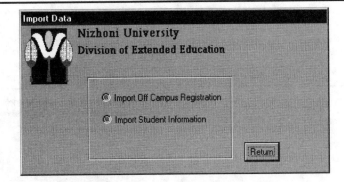

2. Locate the grpStudentsInstructors_AfterUpdate macro, then click in the row that has the **SetValue** action that hides the switchboard and click the Insert Row button (in the toolbar).

3. Click in the Condition cell of the inserted row and enter the condition **grpStudentsInstructors = 5**

4. Select the **OpenForm** action and set the **Form Name** argument to **fdlgImport**

5. Save and close the macro group.

Test the Macro

1. Click the Import Data option button in frmSwitchboard. The fdlgImport mini-switchboard opens and the main switchboard is hidden.

2. Switch to Design view.

Create a Macro to Import the File and Append the Data

You'll create a macro that imports the spreadsheet file using the **TransferSpreadsheet** action and then runs the two append queries to modify and append the data. You run the macro when the Import Off Campus Registration option button is clicked. There are several steps in the process, so you'll create a separate macro named OffsiteGrades and use the **RunMacro** action to run it when the option button is clicked. This example assumes the spreadsheet file is on a floppy disk that you insert in drive A (if your floppy drive is B, alter the macro as required). Before you tell Access to start importing data, you have to make sure the Offsite file has been inserted in drive A. If no disk is in drive A when you begin the import process, Access displays the error message shown in Figure 12.24.

FIGURE 12.24:

The error message when there is no disk in drive A.

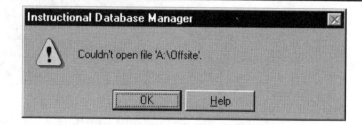

If there is a disk in the drive but the disk doesn't contain a file with the path A:\Offsite, Access displays the error message shown in Figure 12.25.

FIGURE 12.25:

The error message when the disk in drive A doesn't contain the file with path A:\Offsite.

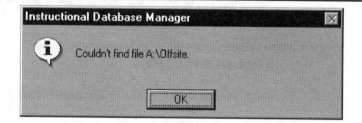

In either case, when you try to import the spreadsheet file using the **Transfer-Spreadsheet** action, Access won't be able to import the file. By design, the **TransferSpreadsheet** action doesn't fail when either of these run-time errors occurs; however, when you try to run the first append query, the **OpenQuery** action fails because the tblOffsite table doesn't exist. Using macros alone, you can't determine if the correct file is in the drive, but you can create an error handler using Visual Basic to detect either error. Table 4.1 indicates that the error codes for these two errors are:

Error Code	Error Message
3051	Couldn't open file '	'
7889	Couldn't find file '	'

Create a Visual Basic Error Handler for an Unavailable Import File

You'll create an error handler to deal with these two errors. In either case, if the error occurs the error handler displays a custom message and sets an *error flag* on the fdlgImport dialog box. When either error occurs, Access runs the error handler and then returns to the next macro action. By setting an error flag on the form, the macro can test to determine if either error occurred, and stop if it has. You'll place an unbound, hidden ErrorFlag text box on the dialog form to hold the value of the flag. When the dialog form opens, the value in the text box is null. If either error occurs, the handler *flags the error* by setting the value of the ErrorFlag text box to 1. (If you want the macro to know which error occurred, you can use the error handler to set the value of the error flag to DataErr instead.)

1. Click in fdlgImport, then switch to Design view; click in the OnError property, then click the Build button and select Code Builder; enter the following lines of code between the two lines of the code template:

```
If DataErr = 3051 Then
      MsgBox "Please insert a disk with the correct file
      ➥in drive A and try again."
      Response = acDataErrContinue
      ErrorFlag = 1
ElseIf DataErr = 7889 Then
      MsgBox "The disk in drive A doesn't contain the
      ➥correct file. Insert the correct disk and try again."
      Response = acDataErrContinue
      ErrorFlag = 1
Else
      Response = acDataErrDisplay
End If
```

2. Choose Run ➤ Compile Loaded Modules, then close the module window.

3. Select the Text Box tool and place a text box in the detail section of fdlgImport.

4. Set the Name property to **ErrorFlag**. When either error occurs, the code sets the value of this control to 1 in the statement `ErrorFlag = 1`.

5. Set the Visible property to No and delete the label.

6. Save the form.

Asking If the Spreadsheet File Has Been Loaded

You can use the MsgBox() function to ask if the correct file has been placed in drive A (refer to Chapter 8, "Data Entry Operations", for more information on the MsgBox() function). Use the following MsgBox() function:

MsgBox("Importing off campus data requires a disk with the file A:\ Offsite to be inserted in drive A. Insert the correct disk in drive A, click Yes to continue. Click No otherwise.", 4+48+256, "Importing Data")

In the second argument, each of the three numbers defines a design characteristic of the message box. The Button Set Type of 4 indicates that Yes and No buttons are displayed, the Icon Type of 48 indicates that the Warning Message icon is displayed, and the Default Type of 256 indicates that the No button is the default. The value returned by the function depends on the button you select: the function returns the value 6 if you select the Yes button and the value 7 if you select the No button.

The OffsiteGrades Macro

The macro begins by asking if the correct file has been loaded into drive A. The macro uses the MsgBox() function in a condition, as follows:

MsgBox("Importing off campus data requires a disk with the file A:\ Offsite to be inserted in drive A. Insert the correct disk in drive A, click Yes to continue. Click No otherwise.", 4+48+256, "Importing Data")>6

If you click the No button, the function returns the value 7, so the condition is true; the macro displays a message that the import process has been aborted and terminates. If you click the Yes button, the function returns the value 6; the macro runs the `TransferSpreadsheet` action to import the file. If Access finds the file, the macro imports the spreadsheet file into a new temporary table. If Access can't find the file, one of the two errors is generated, and the Visual Basic code sets the Error-Flag to 1. The macro tests the value of the ErrorFlag and terminates if the value is 1 (not null). If the value of the ErrorFlag is null, the macro runs the query to append the new student information to tblStudents, then runs the query to append the new class registration data to tlnkClassStudent, and finally deletes the temporary table.

Since the macro takes more than a few seconds, begin the macro with the **Hourglass** action to display the hourglass while the macro runs, and the **Echo** action to turn off screen updating and display a message in the Status Bar. Since the append queries change the data tables, Access displays default confirmation messages while executing each append query. You can use the **SetWarnings** action to suppress the confirmation messages. When the import process is complete, you can use the **MsgBox** action to display a message indicating success. The flow diagram for the final macro, with a few additional **MsgBox** actions to display progress during execution, is shown in Figure 12.26.

The Option Group Macro

You'll run the Offsite Grades macro from the Import Data mini-switchboard. You need to create the macro for the option group on the mini-switchboard. The macro tests the value of the option group, then runs the Offsite Grades macro if the value is 1 or the StudentAddresses macro (which we'll create in the next section) if the value is 2, and finally resets the option group and error flag values to null. Figure 12.27 shows the flow diagram for the macro.

1. Open a new macrosheet and save it as **mfdlgImport**

2. Click in the first Macro Name cell and name the new macro **grpImport_AfterUpdate**

3. Enter the macro shown in Table 12.1.

TABLE 12.1: Macro to import data.

Macro Name	Condition	Action	Action Arguments
grpImport_ AfterUpdate			
	grpImport = 1	RunMacro	**Macro Name**: mfdlgImport.OffsiteGrades
	grpImport = 2	RunMacro	**Macro Name**: mfdlgImport.StudentAddresses
		SetValue	**Item**: grpImport
			Expression: Null
		SetValue	**Item**: ErrorFlag
			Expression: Null

FIGURE 12.26:

Flow diagram for the grpImport_AfterUpdate macro.

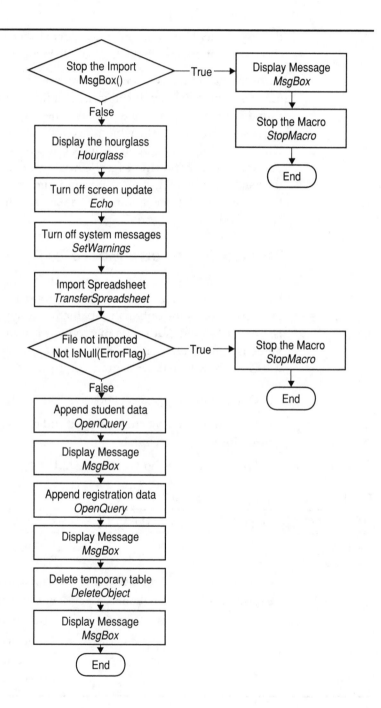

FIGURE 12.27:

Flow diagram for the grpImport_AfterUpdate macro.

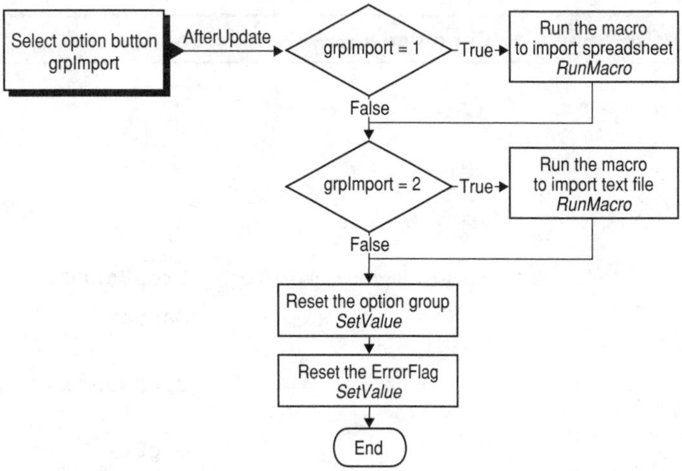

TABLE 12.2: Macro to automate the process to import and append spreadsheet data.

Macro Name	Condition	Action	Action Arguments
OffsiteGrades			
	MsgBox("Importing off campus data requires a disk with the file A:\Offsite to be inserted in drive A. Insert the correct disk in drive A, click Yes to continue. Click No otherwise.", 4+48+256, "Importing Data")>6	**MsgBox**	**Message**: Import aborted
	...	**StopMacro**	
		Hourglass	
		Echo	**Echo On**: No
			Status Bar Text: Importing Off Campus Data
		SetWarnings	
		TransferSpreadsheet	**Transfer Type**: Import

TABLE 12.2: Macro to automate the process to import and append spreadsheet data *(continued)*.

Macro Name	Condition	Action	Action Arguments
			Spreadsheet Type: Microsoft Excel 5-7
			Table Name: tblOffsite
			File Name: A:\Offsite
			Has Field Names: Yes
	Not IsNull(ErrorFlag)	StopMacro	
		MsgBox	**Message**: Spreadsheet imported
		OpenQuery	**Query Name**: qappStudentsImport
		MsgBox	**Message**: New students added
		OpenQuery	**Query Name**: qappClassStudentImport
		MsgBox	**Message**: Classes & grades entered
		DeleteObject	**Object Type**: Table
			Object Name: tblOffsite
		MsgBox	**Message**: Data successfully imported!
			Title: Import Off Campus Registration

4. Click into the Macro Name cell of a new row, and name the new macro **OffsiteGrades**

5. Enter the macro shown in Table 12.2.

6. In the Condition cell of the row that has the **SetWarnings** action, enter **False**. During the trial run of the macro, you enter False in this Condition cell to suppress the execution of the **SetWarnings** action and display the system confirmation messages. You can use the default messages to observe progress during execution of the macro.

7. Save the macro.

Attach and Test the Macro to Import the Data

1. Select fdlgImport and switch to Design view.

2. Select the option group, then click in the AfterUpdate property and select mfdlgImport.grpImport_AfterUpdate.

3. Click in the form's PopUp property and change the value to Yes. You are finished designing the mini-switchboard.

4. Copy the Offsite file from the Automate folder on your hard drive to a floppy disk, then remove the disk from drive A.

5. Switch to Form view; on the mini-switchboard, click the Import Off Campus Registration option button.

6. Click Yes to the first message asking if the file is in drive A. The custom message indicating you need to insert a disk is displayed. When you click OK, the macro will terminate.

7. Click OK, then insert a blank floppy disk into drive A and click the Import Off Campus Registration option button again.

8. Click Yes to the first message. The custom message indicating that the disk doesn't contain the correct file is displayed. When you click OK, the macro will terminate.

9. Click OK, then insert the floppy disk with the Offsite file into drive A and click the Import Off Campus Registration option button again. The message indicating the spreadsheet has been imported is displayed.

10. Click Yes to both of the confirmation statements that are displayed before Access runs the append queries. After appending, the message indicating that the data has been imported successfully is displayed.

11. Click OK.

When you are satisfied that the macro runs correctly, delete the False condition from the row that has the **SetWarnings** action. If you prefer, you can also delete the two **MsgBox** actions that follow the **OpenQuery** actions.

Importing Word Files

This section shows you how to automate the process of importing and modifying a text file. The automation process is very similar to the process you learned in the last section for importing and modifying a spreadsheet file.

In the College database, the field campus keeps track of the home addresses of all students who register for classes at the campus and of all people who request information about the classes that are offered at the campus. Microsoft Word is used to generate a text file of the student information. Along with the Offsite spreadsheet file, the campus has produced the Students tab-delimited text file (partially shown in Figure 12.28).

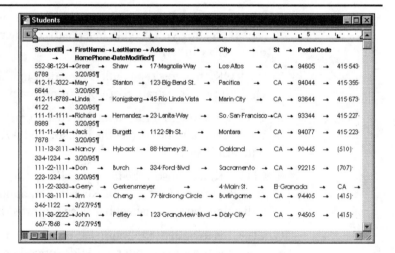

Importing the Text File Interactively

We'll go through the steps for importing the text file interactively, and create the Import Specification that we'll use in the **TransferText** action when we automate the process in the next section.

1. Select the File ➤ Get External Data ➤ Import command and choose Text Files from the Files Of Type list.

2. Select Students and click Import. The Text Import wizard is summoned (Figure 12.29 shows the first dialog box).

FIGURE 12.29:
The Text Import wizard analyzes the format of the text file.

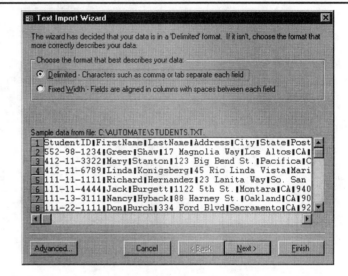

3. Click the Next button. In the next dialog you choose the field delimiter.

4. Click the Tab option, check the First Row Contains Field Names check box, select {none} as the Text Qualifier, and then click Next. In the next dialog you choose to store the data in a new table.

5. Click Next. In the next dialog you can modify the information about each field.

6. Click the PostalCode field, select Text Data Type, and then click Next. In the next dialog you can define a primary key.

7. Choose the No Primary Key option button and click Next. In the next dialog you can name the import table. The College database uses the name tblStudents for the student information data table, so accept Students as the default name for the import table. Before completing the import process, you'll save the import specifications.

8. Click the Advanced button. The import specifications dialog box (see Figure 12.30) indicates the choices you've made.

FIGURE 12.30:

The import specifications for
students.txt.

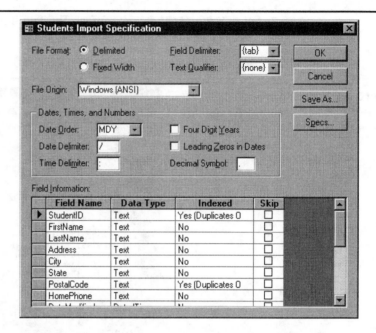

9. Click the Save As button, and then click OK to accept the default name. The
   specifications are saved as Students Import Specification.

10. Click Finish.

Creating a Single Query to Append New Records and Update Existing Records

You've learned how to use the Find Unmatched Query Wizard to create a query that
selects the new students' records, but there is an additional problem: some of the
existing students' address and/or phone information may have changed since the
last time they registered, so in addition to appending the new students, you need
to update the records of the existing students with any new address/phone information. You can create a single query to select records in Students, both for new students and for the existing students whose records need to be updated.

After creating a query to select the records, you convert the query to an update query that performs both operations: appending new records to the end of tblStudents, and updating existing records in tblStudents.

Selecting the New Students

You can create a query to select the new students using the Find Unmatched Query Wizard.

1. In the Database window, select the Students table, then in the toolbar, click the arrow on the New Object button; select New Query, then select Find Unmatched Query Wizard and click OK. In the first dialog you select the table that contains the new student records.

2. Select Students and click Next. In the next dialog you select the table that contains the existing student records.

3. Select tblStudents and click Next. In the next dialog you specify the matching fields.

4. Select StudentID in both lists, then click the double arrow and click the Next button.

5. Click the double arrow (to display all of the fields in the result) and then click the Next button. Accept the default name for the query.

6. Click the Finish button. The query datasheet displays the records of the two new students. (If you didn't work through the last section, the datasheet displays records for five new students.)

Selecting the Records to Update

You can modify this query so that it also selects the records of existing students who have new address information.

The DateModified field indicates when the record was last modified. For each student record in Students, you compare the DateModified value to the DateModified value of the corresponding student record in tblStudents. If the imported value is more recent than the table value, you update the record; otherwise, you don't update. You set criteria for the DateModified field from tblStudents to select the records that need to be updated.

1. Switch to Design view.

2. Check the Show check box for the StudentID field (from the tblStudents table) to show the Student ID of the existing student records that need to be updated.

3. Drag the DateModified field from tblStudents to the next empty Field cell in the design grid, then click in the Or cell below the DateModified field and enter this expression:

   <Students.DateModified

   This criteria selects records for existing students in Students that have been modified more recently than the corresponding records in tblStudents. Criteria in the Or row tell the query to select records that are new *or* records that need to be updated (see Figure 12.31).

4. Switch to Datasheet view. The datasheet displays the records, including the two new student records you just imported and the existing student records that need to be updated.

FIGURE 12.31:
Modify the query so that it selects records that are new or records that need to be updated.

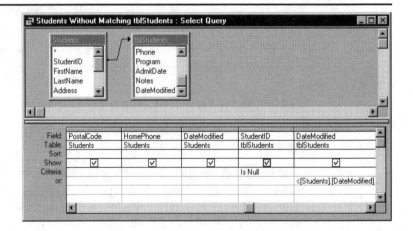

Creating the Update Query

The query displays fields from the Students table. To use this query to update the corresponding fields in tblStudents, you'll delete the fields from Students and replace them with the corresponding fields from tblStudents.

1. Select and delete all of the columns from the Students table.

2. From the tblStudents table, drag the LName, FName, Address, City, State, ZipCode, and Phone to the design grid.

3. In the toolbar, click the Query Type button and select Update.

4. Enter the following in the Update To cells:

Field Cell	Update To
StudentID	Students.StudentID
LName	Students.LastName
FName	Students.FirstName
Address	Students.Address
City	Students.City
State	Students.State
ZipCode	Students.PostalCode
Phone	Students.HomePhone
DateModified	Students.DateModified

5. Save the query as **qupdStudents**. Figure 12.32 shows a portion of the update query in Design view.

6. In the Database window, delete the query Students Without Matching tblStudents.

The qupdStudents query shows the power of Access queries: a single update query appends new records to a table and updates existing records that satisfy a specific criteria.

The update query appends records for new students and updates records for existing students.

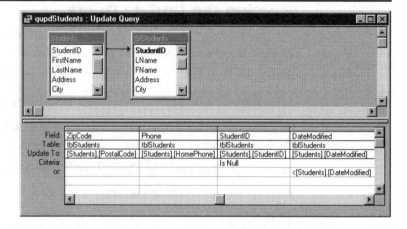

> **NOTE**
>
> This query takes advantage of the ability of the Jet database engine to update outer joins. If a record doesn't exist in tblStudents, the outer join with Students causes a new record to be included in the recordset of the query. When the update runs, the join field is updated and a new record is created in tblStudents.

Automating the Import and Update Procedure

You create a new macro called StudentAddresses (to run the import and update procedure) by copying and modifying the OffsiteGrades macro that you created in the last section.

1. Select and copy all of the rows of the macro OffsiteGrades.

2. Click into an empty row and paste the copied rows.

3. Change the name to **StudentAddresses**, then modify the macro by deleting rows and changing rows as shown in Table 12.3. Changes to the text are shown in italics.

TABLE 12.3: Macro to automate the process to import, append, and update text file data.

Macro Name	Condition	Action	Action Arguments
StudentAddresses			
	MsgBox("Importing off campus data requires a disk with the file A:*Students* to be inserted in drive A. Insert the correct disk in drive A, click Yes to continue. Click No otherwise.", 4+48+256, "Importing Data")>6	MsgBox	**Message**: Import aborted
	...	StopMacro	
		Hourglass	
		Echo	**Echo On**: No
			Status Bar Text: Importing Off Campus Data
		SetWarnings	
		TransferText	**Transfer Type**: Import Delimited
			Specification Name: Students Import Specification
			Table Name: Students
			File Name: A:\Students
			Has Field Names: Yes
	Not IsNull(ErrorFlag)	StopMacro	
		MsgBox	**Message**: Text file imported
		OpenQuery	**Query Name**: qupdStudents
		MsgBox	**Message**: New students added and existing students updated.
		DeleteObject	**Object Type**: Table
			Object Name: Students
		MsgBox	**Message**: Data successfully imported!
			Title: Import Student Information

Test the Import and Update Procedure

1. In the Database window, select and delete the Students table.

2. Copy the file Students from the Automate folder on your hard drive to a floppy disk.

3. Click in the fdlgImport mini-switchboard and then click the Import Student Addresses option button. Access displays the sequence of custom messages, ending with the message that the data was successfully imported (see Figure 12.33).

FIGURE 12.33:

The message displayed by the macro that imports student information.

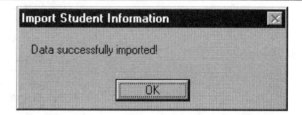

Endnotes

In this chapter you've learned some techniques for working with external data, including how to:

- use the Database Splitter wizard to split an application into a program file and a separate data file

- refresh the links to external tables interactively

- use the built-in string manipulation functions to modify imported data

- use action queries to modify, append, and update data

- avoid the errors that occur when you try to append records with duplicate primary keys, by creating a find unmatched query to select only the new records

- automate the process of importing and modifying data in a spreadsheet or a text file

You also learned an interesting programming technique: how to set an error flag in the Visual Basic error handler and pass information to a macro that a run-time error has occurred.

CHAPTER

THIRTEEN

Closing Out a Session

- Using a mini-switchboard for session operations

- Testing data for completeness

- Changing a form's RecordSource property dynamically

- Inner and outer joins

- Choosing the Cascade Delete Related Records option

- Creating an archive process

In many database applications, you divide time into intervals such as months, quarters, or fiscal years. At the end of an interval, you "close out" the interval by performing a set of database operations that includes testing records for *completeness*, calculating summaries, and archiving records by appending them to historical files and then deleting them from the current files. Completeness means that before closing out a specific time interval, all transactions that should have been entered have been entered (for example, all invoices have been approved for payment, or all billing statements have been sent out).

Session Operations

In the College database, time is divided into four annual sessions: Win, Spr, Sum, and Fall. Completeness means that all classes have been assigned instructors and grades have been assigned to all registered students.

> **NOTE** When you begin the chapter, only the switchboard and the Database window are displayed. Close any other objects.

Adding Session Operations to the Switchboard

You'll create a mini-switchboard for navigation to the three session operations: appointing instructors, assigning grades, and archiving session data. You branch to the mini-switchboard by clicking the Closing Out a Session option button on the main switchboard. You'll place an option group on the new mini-switchboard, with option buttons to display a list of classes without instructors and a list of classes with missing grades, and to run the archive process.

Creating a Mini-Switchboard for Session Operations

1. In the Database window, select zsfdlgMaster, then copy and paste it as **fdlgClosingOut**

2. Open fdlgClosingOut in Design view; make sure the Modal property is set to Yes and the PopUp property is set to No so that you have access to the menus and toolbars. (When you are finished developing this part of the application you can set the PopUp property to Yes.)

3. Set the form's Caption property to **Closing Out a Session** and increase the size of the Detail section to 4.5" wide by 3" tall.

4. Click the Option Group tool, then create an option group 1.75" wide and 1" tall; set its Name property to **grpClosingOut**, and delete its label.

5. Double-click the Option Button tool and create three option buttons within the option group.

6. Set the Caption property of the first label to **Classes without Instructors**, the second label to **Classes without Grades**, and the third label to **Archive Session Data** (you'll use this option button in the next section).

7. Click the Text Box tool and create a text box in the upper right corner of the dialog box; set the Caption property of its label to **Session**, set the Default Value property of the text box to **=Forms!frmSwitchboard!WorkingSession** and then set the Enabled property to No and the Locked property to Yes.

8. Click in the BackColor property, then click the Build button; select light gray and click OK.

9. Move the Return button up so that the option group and the Return button are aligned at the bottom. Figure 13.1 shows the mini-switchboard in Form view.

FIGURE 13.1:
The mini-switchboard for session operations.

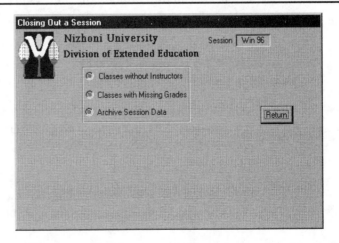

Branching to the Mini-Switchboard from the Main Switchboard

You create a macro that opens the new dialog form, and run the macro when you choose the Closing Out a Session option button on the main switchboard.

1. In the Database window, select and open the mfrmSwitchboard macro group.

2. Select the row of the grpClasses_AfterUpdate macro that has the expression grpClasses = 6 in its Condition cell, and then click the Insert Row button in the toolbar.

3. Click in the Condition cell of the inserted row and enter the condition grpClasses = 5

4. Select the `OpenForm` action and set the `Form Name` argument to fdlgClosingOut

5. Save and close the macrosheet.

Test the Macro

1. Click in the main switchboard.

2. Click the Closing Out a Session option button. The mini-switchboard opens and the main switchboard is hidden.

3. Click the Return button. The mini-switchboard closes and the main switchboard is unhidden.

Finding Classes without Instructors

The College database includes a form that lists classes for which no instructor has been assigned. You use this form when planning a session to keep track of instructor appointments. Each class that is actually held during a session must have an instructor assigned.

1. In the Database window, double-click the form frmClassesMissingData to open it. This form lists classes for which no instructor has been assigned. To

observe how this list is generated, first determine the form's record source.

2. Switch to Design view and note that the RecordSource property is the qry-ClasseswoInstructors query.

3. In the Database window, select the query qryClasseswoInstructors and click the Design button. I created this query, using the Find Unmatched Query Wizard, in order to find records in tblClasses that had no matching records in tlnkClassInstructors (see Figure 13.2). The wizard used an outer join to select all classes and then selected only the classes with a null value for the InstructorID. After the wizard built the query, I added tblCourses to provide the Prefix, Number, and Course Title.

4. Close qryClasseswoInstructors.

FIGURE 13.2:
The qryClasseswoInstructors query selects records in tblClasses without matching records in tblInstructors.

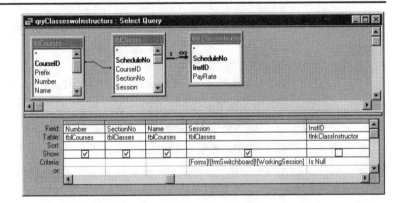

Automating the Process

You can automate the process of appointing an instructor to a particular class by adding detail drill-down buttons to open the frmAppointmentsByClass form (you created this form in Chapter 6 "Creating a Data Entry Form for a Linking Table"). The button's macro carries out the following tasks:

- opens the frmAppointmentsByClass form and synchronizes the form to the class selected in frmClassesMissingData.

- sets the opened form's Tag property to "frmClassesMissingData" so that the form "remembers" that it was opened from the frmClassesMissingData form.

- hides the frmClassesMissingData form.

You modify the macro for the Return button on frmAppointmentsByClass so that the macro tests the value of the form's Tag property. If the Tag property is frmMissingData, the macro closes the form after resetting its Tag property to Null and then unhides frmMissingData.

Adding Detail Drill-Down Buttons

Place a command button in the detail section of frmClassesMissingData and create its macro, and then modify the cmdReturn_Click macro in the mcrGallery macro group.

1. With the Control Wizards tool deselected, click the Command Button tool and draw a small button on the right side of the detail section (just below the Session text box).

2. Set the Name property to **cmdDetail** and set the Caption property to + (plus).

3. Click in the OnClick property, then click the Build button, select Macro Builder, and click OK.

4. Save the new macro sheet as **mfrmClassesMissingData**

5. Click in the first Macro Name cell and name the new macro **cmdDetail_Click**

6. Enter the macro shown in Table 13.1.

TABLE 13.1: The macro for the detail drill-down button.

Macro Name	Action	Action Arguments
cmdDetail_Click		
	OpenForm	**Form Name**: frmAppointmentsByClass
		Where Condition: ScheduleNo=Screen.ActiveForm.ScheduleNo
	SetValue	**Item**: Forms!frmAppointmentsByClass.Tag
		Expression: "frmClassesMissingData"
	SetValue	**Item**: Forms!frmClassesMissingData.Visible
		Expression: No

7. Save the macrosheet.

8. In the Database window, open mcrGallery and modify the cmdReturn_Click macro by inserting the four rows shown in italics in Table 13.2.

9. Save the macrosheet.

TABLE 13.2: The modified macro for the Return button.

Macro Name	Condition	Actions	Action Arguments
cmdReturn_Click			
	IsNull(Screen.Active-Form.Tag)	Close	
	...	SetValue	**Item**: Forms!frmSwitch-board.Visible
			Expression: Yes
	...	StopMacro	
	Screen.ActiveForm.Tag= "frmClassesMissingData"	*SetValue*	*Item*: *Screen.Active-Form.Tag*
			Expression: *Null*
	...	*Close*	
	...	*SetValue*	*Item*: *Forms!frmClasses-MissingData.Visible*
			Expression: *Yes*
	...	*StopMacro*	
		SetValue	**Item**:Screen.Active Form.Tag
			Expression: Null
		Close	

Attach and Test the Macros

1. Click in frmClassesMissingData, then select the cmdDetail button; click in the OnClick property, and select the mfrmClassesMissingData.cmdDetail_Click macro.

2. Save the form and switch to Form view. Figure 13.3 shows the form.

3. Click the button for one of the classes. The synchronized appointment form opens and the list is hidden.

4. Assign an instructor, then note the ScheduleNo for the class and click the Return button. The list is unhidden; note that the class is still on the list even though you assigned an instructor.

FIGURE 13.3:
The list of classes with missing instructors. Clicking a detail drill-down button opens an appointment form for the selected class and hides the list.

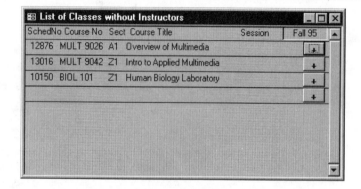

Create a Macro to Requery the Form

To update the list of classes without instructors, requery the frmClassesMissingData form when it becomes the active form.

1. Click in mcrGallery, then click in a new row and name the new macro **Form_Activate**

2. Click in the next row and select the **Requery** action. Leave the argument blank so that the action requeries the form.

3. Save the macro group.

Attach and Test the Macro

1. Click in the frmClassesMissingData form and switch to Design view.

2. Click in the form's OnActivate property, and select mcrGallery.Form_Activate.

3. Save the form.

4. Switch to Form view, then click the drill-down button for a class and assign an instructor.

5. Note the class ScheduleNo and then click the Return button. The class is no longer on the list of classes that have no instructors.

Using the Same Form to Find Classes That are Missing Grades

The second operation that must be complete before closing out a session is the assignment of grades for all students registered in all classes in the session. You can use the same frmClassesMissingData form to display a list of classes that are missing grades, by changing the form's record source to a query that selects these classes instead of classes that are missing instructors.

1. Switch to Design view.

2. Click in the RecordSource property and select qryClasseswoGrades.

3. Change the form's Caption property to **List of Classes with Missing Grades**

4. Save the form and switch to Form view. Figure 13.4 shows the frmClasses-MissingData form displaying the classes.

FIGURE 13.4:
Changing the RecordSource and Caption properties of a form to display two sets of data.

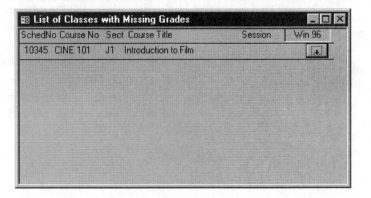

If you click a detail drill-down button, the appointment form corresponding to the class opens. To have the button work correctly, you'll have to modify the macro so that it opens the frmClassList form that you use to assign grades instead of frm-AppointmentByClass. You'll modify the macro later, after you've modified the mini-switchboard to display frmClassesMissingData as a subform.

Observing the Query to Find Classes with Missing Grades

Let's look at how classes are selected for this list of classes with missing grades.

1. In the Database window, select qryClasseswoGrades and click the Design button. Figure 13.5 shows the query in Design view.

FIGURE 13.5:

The qryClasseswoGrades query.

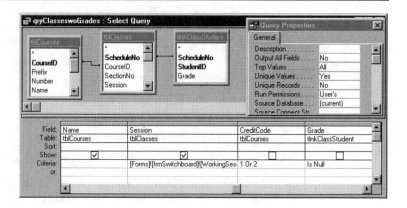

This query was not created using the Find Unmatched Query Wizard. That wizard would help if we were looking for classes *without* students; instead, we are looking for classes *with* students who don't have grades. The query uses an inner join between tblClasses and tlnkClassStudents to provide records for students registered in classes, and uses the Session field from tblClasses to select classes for the working session and the CreditCode field from tblCourses to select classes for which grades are to be assigned. The college offers both credit and non-credit classes;

grades aren't assigned for non-credit classes. The CreditCode for a course can have the following values:

CreditCode	Integer Value
CEU (Continuing Education)	1
Academic Credit	2
Non-Credit	3

The query selects the only the credit classes and only those classes with a null value in the Grade field. The query's UniqueValues property is set to Yes to display only the records for which the combination of all of the fields displayed in the query result is unique; this means that a single record is displayed for a class with missing grades, regardless of the number of missing grades. To see the effect of the UniqueValues property:

1. Change the UniqueValues property to No and switch to Datasheet view. The datasheet includes a record for each student in each class with a missing grade (see Figure 13.6). For example, the class with ScheduleNo 13016 has five students with missing grades.

2. Switch to Design view and change the UniqueValues property to Yes.

3. Save and close the query.

4. Save and close the frmClassesMissingData form.

FIGURE 13.6:
When the UniqueValues property is set to No, the datasheet includes a record for each student in each class with a missing grade. Set the UniqueValues property to Yes to display a single record for each class with missing grades, regardless of the number of missing grades.

ScheduleN	Prefix	Numbe	SectionNo	Course Title	Session
14103	MSFT	9705	Z5	Intro to MS Windows for New Users	Fall 95
12272	MSFT	9706	Z2	Mastering Windows for Experienced Use	Fall 95
12316	MSFT	9709	A1	Intermediate MS Excel	Fall 95
12316	MSFT	9709	A1	Intermediate MS Excel	Fall 95
12316	MSFT	9709	A1	Intermediate MS Excel	Fall 95
12876	MULT	9026	A1	Overview of Multimedia	Fall 95
12876	MULT	9026	A1	Overview of Multimedia	Fall 95
12876	MULT	9026	A1	Overview of Multimedia	Fall 95
13016	MULT	9042	Z1	Intro to Applied Multimedia	Fall 95
13016	MULT	9042	Z1	Intro to Applied Multimedia	Fall 95
13016	MULT	9042	Z1	Intro to Applied Multimedia	Fall 95
13016	MULT	9042	Z1	Intro to Applied Multimedia	Fall 95
13016	MULT	9042	Z1	Intro to Applied Multimedia	Fall 95
10710	CINE	310	Z1	Workshop in Film Production	Fall 95

Record: 1 of 21

Displaying the Lists of Missing Data in the Mini-Switchboard

Either list of classes with missing information can be displayed using the frmClasses-MissingData form just by changing the form's record source. You'll design the fdlgClosingOut mini-switchboard so that the mini-switchboard displays the chosen list as a subform when you click one of the option buttons. By displaying the lists on the mini-switchboard itself, you avoid adding an additional layer to the user interface.

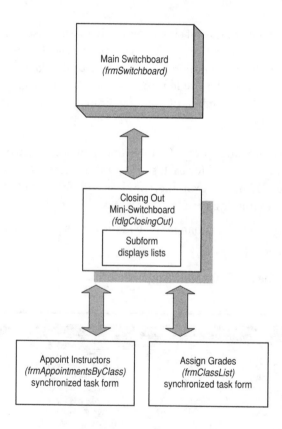

You place the frmClassesMissingData form as a hidden subform on the fdlgClosing-Out mini-switchboard. You create a macro that unhides the subform control and changes the record source of the subform when either of the first two option buttons is selected; the macro runs when you change the value of the option group on the mini-switchboard.

Place the Subform on the Mini-Switchboard

We'll use the Subform/Subreport tool to create a subform control on the mini-switchboard, and set the control's SourceObject property to frmClassesMissingData so that the subform displays this form. Note that there is no linking between the main form and the subform: the main form is unbound so you leave the linking properties blank.

1. In the Database window, select and open fdlgClosingOut in Design view.

2. With the Control Wizards tool deselected, click the Subform/Subreport tool (in the toolbox) and create a subform control 4.3" wide and 1.4" tall.

3. Delete the label and set the subform properties as shown below.

Name	Child
SourceObject	frmClassesMissingData
Visible	No

Create a Macro to Change the Record Source for the Subform

Create a macro that runs when you change the value of the option group (by clicking an option button). If you click either the first or the second option button, the macro changes the subform's record source and unhides the subform control. Use the syntax

subformcontrolname.Form.propertyname

(that is, Child.Form.RecordSource) to refer to the RecordSource property of the form displayed in the subform control. The macro flow diagram is shown in Figure 13.7.

FIGURE 13.7:

The flow diagram for grpClosingOut_AfterUpdate. The macro changes the record source of the subform to display different information.

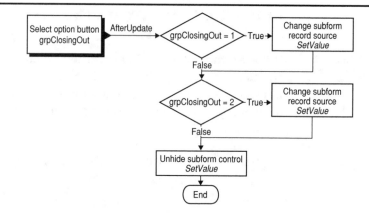

1. Click in the AfterUpdate property of the option group, then click the Build button; select Macro Builder, then click OK and save the new macrogroup as **mfdlgClosingOut**

2. Click in the first Macro Name cell and name the new macro **grpClosing-Out_AfterUpdate**

3. Enter the macro shown in Table 13.3.

4. Save the macro.

TABLE 13.3: The macro for grpClosingOut option group.

Macro Name	Condition	Action	Action Arguments
grpClosingOut _AfterUpdate			
	grpClosingOut = 1	SetValue	**Item**: Child.Form.RecordSource
			Expression: "qryClasseswoInstructors"
	grpClosingOut = 2	SetValue	**Item**: Child.Form.RecordSource
			Expression: "qryClasseswoGrades"
		SetValue	**Item**: Child.Visible
			Expression: Yes

Attach and Test the Macro

1. Click in fdlgClosingOut and select the option group, then select the AfterUpdate property and choose mfdlgClosingOut.grpClosingOut_AfterUpdate.

2. Save the form.

3. Switch to Form view.

4. Click each of the first two option buttons. Figure 13.8 shows the modified fdlgClosingOut form.

FIGURE 13.8:
The fdlgClosingOut mini-switchboard form, displaying the list of classes that have missing grades in a subform control.

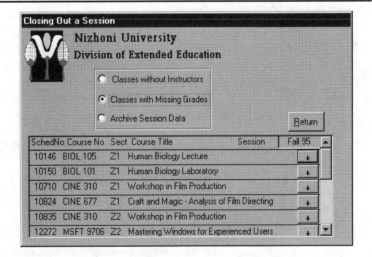

Making the Detail Drill-Down Buttons Work Correctly

Modify the macro that runs when a detail drill-down button on frmClassesMissing-Data is clicked, so that the macro tests which option button has been selected and then opens either frmAppointmentsByClass or frmClassList. Since the drill-down button is on the subform and the option group is on the main form, you can use the Parent property to refer to the option group. To synchronize the opened form and display the record that matches the class selected in the subform, use the following expression in the **Where Condition** argument of the **OpenForm** action:

ScheduleNo = Screen.ActiveForm.Child.Form.ScheduleNo

After opening either form, the macro sets its Tag property to "fdlgClosingOut" so that the form can "remember" that it was opened from this mini-switchboard. Finally, the macro hides the mini-switchboard. Figure 13.9 shows the flow diagram for the revised macro.

FIGURE 13.9:

The flow diagram for the macro that runs when you click the detail drill-down button. The macro uses the Parent property to refer to the option group on the main form.

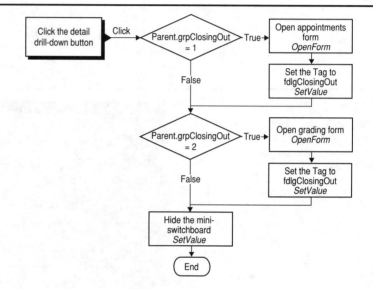

1. Switch to Design view for the mini-switchboard.

2. Click in mfrmClassesMissingData and modify the cmdDetail_Click macro as shown in Table 13.4.

3. Save and close the macrosheet.

TABLE 13.4: The macro for the detail drill-down button refers to the option group on the main form

Macro Name	Condition	Action	Action Arguments
cmdDetail_Click			
	Parent.grpClosingOut = 1	**OpenForm**	**Form Name**: frmAppointmentsByClass **Where Condition**: ScheduleNo=Screen.Active-Form.Child.Form.ScheduleNo

TABLE 13.4: The macro for the detail drill-down button refers to the option group on the main form *(continued).*

Macro Name	Condition	Action	Action Arguments
	...	SetValue	**Item**: Forms!frmAppointmentsBy-Class.Tag
			Expression: "fdlgClosingOut"
	Parent.grpClosingOut = 2	OpenForm	**Form Name**: frmClassList
			Where Condition: ScheduleNo=Screen.Active-Form.Child.Form.ScheduleNo
	...	SetValue	**Item**: Forms!frmClassList.Tag
			Expression: "fdlgClosingOut"
		SetValue	**Item**: Forms!fdlgClosing-Out.Visible
			Expression: No

Also, modify the macro for the Return button so that the macro closes the form after resetting its Tag property to Null and then unhides the fdlgClosingOut mini-switchboard.

1. Click in mcrGallery.

2. Change frmClassesMissingData to **fdlgClosingOut** in the first and third rows you added to the macro: in the Condition cell of the first row and in the **SetValue** action in the third row (refer to Table 13.2).

3. Save and close the macrosheet.

Test the Modified Macros

We are now finished making changes in the fdlgClosingOut mini-switchboard; this is a good time to set the form's PopUp property so that the form becomes a true dialog box.

1. Click in fdlgClosingOut and set the form's PopUp property to Yes.

2. Switch to Form view, click the first option, then select a class and click the detail drill-down button. The corresponding class appointment form is displayed and the mini-switchboard is hidden.

3. Click the Return button. The class appointment form closes and the mini-switchboard is unhidden.

4. Click the second option, then select a class and click the detail button. The corresponding class list is displayed and the mini-switchboard is hidden.

5. Click the Return button—the class list closes and the mini-switchboard is unhidden.

6. Click the Return button again. The mini-switchboard closes and the main switchboard is unhidden.

Session Summary Data

At the end of the time interval, you calculate statistics based on the data accumulated during the interval. For a profit-based business, summary calculations include any statistic that helps to diagnose the health of the business (such as gross revenue, total cost of goods sold, summaries of other costs, and summaries of sales by product). Comparing summaries for several intervals is useful in analyzing the growth of the business. Summary reports are generated as part of the closing out process. Normally, the summary data are calculated and posted to historical summary tables so that the statistics are readily available and you don't have to recalculate them each time you want to review the summary data.

As an example, in the College database, the qryEnrollmentSummary query generates the total enrollment and fees paid for each class. You'll create an append query to post the enrollment summary data to tblEnrollmentSummaryHist as one of the steps in the archive process.

1. In the Database window, double-click the qryEnrollmentSummary query to open it in Datasheet view. Browse through the records.

2. Switch to Design view. The query is based on outer join between qalkCourseClass and tlnkClassStudent (see Figure 13.10). The query is designed as an outer join in order to provide information about every scheduled class, whether or not students are enrolled. The query selects fields from the qalkCourseClass autolookup query to provide course information for a specified class, and fields from the tlnkClassStudent linking table to provide a record for each student enrolled in the class. As a totals query, the query groups the records by class, counts the students, and sums the fees paid in each class.

FIGURE 13.10:
The qryEnrollmentSummary uses an outer join in order to provide information for every scheduled class, whether or not students are enrolled.

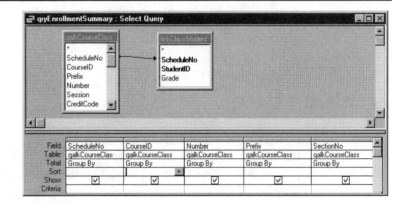

Create an Append Query

You convert this query to an append query that adds records to the tblEnrollmentSummaryHist table. After splitting the database in Chapter 12, this table is in another database, the Colldata data file; however, because the tables are linked you can treat them as though they were in the current database when you create the append query.

1. Choose the Query ➤ Append command. You use the Append dialog to specify the name of the table (see Figure 13.11). (If the table is in another database and is not linked to the current database, you use this dialog to specify the file name.)

FIGURE 13.11:

Use the Append dialog to specify the name and location of the table.

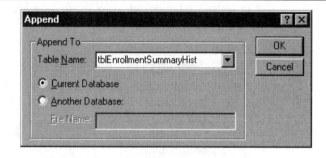

2. Select tblEnrollmentSummaryHist from the Table Name list.

3. Click OK, then select File ➤ Save As and name the new query **qappEnroll-mentSummary**

4. Save and close the query.

Archiving Data

At the end of the time interval, you archive the records by appending them to historical files and then deleting them from the current files. Archiving the records protects their data from inadvertent changes and also improves performance by keeping the current data tables as small as possible. The historical tables can be in the same or in another database.

In the College database, there are three historical data tables and a set of queries for archiving class information for a session.

The Historical Data Tables

The historical data tables store historical data from tblClasses, tlnkClassInstructor, and tlnkClassStudent. The historical tables are named tblClassesHist, tlnkClass-InstructorHist, and tlnkClassStudentHist, respectively, and have structures identical to their current table counterparts.

1. In the Database window, select tblClassesHist and click the Design button.

2. Switch to Datasheet view. The table is empty because no records have been archived.

3. Close the table.

The Append Queries

The append queries (qappClasses, qapplnkClassInst, and qapplnkClassStud) append the records in one of the current tables to its corresponding historical table. The append queries were created before the database was split, but you don't have to modify the query properties in this case because the historical tables are linked.

1. In the Database window, select the qappClasses query and click the Design button. Figure 13.12 shows the query design. You use the asterisk to include all the fields from a field list. When you use the asterisk method, you have to include a separate field in the design grid for any field you are using to sort or select records. In this case, you use the Session field to select records for the working session; the query obtains its selection criteria from the switchboard. The Append To cell below the Session field is blank so that the query won't try to append the field a second time.

FIGURE 13.12:
The qappClasses append query, which appends class records to the historical table.

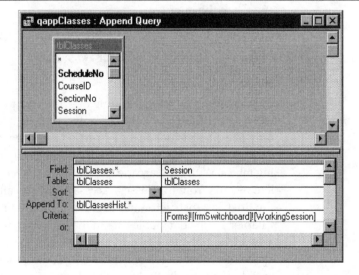

2. Close qappClasses.

3. In the Database window, select qapplnkClassInst and click the Design button. Figure 13.13 shows the query design and the query property sheet. The query uses the tblClasses table to select records for the working session.

FIGURE 13.13:

The qapplnkClassInst append query, which appends class appointment records to the historical table.

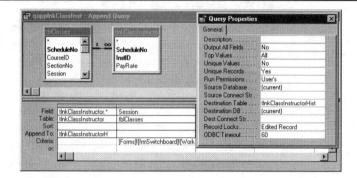

4. Close the query.

5. Open qapplnkClassStud in Design view. This query also uses tblClasses to select records for the working session.

6. Close the query.

How Many Delete Queries Are Needed?

Even though you need separate queries to append records to the three historical tables (tblClassesHist, tlnkClassInstructorHist, and tlnkClassStudentHist), you need only one query to delete the records in the three tables if the Cascade Delete Related Records options are selected for the relationships between tblClasses and both linking tables. With the Cascade Delete Related Records options selected, when you delete records from tblClasses, Access automatically deletes the related records from the tlnkClassInstructor and tlnkClassStudent tables. After splitting the database in Chapter 12, the data tables are in the back-end database and retain the relationships and referential integrity options that were set before splitting. The relationships and options can be changed only from within the back-end database. We'll open the back-end database to check the status of the referential integrity options.

1. Click in the Database window and choose File ➤ Close. The College database closes.

2. Choose File ➤ Open Database, then locate and select the Colldata database and click OK. The Colldata database opens.

3. Click the Relationships button (in the toolbar). The Relationships layout opens. If the layout displays tblClasses, tlnkClassStudent, and tlnkClass-Instructor, then skip the next two steps.

4. Choose Edit ➤ Clear Layout.

5. In the Database window, select tblClasses and drag to the layout, then select and drag tlnkClassInstructor and tlnkClassStudent.

6. Right-click on the relationship line between tblClasses and tlnkClassInstructor, and choose Edit Relationship from the shortcut menu. Make sure that the two Cascade options are selected (see Figure 13.14) and then click OK.

FIGURE 13.14:

When the Cascade Delete Related Records option is set for a relationship, deleting records in the 'one' table automatically deletes related records in the 'many' table.

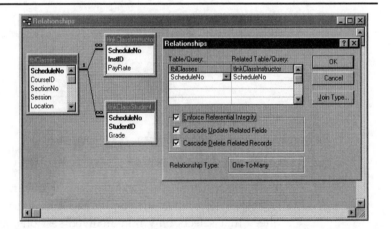

7. Right-click on the relationship line between tblClasses and tlnkClassStudent, and choose Edit Relationship from the shortcut menu; make sure the two Cascade options are selected and then click OK.

8. Close the layout without saving.

9. Close the Colldata database and reopen the College database.

The Delete Query

1. In the Database window, select the qdelClasses query and click the Design button. Figure 13.15 shows the query design. The asterisk method is used to select all the fields, and the Session field is included separately to provide the selection criteria.

FIGURE 13.15:

The qdelClasses query.

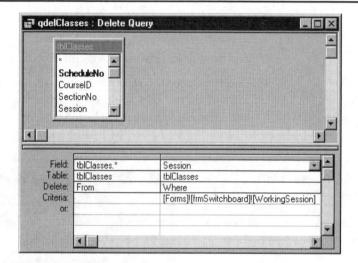

Displaying Only Non-Archived Sessions in the Switchboard

After the records for a session have been archived, the session should no longer be available in the main switchboard's cboWorkingSession combo list. You can create a query that selects only non-archived sessions, and use that query (instead of tblSessions) as the record source for frmSwitchboard and as the row source for the session selection combo box.

1. In the Database window, select tblSessions; click the arrow on the New Object button (on the toolbar), select New Query, then select Design View and click OK.

2. Drag both fields to the design grid. The Archived? field has the Yes/No data type.

3. Enter **No** in the Criteria cell below the Archived? Field cell and clear the Show check box.

4. Save the query as **qrySessions**

5. Click in the switchboard, then switch to Design view.

6. Set the RecordSource property to **qrySessions**

7. Select the cboWorkingSession combo box, and set its RowSource property to **qrySessions**

Designing the Archive Macro

You'll create a macro that archives the records when the Archive Session Data option button on the fdlgClosingOut mini-switchboard is selected. This macro is the longest one in the book and uses many of the macro programming techniques you've learned in previous chapters. The macro carries out the following tasks:

- Hides the subform that displays classes with missing data (the subform may be displayed or may already be hidden when you click the option button).

- Displays a message that the archive process permanently changes the records, and asks you for confirmation before continuing. Use the following MsgBox( ) function in the Condition cell to obtain a response:

   MsgBox("Archiving will permanently delete records and place records in historical tables. You will not be able to undo the archive process, so you should back up the data files. Do you wish to continue? ", 4+48+256, "Archiving Data")>6

The second argument in the MsgBox( ) function indicates that the dialog displays Yes and No buttons (see Chapter 8 for more information on the MsgBox( ) function). If you click the No button, the function returns the value 7, the macro displays a message that the closing out procedure is cancelled, and the macro terminates. If you confirm that you want to continue by clicking the Yes button, the function returns the value 6, and the macro continues.

- Tests to determine if each class has an instructor assigned, and if all students in each class have grades. You can use the DCount( ) function to count the records in the qryClasseswoInstructors and qryClasseswoGrades queries, and then create test conditions as follows:

    DCount("*","qryClasseswoInstructors")>0

    DCount("*","qryClasseswoGrades")>0

    If either test fails, the macro displays a message and terminates. In each case, you can include the number of classes with missing data by concatenating the DCount( ) function with the text message. For example, if there are classes with missing grades you can use the following expression in the **Message** argument of the **Msgbox** action:

    ="There are "&DCount("*","qryClasseswoGrades")&" classes with missing grades. Select the Classes with Missing Grades option and assign grades first."

    If both conditions are met, the macro continues.

- Runs the summary queries and appends the summaries to the historical summary tables.

- Appends the records from tblClasses and the linking tables to the corresponding historical data tables, and deletes the records from the three current tables. The macro displays a message that the archive process was successful.

- Closes the fdlgClosingOut mini-switchboard by running the cmdReturn_Click macro.

- Sets the Archived? field in tblSessions to Yes. The Archived? field is not displayed on frmSwitchboard, so you use the syntax

    Forms!formname!fieldname

    to refer to the field in the **SetValue** action.

- Requeries the cboWorkingSession combo list to remove the archived session from the list.

- Uses the `GoToRecord` action to display the next session in the switchboard; if there are no more sessions, the macro displays a message.

You can include the `Hourglass`, `Echo`, and `SetWarnings` actions before the macro runs the action queries in order to display the hourglass, turn off screen updating, improve performance, and suppress default confirmation messages. Figure 13.16 shows the flow diagram for the macro.

FIGURE 13.16:

The flow diagram for the archive macro.

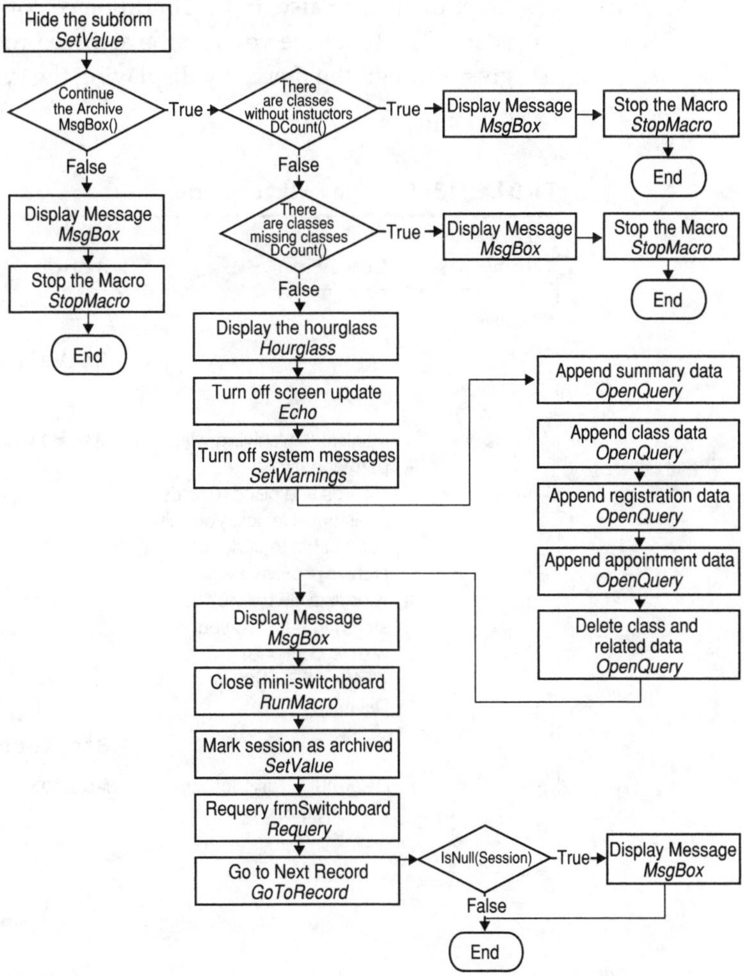

Creating a Macro to Archive Session Data

Create the macro to archive the data for the working session.

1. Click in mfdlgClosingOut, then click in the Macro Name cell of a new row and name the new macro **Archive**

2. Enter the macro shown in Table 13.5.

3. Enter the word **False** in the Condition cell of the row with the `SetWarnings` action. The first time you run the archive procedure, you can observe the progress through the macro by displaying the system messages.

4. Save the macro.

TABLE 13.5: The archive macro.

Macro Name	Condition	Action	Action Arguments
Archive			
		SetValue	**Item**: Child.Visible **Expression**: No
	MsgBox("Archiving will permanently delete records and place records in historical tables. You will not be able to undo the archive process. Back up your data file before archiving data. Do you wish to continue?", 4+48+256, "Archiving Data")>6	MsgBox	**Message**: The archive process is cancelled.
	...	StopMacro	
	DCount("*","qryClasses-woInstructors")>0	MsgBox	**Message**: ="There are " &DCount("*","qryClasses-woInstructors")&" classes without instructors. Select the Classes without Instructors option and appoint instructors first."
	...	StopMacro	

TABLE 13.5: The archive macro (continued).

Macro Name	Condition	Action	Action Arguments
	DCount("*","qryClasseswoGrades")>0	MsgBox	**Message**: ="There are " &DCount("*","qryClasseswoGrades")&" classes with missing grades. Select the Classes with Missing Grades option and assign grades first."
	...	StopMacro	
		Hourglass	
		Echo	**Echo On**: No
			Status Bar Text: Archiving data
		SetWarnings	**Warnings On**: No
		OpenQuery	**Query Name**: qappEnrollmentSummary
		OpenQuery	**Query Name**: qappClasses
		OpenQuery	**Query Name**: qapplnkClassStud
		OpenQuery	**Query Name**: qapplnkClassInst
		OpenQuery	**Query Name**: qdelClasses
		MsgBox	**Message**: The records have been archived successfully!
		RunMacro	**Macro Name**: mcrGallery.cmdReturn_Click
		SetValue	**Item**: Forms!frmSwitchboard!Archived?
			Expression: Yes
		Requery	**Control Name**: cboWorkingSession
		GoToRecord	**Record**: Next
	IsNull(Session)	MsgBox	**Message**: There are no more sessions. Create another session before continuing.

Modify the grpClosingOut_AfterUpdate Macro to Run the Archive Macro

The Archive macro runs when you click the third option button on the Closing Out a Session mini-switchboard. Modify the macro for the option group to run the macro.

1. Click in the Condition cell of the row following the last row of the grpClosing-Out_AfterUpdate macro and enter the condition **grpClosingOut = 3**

2. Select the `RunMacro` action and set the `Macro Name` argument to **mfdlgClosing-Out.Archive**

3. Save the macro.

Test the Macro

1. In frmSwitchboard, select Fall 95 as the Working Session; click the Closing-Out a Session option button, then click the Archive Session Data option button. The custom warning message is displayed.

2. Click the No button. The information that the archive process is cancelled is displayed.

3. Click the OK button. The message box indicating there are classes without instructors is displayed. You must appoint the missing instructors in order to continue.

4. Click OK.

Appoint the Missing Instructors and Reinitiate the Archive Process

1. Click the Classes without Instructors option button.

2. For each class listed, click the detail drill-down button, appoint an instructor, and click the Return button. When there are no more classes, reinitiate the archive process.

3. Click the Archive Session Data option button and then click the Yes button. With all instructors appointed, the macro tests for missing grades and displays the dialog box indicating that grades must be assigned. You must assign the missing grades in order to continue.

4. Click OK.

Assign Missing Grades and Reinitiate the Archive Process

1. Click the Classes with Missing Grades option button.

2. For each class listed, click the detail drill-down button, assign grades, and click the Return button. When there are no more classes, reinitiate the archive process.

3. Click the Archive Session Data option button and then click the Yes button. Access runs the four append queries. As each query executes, the default confirmation dialog boxes, system messages, and warnings are displayed. Make sure to confirm the action queries. After the delete query is executed, the final message box, indicating that the archive process is finished, is displayed. The fdlgClosingOut mini-switchboard closes. The main switchboard is displayed with Win 96 as the working session.

4. Click in the Condition cell of the row that has the `SetWarnings` action and delete the word False. After testing the process you *must* remove the confirmation messages that would allow the user to run some but not all of the archive queries.

Endnotes

In this chapter you added a mini-switchboard to the user interface to navigate to the session operations, including testing data for completeness and archiving the data at the end of a session. Two lists of classes with missing data are displayed in a subform on the mini-switchboard itself in order to minimize the number of branches in the user interface. The form is displayed in the subform control and the form's record source is changed dynamically to display the different lists.

The archive macro appends records to historical tables and then deletes records from the current data tables. The final chores of the archive macro are to update the main switchboard so that the archived session is no longer available as a choice for the working session.

On Your Own

In the exercises, you improve the session operations. You improve performance of the procedures for appointing instructors and assigning grades by requerying the list of classes with missing data only when data is changed. Also, you modify the Archive macro to test for classes in the working session, and abort the archive process if there are none.

Adding to the Application

1. Requery only when necessary.
   The Form_Activate macro created in this chapter requeries the frmClasses-MissingData form whenever the form becomes active, whether or not you appointed an instructor or assigned grades.

   a. Instead, create a macro that requeries the form only if you changed the data in the form you drilled down to.

   b. Trigger the macro from the appropriate event on the appointment or class list form. The macro tests the form's Dirty property to determine if the data has been changed, and requeries the frmClassesMissingData form only if it has.

2. Are there classes to archive?
   In this exercise, you modify the Archive macro to determine if there are any classes for a session before continuing with the archive process.

   a. Create a new query named **qryClasses** based on tblClasses. Drag ScheduleNo and Sessions to the design grid, and set the Sessions criteria cell to select classes for the working session.

b. Use the DCount( ) function to determine the number of classes in the working session.

c. Open the mfdlgClosingOut macrosheet and insert new second and third rows in the Archive macro. In the new second row, enter the condition that the number of classes in the working session is less than or equal to zero. If this condition is true, display a message that "There are no classes in the working session. The archive process is aborted." Enter an ellipsis in the condition cell of the new second row and stop the macro.

d. To test your modification, type **break** into the Macro Name cell of the next row so that the macro stops immediately after your modification. Select a session with no classes (Spr 97) in the switchboard, then click the Closing Out a Session option button, and click Archive Session Data in the Closing Out mini-switchboard. Your custom message is displayed. Close the mini-switchboard, select a session with classes, and go through the steps again. This time your message isn't displayed.

e. After testing your modification, delete the word **break** in the Macro Name cell.

FOURTEEN

Embellishing Reports with Macros

- Utilizing the `Format` and `Print` events

- Accumulating a page total

- Adding a report to the user interface

When you print a report, Access acknowledges several events that you can use to trigger macros that embellish the report. You can highlight important information, omit unimportant information, or display the results of additional calculations. In this chapter, you learn how to highlight information and how to place page totals in a report's page header or footer.

> **NOTE** When you begin this chapter, only the switchboard and the Database window should be displayed. Close any other objects.

Highlighting Information Dynamically

Each section in a report recognizes a **Format** event when Access has determined which information goes into the section, but before Access lays out the section; therefore, a macro triggered by the **Format** event for a section can use the information in the section. As special cases, a macro triggered by the **Format** event for a group header section can use the information in the first record of its detail section as well as information in the group header, and a macro triggered by the **Format** event for a group footer section can use the information in the last record of its detail section as well as information in the group footer.

A macro triggered by a section's **Format** event can use the section information to change formatting properties (for the section and for the controls in the section) such as Visible, HideDuplicates, CanGrow, and KeepTogether. After the macro changes the property settings, Access uses the new settings to lay out the section on the page. For example, the macro can test data in the section and then hide or display a control in the section based on the result, or the macro can use the **Cancel-Event** action to prevent the section from appearing in the report.

In the College database, the Enrollment Summary report (rptEnrollmentSummary) collects enrollment and fee information and calculates totals for each program.

1. In the Database window, double-click the rptEnrollmentSummary report to open it in Print Preview. Figure 14.1 shows a portion of the report. The report groups enrollment and fee data by program for the working session.

FIGURE 14.1:
The rptEnrollmentSummary report.

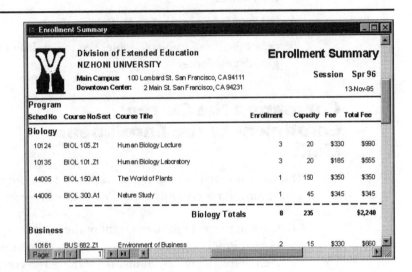

When the enrollments in a program fall below a planned level of 50% of total capacity, the college director examines the classes in the program so as to plan schedule and staffing changes. You can highlight this information by displaying a label beside the enrollment data for any program that has total enrollments less than the minimum level. You place a label next to the program totals in the group footer section, and create a macro that determines whether the label is displayed. The decision to display or hide the label is made *dynamically* (that is, the decision depends on the enrollments that are current when you generate the report).

Placing the Label

Place a label in the ProgramName group footer.

1. Switch to Design view, and click the Label tool.

2. Click in the ProgramName footer, just to the right of the text box named Prog-Totals (the text box containing the expression =[ProgramName]& " Totals"), to create a label, and set the label's Caption property to **are Below Target** …

3. On the Formatting toolbar, click the Bold button, then select Arial in the Font Name list and 10 in the Font Size list; finally, click the arrow on the Fore Color button and select Red. (If you don't have a color printer, this red label will print in a shade of gray. To emphasize the label click the Italic button on the toolbar.)

4. Set the Name property to **lblBelow**

5. Select the ProgramName footer section and set the Name property to **ProgramNameFooter**

Comparing the Current Enrollment to the Enrollment Limit

The current enrollment and total capacity for a program are calculated using the Sum() function in controls in the ProgramName group footer.

1. Click in the text box to the right of the label you just placed. This text box, named ProgEnroll, contains the current enrollment total for a program (the sum of the current enrollments for the classes offered by a program). Note that the ControlSource property is set to the expression

    = Sum([Enrollment])

2. Click in the text box to the right of ProgEnroll. This text box, named ProgCapacity, contains the total capacity for a program (the sum of the enrollment limits for classes offered by the program). Note that the ControlSource property is set to the expression

    = Sum([EnrollLimit])

Creating the Macro to Compare the Enrollments

You create a macro to compare the current total enrollment to the total capacity for each program. If the value in the ProgEnroll text box is less than 50% of the value in the ProgCapacity text box, the macro sets the Visible property of the label to Yes; otherwise, the macro sets the Visible property to No. You run the macro when Access has determined which data goes into the ProgramNameFooter section, and has calculated the sums in the ProgEnroll and ProgCapacity text boxes, but before Access actually lays out the section for previewing or printing (that is, when the ProgramNameFooter section recognizes its **Format** event).

1. Open a new macrosheet and save it as **mrptEnrollmentSummary**

2. Click in the Macro Name cell in the first row and name the new macro **ProgramNameFooter_Format**

3. Enter the macro shown in Table 14.1.

4. Save the macro.

TABLE 14.1: The macro to test the enrollment and display a label.

Macro Name	Condition	Action	Action Arguments
ProgramName-Footer_Format			
	ProgEnroll < .5 * ProgCapacity	**SetValue**	**Item**: lblBelow.Visible
			Expression: Yes
	Not ProgEnroll < .5 * ProgCapacity	**SetValue**	**Item**: lblBelow.Visible
			Expression: No

Attach and Test the Macro

1. Click in the report and select the ProgramNameFooter section.

2. Click in the OnFormat property and select the mrptEnrollmentSummary.ProgramNameFooter_Format macro.

3. Save the report.

4. Switch to Print Preview. Browse through the report and observe the label for those programs that are below target.

Adding the Report to the User Interface

You can open the report from the fdlgClassReports mini-switchboard by adding an option button to the option group. When you select the option button, you run a macro that unhides command buttons that allow you to view the report in Print Preview or to print the report.

Place the Option and Command Buttons

1. In the main switchboard, click the Reports button in the Classes option group. The fdlgClassReports mini-switchboard is displayed.

2. Switch to Design view.

3. Click the Option Button tool and place a new button in the option group.

4. Set the label to **Enrollment Summary**

5. Click the Command Button tool, then place two buttons (0.75" wide and 0.2" tall) just above the Return button, and set their properties as follows:

Button	Name	Caption	Visible
Button1	cmdPreview	Print Pre&view	No
Button2	cmdPrint	&Print	No

6. Save the form.

Create the Macro for the Option Button

Create a macro that displays the print command buttons when the new option button is selected.

1. Select the option group, then click in the AfterUpdate property and click its Build button. The mfdlgClassReports macro group opens.

2. Modify the grpClassReports_AfterUpdate macro as shown in Table 14.2.

3. Save the macro group.

Test the Macro

1. Click in fdlgClassReports and switch to Form view.

2. Click the Enrollment Summary option button. Figure 14.2 shows the dialog box after you click the option button and the print command buttons are visible.

TABLE 14.2: The macro for the option group on the Class Reports mini-switchboard.

Macro Name	Condition	Action	Action Arguments
grpClassReports_AfterUpdate			
	grpClassReports = 1	`OpenForm`	**Form Name**: fdlgClassLists
	...	`Close`	**Object Type**: Form
			Object Name: fdlgClassReports
	grpClassReports = 2	`SetValue`	**Item**: cmdPreview.Visible
			Expression: Yes
	...	`SetValue`	**Item**: cmdPrint.Visible
			Expression: Yes

FIGURE 14.2:

Clicking the Enrollment Summary option unhides the print command buttons.

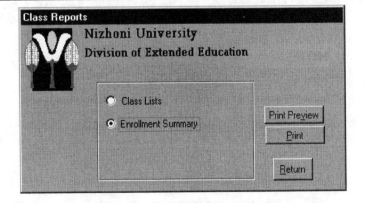

Create the Macros for Print Preview

You'll create two macros. When you click the Print Preview button, the first macro hides the mini-switchboard and displays the report in Print Preview (see Figure 14.3). When you close the Print Preview window (and the report recognizes the `Close` event), another macro determines if the fdlgClassReports mini-switchboard is open and unhides the form if it is open. Figure 14.4 shows the flow diagram for the Report_Close macro.

1. Click in the Class Reports mini-switchboard and switch to Design view.

FIGURE 14.3:

Flow diagram for cmdPreview_Click and Report_Close.

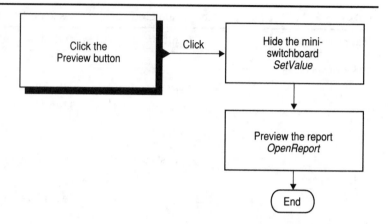

FIGURE 14.4:

Flow diagram for Report_Close.

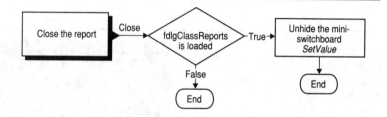

2. Click in mfdlgClassReports.

3. Click in the Macro Name cell of a new row and name the new macro **cmdPreview_Click**

4. Enter the macro shown in Table 14.3.

5. Save the macro group.

6. Open the mrptEnrollmentSummary macrosheet.

7. Click in the Macro Name cell of a new row and name the new macro **Report_Close**

8. In the next row, click in the Condition cell and enter **IsLoaded("fdlgClassReports")**. You have to test this condition before unhiding the form because the `SetValue` action fails if you try to unhide a closed form.

TABLE 14.3: The cmdPreview_Click macro hides the dialog form and opens the report.

Macro Name	Action	Action Arguments
cmdPre-view_Click		
	SetValue	**Item**: Screen.ActiveForm.Visible
		Expression: No
	OpenReport	**Report Name**: rptEnrollmentSummary
		View: Print Preview

9. In the Action cell of the same row, select the **SetValue** action and set its arguments as follows:

Item	Forms!fdlgClassReports.Visible
Expression	Yes

10. Save the macro.

Attach and Test the Macros

1. In the Database window, select rptEnrollmentSummary and open it in Design view.

2. Click in the report's OnClose property and select mrptEnrollmentSummary.Report_Close.

3. Save and close the report.

4. Click in fdlgClassReports, then click the cmdPreview button; click in the OnClick property and select mfdlgClassReports.cmdPreview_Click.

5. Save the form and switch to Form view.

6. On the mini-switchboard, click the Enrollment Summary option button, then click the Print Preview button. The dialog form is hidden and the report is opened in Print Preview.

7. Click the Close box on the report. The report closes and the mini-switchboard is unhidden.

Create the Macro for the Print Button

When you click the Print button, the macro prints the report. The macro doesn't need to hide the mini-switchboard because the report isn't displayed.

1. Switch to Design view.

2. Click in mfdlgClassReports, then click in the Macro Name cell of a new row and name the new macro **cmdPrint_Click**

3. In the next row, select the `OpenReport` action and set its arguments as follows:

`Report Name`	rptEnrollmentSummary
`View`	Print

4. Save the macro.

Attach and Test the Macro

1. Click in fdlgClassReports, then click the cmdPrint button; click in the OnClick property and select mfdlgClassReports.cmdPrint_Click.

2. Click in the form's PopUp property and change the value to Yes. You are finished designing this dialog box.

3. Save the form and switch to Form view.

4. Select the Enrollment Summary option and click the Print button. The report is printed.

5. Click the Return button. The mini-switchboard closes and the main switchboard is unhidden.

Calculating Page Totals

The rptEnrollmentSummary report includes subtotals for each program and a grand total for all programs. You calculate both kinds of totals in calculated controls that use the same expression. For example, you calculate current enrollment totals using the expression

=Sum([Enrollment])

as the ControlSource property of a calculated control—the location of the control determines which records are used in the calculation. When you place the control in a group header or footer, only the records for the group are included in the calculation; when you place the control in the report header or footer, all of the records in the report are included. In the Enrollment Summary report, there are subtotals for each program group in the group footer, and there are grand totals in the report footer.

1. In the Database window, select rptEnrollmentSummary and click the Design button.

2. Click in the ProgEnroll text box (in the ProgramNameFooter section). Observe the ControlSource property that calculates the current enrollment subtotal for a program:

   =Sum([Enrollment])

3. Click in the GrandTotalEnrollment text box in the Report Footer section (to the right of the label containing the text "Grand Totals:"). Observe that the ControlSource property that calculates the current enrollment grand total for all programs is the same expression:

   =Sum([Enrollment]

Sometimes you want to calculate page totals in addition to, or instead of, group and report totals. A report has page header and footer sections in addition to the other sections, so you might expect to use a calculated control in a page header or footer section to calculate page totals; however, before you can use a calculated control in a section, you have to know which records are included in the calculation. Access knows which records are in a group and which records are in the report, so you can use calculated controls for group totals in a group header or footer and for report totals in a report header or footer. In these cases, Access does the group and report calculations *before* laying out the pages of the report. But, since Access doesn't know which records are on a page until *after* the page has been laid out, Access doesn't know which records to include in the calculation of page totals; as a result, you can't use calculated controls for page totals in page header and footer sections.

The event that a section recognizes after the section has been laid out, but before the section is printed or displayed in Print Preview, is the `Print` event. You can use the `Print` event to trigger a macro that uses information that depends on how the section is laid out. For example, a macro triggered by the **Print** event of the page footer can use the value of the current page number.

To calculate the page total for enrollment, you can place an unbound text box in the page footer and use it to accumulate the total enrollment for the page as Access lays out the records of the page. You create two macros triggered by **Print** events to calculate a page total, as follows:

- The first macro sets the value in the unbound text box to zero when a new page starts. A new page starts after Access lays out the page header (and the page header section recognizes the **Print** event). Therefore, you can trigger this macro with the **Print** event of the page header section.

- The second macro creates a running total, by increasing the value in the text box by the enrollment value in each record, as soon as Access has laid out the record (and the detail section recognizes the **Print** event). After Access has laid out the last record for the page, the unbound text box contains the total enrollment for the page.

After laying out the last record for the page, Access prepares to lay out the page footer (including the unbound text box containing the total enrollment for the page). The page footer recognizes the **Format** event before formatting and then the **Print** event after formatting. After laying out the page footer for a page, Access lays out the page header for the next page and begins the accumulation for its enrollment page total by running the first macro to initialize the unbound text box in its page footer.

Placing the Unbound Text Box to Accumulate the Page Total

First, place an unbound text box and a label in the page footer section.

1. Click the Label tool, then click in the page footer section (just below the label containing the text "are Below Target…") and type into the new label **Page Total for Enrollment**

2. Click the Text Box tool, then click in the page footer section (below the text box for program enrollment total) and create a new text box 0.5" wide.

3. Set the Name property of the new unbound text box to **PageEnrollTotal**

Create the Macros to Calculate the Page Total

Create the two macros to initialize the text box and accumulate the enrollment total for the page.

1. Click in the mrptEnrollmentSumary macrosheet, then click in the Macro Name cell of a new row and name the new macro **PageHeader_Print**

2. Enter the first macro shown in Table 14.4.

3. Click in the Macro Name cell of a new row, then name the next new macro **Detail_Print** and enter the second macro shown in Table 14.4.

4. Save the macro group.

TABLE 14.4: Macros to calculate a page total. The first macro initializes the page total when the page header for the page is laid out. The second macro increases the page total by the value in the record after the record is laid out.

Macro Name	Action	Action Arguments
PageHeader_Print		
	SetValue	**Item**: PageEnrollTotal
		Expression: 0
Detail_Print		
	SetValue	**Item**: PageEnrollTotal
		Expression: PageEnrollTotal + Enrollment

Attach and Test the First Macro

1. Click in the OnPrint property of the Page Header and select the macro mrptEnrollmentsummary.PageHeader_Print.

2. Switch to Print Preview and observe that the value of the unbound text box is zero.

3. Switch to Design view.

Attach and Test the Second Macro

1. Click in the Detail section, then click in the OnPrint property and select the macro mrptEnrollmentSummary.Detail_Print.

2. Switch to Print Preview. Observe that the unbound text box contains the enrollment total for each page (see Figure 14.5).

FIGURE 14.5:

Page Totals for Enrollment.

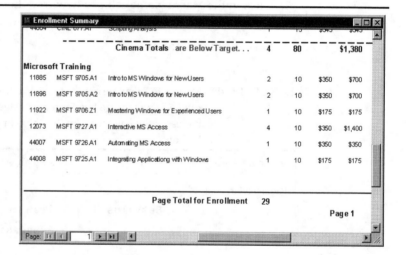

Modify the Process for When There Are No Classes

If you select a session for which no classes are scheduled, you find that the Detail_Print macro fails. To avoid macro failure, determine if there are classes by using the **NoData** event (recognized by the report when its recordset is empty). You use the **NoData** event to trigger a macro that displays a message and then uses the **CancelEvent** action to cancel the printing process.

Create a Macro for the NoData Event

1. Click in Macro Name cell of an empty row in mrptEnrollmentSummary, and name the new macro **Report_NoData**

2. In the next row, select the `MsgBox` action and set the `Message` argument to **There are no enrollments for the session.**

3. In the next row, select the `CancelEvent` action.

4. Save the macrosheet.

Attach and Test the Macro

1. Click in rptEnrollmentSummary, switch to Design view, then click in the OnNoData property and select the mrptEnrollmentSummary.Report_NoData macro.

2. Save and close the report.

3. In the main switchboard, select Spr 97 as the Working Session.

4. Select the Reports option button in the Classes option group, and select Enrollment Summary.

5. Click the Print Preview command button. The custom message is displayed.

6. Click OK. The Class Reports mini-switchboard is displayed.

7. Click Return. The mini-switchboard closes and the main switchboard is unhidden.

Endnotes

In this chapter you learned:

- How to use the `Format` event to embellish a report. Because a section recognizes the `Format` event when Access knows what data goes into the section but before laying out the section, you can use this event to trigger a macro that uses the data in the section to change the layout.

- How to use the `Print` event to update page totals. Because a section recognizes the `Print` event when Access has laid out the report section but before

displaying or printing the section, you can use this event to trigger a macro
that updates a text box in the page footer with data from each record laid out
on the page.

On Your Own

In the exercises, you add to the application by creating an enrollment report to highlight low enrollments and by creating a page total for student fees on the enrollment
summary report. Also, you create simple macros to explore the various report
events.

Adding to the Application

1. Create a low enrollment report.

   a. In the Database window, copy the rptEnrollmentReport report and
      paste it as rptLowEnrollment. Change the label in the header to **Low
      Enrollment Report**

   b. Place a label near the right edge of the detail section and set its Caption
      property to **Under Enrolled**

   c. Set the ForeColor property to red and the Name property to **lblUnder-
      Enrolled**

   d. Create a new macro group named **mrptLowEnrollment**, and a macro
      named **Detail_Format** that tests the value of the enrollment. If enroll-
      ment is less than 5, the macro sets the label's Visible property to Yes;
      otherwise, the macro sets the label's Visible property to No.

   e. Attach the macro to the OnFormat property of the Detail section.

   f. Open the report in Print Preview to test the macro.

2. Create a page total for fees.

   In this exercise, you place an unbound text box in the Page Footer of rptEnrollmentSummary to accumulate total fees for each page.

   a. Place an unbound text box in the Page Footer of rptEnrollmentSum-
      mary, just below the program fee total, and set the Name property to

PageFeeTotal. You use this control to accumulate values of the TotalFee control in the detail section that contains the total fees for each course.

b. Modify the mrptEnrollmentSummary (created in this chapter) by adding a row to the PageHeader_Print macro: add a **SetValue** action to initialize the value in PageFeeTotal.

c. Add a row to the Detail_Print macro (created in this chapter): add a **SetValue** action to increment the PageFeeTotal using the expression PageFeeTotal + TotalFee.

Extending the Concepts

1. Explore Report events.

You can observe the occurrence of a report's events by creating a set of macros that display a message for each event, and then triggering each macro with its corresponding event.
For the rptEnrollmentSummary report:

a. Create a macro for each report and report section event with a single **MsgBox** action to display the section and name of the event as its **Message** argument. For example, for the detail section, create the three macros:

Macro Name	Action	Action Argument
Detail_Format	**MsgBox**	Message: Detail Format event
Detail_Print	**MsgBox**	Message: Detail Print event
Detail_Retreat	**MsgBox**	Message: Detail Retreat event

For the events that already have a macro, insert a new first row for the macro, then select the **MsgBox** action and display the section and name of the event as the **Message** argument.

b. Attach each macro to its corresponding event. Save the report.

c. Explore the events by selecting a working session with enrollments and a working session without enrollments (Spr 97).

d. When you are finished exploring, enter the word **False** in the condition cell for each **MsgBox action so that the action won't be executed.**

CHAPTER

FIFTEEN

Controlling the User Interface

- Understanding the built-in command environment

- Creating custom menu bars and shortcut menus

- Using the Menu Builder

- Creating custom toolbars

- Customizing key assignments with an AutoKeys macro

- Disabling keyboard shortcuts

In previous chapters of this book you learned how to create a user interface that includes main and mini-switchboard forms, navigation paths that use command buttons and option groups to provide choices, and selection procedures that use combo boxes and custom dialog boxes to select records. To restrict users to the forms and navigation paths as you designed them, you must control access to menu commands and toolbar buttons. This chapter shows you how to build your own restricted menus and toolbars; how to hide the built-in menus and toolbars, and replace them with your custom versions; and how to make custom keyboard assignments.

> **NOTE** When you begin this chapter, only the switchboard and the Database window should be displayed. Close any other objects.

The Built-in Command Environment

When you work interactively, Access provides a set of built-in commands and makes them available in four ways:

- as items on menus (on built-in menu bars) that you choose with the mouse or access key combinations

- as items on built-in shortcut menus that you click with the mouse

- as buttons on built-in toolbars that you click with the mouse

- as built-in keyboard combinations that you press

The Built-in Menu Bars

Nearly all of the commands that are built into Access are arranged in *menus*. You display a menu by clicking on the menu's name in the *menu bar* below the title bar. Each view of a database object has its own menu bar that contains the menus and the menu commands appropriate to that view. For example, the Form view menu bar includes menus with *menu names*: File, Edit, View, Insert, Format, Records,

Tools, Window, and Help. The commands in a menu are grouped by using *separator bars*. A command can have a *submenu* with its own commands (a right-pointing arrow next to a command indicates that the command has a submenu). A submenu includes its own commands, which can also be grouped by using separator bars. Figure 15.1 shows the menu bar for Form view, and displays the Edit menu and the submenu for the Go To command.

By default, Access displays the set of built-in menu bars with all of the commands you have been using. Access also has a *reduced set of built-in menus* that you can display instead. The reduced set includes only the commands that are useful when you are working with a custom database application in views other than Design view—it doesn't include the menu bars for any Design view, and eliminates several other commands. Figure 15.2 shows the reduced menu bar for Form view; this menu bar doesn't include the View or Tools menus. The figure shows the reduced File menu.

FIGURE 15.1:

The built-in Form view menu bar. The commands in a menu are grouped by using *separator bars*. A command that has a submenu is displayed with a right-pointing arrow.

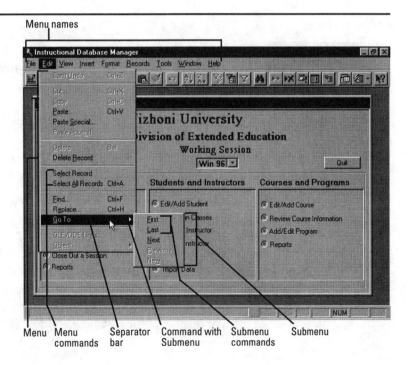

Menu names

Menu | Menu commands | Separator bar | Command with Submenu | Submenu commands | Submenu

FIGURE 15.2:

The reduced built-in Form view menu bar.

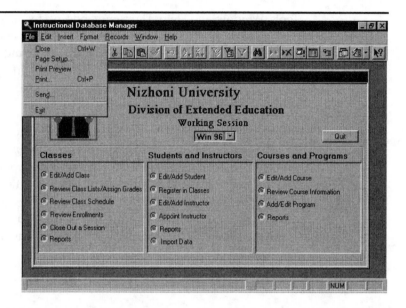

NOTE

When you display the reduced set of menus, the commands that are missing from the menus are only hidden so that you can't use them interactively; however, you can still use them in macros and Visual Basic programming.

You can elect to display the reduced set of built-in menus by clearing the Allow Full Menus check box in the Startup dialog (see Figure 15.3).

You can use the reduced set of built-in menu bars when you are creating a custom application for others to use. In the simplest case, you can elect the reduced set of built-in menus and also hide all of the built-in toolbars by clearing the Allow Built-in Toolbars check box. With these choices, after you have started up the database you can't get to the Design view of any database object by using a menu command, but you can still display the Database window by pressing F11 or ALT+F1. Once the Database window is displayed you can open any database object in Design view. You can prevent display of the Database window (after the database is started up) by clearing the Use Access Special Keys and Display Database Window check boxes in the Startup dialog box. You can display the full Startup dialog box, shown in Figure 15.4, by clicking the Advanced button.

FIGURE 15.3:

Using the Startup dialog to display the reduced set of built-in menus.

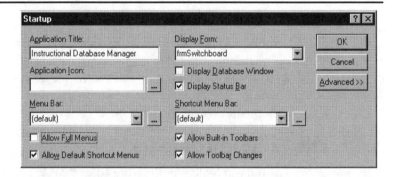

FIGURE 15.4:

Using the Startup dialog box to disable function key access to the Database window.

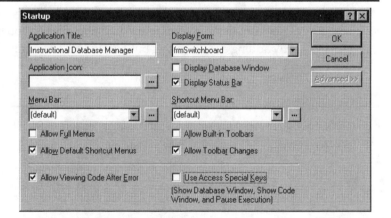

NOTE Once you have cleared the Allow Full Menus, Allow Built-in Toolbars, Display Database Window, and the Use Special Access Keys check boxes in the Startup dialog box, you won't be able to display the Database window after the database is started up. Note that you can still bypass the Startup settings by pressing the SHIFT key when you first open the database.

You can also display a form or a report without a menu bar. See the exercise at the end of this chapter.

The Built-in Shortcut Menus

Some of the built-in commands are arranged in shortcut menus that you display by right-clicking with the mouse—each view has its own shortcut menu. In Form view there is a separate built-in shortcut menu for controls in addition to the shortcut menu for the form. Figure 15.5 shows the shortcut menus that appear when you click on the switchboard and on its controls.

The Built-in Toolbars

The built-in toolbar buttons are equivalent to many of the menu commands. Each view of a database object has its own built-in toolbar, which Access displays by default when the view is the current view. Toolbars provide a convenient, visual display of the more commonly used commands; you can modify the built-in toolbars by adding and removing buttons. In previous chapters you modified several toolbars to include buttons from other toolbars (such as the Run button you placed on the

FIGURE 15.5:

The shortcut menus for the switchboard.

Form view toolbar) and buttons that aren't displayed in any default toolbar (such as the Run Macro button you placed on several toolbars). Figure 15.1 shows a portion of the built-in Form view toolbar which was modified to include the Run Macro, Debug window, and Single Step buttons.

The Built-in Key Combinations

Access includes a large set of shortcut key combinations that make your work more efficient. Most Windows applications have a common set of basic keyboard shortcuts, such as CTRL+X, CTRL+C, and CTRL+V for the Cut, Copy, and Paste commands and F1 for context-sensitive help. In addition, Access has a set of its own shortcuts, such as F11 to bring the Database window to the front, CTRL+G to display the Debug window, and F6 to toggle between controls on a main form and a subform.

Access to Built-in and Custom Commands

Some built-in commands are available in all four ways. An example is the Copy command, which is available as a menu command in the Edit menu, as a menu command on shortcut menus for controls on forms, as the Copy toolbar button, and as the CTRL+C keyboard shortcut. Other built-in commands are only available in one or two ways. For example, to open the Zoom box you can either use the Zoom command on the shortcut menu or press the SHIFT+F2 keyboard combination; there is neither a command on a menu bar menu nor a Zoom toolbar button.

This chapter shows you how to control the four ways to access the built-in commands, and how to use macros to create a custom command and make the custom command available in any of the four ways. With the tools you learn in this chapter, you can gain control over the commands you provide in your custom database application.

Creating a Custom Menu Bar

You can create a custom menu bar that includes both built-in menu commands and your own custom commands. You can display a custom menu bar in two ways:

- Create an individual custom menu bar and attach it to a specific form or report. The menu bar is displayed whenever the form or report is the active object.

- Create a *global menu bar* that is displayed in all windows except for those forms and reports that have their own individual custom menu bars.

Whether you are using macros or Visual Basic programming for your application, you can only use macros to create custom menu bars. You create two kinds of macros for each custom menu bar:

- A *menu bar macro* for the menu bar itself, to specify which menu names appear on the menu bar.

- A *menu macro group* for each of the menus and submenus. The macro group contains a macro for each of the commands that appear on the menu or submenu.

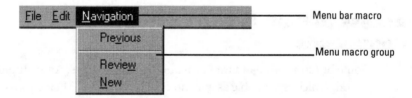

Creating an Individual Menu Bar for frmRegistration

We'll create a custom menu bar for frmRegistration that provides custom menu commands equivalent to the five command buttons on the form, and an Edit menu that provides the three built-in commands Cut, Copy, and Paste. Figure 15.6 shows the frmRegistration form.

We'll arrange the five custom commands and the three built-in commands in three menus, as follows:

File	Edit	Navigation
Print	Cut	Previous
Return	Copy	New
	Paste	Review

FIGURE 15.6:

The five command buttons on the
frmRegistration form.

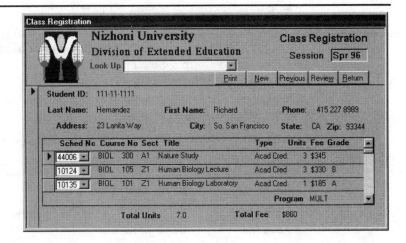

Creating the Menu Bar Macro

The menu bar macro is stored in its own macrosheet, and contains an **AddMenu** action for each of the menu names. The arguments of the **AddMenu** action are

Menu Name	The name of the menu as you want it to appear in the menu bar. To create an access key for the menu, type an ampersand to the left of the letter you want to use for the access key.
Menu Macro Name	The name of the macro group for the menu.
Status Bar Text	The text you want displayed in the Status Bar when you select this menu.

1. Open a new macrosheet and save it as **mmnuRegistration**. The mmnu tag indicates a menu bar macro.

2. In the toolbar, click the Macro Names button to hide the Macro Name column. The menu bar macro is a single macro stored in its own macrosheet. (The macro can include conditions that you can use to show or hide a menu, so you display the Condition column.)

3. Enter the macro shown in Table 15.1. When you name the macro group for a menu, use the name of the menu bar macro followed by an underscore and (part of) the menu name; for example, mmnuRegistration_File is the name of the macro group for the File menu.

4. Save the macro.

TABLE 15.1: The menu bar macro for frmRegistration.

Action	Action Arguments
AddMenu	Menu Name: &File
	Menu Macro Name: mmnuRegistration_File
AddMenu	Menu Name: &Edit
	Menu Macro Name: mmnuRegistration_Edit
AddMenu	Menu Name: &Navigation
	Menu Macro Name: mmnuRegistration_Navigation

Creating the Menu Macro Groups

Next, you create a macro group for each menu, and create a macro within the group for each command you want to display in the menu. Use the name of the command as the name of the macro; for example, in the mmnuRegistration_File macro group, you'll create macros named &Print an &Return.

The Edit Menu Macro Group

The Edit menu runs built-in menu commands. Use the DoMenuItem action to run a built-in menu command in a custom menu.

1. Open a new macrosheet and save it as **mmnuRegistration_Edit**

2. In the toolbar, click the Conditions button to hide the Condition column. (A menu macro group can't include conditions.)

3. Enter the macro group shown in Table 15.2.

4. Save the macro group.

TABLE 15.2: The menu macro group for mmnuRegistration_Edit. Each macro runs the **DoMenuItem** action for the corresponding built-in menu command.

Macro Name	Action	Action Arguments
Cu&t	DoMenuItem	**Menu Bar**: Form
		Menu Name: Edit
		Command: Cut
&Copy	DoMenuItem	**Menu Bar**: Form
		Menu Name: Edit
		Command: Copy
&Paste	DoMenuItem	**Menu Bar**: Form
		Menu Name: Edit
		Command: Paste

The File Menu Macro Group

Each custom command in the File menu has a macro that uses the **RunMacro** action; it runs the same macro as the corresponding command button on the frmRegistration form.

1. Click in frmRegistration and switch to Design view.

2. Select the Print button, then click in the OnClick property and observe that the macro is mfrmRegistration.cmdPrint_Click.

3. Select the Return button, then click in the OnClick property and observe that the macro is mcrGallery.cmdReturn_Click.

4. Open a new macrosheet and save it as **mmnuRegistration_File**

5. Enter the macro group shown in Table 15.3.

6. Save the macro group.

TABLE 15.3: The menu macro group for mmnuRegistration_File. Each macro uses the **RunMacro** action to run the macro for the corresponding command button on the form.

Macro Name	Action	Action Arguments
&Print		
	RunMacro	Macro Name: mfrmRegistration.cmdPrint_Click
&Return		
	RunMacro	Macro Name: mcrGallery.cmdReturn_Click

The Navigation Menu Macro Group

The Navigation menu also runs custom menu commands. Include a separator bar between the Previous command and the New and Review commands (which open the frmStudents form). To display a separator bar in the menu, you use a hyphen in the Macro Name cell and a blank action cell (as shown in Table 15.4).

1. Click in frmRegistration and switch to Design view. Observe the macros for the New, Review, and Previous buttons.

2. Open a new macrosheet and save it as **mmnuRegistration_Navigation**

3. Enter the macro group shown in Table 15.4.

4. Save the macro group.

Attaching an Individual Menu Bar

When a form (or report) has the focus, you display a custom menu bar by setting the form's (or report's) MenuBar property to the menu bar macro.

1. Click in frmRegistration and select the form; click in the MenuBar property and select mmnuRegistration.

2. Save the form and switch to Form view. Figure 15.7 shows the custom menu bar.

TABLE 15.4: The menu macro group for mmnuRegistration_Navigation. Each macro uses the **RunMacro** action to run the macro for the corresponding command button on the form.

Macro Name	Action	Action Arguments
Pre&vious		
	RunMacro	**Macro Name**: mcrGallery.cmdPrevious_Click
Revie&w		
	RunMacro	**Macro Name**: mfrmRegistration.cmdReview_Click
&New		
	RunMacro	**Macro Name**: mfrmRegistration.cmdNew_Click

FIGURE 15.7:

Displaying the custom menu bar for frmRegistration.

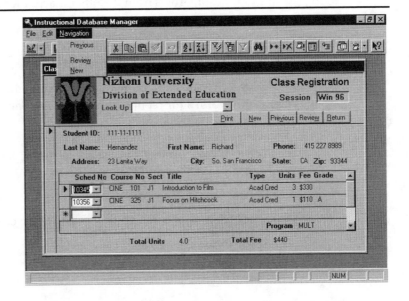

Creating a Custom Shortcut Menu

To create a custom shortcut menu: create a shortcut menu macro that has a single AddMenu action, and a single macro group for the commands displayed in the menu. Because a shortcut menu doesn't have a title bar, the name you enter in the Menu Name argument of the AddMenu action isn't displayed.

You'll create a shortcut menu for frmRegistration that displays all five custom commands.

1. Open a new macrosheet and save it as **mmnusRegistration**. We'll use the mmnus tag for a menu macro for a shortcut menu.

2. Select the AddMenu action and set the Menu Name argument to **Short**

3. Set the Menu Macro Name argument to **mmnusRegistration_Short**

4. Open a new macrosheet and save it as **mmnusRegistration_Short**

5. Enter the macro shown in Table 15.5. Create the rows of this macro by copying and pasting rows from the other macro menu groups.

6. Save both macrosheets.

Attaching the Shortcut Menu

To display a custom shortcut menu when you right-click in the active form (or report), set the form's (or report's) ShortcutMenuBar property to the shortcut menu macro.

1. Click in frmRegistration, and select the form; click in the ShortcutMenuBar property and select mmnusRegistration.

2. Save the form and switch to Form view.

3. Right-click in the form. Figure 15.8 shows the custom shortcut menu.

4. Choose Return.

TABLE 15.5: The shortcut menu macro group for mmnusRegistration. Each macro uses the **RunMacro** action to run the same macro as the corresponding command button on the form.

Macro Name	Action	Action Arguments
&Print		
	RunMacro	**Macro Name**: mfrmRegistration.cmdPrint_Click
&Return		
	RunMacro	**Macro Name**: mcrGallery.cmdReturn_Click
Pre&vious		
	RunMacro	**Macro Name**: mcrGallery.cmdPrevious_Click
Revie&w		
	RunMacro	**Macro Name**: mfrmRegistration.cmdReview_Click
&New		
	RunMacro	**Macro Name**: mfrmRegistration.cmdNew_Click

Using the Menu Builder

You can use the Menu Builder to create custom menu bars and shortcut menus. You specify the design of the menu bar, menus and submenus by using the series of dialogs that the Menu Builder displays. When you finish designing the menu bar, the Builder creates the menu bar macro and the menu macro groups according to your specifications.

Use the Menu Builder to create a simple menu bar that you'll use as a global menu bar.

FIGURE 15.8:

Displaying the custom shortcut menu for frmRegistration.

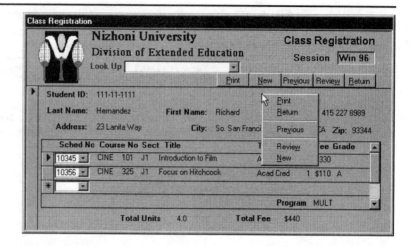

1. Choose Tools ➤ Add-ins ➤ Menu Builder. The first dialog lists all the macro groups in the application.

2. Click the New button. The next dialog displays a list of the built-in menu bars. You can select <Empty Menu Bar> to start from scratch, or select one of the built-in menu bars to use as a template. You'll select the Database menu bar, which is the menu bar displayed by default when the Database window is the active window.

3. Select Database and click OK. The next dialog is the New Menu Bar dialog shown in Figure 15.9.

The list box displays the names of the menus, commands, submenus, and submenu commands. The symbol preceding a name indicates its function (see Table 15.6).

Use the up and down arrow buttons to move through the list; use the left and right arrow buttons to change the level of indentation. A name that isn't indented is a menu name, a name at one level of indentation is a menu command, and a name at two levels of indentation is a submenu command. The list in Figure 15.9 shows two levels of indentation, but you can use additional levels. Use the Next button to move down the list, the Insert button to insert a new item, and the Delete button to delete the selected name. If a command is directly followed by one or more items indented to the next level, the command has a submenu and is shown with a right-pointing arrow in the menu; the indented items are displayed in the submenu.

FIGURE 15.9:

Use the New Menu Bar dialog to design a custom menu bar.

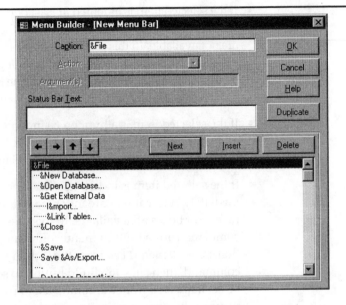

TABLE 15.6: The Menu Builder symbols. The symbol preceding a name indicates its function.

Symbol	Description
&	Indicates that the letter immediately to the right is the access key.
...	One level of indentation indicates a menu command
..._	Indicates a separator bar between two menu commands
......	Two levels of indentation indicates a submenu command
......_	Indicates a separator bar between two submenu commands

When you select an item in the Menu Builder's list box, it is displayed in the Caption edit box at the top of the dialog and is available for editing. The item's role in the list determines whether the Action and Argument edit boxes are available, as follows:

- If the selected item is not indented, the Action and Argument edit boxes are not available. The Menu Builder creates the menu bar macro based on the non-indented items, and includes an **AddMenu** action for each one.

- If the selected item is indented at least one level and has items immediately below it that are indented at the next level, the Action and Argument edit boxes are not available. In this case the selected item has a submenu, so Access displays the selected item with a right-pointing arrow and displays the items indented at the next level in a submenu. The Menu Builder includes an **AddMenu** action in the menu macro group to create the submenu for the selected item.

- If the selected item is a hyphen (-) indented at least one level, Access displays a separator bar. The Menu Builder includes a row in the macro group with a hyphen in the Macro Name cell and a blank in the Action cell.

- If the selected item is indented at least one level and doesn't have items immediately below it that are indented at the next level, the Action and Argument edit boxes are available. In this case you can specify whether the command runs a built-in menu command, a macro, or a Visual Basic function. Select **DoMenuItem** from the Action combo list to run a built-in menu command, then click the Build button to set the arguments (see Figure 15.10). Select **RunMacro** from the combo list to run a macro, then enter the full macro name in the Argument edit box. Select **RunCode** in the combo list to run a Visual Basic function, and enter the function name in the Argument edit box.

FIGURE 15.10:

Using the Menu Builder to run a built-in menu command.

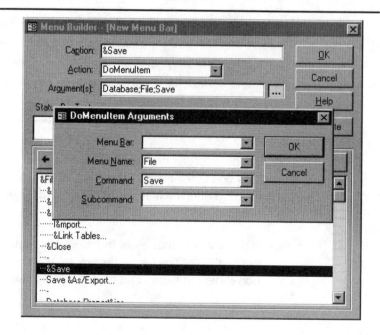

Design the Global Menu Bar

You'll create a menu bar with two menus, and menu commands as follows:

File	Edit
Page Setup	Cut
Print Preview	Copy
Print	Paste
Exit	

1. In the Menu Builder list box, select the &New Database command, then click the Delete button above the list box. You'll delete most of the items in the File menu.

2. Select and delete all of the items under &File except:

   Page Set&up

   Print Pre&view

   &Print

   -

   E&xit

3. Select and delete all of the items under ~&Edit except:

   Cu&t

   &Copy

   &Paste

4. Delete the remaining menus: View, Insert, Tools, Window, Help, and all their sub-items.

5. Click OK and name the menu bar **mmnuGlobal**. The Menu Builder creates the menu bar macro and the two menu macro groups.

The Menu Bar Macro and Macro Groups

1. In the Database window, observe the three new macro objects:

   mmnuGlobal

   mmnuGlobal_File

   mmnuGlobal_Edit

2. Select the menu bar macro, mmnuGlobal, and click the Design button. The macro contains an **AddMenu** action for the two menus you designed. The first **AddMenu** action adds the menu named &File and specifies mmnuGlobal_File as the macro group for the menu commands.

3. Close the macrosheet.

4. Select the macro group mmnuGlobal_File and click the Design button. There is a macro for each command you have selected and a row for the separator bar (see Figure 15.11).

FIGURE 15.11:

The menu macro group for the File menu.

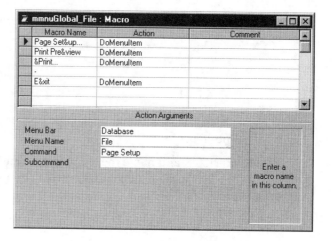

5. Click in the third row. This macro tells Access what to do when you select the Print command from your custom File menu: The **DoMenuItem** action runs the built-in Print command on the built-in File menu on the built-in Database menu bar.

6. Close the macro group.

NOTE   When you create a custom menu bar you can include any built-in command, but Access can only run a command that is appropriate to the current view. For example, you can include the View ➤ Macro Names command (from the built-in Macro menu bar) on a custom global menu bar, but for all views other than macro Design view (when a macrosheet is active), the command is grayed out and unavailable.

Using the Menu Builder is often the easiest way to create custom menu bars and shortcut menus. Not only can you use the Builder to create a custom menu bar and edit the macros, you can also create a menu bar manually and then use the Builder to edit it—provided that you follow the Builder's rules:

- You must name a menu macro group using the menu bar macro name, followed by an underscore and the menu name (without the ampersand).

- Each row in the menu macro group must contain an **AddMenu** action and no conditions.

- Each macro in a menu macro group must have a single macro action, and the action must be **DoMenuItem**, **RunMacro**, or **RunCode**.

- There can be no blank rows or rows containing only comments.

Displaying a Custom Global Menu Bar

You use the Startup dialog to specify the global menu bar.

1. Choose Tools ➤ Startup.

2. Select mmnuGlobal from the macro objects displayed in the Menu Bar combo list (see Figure 15.12). The new global menu takes effect the next time you open the database.

FIGURE 15.12:

Assigning a global menu bar in the Startup dialog.

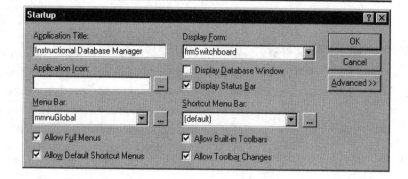

3. Click OK.

4. Click the Close button in the Database window.

5. Open the College database. The custom global menu bar is displayed.

> **NOTE**
> When you have assigned a custom global menu, you can display the built-in menus by pressing CTRL+F11; however, if you clear the Use Access Special Keys option in the Startup dialog, this key sequence is disabled and the built-in menu bars are not available.

Using Custom Toolbars

Toolbars make your application easier to learn and use by providing convenient visual access to commands:

- You can use toolbars to provide alternative access to menu commands (just as the built-in toolbars provide alternate access to the built-in menu commands).

- Toolbars can also provide alternative access to commands that you run by clicking command or option buttons on forms.

- You can design a switchboard to be a custom toolbar instead of a form, and include custom toolbar buttons to navigate to the task forms in your application.

There are several ways you can change the toolbars in your application:

- You can create a custom toolbar button that opens a specific database object, such as a form or report, or that runs a macro.

- You can customize a built-in toolbar by adding or removing built-in buttons and by adding custom buttons.

- You can create custom toolbars with built-in and custom buttons for any of the forms and reports of your application.

- You can hide any, or all, of the built-in toolbars.

Hiding the Built-in Toolbars

You can hide the built-in toolbars by clearing the Allow Built-In Toolbars check box in the Startup dialog.

1. Press F11 to display the Database window.

2. Choose Tools ➤ Startup and clear the Allow Built-in Toolbars check box (see Figure 15.4). This change takes effect the next time you open the database.

3. Click the Close button in the Database window.

4. Open the College database. The toolbars are hidden.

5. Press F11 to display the Database window, and then press CTRL+F11. The built-in menu bar is displayed.

Creating a Custom Toolbar

Create a custom toolbar with custom and built-in buttons for the frmClasses form. You'll include the built-in Cut, Copy, and Paste buttons, and some custom toolbar buttons, as alternates to the command buttons on the form.

1. Select the View ➤ Toolbars command.

2. Click New, then save the custom toolbar as **tbarClasses,** and click OK.

3. Click the Customize button. The Customize Toolbars dialog box contains all of the available buttons, arranged by the categories listed in the list box. A very small empty toolbar appears somewhere to the left of the dialog box (see Figure 15.13).

FIGURE 15.13:

Creating a new toolbar.

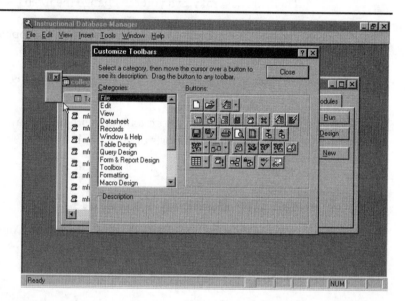

4. Select the Edit category.

5. Drag the Cut button out of the dialog box, and drop it on the toolbar.

6. Drag the Copy button to the toolbar, and drop it on top of and slightly to the right of the first button. When you release the mouse button, the Copy button is placed to the right of the Cut button. With the Customize Toolbars dialog box open, you can rearrange buttons by dragging them to new locations on the toolbar.

7. Drag the Paste button to the toolbar.

8. In the Customize Toolbars dialog box, select the All Macros category. The Objects list box displays all the macro objects in the application.

9. Select mcrGallery.cmdPrevious_Click, then drag it to the toolbar and release it to the right of the Paste button.

10. Similarly, select and drag buttons for mfrmClasses.cmdReviewCourse_Click and mcrGallery.cmdReturn_Click to the toolbar.

Changing the Toolbar Button Image

Since the three custom buttons all display the same image, you'll customize their images.

1. Be sure the Customize Toolbars dialog box is still displayed.

2. In the custom toolbar, right-click the first custom macro button, and click the Choose Button Image command from the shortcut menu.

3. Select the left-pointing arrow button, and change the Description text to **Previous** (see Figure 15.14).

4. Click OK. The button image is the left-pointing arrow, and the ToolTip reads Previous.

5. Right-click the second custom macro button, then click Choose Button Image; select the Form button, change the Description text to **Review Course**, and click OK.

FIGURE 15.14:

Changing the custom button image.

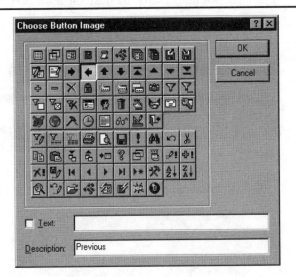

6. Right-click the third custom macro button, then click Choose Button Image; select the Open Door button, change the Description text to **Return**, and click OK.

7. Click the Close button on the Customize Toolbars dialog box.

Docking and Undocking the Custom Toolbar

You can drag a custom toolbar anywhere on the screen and drop it in a new location. When you drag the toolbar to an edge of the screen and drop it, the toolbar remains "docked" until you move it again.

1. Drag the new toolbar to the top edge of the screen and release the mouse button. The toolbar is now docked at the top of the screen. Figure 15.15 shows the new custom toolbar.

FIGURE 15.15:

Docking the custom toolbar beneath the menu bar.

2. To "float" the toolbar (the opposite of docking), click in the toolbar (but not on a button), then drag the toolbar away from the edge of the screen and release it.

3. Dock the toolbar at the top of the screen again.

Displaying Custom Toolbars

You control the display of a custom toolbar in one of two ways:

- Use the Toolbars dialog to specify when you want the toolbar displayed (in the same way that you control the display of a built-in toolbar).

- Attach the toolbar to an individual form (or report) with a pair of macros to show and hide the toolbar when the form (or report) becomes active and inactive, respectively.

Creating Macros to Show and Hide a Custom Toolbar

Create a pair of macros to show and hide a custom toolbar, and run them when the form recognizes the **Activate** and **Deactivate** events, respectively.

1. In the Database window, select mfrmClasses and click the Design button.
2. Click in a new row and enter the macros shown in Table 15.7.
3. Close and save the macrosheet.

TABLE 15.7: The macros to show and hide a custom toolbar.

Macro Name	Action	Action Arguments
Form_Activate		
	ShowToolbar	**Toolbar Name**: tbarClasses
		Show: Yes
Form_Deactivate		
	ShowToolbar	**Toolbar Name**: tbarClasses
		Show: No

Attach and Test the Macros

1. In the Database window, select the frmClasses form and click the Design button.
2. Click in the form's OnActivate property and select mfrmClasses.Form_Activate.
3. Click in the form's OnDeactivate property and select mfrmClasses.Form_Deactivate.
4. Save the form and switch to Form view. The custom toolbar is displayed.
5. Click the Review Course button in the toolbar. The frmCoursesView form is displayed.
6. Click the Return button on the frmCoursesView form.

7. Click the Previous button in the toolbar. The default error message shown in Figure 15.16 is displayed.

FIGURE 15.16:

The error message displayed when you click the Previous toolbar button.

The problem is that the Previous toolbar button runs a macro that we designed to be run from a command button on the form. We used the short syntax to refer to the controls on the form. In order to run the macro from a button on the toolbar, you must use the full syntax. You can use the Screen object to refer to controls on the active form so that the macros are still reusable.

> **TIP**
>
> To avoid having to toggle between the custom and built-in meuus, close the database and then reopen with the SHIFT key pressed to bypass the startup options.

Modify the Control References to Run a Macro from a Toolbar Button

1. In the Database window, click the Close button.

2. With the SHIFT button pressed, open the College database.

3. Select mcrGallery and click the Design button.

4. Modify the macro as shown in Table 15.8. You don't modify the `GoToControl` action because the `Control Name` argument requires the short syntax.

5. Save and close the macro.

TABLE 15.8: Use the full syntax for the control references for a toolbar macro.

Macro Name	Condition	Action	Action Arguments
cmdPrevious_Click			
	Screen.ActiveForm.PrimaryID.Enabled = Yes	RunMacro	**Macro Name**: mcrGallery.Previous
	...	StopMacro	
		SetValue	**Item**: Screen.ActiveControl.PrimaryID.Enabled
			Expression: Yes
		RunMacro	**Macro Name**: mcrGallery.Previous
		SetValue	**Item**: Screen.ActiveControl.PrimaryID.Enabled
			Expression: No
Previous			
	IsNull(Screen.Active-Form.PreviousID)	StopMacro	
		GoToControl	**Control Name**: PrimaryID
		FindRecord	**Find What**: =Screen.ActiveForm.PreviousID
		GoToControl	**Control Name**: cboFind

Test the Macro

1. In the Database window, double-click frmSwitchboard.

2. Select the Add/Edit Classes button.

3. Select another class in the combo list and click the Previous button in the toolbar. The new macro runs and displays the previous class.

Creating Custom Key Assignments

You can customize keyboard shortcuts in two ways: by defining access keys and by assigning custom key assignments with a macro.

Access Keys

You create access keys by inserting an ampersand just before the selected letter in a command button caption, menu command, or label. Pressing the key combination ALT+letter is an alternative to clicking the command button or selecting a menu command. When you define an access key for a label, pressing the access key moves the focus to the next control that can have the focus; if the label is attached to a control, the focus moves to the control.

1. In the Database window, select frmStudents and click the Design button.

2. Select the labels and modify their Captions as follows:

Student&ID	&City	&Zip
&Program	&State	P&hone
&Last Name	&Address	Admit &Date
&First Name	&Notes	

3. Save the form and switch to Form view (see Figure 15.17).

4. Test the access keys.

Access keys are part of the standard Windows interface design convention, so you don't have to provide additional instructions.

Creating a Key Assignment Macro

Access has a large set of default key combination assignments, such as CTRL+G to display the Debug window or F11 to display the Database window. You can create a macro group to assign custom commands to key combinations. You use a special

FIGURE 15.17:

When you define an access key for a label, pressing the access key moves the focus to the next control that can have the focus.

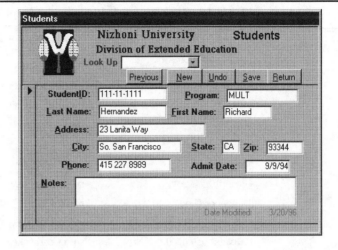

name, AutoKeys, for the macro group. When you press a key combination, Microsoft Access looks for an AutoKeys macro and runs the macro assigned to the combination (if there is one). You can use the AutoKeys macro to make key assignments in addition to, or in place of, the default key assignments. You can include conditions if you want a key assignment to be effective only if preconditions are met. The macro you assign to a key combination takes precedence over the default key assignment: you can use this feature to control the interface by disabling certain default key assignments. You name a macro in the AutoKeys group by entering the key or key combination in the Macro Name cell and using the **SendKeys** codes (see Chapter 7). Not all key combinations are available for assignment; Table 15.9 lists the key combinations you can use in an AutoKeys macro.

NOTE

Notice that the ALT+ key combinations are missing from the list. This means that you can't use the AutoKeys macro to disable the ALT+F4 combination that quits Access or the ALT+F1 combination that displays the Database window. You can, however, reassign any of the ctrl~+ letter combinations—including CTRL+C and CTRL+V! You should avoid reassigning these standard Windows defaults, though, in order to make your application consistent with other Windows applications.

TABLE 15.9: Key combinations for the AutoKeys macro.

SendKeys Code	Key Combination
^A or ^2	CTRL+ any letter or number key
{F1}	Any function key
^{F1}	CTRL+ any function key
+{F1}	SHIFT+ any function key
{insert}	INSERT key
^{insert}	CTRL+ INSERT key
+{insert}	SHIFT+ INSERT key
{Delete} or {Del}	DELETE key
^{Delete} or ^{Del}	CTRL+ DELETE key
+{Delete} or +{Del}	SHIFT+ DELETE key

In this book, you've learned a number of ways to control how a form can be closed, including:

- creating a custom button to close the form

- setting form properties to remove the default Control Box and Close Button controls

- creating custom menus without the Close command

However, you can still close the form by pressing CTRL+F4. You've also learned to control how a record can be deleted, by:

- creating a custom command button

- creating custom menus without the Delete commands

But you can still initiate a deletion by pressing the DELETE key.

You'll give some finish to your application by creating an AutoKeys macro that disables the CTRL+F4 and DELETE key combinations.

Creating an AutoKeys Macro Group

1. Open a new macrosheet and save it as **AutoKeys**

2. Click in the first Macro Name cell and enter ^{F4}. This is the **SendKeys** code for CTRL+F4.

3. Select the **StopMacro** action. To disable the key assignment, you stop the macro without taking any other action.

4. Click in the next row, enter {Del} in the Macro Name cell and select the **Stop-Macro** action.

5. Save the macro.

Test the Macro

The AutoKeys macro takes effect immediately.

1. Click in the frmSwitchboard form and press CTRL+F4. The form doesn't close.

2. Click the Add/Edit Class option button, select the record, and press DELETE. There is no response.

Endnotes

In this chapter, you have learned ways to control the command environment of your application, including:

- setting startup conditions to eliminate access to the Database window

- replacing the built-in menu bars and shortcut menus with reduced menu bars or custom menu bars

- replacing the built-in toolbars with custom menu bars

- making custom key assignments to disable built-in assignments

Using these techniques, you can provide only the commands required to use your application and no more. By removing the other built-in commands, you

- make the application easier to use

- avoid inadvertent changes to the database objects that could break the application

- protect the data by controlling the data entry operations

The next chapter shows you additional ways to protect your application and data.

On Your Own

In the exercise you learn how to display a form without a menu bar.

Adding to the Application

1. Display a form without a menu bar.

    You can display a form or a report without a menu bar by creating an empty menu bar macro.

    a. Open a new macrosheet and save the empty sheet as **mmnuNoMenu**

    b. Open a mini-switchboard, such as fdlgClassReports, in Design view and set the MenuBar property to **mmnuNoMenu**

    c. Switch to Form view. The mini-switchboard is displayed without a menu bar.

    d. Give the same treatment to the other mini-switchboard forms in the application.

CHAPTER

SIXTEEN

The Finishing Touches

- Protecting the application with passwords

- Preventing access to the Database window

- Documenting your application with the Database Documentor

- Setting command-line options for automatic backup and compacting

- Understanding the limitations of macro programming

In Chapter 15, "Controlling the User Interface," you learned to control the user interface by replacing built-in menus and toolbars with custom menus and toolbars and by disabling certain keyboard shortcuts. Nevertheless, these methods have not protected your application from inadvertent changes. For example, you can bypass the Startup options by pressing SHIFT when you open the database, and you can press ALT+F1 to display the Database window; either of these key combinations provides access to the Database window and risk of damage to the application's design.

Protecting Your Application

Access provides several methods you can use to protect the application from inadvertent design changes and from unauthorized use of the objects in the application. You can

- use a password to protect the application from unauthorized use

- hide objects in the Database window

- set options in the Startup dialog that help minimize access to the Database window

- implement user-level security

- encrypt the application

Protecting Your Application with a Password

You can prevent unauthorized people from opening your application by defining a password. Before you can set a password you need to establish exclusive access to the database.

1. In the Database window, click the Close box to close the database.

2. Choose File ➤ Open Database; check the Exclusive option (see Figure 16.1), then select College and click Open.

FIGURE 16.1:

Check the Exclusive option in the Open dialog to establish exclusive access to the database.

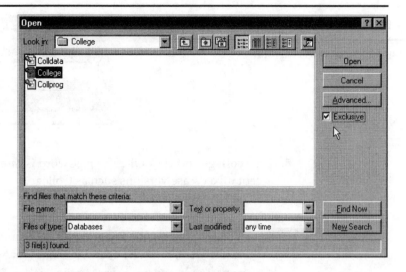

3. Choose <u>T</u>ools ➤ Security ➤ Set <u>D</u>atabase Password. Use the Set Database Password dialog to set a password (see Figure 16.2).

FIGURE 16.2:

Use the Set Database Password dialog to set a password.

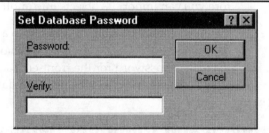

4. In the Password edit box, type **college** as your password.

5. In the Verify edit box, type **college** again and click OK.

6. In the Database window, click the Close box.

7. Choose File, and from the bottom of the File menu, choose College to open the database. The Password Required dialog is displayed (see Figure 16.3).

FIGURE 16.3:

You must type the correct password
before the application can open.

8. Type **college** and click OK. The password is *case-sensitive* and Access won't accept mixed-case versions such as College.

WARNING Make sure you record your password somewhere. If you forget or lose the password, you can't open the database. Also, anyone who knows the password and has access to the Tools ➤ Security ➤ Set Database Password command can change or clear the password.

When you establish a password for a database, you have to enter the password before you can import its objects into another database or compact it.

When you separate an application into a program file (the *front-end database*) and a data file (the *back-end database*), you can only use the Set Database Password dialog to create a password for the front-end database; you need Visual Basic to establish a separate password for the back-end database.

Hiding and Unhiding Database Objects

When you set a password, you protect the application only from being opened by unauthorized people. Once the application is open, you need additional measures to protect the application from changes. One simple technique is to hide database objects to prevent them from inadvertent changes.

1. In the Database window, select the object you want to hide.

2. Display the property sheet by choosing <u>V</u>iew ➤ <u>P</u>roperties, then check the Hidden check box (see Figure 16.4) and click OK. The object no longer appears in the Database window.

FIGURE 16.4:

Using a database object's property sheet to hide the object.

FIGURE 16.4:

Using a database object's property sheet to hide the object.

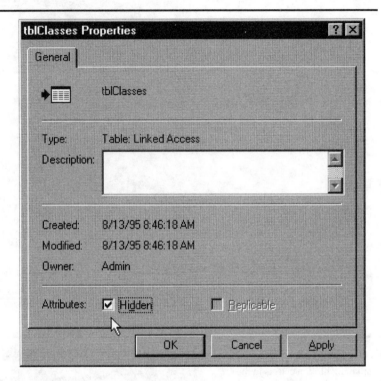

3. Choose <u>T</u>ools ➤ <u>O</u>ptions and click the View tab (see Figure 16.5).

4. Check the Hidden Objects check box to show all hidden Database objects, and then click OK. Figure 16.6 shows the Database window, with the hidden objects shown with dimmed outline.

5. Select the object you want to unhide, then display the property sheet by choosing View ➤ Properties; clear the Hidden option (see Figure 16.4) and click OK. The object is restored to its unhidden state.

FIGURE 16.5:

Using the Options dialog to show all hidden Database window objects with dimmed outline.

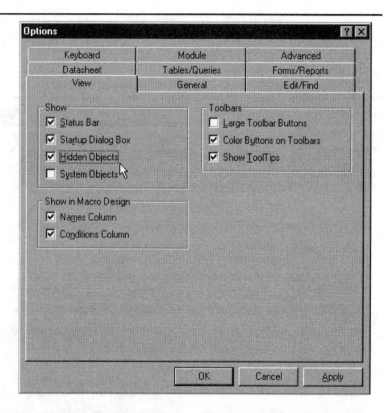

FIGURE 16.6:

Displaying hidden objects in the Database window.

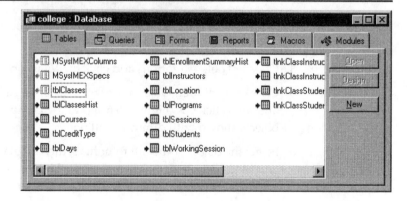

WARNING Anyone with access to the <u>V</u>iew ➤ <u>P</u>roperties and <u>T</u>ools ➤ <u>O</u>ptions commands can unhide database objects.

Minimizing Access to the Database Window

You can disable the keys that display the Database window by clearing the Use Access Special Keys check box in the advanced version of the Startup dialog (see Figure 16.7).

FIGURE 16.7:
Clearing the Use Access Special Keys check box to lock users out of the Database window after the database is started up. Note that you can still regain full access to the database by holding down the SHIFT key when you start the database.

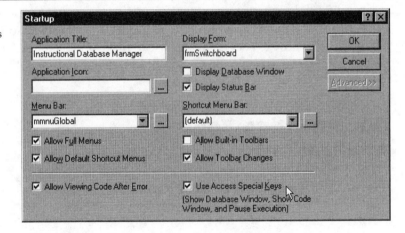

If you clear both the Display Database Window and the Use Access Special Keys check boxes, the Database window is not accessible after the database has been opened. If you specify a custom global menu bar and clear the Use Access Special Keys check box, the built-in menu bar is not accessible. A simple strategy to minimize access to the Database window is to clear the Display Database Window and Allow Built-In Toolbars check boxes, elect the reduced set of built-in menus (or display a custom global menu with similarly reduced commands), and clear the Use Access Special Keys check box.

NOTE   Unfortunately you cannot disable the Bypass (SHIFT) key in Microsoft Access for Windows 95, so users can easily bypass the startup options that you set. The only way to disable the SHIFT key is to use Microsoft's Access Developer's Toolkit (ADT).

Protecting Your Application with User-Level Security

Access provides a way to secure your application by granting specific permissions to the different people who use your database. You can learn more about the Microsoft Access security model in Chapter 14 of the *Building Applications with Microsoft Access for Windows 95* user's manual. (You can order this manual and the Access Developer's Toolkit directly from Microsoft.) The chapter also describes how to encrypt a database to make it indecipherable by an application other than Access.

Documenting Your Application

You can create reports that document the properties of the database objects by using the Database Documentor.

1. Choose Tools ➤ Analyze ➤ Documentor. Use the Select Objects dialog to select the objects you want to document (see Figure 16.8).

2. Select Macros from the Object Type list, and click the Options button. Use the Print Macro Definition dialog box (see Figure 16.9) to select report options, then click OK.

3. In the Objects list, select the macros you want to document, then click OK. Access generates a report for the selected macros. Figure 16.10 shows a portion of the report to document the mcrGallery macro group.

FIGURE 16.8:

Use the Select Objects dialog to select the objects you want to document. Click the Options button to display the available report choices.

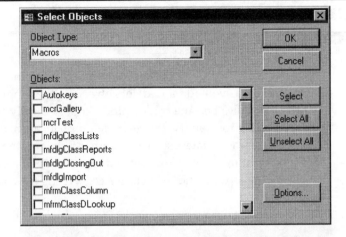

FIGURE 16.9:

Use the Print Macro Definition dialog to select report options.

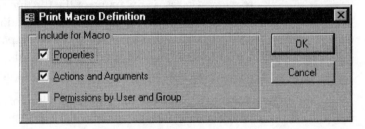

FIGURE 16.10:

A report generated by the Database Documentor.

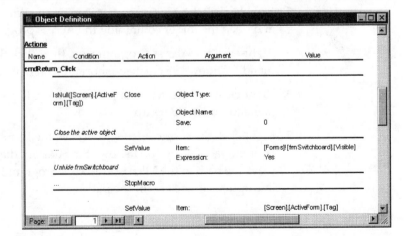

Automating the Backup and Compacting Operations

Back up your data and program files to another media on a regular basis. Additionally, as you add and delete objects to the program file and records to the data file, the files become fragmented, so periodically you should defragment the files as well. You can use the *command-line options* to automate both backing up and compacting a database. The command-line options let you specify how you want to start up Access. You can start Access, open a database, compact the database to a backup file, and then close Access using the command-line option:

source database/compact *target database*

where *source database* is the name of the file (including path) you want to compact, and *target database* is the name of the file (including path) you are backing up to; if you omit a target database name, the file is compacted to the original name. You can create a custom icon for the operation and display it along with the custom icon that represents your database application (see Chapter 2, "Building a User Interface").

As an example, we'll automate the operations of compacting the data file and backing it up to a floppy disk.

1. Close all instances of Access.

2. Double-click the My Computer icon on the Windows 95 desktop, then locate and open the folder containing the Access program file (Msaccess.exe).

3. Right-click the Access program icon, then click the Create Shortcut command. Windows 95 creates a shortcut icon named Shortcut to MsAccess.

4. Right-click the shortcut icon, then click the Rename command and set the name to **College Backup**

5. Right-click the shortcut icon, then click the Properties command and click the Shortcut tab. Figure 16.11 shows the Shortcut dialog box. The Target box displays the path to the Microsoft Access program file. You add the command-line options to the end of the path.

FIGURE 16.11:

Using the Shortcut dialog to set command-line startup options.

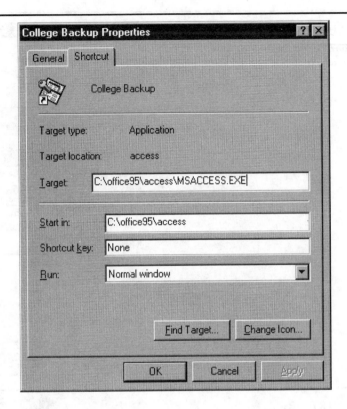

6. Click to the right of the entry in your Target box and add the following command-line option (your data file may be in a different path):

   c:\automate\colldata.mdb/compact a:\colldata.mdb

7. Click the Change Icon button. If necessary, click the Browse button, locate the Windows\system\shell32.dll file and click OK.

8. Select the tree icon and click OK. Figure 16.12 shows a portion of the command-line options and the new icon.

9. Drag the shortcut icon to the desktop, next to the College shortcut icon you created in Chapter 1. Figure 16.13 shows a portion of the desktop.

10. Insert a blank disk in drive A, then double-click the College Backup icon. The Access startup screen flashes briefly, the status bar indicates the file is being compacted, and then Access closes.

FIGURE 16.12:

Setting the properties of the shortcut icon.

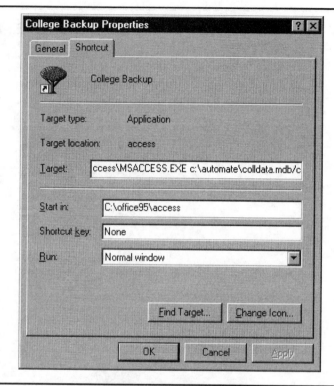

FIGURE 16.13:

The application and backup icons on the Windows 95 desktop.

If you start the backup without inserting a disk, a Disk Error message is displayed. If the disk in drive A contains the Colldata.mdb file, Access replaces it with the new version without displaying a message. If there isn't enough space on the disk in drive A, Access displays the message "Not enough space on disk."

When Do You Need Visual Basic?

For many people, the answer is never! This book has shown you how to automate a database and create a custom application by using macro programming and a simple Visual Basic error handler. You've used macros to create and control a custom user interface that provides easy access to the tasks of the database. You've created macros to open forms, automate data entry, import and modify data, find specific records and groups of records, archive data, and print and embellish reports. You've used a Visual Basic error handler to trap and deal with specific errors and suppress default messages.

But there are times when macro programming alone is insufficient to accomplish a task, and times when using Visual Basic is more efficient. Here are some of the reasons for using Visual Basic:

To Create Custom Functions   Access includes a large set of built-in functions that you can use together with operators to create complex expressions. Sometimes an expression that you need to use in several places is long and complex. Rather than retyping a complex expression, you can create your own custom function. You use custom functions the same way you use the Access built-in functions. In Chapter 5, you imported a module containing custom functions from the Orders sample database and used several of its custom functions.

To Handle More Complex Decisions   The built-in decision functions, conditions in macros, and the `RunMacro` action for repeated operations provide convenient ways to handle simple decisions. If you need more complex decision structures, you may still be able to use macros, but using Visual Basic often results in a more efficient solution.

To Trap Errors   Because of the limited error handling in macro programming, the approach we have taken is to avoid most errors by anticipating them. We used a simple Visual Basic error handler to suppress default error messages when macros alone were insufficient. As unanticipated errors occur, you can often troubleshoot and modify the application by using macros to avoid future occurrences. Nevertheless, external events that you can't prevent or anticipate may occur: a file may be deleted, the power may shut down while a macro is running, or a network connection may be lost. The most important reason for including Visual Basic in your application is its ability to handle unexpected and unanticipated errors. With Visual Basic you can include error handling in the individual event procedures you create, in addition to the single form-level error handler you've used in this book.

To Provide Hard-Copy Documentation   The documentation for macros that is created by the Database Documentor is not as convenient to use as a printout of Visual Basic code. For large or complicated applications, easy-to-use hardcopy documentation is essential.

To Create and Manipulate Objects   In most cases you create and manipulate objects interactively (that is, in the object's Design view). There are times, however, when it is useful to define or modify an object automatically when the application is running. For example, the wizards create objects to your specifications: the Form Wizard creates forms and the Combo Box Wizard creates combo boxes. The built-in wizards are written in Visual Basic. You may want to create a custom wizard that is specific to your application. Using Visual Basic, you can create and manipulate any of the objects in the database, including the database itself.

To Perform Actions Not Available with Macros   There are some actions that cannot be carried out efficiently, or at all, with macros alone. An important example is *transaction processing*. A *transaction* is a set of operations that you handle as a single unit: either you carry out all of the operations in the set or you don't carry out any of them. If you begin the transaction and one of the operations fails, then you return the data to the state it was in before you started any of the operations. A good candidate for transaction processing is the archive process: you append records to historical tables and then delete them from the current data tables. Either both operations occur or you don't want either to occur. In the Archive macro of Chapter 13, "Closing Out a Session," you run three append queries followed by a delete query; if the power fails while you are running one of the queries, the archive operation is only partially completed. While you can modify the Archive macro so that you can simply run it again, you can consider using Visual Basic to run all of the queries as a single transaction. In a Visual Basic transaction, all of the operations of the transaction are run in memory; if an operation fails, the transaction is aborted, leaving the data tables as they were before the transaction began; if all operations are successful, the results of the transaction are updated to the data tables. Another benefit of transaction processing is greatly increased performance: because the operations run in memory, the results for all of the operations involved in the transaction are written to the disk in a single operation when the transaction is finished; without transaction processing, the results of the individual operations are written to the disk separately.

To Pass Arguments to Your Code   With macros, you set the action arguments in the lower pane of the Macro window when you create the macro. You can't change these arguments when the macro is running and you can't use variables in the action arguments. These limitations prevented certain macros from being reusable. For example, the macros for deleting records that we created in Chapter 8 referred to specific fields and specific tables by name; you have to modify these macros for each data entry form. Other macros that we created are reusable because we used the Screen object instead of references to specific controls and forms. Using the Screen object has the same effect as using a variable. Visual Basic provides additional, more efficient ways to change the arguments in your code when the code is running and to use variables in the arguments.

To Optimize Performance   There are features of Visual Basic, such as additional *methods* (the Visual Basic version of macro actions) and compiling, that result in better performance than the corresponding macros-only approach. For example, Visual Basic includes a method to locate a record, called **Seek**, which is significantly faster than the **FindRecord** action. As noted above, transaction processing is typically much faster than running separate operations. Another performance gain is possible because the code you write in Visual Basic is compiled. *Compiling* checks the code for certain types of errors and converts the code into a form that Access can execute more efficiently. In macro programming, the individual macro actions have been designed for optimal performance, but the macros you create are not compiled.

To Work Outside Microsoft Access   With macros, your work outside Access is extremely limited. You can use the **RunApp** action to launch another Windows or MS-DOS-based application, but once the application is open you are limited to working interactively with it. Using Visual Basic, you can automate the other application with *OLE Automation* or *dynamic data exchange (DDE)*. Using Visual Basic, you can also communicate with the Windows *application programming interface (API)* using functions in the *dynamic-link libraries (DLLs)*. For example, you can check to see if a file exists, determine the display driver, or determine if other applications are running.

If you find your application is limited by macros and the Access built-in functions, or if you simply want to explore the more powerful capabilities of Access, then you can turn to Visual Basic with its nearly limitless capabilities. You can even leverage the time you have spent designing, creating, and testing macros by converting them to Visual Basic code.

Endnotes

In this chapter, you've learned several simple ways to protect an application, including:

- using a password

- hiding Database window objects

- setting startup options to minimize access to the Database window

You've learned how to perform database maintenance tasks, including:

- using the Documentor to print macros and other database object information

- using command-line options to automate compacting and backing up your data file

This chapter brings the book to an end, with a discussion of the limitations of macro programming so that you can glimpse the path ahead if you find you are nearing the limits.

Congratulations! In finishing all of the chapters in this book, you've learned how to turn an interactive database into a complete application with its own identity in the desktop and its own user interface that lets any novice computer user do productive work. You've learned enough about interface design to understand that interface design is as much art as science. You've learned how to automate tasks using the power of Access queries and macro programming. You've even learned a smidgen of Visual Basic—just enough to prevent a few errors and error messages that you couldn't prevent using just macros. If you haven't been trying to apply the techniques you've learned while automating the College database to your own databases, now is the time to begin. Just remember: like any skill—use it or lose it!

On Your Own

In the last exercise of the book, you'll use the command-line startup option to automate backing up and compacting a program file.

Adding to the Application

1. Automate the back up and compacting of the program file.

    a. Follow the steps in the section "Automating the Backup and Compacting Operation" to create a command-line startup option for the College database and a shortcut icon.

APPENDIX

A

Referring to Objects

Microsoft Access calls anything that can have a name an *object*. An Access database is composed of myriad objects; it is helpful to understand how these objects are arranged and related. Objects are organized using the basic idea that an object can contain other objects. A *collection* is an object that holds a set of objects of the same type. Here are some examples of objects and collections terminology:

- each field in a table is a **Field** object

- each table is a **TableDef** object

- the set of all fields in a table is the **Fields** collection of the table, so a table is a **TableDef** object containing a **Fields** collection of the **Field** objects in the table.

- each control on a form or report is a **Control** object

- each open form is a **Form** object

- each open report is a **Report** object

- the set of all of the controls on a form or report is the **Controls** collection for the form or report, so an open form is a **Form** object containing a **Controls** collection of the **Control** objects in the form.

The Application Engine

Access has two major components. The first component, called the *Application engine*, controls the end-user interface, open forms and reports, and programming with macros and Visual Basic. The second component, called the *Jet database engine*, handles all the data management, including the storage of data in tables and the indexes, queries, and relationships needed to manipulate the data. The Jet database engine also stores the definitions of all of the objects defined either by the application engine or the Jet database engine.

The Application engine consists of the following objects, referred to as the *Microsoft Access Objects*:

Application   refers to the active Microsoft Access itself.

Control	refers to a control on a form or report. Controls include labels, text boxes, combo boxes, list boxes, check boxes, option buttons, option groups, command buttons, lines, and rectangles.
Form	refers to a specific open form or subform.
Report	refers to a specific open report of subreport.
Screen	refers to the the specific form, report, or control that currently has the focus or to the control that last had the focus.
DoCmd	refers to the object used in Visual Basic to run macro actions.

The Application engine also has collections, including:

Controls	the set of controls on a form or report
Forms	the set of all open forms
Reports	the set of all open reports

The Jet Database Engine

The Jet database engine also uses a hierarchy of objects and collections in its organization of your database. The Jet database engine includes the set of 31 objects referred to as the *data access objects* (or *DAO*). Sixteen of the data access objects are:

TableDef	refers to a saved table in a database.
QueryDef	refers to a saved query in a database.
Recordset	refers to a set of records defined by a tables or query.
Relation	refers to the relationship between two tables or query fields.
Field	refers to a field in a table, query, recordset, index, or relation.

Index	used to specify the ordering of records that are returned for an updateable recordset based on a single table, and whether duplicate records are accepted. The Jet engine uses indexes when it joins tables and creates recordsets.
Parameter	refers to a value that you must enter as a criteria in a parameter query before the query can be run.
Property	refers to a property of an object.
Container	is an object that contains information about other objects.
Document	refers to information that the Jet database engine keeps about a database, a saved table or query, or a saved relationship such as the object's name, date, and time the object was created and modified, who created the object, and who has permission to use the object.
Database	refers to the open database.
DBEngine	refers to the Jet database engine.
Workspace	refers to the active Jet database engine session.
Error	refers to details about data access errors.
User	refers to a user account in the Jet database engine's current workgroup.
Group	refers to a group account in the Jet database engine's current workgroup.

In addition, each of the data access objects except the **DBEngine** has a corresponding collection; for example, the **Properties** collection of an object is the set of properties of the object and the **Indexes** collection of a TableDef object is the set of all stored indexes for the table. A collection is also an object.

The Syntax for Referring to Objects and Properties

When you refer to an object that belongs to a collection, you can identify it as an element of that collection by using the syntax

collectionname![objectname]

where the exclamation point operator indicates that the object is an element of the collection. If the object's name includes spaces or special characters, you must enclose the name in square brackets. In most cases, Access will automatically place square brackets around object names when square brackets are required.

Each object has a set of properties that you can use to specify its characteristics. When you want to refer to a property of an object, you use the dot operator syntax

objectname.propertyname

The properties of an object that you can set in Design view are listed in the object's property sheet.

Referring to a Form or Report

When you first open a database, the Application engine relies on the Jet database engine to supply the names of all the tables, queries, forms, reports, macros, and modules displayed in the collections in the database window. The Application engine creates the two special collections, *Forms* and *Reports*, to keep track of all of the forms and reports, respectively, that are open at any moment.

Use the Debug Window to Test Object References

You can use the Debug window to test the syntax of an object reference. As examples, you can observe the examples of the object references in the following sections.

1. Open frmRegistration and frmStudents in Form view and press CTRL+G. The Debug window opens.

2. To test a reference to a control or property, type the question mark (?) followed by the object reference, and then press ENTER. The next line displays the value of the reference. Figure A.1 shows several examples.

NOTE You can't use the Debug window to test references for the Screen object. When you test references in the Debug window, it (the Debug window) is the active object.

FIGURE A.1:
Use the Debug window to test object references. Type a question mark (?) followed by the object reference, then press ENTER.

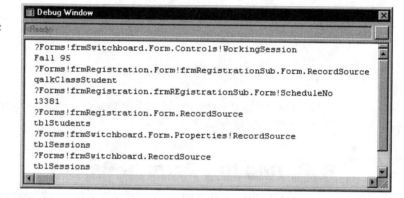

```
Debug Window                                                      ☒
<Ready>                                                          [...]
?Forms!frmSwitchboard.Form.Controls!WorkingSession
Fall 95
?Forms!frmRegistration.Form!frmRegistrationSub.Form.RecordSource
qalkClassStudent
?Forms!frmRegistration.frmREgistrationSub.Form!ScheduleNo
13381
?Forms!frmRegistration.Form.RecordSource
tblStudents
?Forms!frmSwitchboard.Form.Properties!RecordSource
tblSessions
?Forms!frmSwitchboard.RecordSource
tblSessions
```

Using the Forms and Reports Collections

You can refer to a form or report only if it is open. When you want to refer to a form or a report you must first specify which collection contains the object. An open form is a member of the **Forms** collection, so you use the syntax:

Forms![formname]

to refer to the form named formname. For example,

Forms!frmStudents

refers to the (open) form frmStudents. Similarly, to refer to an open report named reportname you use the syntax:

Reports![reportname]

for example,

Reports!rptStudentProgram

Referring to Form and Report Properties

A form or report has properties that define its characteristics. To refer to a property of a form you follow the object name by the dot operator and the property name, using the syntax

Forms![formname].[propertyname]

For example,

Forms!frmStudents.RecordSource

refers to the RecordSource property of the (open) frmStudents form. Object properties that you can set in Design view are listed in the object's property sheet. Many objects have properties that you can't set in Design view, so they are not listed in the property sheet; for example, Dirty and NewRecord are read-only run-time form properties.

Properties of an Object that Represent Other Objects

There are object properties that you can use to refer to another object. For example, the **Screen** object has four properties that let you refer to specific objects:

Screen property	Refers to
ActiveForm	the form that contains the control that has the focus, or the form that has the focus.

Screen property	Refers to
ActiveReport	the report that contains the control that has the focus, or the report that has the focus.
ActiveControl	the control that has the focus.
PreviousControl	the control that had the focus just before the control that currently has the focus.

Controls also have properties that let you refer to another object. A control's **Parent** property refers to the object that contains the control. As examples, an option button's Parent property refers to the option group that contains the button and a subform control's Parent property refers to the form that contains the subform. The control properties that you can use to refer to other objects are:

Control property	Refers to
Parent	the object that contains the control.
Section	the section of a form or report in which the control is located.

Subform/Subreport controls have two additional properties that you can use to refer to the forms or reports they display:

Subform/Subreport control property	Refers to
Form	the form displayed by a subform/subreport control on a form or report and specified in the subform/subreport control's SourceObject property.
Report	the report displayed by a subform/subreport control on a report and specified in the subform/subreport control's SourceObject property.

Forms and reports also have properties that refer to objects:

Form or report property	Refers to
Form	refers to the form itself.
Report	refers to the report itself.
Me	refers to the form or report itself (used only in Visual Basic and not in macro programming).
Module	refers to the form's or report's module.
RecordsetClone	refers to a clone of the recordset underlying the form (used only in Visual Basic and not in macro programming).

WARNING Note the multiple meanings of the word Form: as the Form object to represent an open form, as the Form property of a form to refer to the form itself, and as the Form property of a subform/subreport control to refer to the form displayed in the control; unfortunately, there are other examples of words with multiple meanings.

Referring to a Control

Because a control is a member of the *Controls* collection, you can refer to a control on a form using the syntax:

Forms![formname].Controls![controlname]

You can even include the *Form* property that refers to the form itself in the reference, as follows:

Forms![formname].Form.Controls![controlname]

However, for a form, Access assumes that you are referring to the Form property by default, so you don't have to include the Form property explicitly. A *default property* is the property Access assumes when you don't explicitly specify a property name. An object can also have a *default collection* that Access assumes when you specify a member of a default collection without specifying the collection. For forms and reports, the Controls collection is the default collection. Technically, you can use any of the four expressions

Forms![formname].Form.Controls![controlname]

Forms![formname].Form![controlname]

Forms![formname].Controls![controlname]

Forms![formname]![controlname]

to refer to a control on a form, and any of four analogous expressions to refer to a control on a report. It is fastest to use the last expression; we refer to this one as the *full identifier syntax* or the *qualified identifier* for referring to a control on a form.

Using the Form Property to Refer to a Control on a Subform

To refer to a subform control on a form, the full identifier syntax becomes

Forms![formname]![subformcontrolname]

When you refer to the form displayed in the subform control, you use the Form property of the subform control. For example, to refer to a property of a subform you use the syntax

Forms![formname]![subformcontrolname].Form.[propertyname]

For example,

Forms!frmRegistration!frmRegistrationSub.Form.RecordSource

refers to the RecordSource property of the subform displayed in the subform control named frmRegistrationSub on the frmRegistration form (frmRegistrationSub is also the name of the subform in this case, but it isn't necessary that the subform and the subform control have the same name). The Form property of a subform/subreport control is not its default property, so you must include the Form property in the reference.

To refer to a control on a form displayed in a subform control, first you use the subform control's Form property to refer to the form it displays, and then you refer to the control on the form, as follows:

Forms![formname]![subformcontrolname].Form![controlname]

This expression is the full identifier syntax for a control on a form or a subform. For example,

Forms!frmRegistration!frmRegistrationSub.Form!ScheduleNo

refers to the ScheduleNo control on the form displayed in the frmRegistrationSub subform control on the frmRegistration form.

If you really wanted to, you could include explicit references to the Controls collections of both the form and the subform in the reference, as follows:

Forms![formname].Controls![subformcontrolname].Form.Controls![controlname]

and if you really wanted to, you could include the Form property of the main form, too:

Forms![formname].Form.Controls![subformcontrolname].Form.Controls![controlname]

But, fortunately, there is no reason to use any but the briefest expression for the full identifier syntax.

Referring to a Control's Properties

When you refer to a property of a control, you follow the control's name with the dot operator and the name of the property. For example,

Forms!frmStudents!LastName.Visible

refers to the Visible property of the LastName control on the frmStudents form, and

Forms!frmRegistration!frmRegistrationSub.Form!ScheduleNo.Enabled refers to the Enabled property of the ScheduleNo control on the form displayed in the frmRegistrationSub subform control on the frmRegistration form.

Just as the Form property is the default property for a form, a control also has a default property. The default property for a text box is the Text property. If you want to refer to the value in the text box, you could use either of the following equivalent expressions:

Forms!frmStudents!LastName.Text

Forms!frmStudents!LastName

Normally, you use the last expression as the full identifier syntax to refer to a control on a form.

Referring to a Control on the Active Form or Report

When you refer to a specific control on the active form, you can use a *short syntax* and refer to the control simply as

[controlname]

For example, you can use

LastName

if frmStudents is the active form, and

frmRegistrationSub.Form!ScheduleNo

if frmRegistration is the active form.

When you refer to the active control on the active form, you can use the Screen object and refer to the control as

Screen.ActiveControl

Deciding When to Use the Full Syntax versus the Short Syntax

Usually you can use the full syntax without problems, but there are exceptions when you have to use the short syntax. For example, you must use the short syntax in the `Control Name` argument of the `GoToControl` macro action to specify the name of the control on the active object that you want to move the focus to.

Referring to a Field on a Form

To refer to a field in the table or query that is the record source for the form, you use the syntax:

Forms![formname]![fieldname]

You can use this reference whether or not the field is displayed in a control on the form.

Referring to a Field in a Table or Query

When you refer to fields in a table or query, you follow the object name with the field name, using the syntax:

[tablename]![fieldname]

For example,

tblCourses!Prefix

refers to the Prefix field in the table tblCourses.

Referring to a Macro in a Macro Group

When you refer to a macro in a macro group, you follow the macro group name with the macro name, as follows:

[macrogroupname].[macroname]

For example,

mfrmRegistration.cmdNew_Click

refers to the cmdNew_Click macro in the macro group mfrmRegistration.

APPENDIX

B

Macro Actions

The 49 macro actions, along with their arguments and purposes, are shown in Table B.1.

TABLE B.1: The Macro Actions.

Action	Argument	Function
AddMenu	Menu Name Menu Macro Name Status Bar Text	Adds a menu to a custom menu bar or adds a custom shortcut menu.
ApplyFilter	Filter Name Where Condition	Selects the records available to a form or report by using a filter, query, or SQL WHERE clause.
Beep	(no arguments)	Produces a beep for use in warnings or alerts.
CancelEvent	(no arguments)	Cancels the default processing that follows an event.
Close	Object Type Object Name Save	Closes the active window or a specified window.
CopyObject	Destination Database New Name Source Object Type Source Object Name	Creates a copy of the specified database object, in another database or in the original database using a different name.
DeleteObject	Object Type Object Name	Deletes the specified object. Leave the arguments blank to delete a selected object in the Database window.
DoMenuItem	Menu Bar Menu Name Command Subcommand	Runs a command on a built-in menu bar if the menu bar is appropriate for the view that is current when you want to carry out the command.
Echo	Echo On Status Bar Text	Turns screen updating on or off during macro execution. If you turn screen updating off, Access resumes screen updating when the macro is finished.

TABLE B.1: The Macro Actions *(continued).*

Action	Argument	Function
FindNext	(no arguments)	Finds the next record specified by the **FindRecord** action or the Find command.
FindRecord	Find What Match Match Case Search Search As Formatted Only Current Field Find First	Finds the next record after the current record that satisfies the specified criteria.
GoToControl	Control Name	Moves the focus to the specified field or control in the current record of the active form, table or query. Requires the short syntax. Use the **GoToControl** action twice to move the focus to a control on a subform, first to move to the subform control and second to move to the control.
GoToPage	Page Number Right Down	Selects the first field on the designated page in a multi-page form.
GoToRecord	Object Type Object Name Record Offset	Makes the specified record the current record in an open form, table, or query.
Hourglass	Hourglass On	Displays an hourglass instead of the mouse pointer while the macro runs.
Maximize	(no arguments)	Maximizes the active window.
Minimize	(no arguments)	Minimizes the active window to an icon within the Access window.

TABLE B.1: The Macro Actions *(continued)*.

Action	Argument	Function
MoveSize	Right Down Width Height	Moves or changes the size of the active window.
MsgBox	Message Beep Type Title	Displays a warning or informational message box and waits for you to click the OK button.
OpenForm	Form Name View Filter Name Where Condition Data Mode Window Mode	Opens or activates a form in one of its views. You can restrict the records, specify the editing mode, and specify whether the form acts as a modal or pop-up dialog.
OpenModule	Module Name Procedure Name	Opens the specified module and displays the specified procedure.
OpenQuery	Query Name View Data Mode	Opens a select or crosstab query or runs an action query.
OpenReport	Report Name View Filter Name Where Condition	Opens a report in the view you specify. You can restrict the records before printing.
OpenTable	Table Name View Data Mode	Opens or activates a table in the view you specify. You can specify the data entry or edit mode for tables in Datasheet view.
OutputTo	Object Type Object Name Output Format Output File Auto Start	Copies the data in the specified object to a Microsoft Excel (.XLS), rich-text format (.RTF), or DOS text (.TXT) file.
PrintOut	Print Range Page From Page To Print Quality Copies Collate Copies	Prints the active datasheet, report, or form.

TABLE B.1: The Macro Actions *(continued)*.

Action	Argument	Function
Quit	Options	Exits from Access and saves unsaved objects according to the options you specify.
Rename	New Name Object Type Old Name	Renames the object selected in the Database window.
RepaintObject	Object Type Object Name	Forces any pending recalculations, and updates screen for the controls on the specified database object or the active object if the arguments are blank. This action does not show new, changed, or deleted records in the database object's underlying source.
Requery	Control Name	Updates the data in the specified control by rerunning the query of the control if the control is based on a query, or by rereading the table if the control is based on a table. This action displays new, changed, or deleted records. Leave the argument blank to requery the source of the active object.
Restore	(no arguments)	Restores a maximized or minimized window to its previous window.
RunApp	Command Line	Runs a Windows or DOS-based application.
RunCode	Function Name	Runs a Visual Basic function procedure.

TABLE B.1: The Macro Actions *(continued)*.

Action	Argument	Function
RunMacro	Macro Name Repeat Count Repeat Expression	Runs the specified macro. Enter the full name of the macro including the group name. Use the Repeat arguments to specify how many times to run the macro.
RunSQL	SQL Statement	Runs an action query or a data-definition query as specified by the SQL statement.
Save	Object Type Object Name	Saves the specified database object. Leave the arguments blank to save the active database object.
SelectObject	Object Type Object Name In Database Window	Selects a specified database object.
SendKeys	Keystrokes Wait	Sends keystrokes to Access or to any active Windows-based application.
SendObject	Object Type Object Name Output Format To Cc Bcc Subject Message Text Edit Message	Sends the specified datasheet, form, report, or module (but not a macro) in an electronic mail message. You must have a MAPI-compliant mail application to use this action.
SetMenu Item	Menu Index Command Index Subcommand Index Flag	Sets the state of a menu item on a custom menu. Use this action to check or gray out a command or to undo these settings.

TABLE B.1: The Macro Action *(continued).*

Action	Argument	Function
SetValue	Item Expression	Sets the value of a field, control, or property on a form, form datasheet, or a report. You can't use this action to set the value of a calculated control on a form or report or a bound control on a report.
SetWarnings	Warnings On	Turns default warning messages on or off. This action does not suppress error messages or screen dialogs that require you to enter text or select an option.
ShowAll Records	(no arguments)	Removes any filters and requeries the active object.
Show Toolbar	Toolbar Name,Show	Displays the specified built-in or custom toolbar.
StopAllMacros	(no arguments)	Stops all macros that are currently running.
StopMacro	(no arguments)	Stops the current macro.
TransferDatabase	Transfer Type Database Type Database Name Object Type Source Destination Structure Only	Imports data from another database or exports data to another database or links a table to the current database from another database.
TransferSpreadsheet	Transfer Type Spreadsheet Type Table Name File Name Has Field Names Range	Imports data from a spreadsheet file or exports Access data to a spreadsheet file.
TransferText	Transfer Type Specification Name Table Name File Name Has Field Names	Imports data from a text file or exports Access data to a text file.

APPENDIX

C

Access Events

Appendix C covers events as they apply to different objects in your database.

Events for Controls on Forms

A control on a form recognizes events when the control gains or loses the focus and when you change the data and the control is updated. Table C.1 shows the nine focus and data events and Table C.2 shows the mouse and keyboard events.

TABLE C.1: The focus and data events for controls on forms.

Event	The event is recognized...	Additional comments
Enter	when you go to a control but before the control has the focus.	Occurs for the first control on a form when the form first opens; thereafter, the event occurs only when a control receives the focus from another control on the same form. The event doesn't occur if you switch to another form and then switch back to the same control on the first form.
GotFocus	after the control has received the focus.	Occurs every time a control receives the focus. The control displays its characteristic appearance when it has the focus.
Change	when you change a character in a text box or the text box part of a combo box.	Does not occur when a value in a calculated control changes or when you select a value from a combo list.
NotInList	after you enter a value in a combo box that is not on the combo list and then attempt to move to another control or save the record.	The LimitToList property must be set to Yes.
BeforeUpdate	when Access recognizes changed data in the control buffer, and just before updating the changed data to the record buffer.	Changing data in a control by using a macro or Visual Basic doesn't trigger the BeforeUpdate event for the control.

TABLE C.1: The focus and data events for controls on forms (*continued*).

Event	The event is recognized...	Additional comments
AfterUpdate	when Access recognizes changed data in the control buffer, and just after updating the changed data to the record buffer.	Changing data in a control by using a macro or Visual Basic doesn't trigger the **AfterUpdate** event for the control.
Exit	when you leave the control but before the control loses the focus.	Occurs for the control on a form that has the focus when the form closes; before that, the event occurs only when a control loses the focus to another control on the same form.
LostFocus	after the control loses the focus.	The **LostFocus** event is recognized every time a control loses the focus.
Updated	when the data in an OLE object has changed.	The order of this event depends on the application that was used to create the OLE object.

TABLE C.2: Mouse and keyboard events.

Event	The event is recognized...	Additional comments
Click	when you press and release the left mouse button.	For a command button, the **Click** event is recognized when you choose the button. For a control, the Click event occurs when you click the control or press the control's access key.
DblClick	when you press and release the left mouse button twice within the double-click time limit setting.	When you double-click a control you trigger the **Click** event, then the **DblClick** event. Double-clicking a command button also triggers a second **Click** event after the **DblClick** event.
MouseDown	when you press a mouse button.	Using Visual Basic, you can determine which mouse button is pressed.
MouseUp	when you release a mouse button.	Using Visual Basic, you can determine which mouse button was pressed.

TABLE C.2: Mouse and Keyboard events *(continued)*.

Event	The event is recognized...	Additional comments
MouseMove	when you move the mouse pointer over the object.	
KeyDown	when you press a key or send a keystroke using **SendKeys** while a control or form has the focus.	
KeyPress	when you press and release a key or key combination that produces a standard ANSI character, or send a keystroke using **SendKeys** that produces a standard ANSI character, while a control or form has the focus.	
KeyUp	when you release a key or after the keystroke is sent.	

Events for Forms and Form Sections

A form recognizes the window and focus events shown in Table C.3 when you open, close, or resize the form or when the form gains or loses the focus. A form recognizes events when a record gains or loses the focus, when you change the data and the record is updated, when you create a new record or delete an existing record and when you apply or remove a filter. A form recognizes **Error** and **Timer** events. Table C.4 shows the data and filter events; Table C.5 shows the **Error** and **Timer** events.

> **NOTE**
> When you update a control by moving to a different record or by choosing <u>R</u>ecords➤Save Rec<u>o</u>rd, first the control recognizes BeforeUpdate and AfterUpdate events as Access updates the changed data in the control buffer to the record buffer, and then the form recognizes BeforeUpdate and AfterUpdate events as Access updates the changed data in the record buffer to the table fields in memory.

TABLE C.3: Window and focus events for forms.

Event	The event is recognized...	Additional comments
Open	when you first open the form but before the first record is displayed.	
Load	after the records are loaded from memory and displayed.	
Resize	when the form is first displayed and just after you change the size of the form.	
Activate	when the form receives the focus and becomes the active window, except when the form receives the focus from a form whose PopUp property is set to Yes or from a window in another application.	The **Activate** event is recognized only when the form is visible.
GotFocus	when the form has received the focus.	The **GotFocus** event is recognized by a form only if all controls on the form are disabled or hidden.
Unload	when you close a form and its records are unloaded, but before the form is removed from the screen.	
LostFocus	when the form has lost the focus.	The **LostFocus** event is recognized by a form only if all controls on the form are disabled or hidden.
Deactivate	when a form loses the focus to another window in Access, except a dialog or a form whose PopUp property is set to Yes.	The **Deactivate** event is not recognized when the form loses the focus to another application.
Close	when you close a form and it is removed from the screen.	

TABLE C.4: Data and filter events for records on forms.

Event	The event is recognized...	Additional comments
Current	when the focus moves to a record or when you refresh a form or requery the form's record source.	The **Current** event occurs both when a form is first opened and whenever the focus moves to another record. The **Current** event is followed automatically by the **Enter** event recognized by the first control in the record to receive the focus.
BeforeInsert	after you type the first character into a new record.	The **BeforeInsert** event doesn't occur if you set the value of a control using a macro or Visual Basic.
BeforeUpdate	when Access recognizes changed data in the record buffer and just before updating the changed data to the table fields stored in memory.	If you change data in a control with a macro or Visual Basic, the control's **BeforeUpdate** event doesn't occur, but when you try to save the record, the form's **BeforeUpdate** event does occur.
AfterUpdate	when Access recognizes changed data in the record buffer and just after updating the changed data to the table fields stored in memory.	If you change data in a control with a macro or Visual Basic, the control's **AfterUpdate** event doesn't occur, but when you try to save the record, the form's **AfterUpdate** event does occur.
AfterInsert	after a new record is saved in memory.	
Delete	when you take a step to delete an existing record, but before the record is deleted.	
BeforeDelConfirm	after the record is removed from the screen and the data is placed in a record buffer, and just before Access displays the confirmation dialog.	

TABLE C.4: Data and filter events for records on forms *(continued)*.

Event	The event is recognized...	Additional comments
AfterDelConfirm	after the record is deleted from memory or after the deletion is canceled and the record is displayed on the screen.	
Filter	when you initiate a filter with Filter By Form or Advanced Filter/Sort command, but before the Filter or Filter by Form window is displayed.	The **Filter** event is not recognized when you use the Filter by Selection command. You can use this event to hide or disable controls in the Filter By Form window, or to display a custom filter window instead of the default filter windows.
ApplyFilter	when you apply a filter using Apply Filter/Sort or Filter by Selection, but before the filtered records are displayed; or when you remove a filter using Remove Filter/Sort, but before the filtered records are removed; or when you close the Filter window without applying the filter.	You can use this event to change the form before the filter is applied, for example to hide or disable controls.

Events for Reports and Report Sections

A report recognizes events when you open or close the report, when the report gains or loses the focus, and when Access detects an error and the report has the focus. Table C.6 shows the events for reports. Additionally, report sections recognize the events shown in Table C.7.

For more information on events, see Chapter 6 of *Building Applications with Microsoft Access for Windows 95* (Microsoft Press). You can see events as they occur by working with the ShowEvents and EventHistory forms in the Orders sample application. As you work with the ShowEvents form to trigger events, the EventHistory form records the object that recognizes the event and name of the event.

TABLE C.5: Error and Timer events.

Event	The event is recognized...	Additional comments
Error	when Access detects a run-time error while the application is running and the form is active.	The **Error** event is not recognized when the error is a run-time error in Visual Basic.
Timer	when the specified time interval passes.	You set the TimerInterval property of the form to specify the interval.

TABLE C.6: Events for Reports.

Event	The event is recognized...	Additional comments
Open	when you first open the report but before the report is displayed or printed.	
Activate	when the report receives the focus and becomes the active window.	This event is not recognized when the report receives the focus from a dialog form or a form whose PopUp property is set to Yes.
Deactivate	when a report loses the focus to another window in Access, except a dialog or a form whose PopUp property is set to Yes.	The **Deactivate** event is not recognized when the report loses the focus to another application.
Close	when the report is removed from the screen.	
NoData	when you open a report and Access recognizes that there are no records in the recordset, but before printing the report and before the first **Page** event for the report.	You can use this event to cancel printing a blank report. This event doesn't occur for subreports.
Page	when you first open a report, after Access formats a page but before the page is printed or displayed.	This event occurs after all **Format** and **Print** events for the page, but before the page is displayed. You can use this event to add graphic elements such as borders.
Error	when Access detects a run-time error, if the report has the focus.	The **Error** event does not occur when the error is a run-time error in Visual Basic.

TABLE C.7: Print events for report sections.

Event	The event is recognized...	Additional comments
Format	when Access has determined the data for a section but before the section is formatted.	For a report detail section, the **Format** event occurs for each record in the section; a macro triggered by the **Format** event of the detail section has access to data in the current record.
Retreat	when Access returns to a previous report section during formatting.	The **Retreat** event occurs for each section Access passes while retreating. For each of these sections the **Format** event occurs again as Access prepares to reformat the sections.
Print	after Access formats the report section but before the section is printed.	For a report detail section, the **Print** event occurs for each record in the section; a macro triggered by the **Print** event or the detail section has access to data in the current record.

APPENDIX

D

The College Database Objects

Tables D.1, D.2, D.3, and D.4 give the names and descriptions of the tables, queries, forms, and reports in the College database.

TABLE D.1: The Tables.

Table Name	Primary Key	Purpose and Description
tblClasses	ScheduleNo	Table to store class data.
tblClassesHist	ScheduleNo	Table to store archived class data.
tblCourses	CourseID	Table to store data for approved courses.
tblCreditType	TypeCode	Lookup table for course credit type. Needed to relate option group numerical values to text values.
tblDays		List of day combinations for combo box on frmClasses.
tblEnrollmentSummaryHist		Table to store enrollment summary data for a session. Updated during the archive process.
tblInstructors	InstructorID	Table to collect name, address information, faculty status, and biographical data for instructors.
tblLocation	LocID	Lookup table of campus locations. Required to provide text value lookups for option group numerical values.
tblPrograms	ProgramID	Table to store data for programs including director's name and program description.
tblSessions		Table to store the session name and archive status.
tblStudents	StudentID	To store name, address information, major program, and comments for students and prospective students.

TABLE D.1: The Tables (*continued*).

Table Name	Primary Key	Purpose and Description
tlnkClassInstructor	ScheduleNo InstructorID	The linking table for the many-to-many relationship between classes and instructors. Each record corresponds to the appointment of an instructor to teach a class.
tlnkClassInstructorHist	ScheduleNo InstructorID	Stores the archived records from tlnkClassInstructor.
tlnkClassStudent	ScheduleNo StudentID	The linking table for the many-to-many relationship between students and classes. Each record corresponds to the registration of a student in a class.
tlnkClassStudentHist	ScheduleNo StudentID	Stores the archived records from tlnkClassStudent.

TABLE D.2: The Queries.

Query Name	Purpose and Description
qalkClassInstructor	Autolookup query, based on tblClasses and tlnkClassInstructor, to look up class information when an instructor is appointed to a class. Includes tblCourses to provide course information for the class.
qalkClassStudent	Autolookup query, based on tblClasses and tlnkClassStudent, to look up class information when a student is registered in a class. Includes tblCourses to provide course information for the class.
qalkCourseClass	Autolookup query, based on tblCourses and tblClasses, to look up course information for a specified class. Includes the lookup tables tblPrograms, tblCreditType and tblLocation to provide text equivalents of the codes.
qalkCourseClass0	Autolookup query, based on tblCourses and tblClasses, to look up course information for a specified class. Displays codes for program, credit type and location (doesn't include any lookup tables).
qalkInstructorClass	Autolookup query, based on tblInstructors and tlnkClassInstructor, to look up instructor information for a designated class. Includes tblClasses to select records for the working session.
qalkStudentClass	Autolookup query, based on tblStudents and tlnkClassStudent, to look up student information for a designated class. Includes tblClasses to select records for the working session.

TABLE D.2: The Queries *(continued)*.

Query Name	Purpose and Description
qappClasses	Append query to append records from tblClasses to tblClassesHist.
qapplnkClassInst	Append query to append records from tlnkClassInstructor to tlnkClassInstructorHist.
qapplnkClassStud	Append query to append records from tlnkClassStudent to tlnkClassStudentHist.
qdelClasses	Delete query to delete records from tblClasses.
qlkpClasses	Lookup query for combo list of classes for the working session. Includes tblCourses to provide course information.
qlkpInstructorName	Lookup query for combo list of instructors' names.
qlkpStudentName	Lookup query for combo list of students' names.
qryClasseswoGrades	Select query to select classes with missing grades.
qryClasseswoInstructors	Select query to select classes with without instructors.
qryCourses	Select query to sort tblCourses by prefix and number. Includes tblCreditType to display credit type with in text values.
qryEnrollment	Select query to provide the records for enrollment reports. Based on qalkCourseClass and qalkStudentClass. Each record provides class, course, and student information for a student registered in a class.
qryEnrollmentSummary	Totals query, based on tlnkClassStudent and qalkCourseClass, that calculated current enrollment for each class.
qryListofClasses	Select query, based on tblClasses and tblCourses, to provide class and course information for frmListofClasses

TABLE D.3: The Forms.

Form Name	Record Source	Purpose and Description
frmAppointments	tblInstructors	The form for making instructor appointments.
frmAppointmentsSub	qalkClassInstructor	Subform for frmAppointments displays class information when instructor is appointed to a class.
frmClasses	qalkCourseClass0	Data entry form for Classes. When you select a course from a combo box, the course information is looked up automatically.

TABLE D.3: The Forms *(continued)*.

Form Name	Record Source	Purpose and Description
frmClassesMissingData	qryClasseswoInstructors	Displays classes for which instructors haven't been appointed.
frmClassList	qlkCourseClass0	This form displays class information, calculates total enrollment, and includes subform controls to display instructor(s) names and the students registered in the class.
frmClassListSubInst	qalkInstructorClass	Used as a subform for frmClassList to provide names of instructor (s) appointed to teach a class.
frmClassListSubStud	qalkStudentClass	Used as a subform for frmClassList to provide names of students and grades for students registered in a class.
frmClassSchedule	qalkCourseClass	Form to display class data with corresponding course information in a tabular form.
frmCourseList	qryCourses	Form to display a list of courses sorted by prefix and number.
frmCourses	tblCourses	Data entry form for Courses.
frmCoursesView	tblCourses	Form to review course information.
frmEnrollmentSummary	qryEnrollmentSummary	Form displays enrollment and fee revenue totals for each class in the working session.
frmInstructors	tblInstructors	Data Entry form for Instructors.
frmListofClasses	qryListofClasses	Form to display a list of classes that have been scheduled for the working session.
frmPrograms	tblPrograms	Data Entry Form for Program information.
frmRegistration	tblStudents	Main form for the registration process. Displays student information and a subform control to display the classes a student is registered in.
frmRegistrationSub	qalkClassStudent	Subform for frmRegistration to display class information when a student is registered in a class.
frmStudents	tblStudents	Data Entry Form for student information.
frmSwitchboard	tblSession	Form to select the working session.

TABLE D.4: The Reports.

Report Name	Record Source	Purpose and Description
rptClassList	qalkCourseClass	Report to provide a printed class list. Includes course information and subreport controls to display subreports for instructors, students, and grades.
rptClassListSub-Instructor	qalkInstructorClass	Report used as a subreport for rptClassList and rptClassSchedule to display instructors names.
rptClassListSub-Student	qalkStudentClass	Report used as a subreport for rptClassList to display students names and grades.
rptClassSchedule	qalkCourseClass	Grouped report to display class schedule information. Contains a subreport control to display rptClassListSubInstructor with instructor(s) name.
rptCourseList	qryCourses	Report a list of courses with units, prerequisites, and description.
rptEnrollmentReport	qryEnrollmentSummary	Report displays enrollment totals for each class in the working session.
rptEnrollment-Summary	qryEnrollmentSummary	Grouped report providing enrollment, enrollment limit, and fees paid for each class (grouped by program).
rptStudentProgram	qryEnrollment	Report to display class registration information for a student.

APPENDIX

E

Index to the Tables in the Book

Table E.1 is an index to the tables in the book.

TABLE E.1: The Tables in the Book

TABLE E.1: The Tables in the Book *(continued)*

Table	Description	Page
Table 7.1:	The **Keystrokes** argument for the **SendKeys** action for moving among records.	267
Table 7.2:	Automating the process of finding a record by using a combo box.	277
Table 7.3:	The macro to undo the find and then return to the previous record.	283
Table 7.4:	The logical navigation macros, to find a record and then return to the previous record.	285
Table 7.5:	Modify the cmnd Review_Click macro to hide the logical navigation controls.	290
Table 8.1:	A macro to validate the uniqueness of the primary key value when you try to update the primary key control.	302
Table 8.2:	A macro to validate the uniqueness of the primary key value and display a primary key violation form.	304
Table 8.3:	A macro to display a new record. The macro determines if the current record is the new record before issuing the command.	307
Table 8.4:	A macro to undo a change. This macro determines if the record has been changed before issuing the command.	309
Table 8.5:	The macro to save a record.	311
Table 8.6:	The macro to test a validation rule before updating the record.	313
Table 8.7:	The macro to delete a record when the Cascade Delete Related Records option is not selected. If there are no related records in a related table, the macro issues the command to delete the record.	323
Table 8.8:	The macro to test for records in a related table before deleting a record.	325
Table 8.9:	The macro to delete a record when the Cascade Delete Related Records option is selected. The macro displays message boxes with the numbers of records in related tables and offers a choice to delete the record and all related records or stop without deleting.	333
Table 8.10	The macro to allow or prevent deletion of a record and its related records when the Cascade Delete Related Records option is selected. The macro displays the numbers of records in related tables that would be deleted, and provides the choice to continue or cancel the deletion.	335
Table 8.11:	Macro to automatically fill a new record with data from a previous record .	342

TABLE E.1: The Tables in the Book *(continued)*

TABLE E.1: The Tables in the Book *(continued)*

Table	Description	Page
Table 13.3:	The macro for grpClosingOut option group.	504
Table 13.4:	The macro for the detail drill-down button refers to the option group on the main form.	506
Table 13.5:	The archive macro.	518
Table 14.1:	The macro to test the enrollment and display a label.	529
Table 14.2:	The macro for the option group on the Class Reports mini-switchboard.	531
Table 14.3:	The cmdPreview_Click macro hides the dialog form and opens the report.	533
Table 14.4:	Macros to calculate a page total. The first macro initializes the page total when the page header for the page is laid out. The second macro increases the page total by the value in the record after the record is laid out.	537
Table 15.1:	The menu bar macro for frmRegistration.	552
Table 15.2:	The menu macro group for **mmnuRegistration_Edit.** Each macro runs the **DoMenuItem** action for the corresponding built-in menu command.	553
Table 15.3:	The menu macro group for **mmnuRegistration_File**. Each macro uses the **RunMacro** action to run the macro for the corresponding command button on the form.	554
Table 15.4:	The menu macro group for **mmnuRegistration_Navigation**. Each macro uses the **RunMacro** action to run the macro for the corresponding command button on the form.	555
Table 15.5:	The shortcut menu macro group for **mmnusRegistration**. Each macro uses the **RunMacro** action to run the macro as the corresponding command button on the form.	557
Table 15.6:	The Menu Builder symbols. The symbol preceding a name indicates its function.	559
Table 15.7:	The macros to show and hide a custom toolbar.	569
Table 15.8:	Use the full syntax for the control references for a toolbar macro.	571
Table 15.9:	Key combinations for the **Autokeys** macro.	574
Table B.1	The macro actions.	610
Table C.1	The focus and data events for controls on forms	618
Table C.2	Mouse and keyboard events	619

TABLE E.1: The Tables in the Book *(continued)*

Table	Description	Page
Table C.3	Window and focus events for forms	621
Table C.4	Data and filter events for records on forms	622
Table C.5:	**Error** and **Timing** Events	624
Table C.6:	Events for reports	624
Table C.7:	Print events for report sections	625
Table D.1:	The Tables	628
Table D.2:	The Queries	629
Table D.3:	The Forms	630
Table D.4:	The Reports	632
Table E.1:	The Tables in the Book	634

INDEX

Note to the Reader: Throughout this index **boldface** page numbers indicate primary discussions of a topic. *Italic* page numbers indicate illustrations.

Symbols

& (ampersand), in Caption property text, 93
* (asterisk), to include all fields in query, 511, 514
= (equal sign), 85, 171
"" (zero-length string), 124
∞ (infinity), 16

A

Access, components of, 155
access keys, 93
   defining, **572**
Access Visual Basic. *See* Visual Basic
Access working environment, customizing, **25–43**
acDataErrContinue constant, 157
acDataErrDisplay constant, 157
action arguments
   default, 95
   in Macro window, 76
Action column, in Macro window, 74, *75*
Action Failed dialog, **144–145**, *145*, 155, *284*, 348, *349*

actions. *See* macro actions
Activate event, 65, 423, 569, *621*, *624*
active control, setting color of, 369
active form
   attaching shortcut menu to, **556**
   moving focus within, 263
   moving to record on, **267–268**
   moving to record on subform, **268**
   moving to specific control, **260–262**
   moving to subform controls on, **261–262**
   reference to control, **606–607**
active object
   requery of, 357
   unqualified reference to, 176–177
active window
   action to close, 94
   automatic data update, 354
ActiveControl_AfterUpdate macro, *172*
ActiveControl screen property, 602
ActiveForm Screen property, 601
ActiveReport Screen property, 602
AddMenu action, 551, 556, *610*
aesthetics, in user interface design, 50
AfterDelConfirm event, **235**
AfterInsert event, 356, *622*
AfterUpdate event, 65, 66, 67, 115, *619*, 620, *622*
   subform recognition, 233

B

C

E

F

G

H

I

M

P

Q

R

u

Content of the Disk

The companion 3½" floppy disk contains the files you need to work along with the book's tutorial. To install the files you need Microsoft Windows 95 and Microsoft Access for Windows 95. The disk includes two folders, Automate and Gallery.

The Automate folder contains the three files you work with in the book:

- **College.mdb** is the interactive database that you'll develop into an automated application in the chapters—it contains all the tables, queries, forms, and reports for the College database example.

- **Offsite.xls** is the spreadsheet file you'll import in Chapter 12.

- **Students.txt** is the text file you'll import in Chapter 12.

The Gallery folder is a reference file that contains the **gallery.mdb** database, which includes the form masters and the galleries of reusable controls and macros that you create in the book.

See the introduction for more information about the disk.